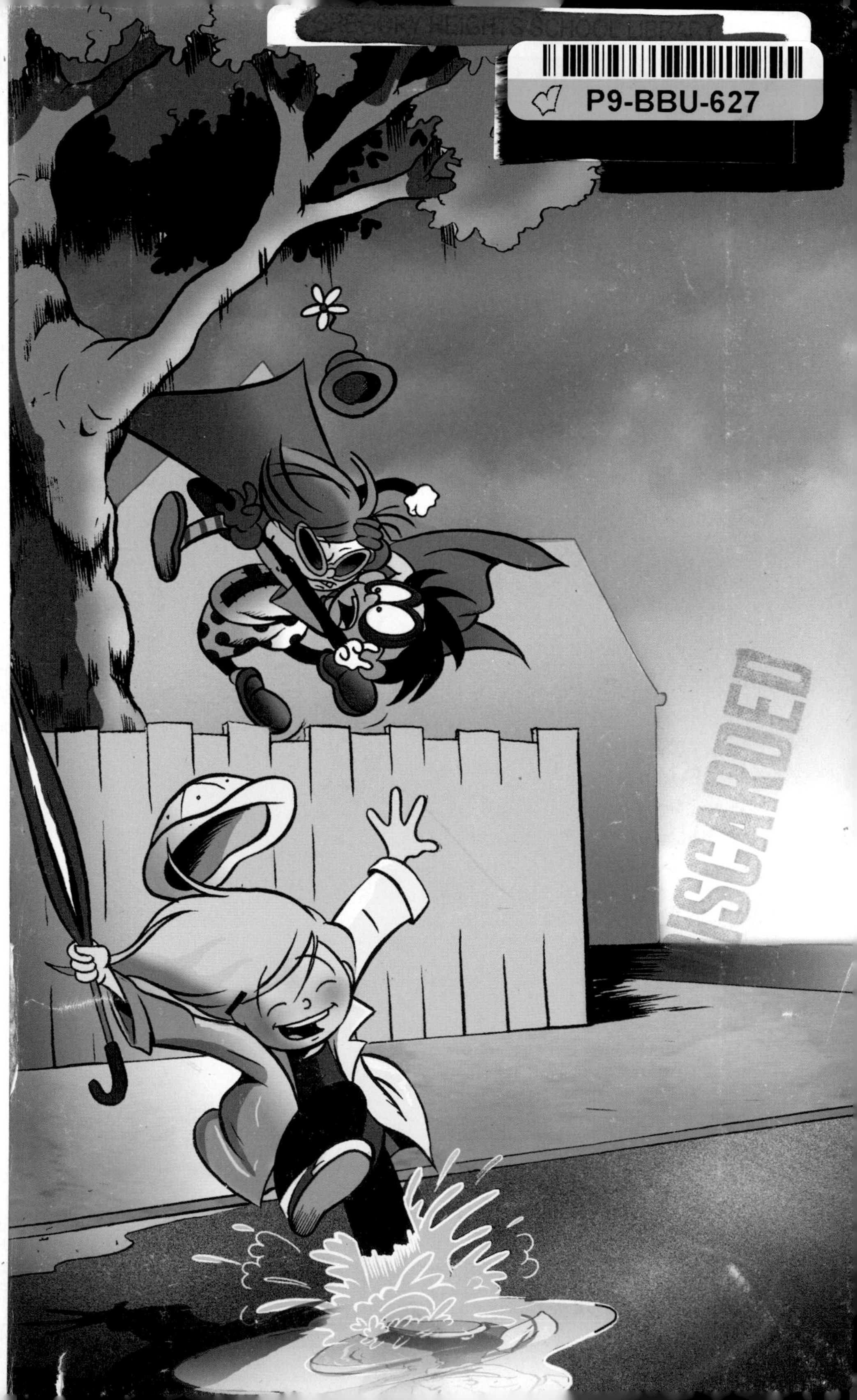

A Publication of **Renaissance Press**

Amelia Rules! Volume Two: What Makes You Happy

TM and Copyright © 2006 Jimmy Gownley
All Rights Reserved

Portions of this book originally appeared in
Amelia Rules! comic books published by Renaissance Press

Introduction Copyright © Mark Crilley

Cover art and design
Copyright © Jimmy Gownley

A Renaissance Press Book

**Renaissance Press
PO Box 5060
Harrisburg, PA 17110**

www.ameliarules.com

ISBN 0-9712169-4-0 (softcover)
ISBN 0-9712169-5-9 (hardcover)

Previously published by ibooks, inc. 2003

First Renaissance Press edition 2006
10 9 8 7 6 5 4 3 2 1

**Editor: Michael Cohen
Marketing and Promotion: Karen Gownley
Director of Publishing and Operations: Harold Buchholz
Brand Manager: Ben Haber**

Special Thanks to Liz Sumner

Printed in Korea

Other Books in This Series:

Amelia Rules! The Whole World's Crazy
ISBN 0-9712169-2-4 (softcover)
ISBN 0-9712169-3-2 (hardcover)

Amelia Rules! Superheroes
ISBN 0-9712169-6-7 (softcover)
ISBN 0-9712169-7-5 (hardcover)

To order additional volumes from Renaissance Press, visit us at ameliarules.com
or to find the comic shop nearest you call 1-888-comicbook

AMELIA RULES!
WHAT MAKES YOU HAPPY

By
JIMMY GOWNLEY

RENAISSANCE
PRESS

·a Renaissance Press book·

Dedication:

To my beautiful new baby girls:

Stella Mary and
Anna Elizabeth

and to their wonderful mother, Karen.

You're what make ME happy.

INTRODUCTION

Amelia Rules! is simply one of the best all-ages comics I've ever seen. It succeeds on so many different levels, I'm sure anyone who gives it a chance will fall for it hook, line, and sinker. Jimmy Gownley understands the full potential of comic book storytelling in a way that few of his peers do, and he wastes no time in getting every ounce of potential out of every square inch of the page. I don't know exactly how he does it, and he does it with astonishing consistency from one issue to the next–so the best I can do is point out a few examples of what I'm talking about.

Take the sequence in *What Makes You Happy* where Reggie launches into his hilarious definition of Artisticus Pretentious. Tossing the comic book's cherished panels and word balloons out the window, Gownley combines a graph-paper background, a wickedly funny mock-dictionary definition ("If possible the work should look as if it were done by a deranged toddler."), and wonderfully spare drawings to illustrate the words. *Amelia Rules!* would rule even without such sequences, but, for me, this use of unconventional storytelling techniques is what really makes the series shine.

Here's another example, and one that makes full use of Gownley's considerable talents as a writer, illustrator, and computer colorist. In *Her Three Kisses*, when Amelia recounts what she picked up from a conversation about her late great aunt Sarah, the reader is treated to a series of tributes to comic book greats, old and new. First we get the traditional comic book approach, but then things cut loose: the comic book page is invaded by three spot-on comic strip homages to *Peanuts*, *Doonesbury*, and *Dilbert*. In each instance, Gownley's quality of line perfectly emulates the source material, and, in a fine example of computer savvy being put to its proper use, the presentation creates the illusion that each strip is freshly clipped from the paper. (Details are always just right in this comic: the *Peanuts* "paper" is yellowed with age.)

But this series knows when to knock the reader out with bravura sequences and when to keep things subtle. Take the page from *Life During Wartime* in which Amelia walks home alone. Here we get a mood, an atmosphere, expertly conjured up with a limited color palette, simple,clear narration, and a final panel that is, to a certain extent, the page itself. I love how a border is drawn around the full moon, allowing it to come into the sequence once, then reappear at the end without being drawn a second time. Here's a comic that knows the meaning of "less is more."

All right, then. I'll stop before I spoil any more surprises. Now it's time for you to sit back and enjoy the marvelous comic book gem that is *Amelia Rules!* And if you find yourself reaching the end and wondering how on earth Jimmy Gownley did it, well, that makes two of us.

Mark Crilley
Author/Illustrator of the *Akiko* books

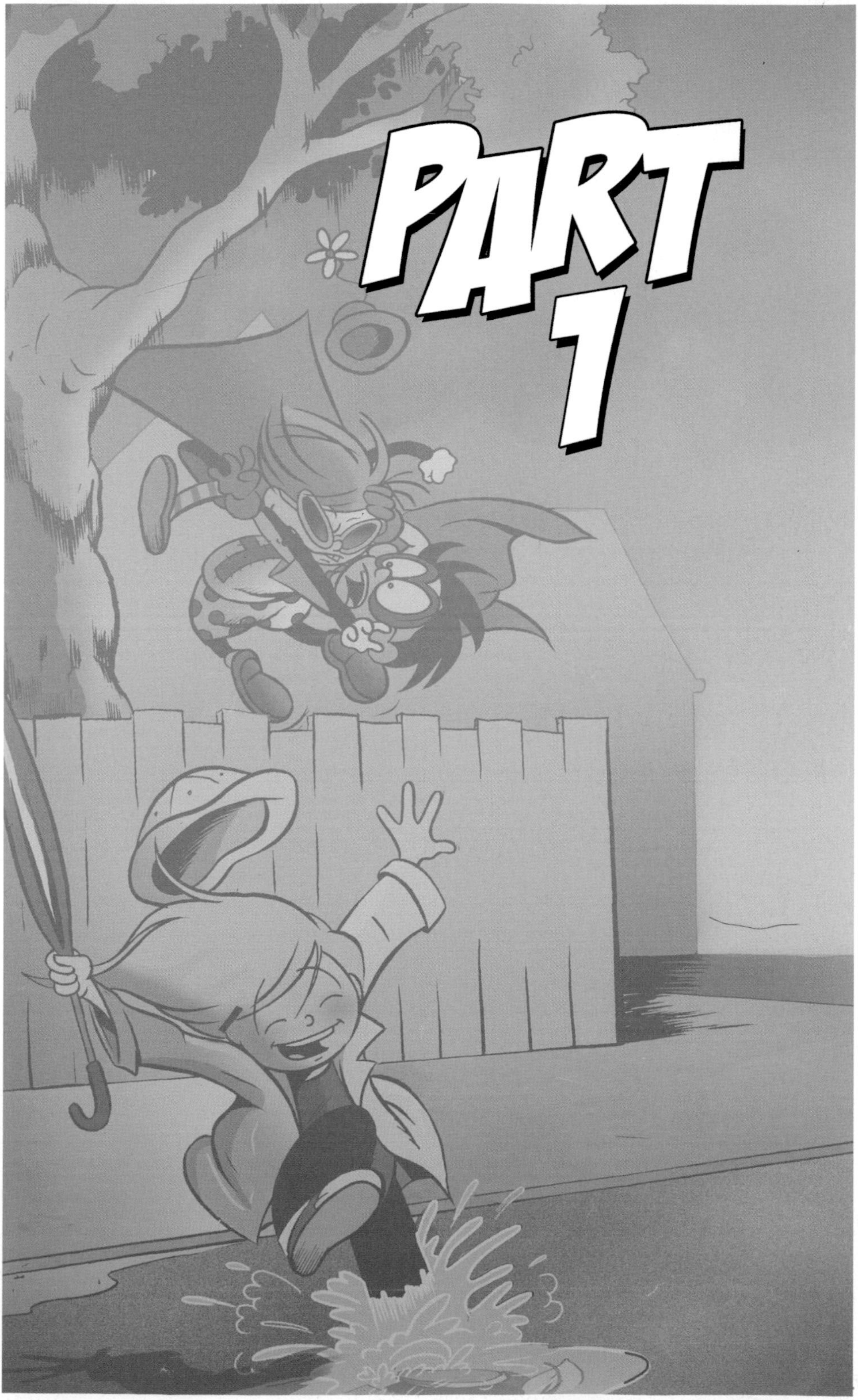
PART 1

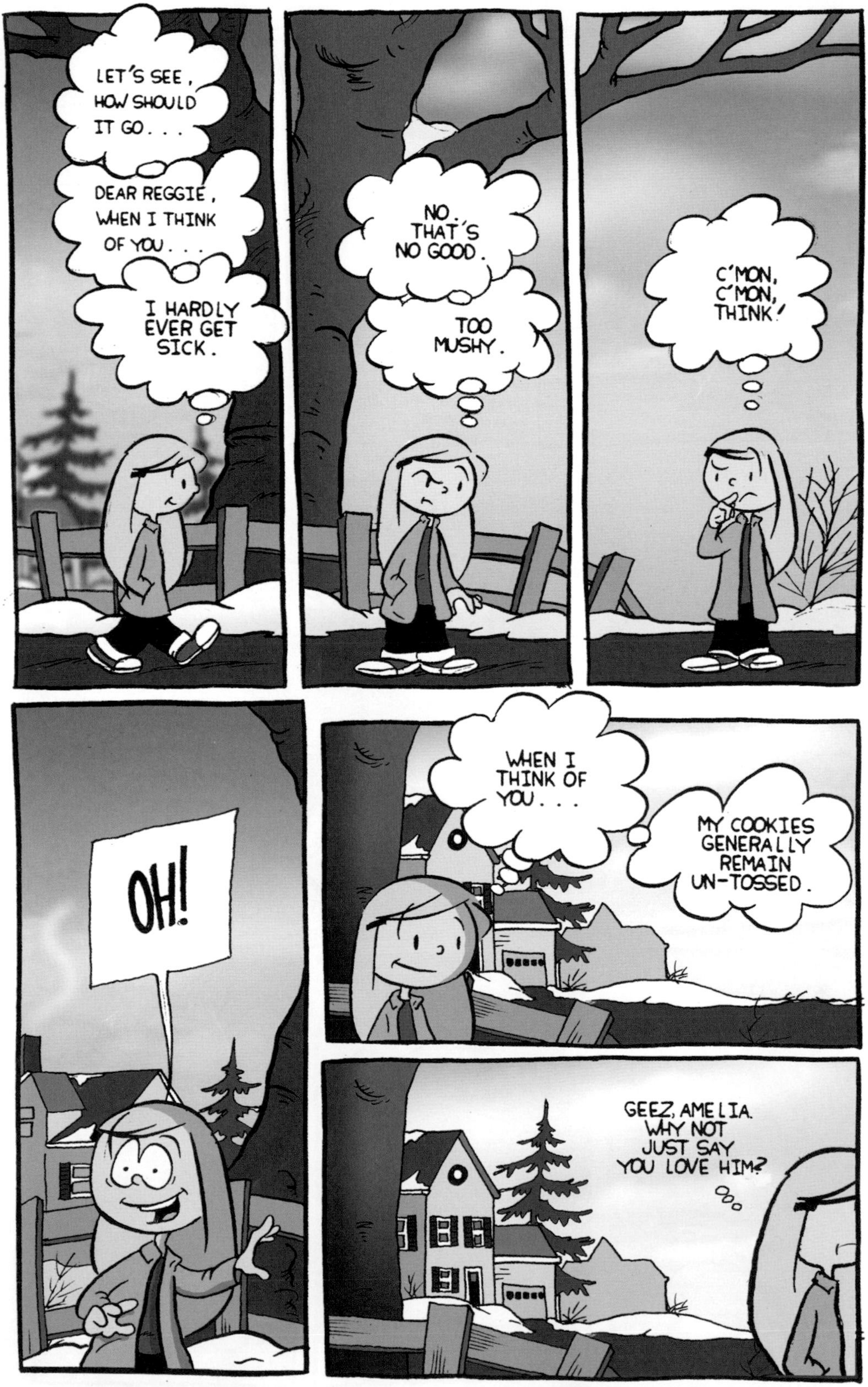
LET'S SEE, HOW SHOULD IT GO . . .
DEAR REGGIE, WHEN I THINK OF YOU . . .
I HARDLY EVER GET SICK.
NO. THAT'S NO GOOD.
TOO MUSHY.
C'MON, C'MON, THINK!
OH!
WHEN I THINK OF YOU . . .
MY COOKIES GENERALLY REMAIN UN-TOSSED.
GEEZ, AMELIA. WHY NOT JUST SAY YOU LOVE HIM?

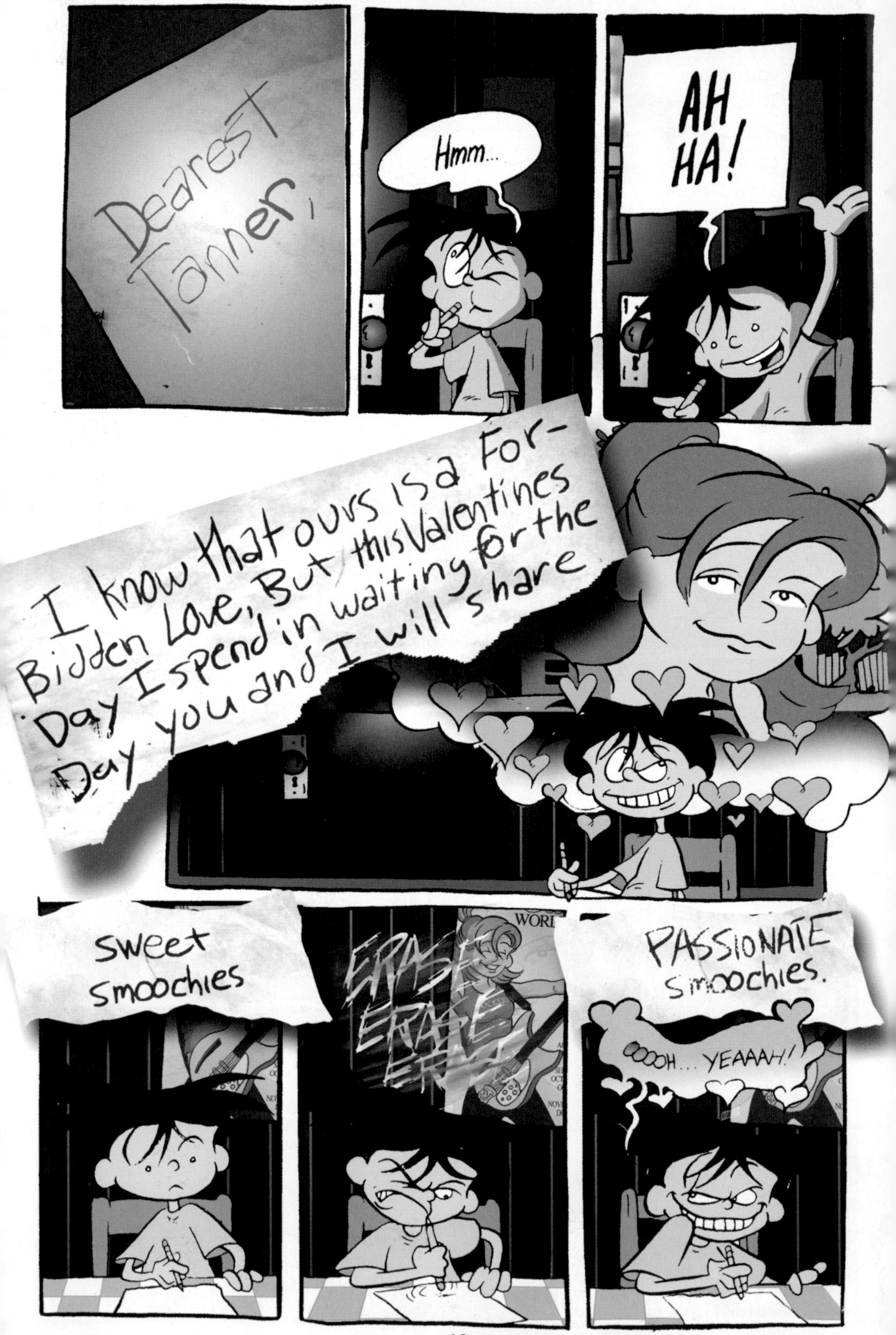
Dearest Tanner,
Hmm...
AH HA!
I know that ours is a For-
Bidden Love, But this Valentines
Day I spend in waiting for the
Day you and I will share
sweet smoochies
ERASE ERASE ERASE
PASSIONATE smoochies.
OOOOH... YEAAAH!

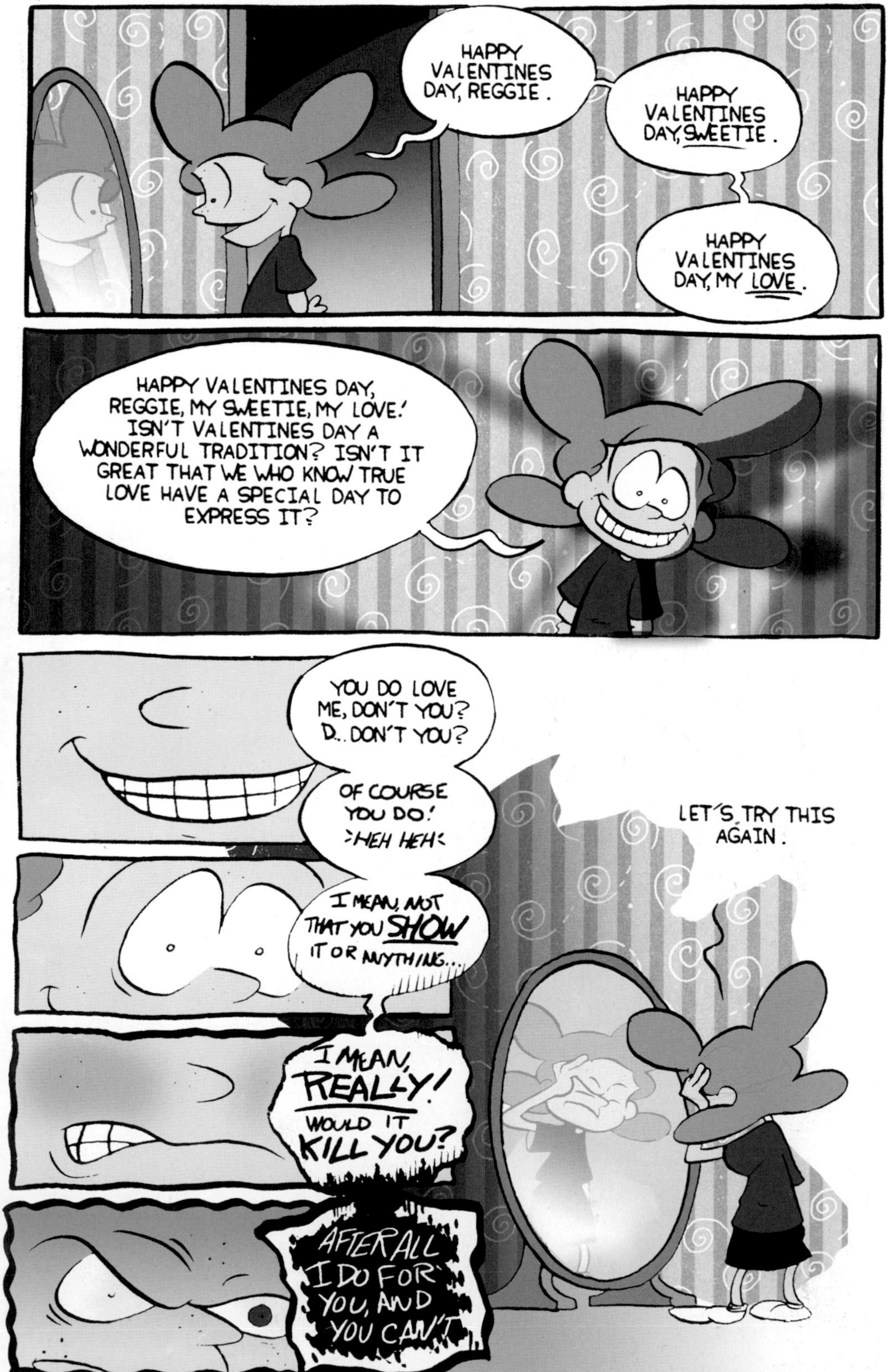
HAPPY VALENTINES DAY, REGGIE.
HAPPY VALENTINES DAY, SWEETIE.
HAPPY VALENTINES DAY, MY LOVE.
HAPPY VALENTINES DAY, REGGIE, MY SWEETIE, MY LOVE! ISN'T VALENTINES DAY A WONDERFUL TRADITION? ISN'T IT GREAT THAT WE WHO KNOW TRUE LOVE HAVE A SPECIAL DAY TO EXPRESS IT?
YOU DO LOVE ME, DON'T YOU? D...DON'T YOU?
OF COURSE YOU DO! >HEH HEH<
I MEAN, NOT THAT YOU SHOW IT OR ANYTHING...
I MEAN, REALLY! WOULD IT KILL YOU?
AFTER ALL I DO FOR YOU, AND YOU CAN'T
LET'S TRY THIS AGAIN.

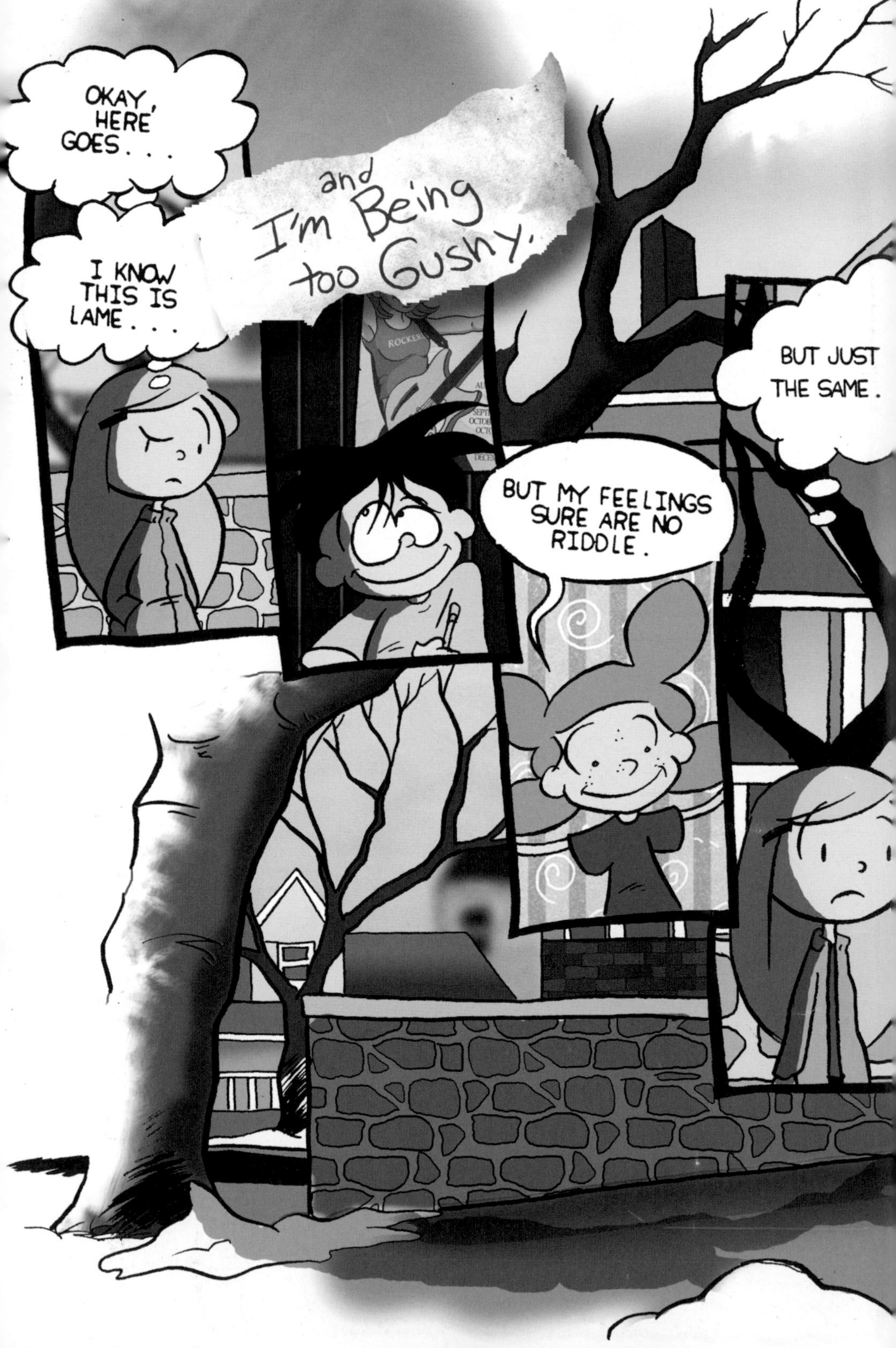
OKAY, HERE GOES. . . .
I KNOW THIS IS LAME. . . .
and I'm Being too Gushy.
BUT MY FEELINGS SURE ARE NO RIDDLE.
BUT JUST THE SAME.

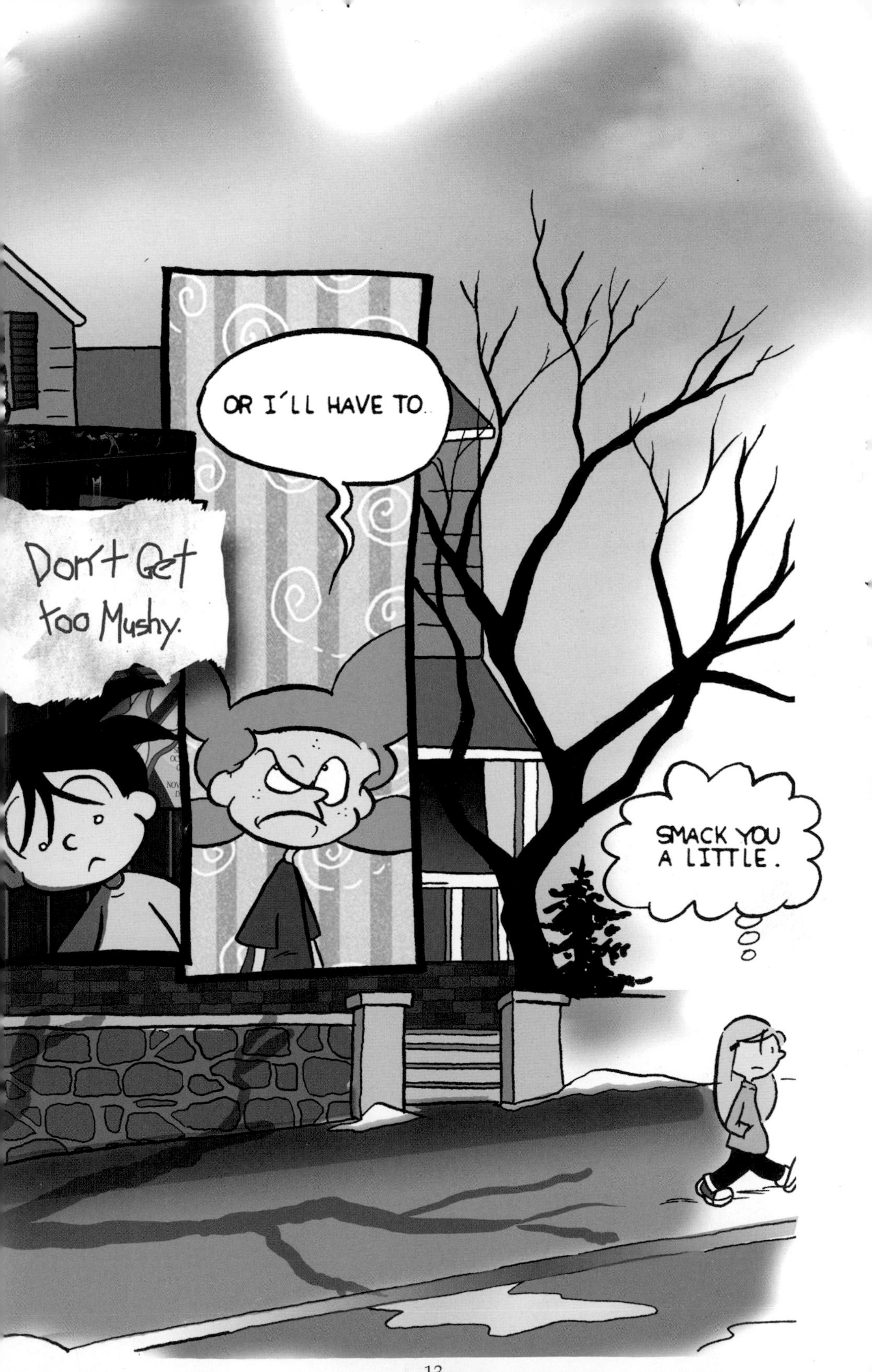
Don't Get too Mushy.
OR I'LL HAVE TO.
SMACK YOU A LITTLE.

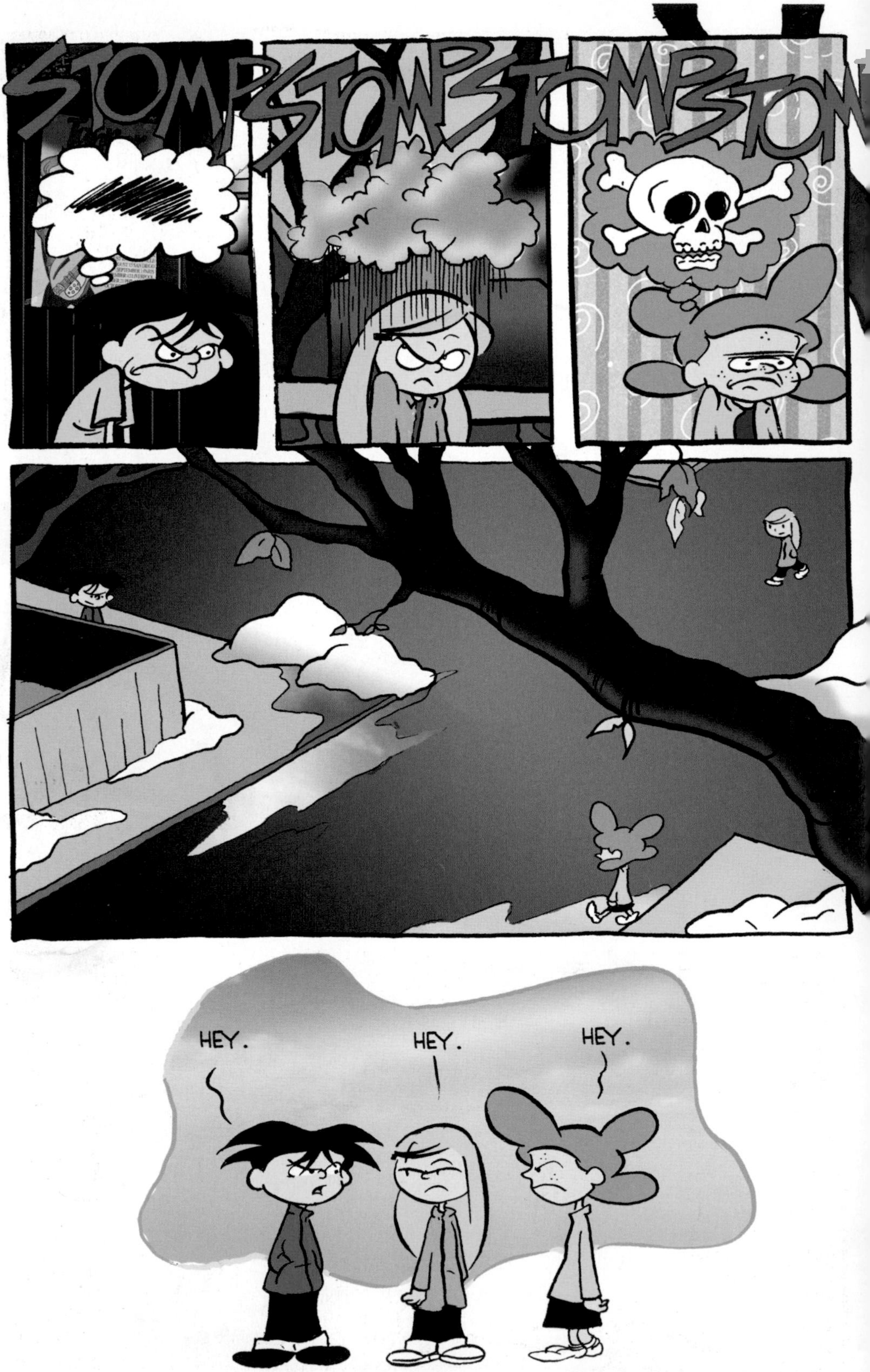
STOMP STOMP STOMP STOMP
HEY.
HEY.
HEY.

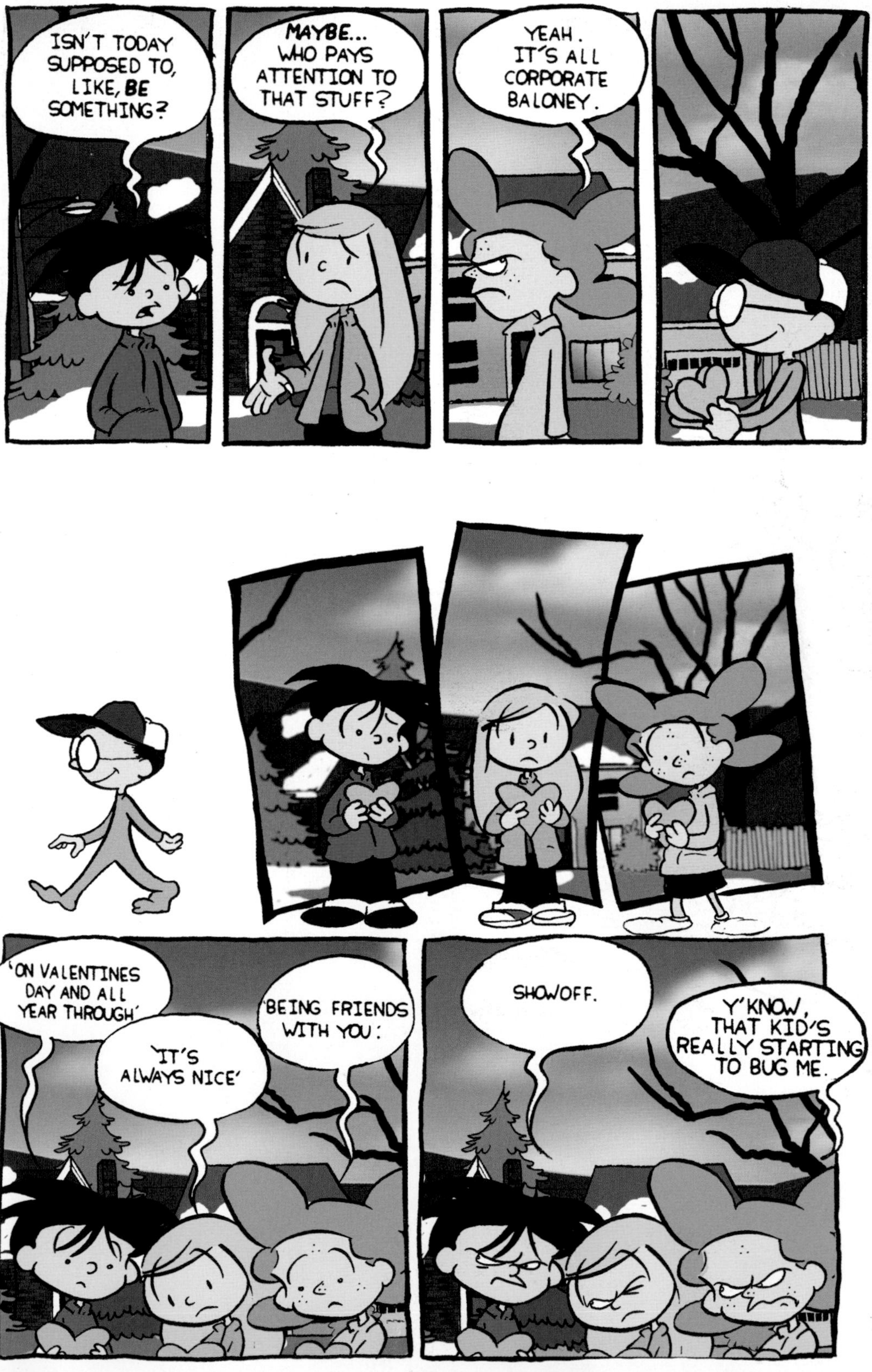
ISN'T TODAY SUPPOSED TO, LIKE, BE SOMETHING?
MAYBE... WHO PAYS ATTENTION TO THAT STUFF?
YEAH. IT'S ALL CORPORATE BALONEY.
'ON VALENTINES DAY AND ALL YEAR THROUGH'
'IT'S ALWAYS NICE'
'BEING FRIENDS WITH YOU'.
SHOWOFF.
Y'KNOW, THAT KID'S REALLY STARTING TO BUG ME.

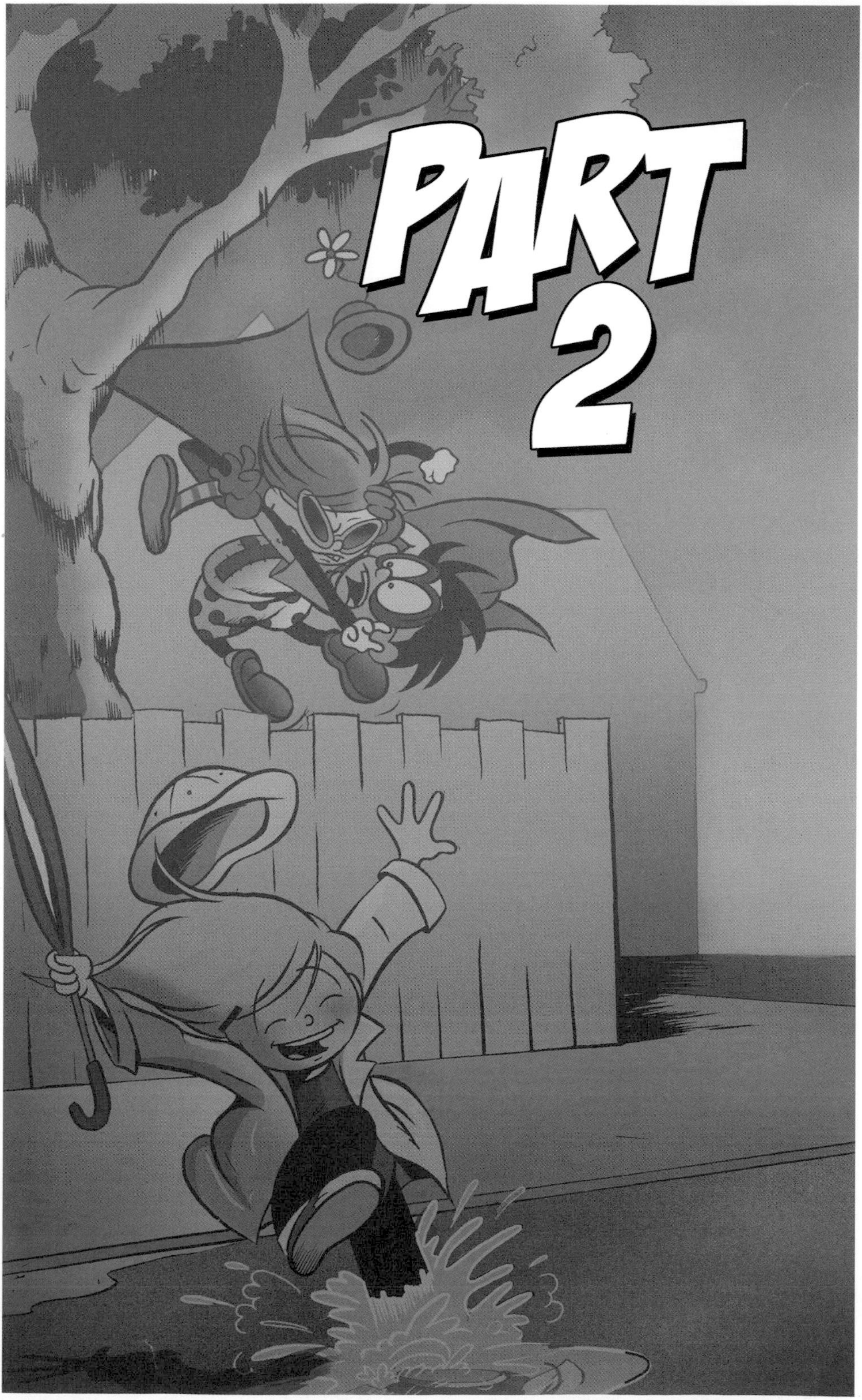
PART 2

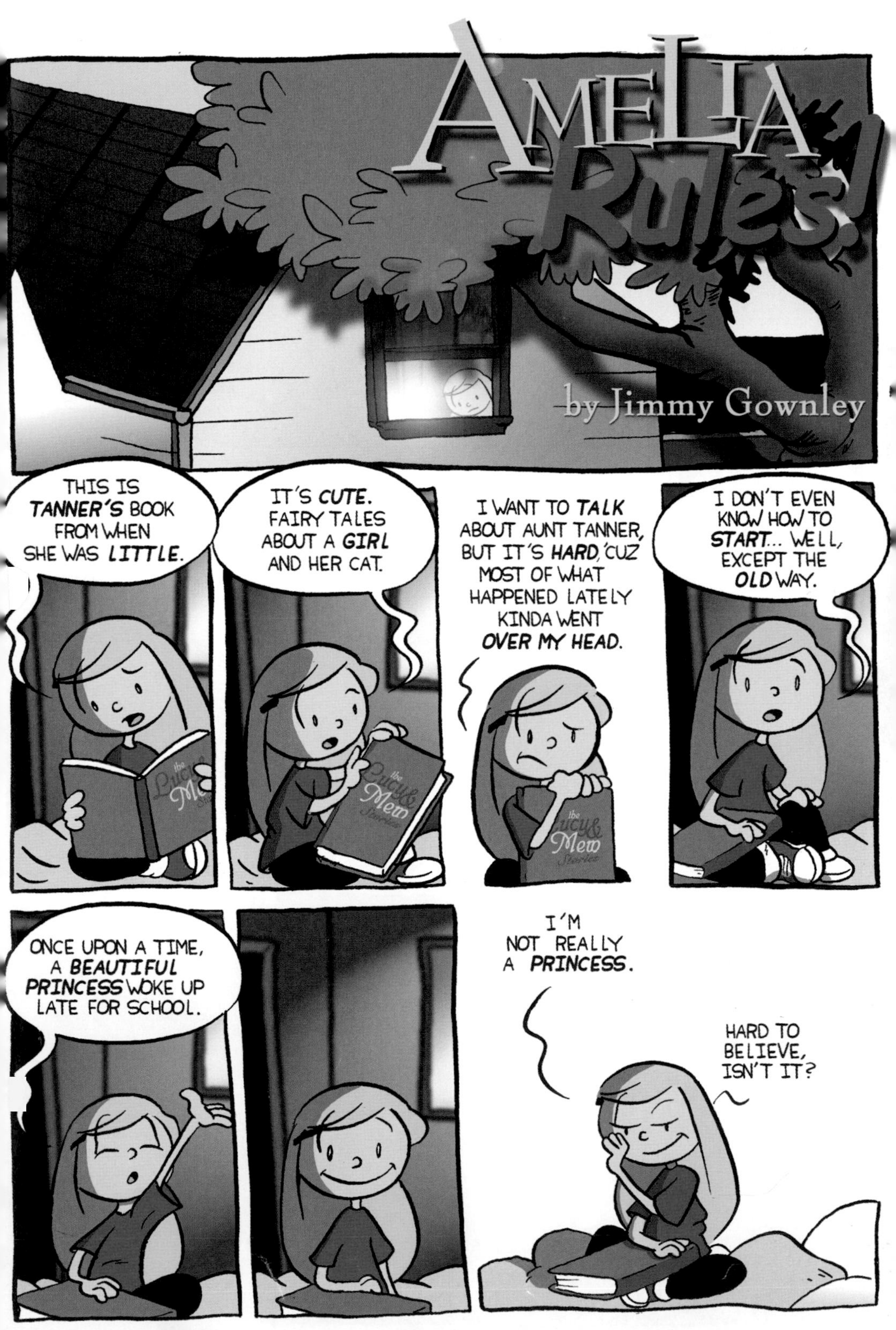
AMELIA Rules!
by Jimmy Gownley
THIS IS TANNER'S BOOK FROM WHEN SHE WAS LITTLE.
IT'S CUTE. FAIRY TALES ABOUT A GIRL AND HER CAT.
I WANT TO TALK ABOUT AUNT TANNER, BUT IT'S HARD, 'CUZ MOST OF WHAT HAPPENED LATELY KINDA WENT OVER MY HEAD.
I DON'T EVEN KNOW HOW TO START... WELL, EXCEPT THE OLD WAY.
ONCE UPON A TIME, A BEAUTIFUL PRINCESS WOKE UP LATE FOR SCHOOL.
I'M NOT REALLY A PRINCESS.
HARD TO BELIEVE, ISN'T IT?

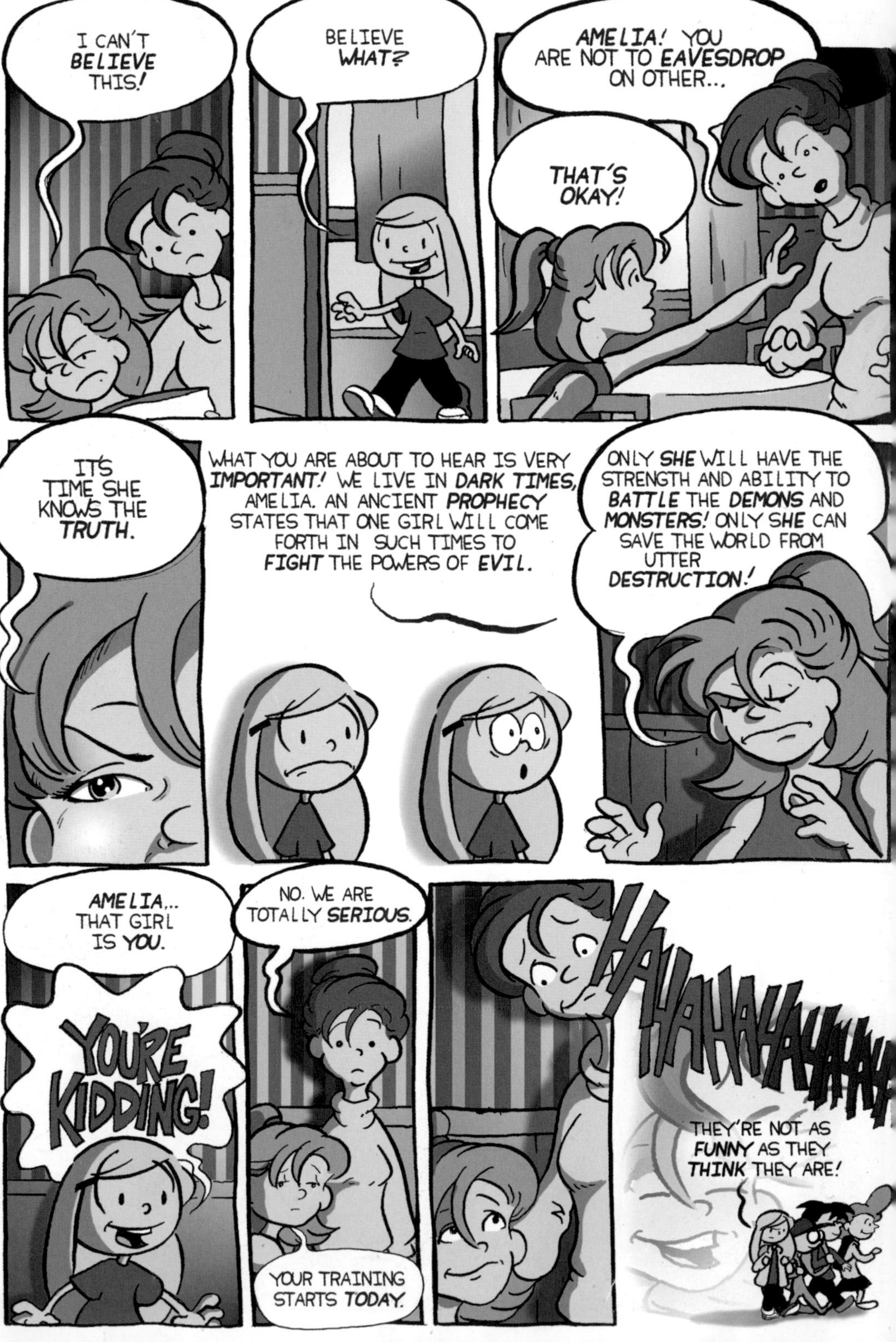
I CAN'T BELIEVE THIS!
BELIEVE WHAT?
AMELIA! YOU ARE NOT TO EAVESDROP ON OTHER...
THAT'S OKAY!
IT'S TIME SHE KNOWS THE TRUTH.
WHAT YOU ARE ABOUT TO HEAR IS VERY IMPORTANT! WE LIVE IN DARK TIMES, AMELIA. AN ANCIENT PROPHECY STATES THAT ONE GIRL WILL COME FORTH IN SUCH TIMES TO FIGHT THE POWERS OF EVIL.
ONLY SHE WILL HAVE THE STRENGTH AND ABILITY TO BATTLE THE DEMONS AND MONSTERS! ONLY SHE CAN SAVE THE WORLD FROM UTTER DESTRUCTION!
AMELIA... THAT GIRL IS YOU.
YOU'RE KIDDING!
NO. WE ARE TOTALLY SERIOUS.
YOUR TRAINING STARTS TODAY.
HAHAHAHAHAHAHAH
THEY'RE NOT AS FUNNY AS THEY THINK THEY ARE!

What Makes You Happy

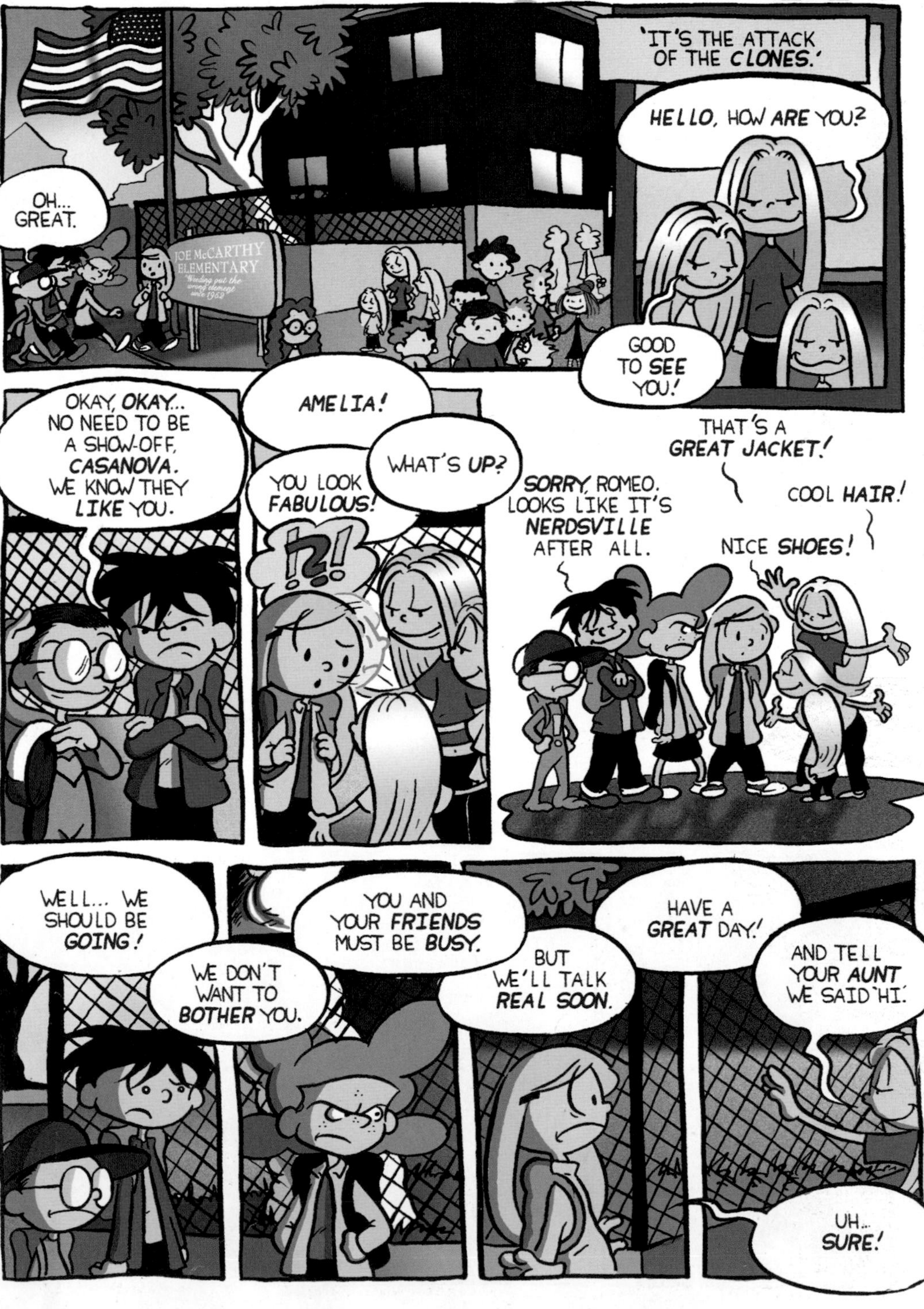

OH... GREAT.
JOE McCARTHY ELEMENTARY
'IT'S THE ATTACK OF THE CLONES.'
HELLO, HOW ARE YOU?
GOOD TO SEE YOU!
OKAY, OKAY... NO NEED TO BE A SHOW-OFF, CASANOVA. WE KNOW THEY LIKE YOU.
AMELIA!
YOU LOOK FABULOUS!
WHAT'S UP?
!?!
SORRY, ROMEO. LOOKS LIKE IT'S NERDSVILLE AFTER ALL.
THAT'S A GREAT JACKET!
COOL HAIR!
NICE SHOES!
WELL... WE SHOULD BE GOING!
WE DON'T WANT TO BOTHER YOU.
YOU AND YOUR FRIENDS MUST BE BUSY.
BUT WE'LL TALK REAL SOON.
HAVE A GREAT DAY!
AND TELL YOUR AUNT WE SAID 'HI.'
UH... SURE!

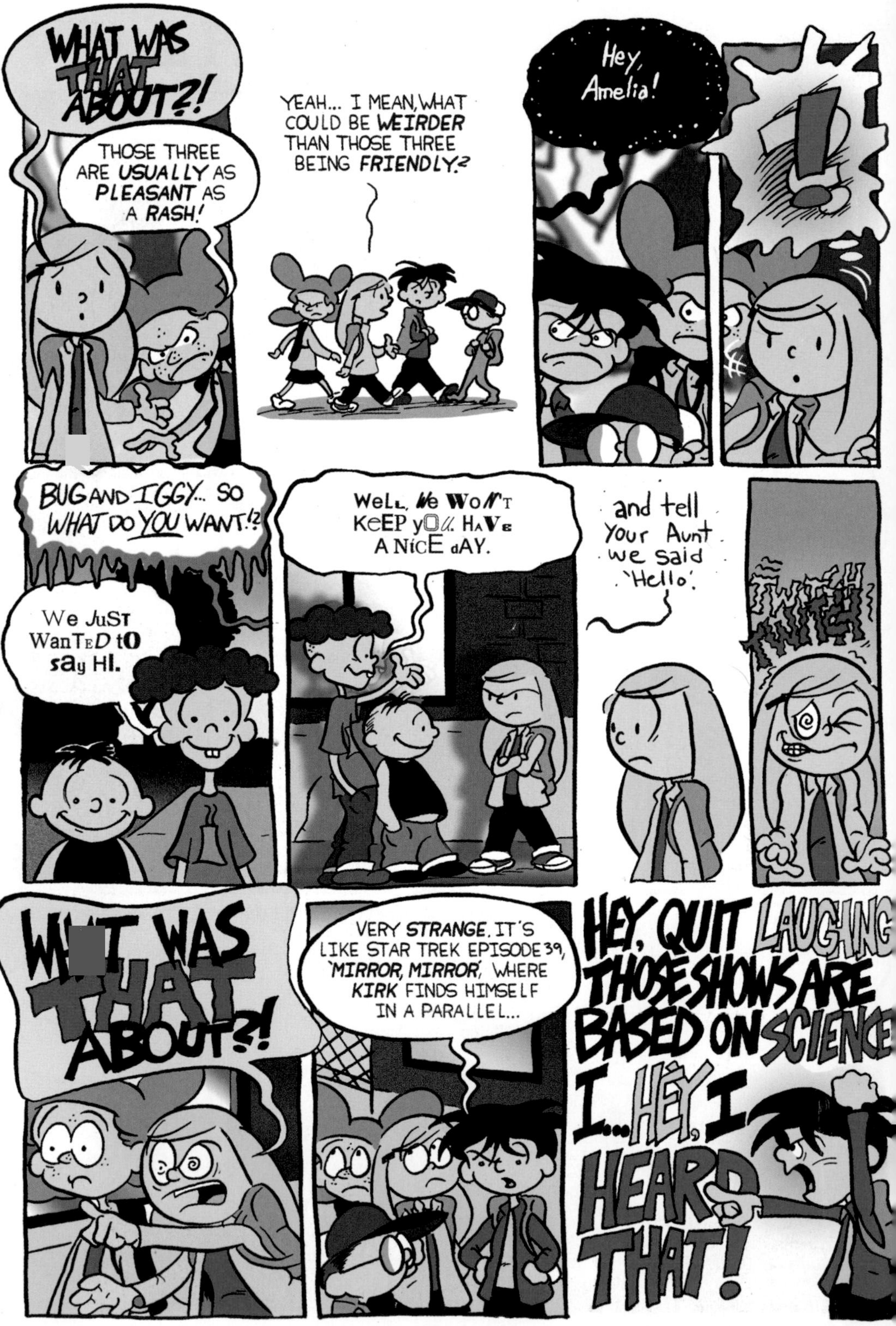
WHAT WAS THAT ABOUT?!
THOSE THREE ARE USUALLY AS PLEASANT AS A RASH!
YEAH... I MEAN, WHAT COULD BE WEIRDER THAN THOSE THREE BEING FRIENDLY?
Hey, Amelia!
!
BUG AND IGGY... SO WHAT DO YOU WANT!?
We JuST WanTeD tO say HI.
WeLL, We WoN'T KeEP yOU. HaVe A NicE dAY.
and tell Your Aunt we said 'Hello'.
TWITCH TWITCH
W[redacted]T WAS THAT ABOUT?!
VERY STRANGE. IT'S LIKE STAR TREK EPISODE 39, 'MIRROR, MIRROR', WHERE KIRK FINDS HIMSELF IN A PARALLEL...
HEY, QUIT LAUGHING THOSE SHOWS ARE BASED ON SCIENCE I... HEY, I HEARD THAT!

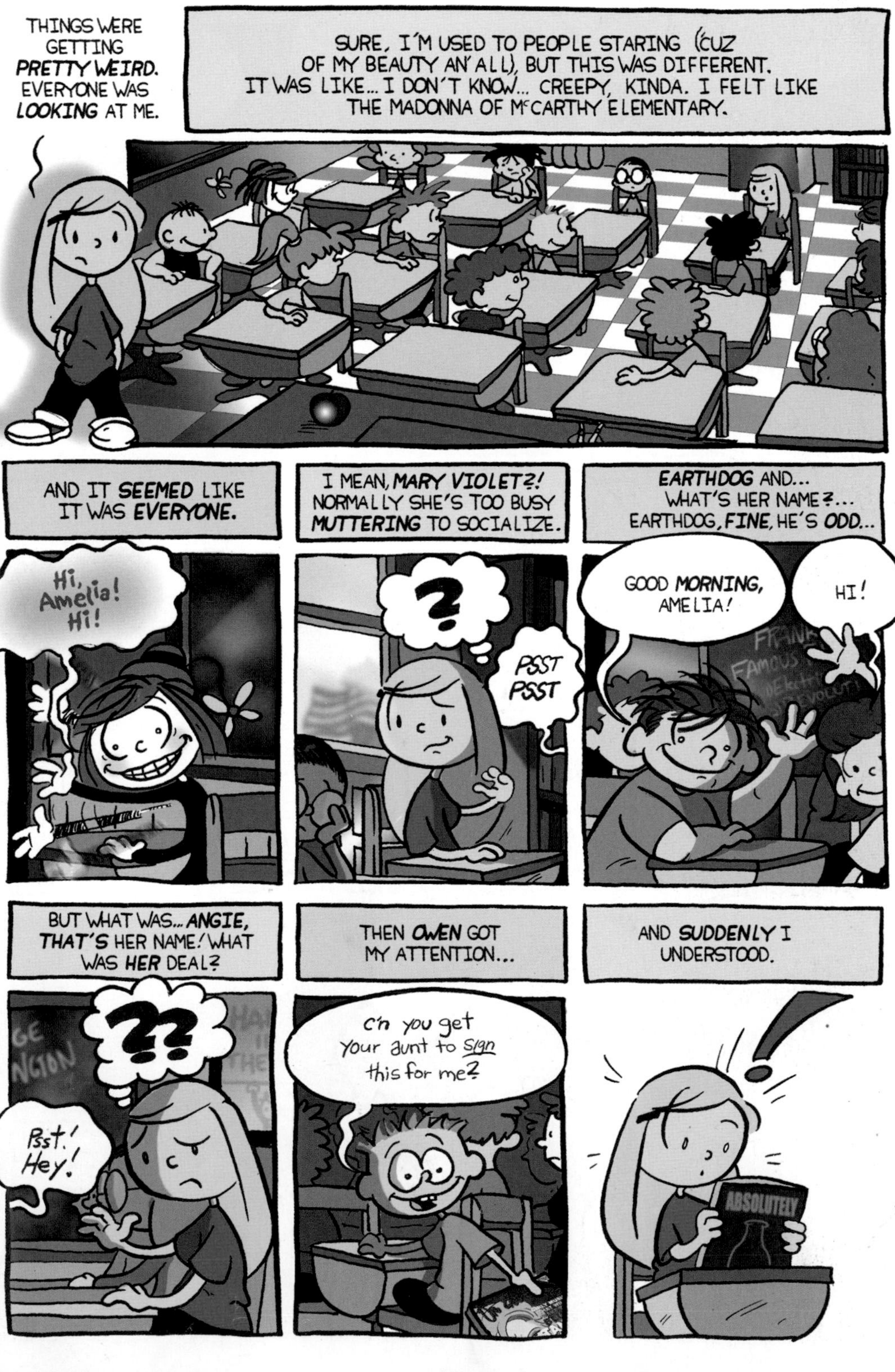

THINGS WERE GETTING PRETTY WEIRD. EVERYONE WAS LOOKING AT ME.
SURE, I'M USED TO PEOPLE STARING ('CUZ OF MY BEAUTY AN' ALL), BUT THIS WAS DIFFERENT. IT WAS LIKE... I DON'T KNOW... CREEPY, KINDA. I FELT LIKE THE MADONNA OF McCARTHY ELEMENTARY.
AND IT SEEMED LIKE IT WAS EVERYONE.
Hi, Amelia! Hi!
I MEAN, MARY VIOLET?! NORMALLY SHE'S TOO BUSY MUTTERING TO SOCIALIZE.
?
PSST PSST
EARTHDOG AND... WHAT'S HER NAME?... EARTHDOG, FINE, HE'S ODD...
GOOD MORNING, AMELIA!
HI!
BUT WHAT WAS... ANGIE, THAT'S HER NAME! WHAT WAS HER DEAL?
??
Psst! Hey!
THEN OWEN GOT MY ATTENTION...
c'n you get your aunt to sign this for me?
AND SUDDENLY I UNDERSTOOD.
!
ABSOLUTELY

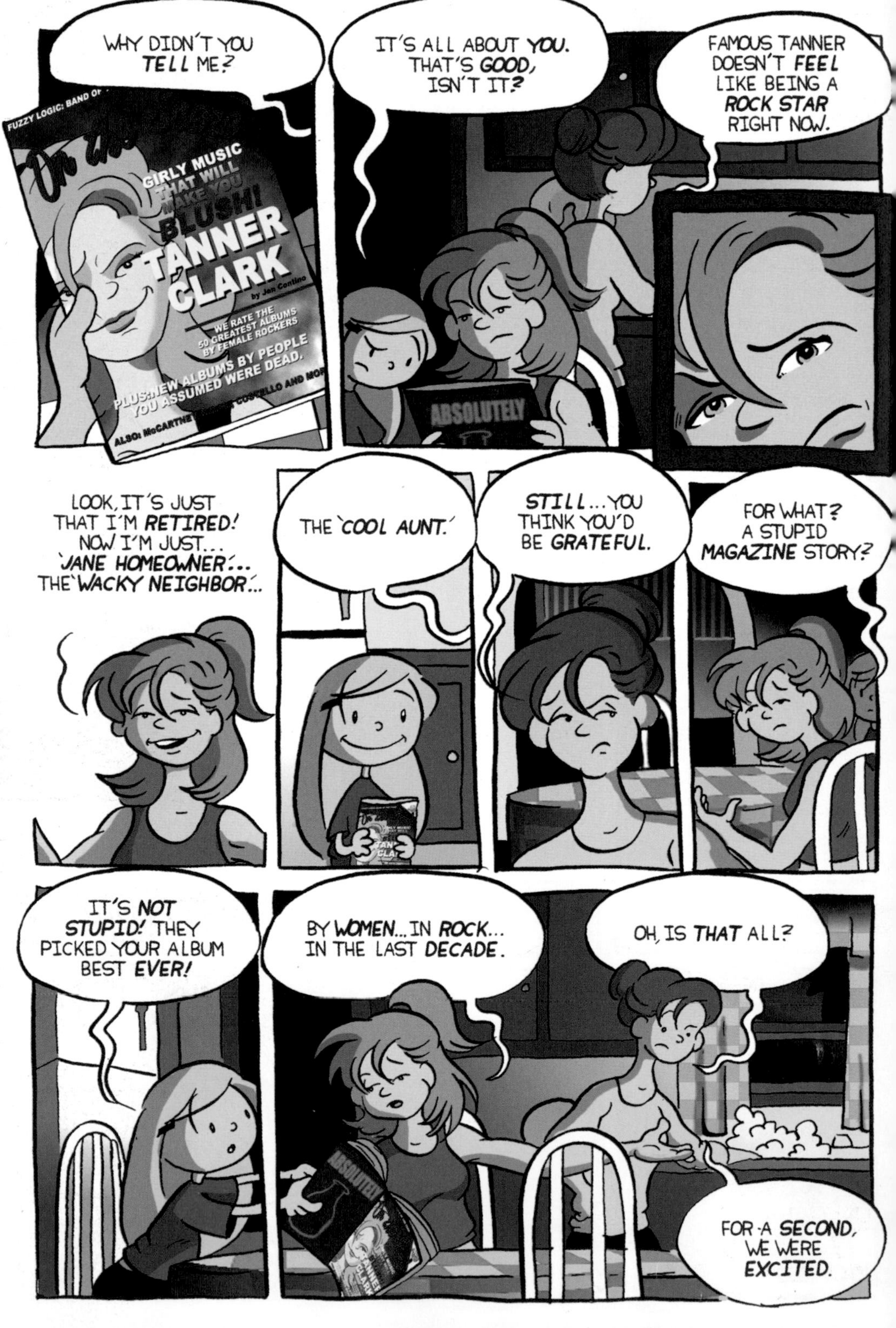
WHY DIDN'T YOU TELL ME?
FUZZY LOGIC; BAND OF
On the
GIRLY MUSIC THAT WILL MAKE YOU BLUSH! TANNER CLARK
by Jen Contino
WE RATE THE 50 GREATEST ALBUMS BY FEMALE ROCKERS
PLUS: NEW ALBUMS BY PEOPLE YOU ASSUMED WERE DEAD.
IT'S ALL ABOUT YOU. THAT'S GOOD, ISN'T IT?
ABSOLUTELY
FAMOUS TANNER DOESN'T FEEL LIKE BEING A ROCK STAR RIGHT NOW.
LOOK, IT'S JUST THAT I'M RETIRED! NOW I'M JUST... 'JANE HOMEOWNER'... THE 'WACKY NEIGHBOR'...
THE 'COOL AUNT.'
STILL... YOU THINK YOU'D BE GRATEFUL.
FOR WHAT? A STUPID MAGAZINE STORY?
IT'S NOT STUPID! THEY PICKED YOUR ALBUM BEST EVER!
BY WOMEN... IN ROCK... IN THE LAST DECADE.
OH, IS THAT ALL?
FOR A SECOND, WE WERE EXCITED.

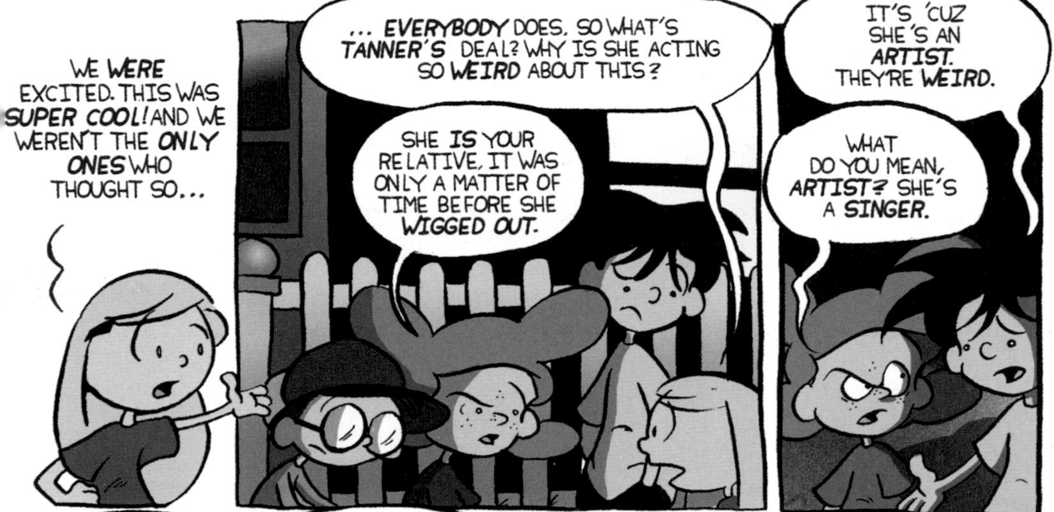
WE WERE EXCITED. THIS WAS SUPER COOL! AND WE WEREN'T THE ONLY ONES WHO THOUGHT SO...
SHE IS YOUR RELATIVE, IT WAS ONLY A MATTER OF TIME BEFORE SHE WIGGED OUT.
... EVERYBODY DOES. SO WHAT'S TANNER'S DEAL? WHY IS SHE ACTING SO WEIRD ABOUT THIS?
IT'S 'CUZ SHE'S AN ARTIST. THEY'RE WEIRD.
WHAT DO YOU MEAN, ARTIST? SHE'S A SINGER.

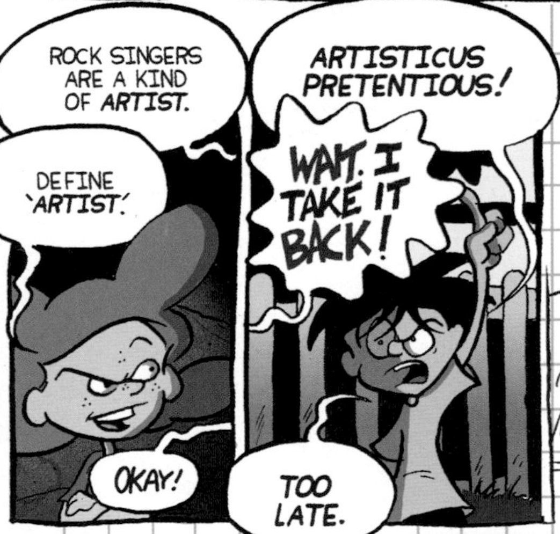
ROCK SINGERS ARE A KIND OF ARTIST.
DEFINE 'ARTIST.'
OKAY!
ARTISTICUS PRETENTIOUS!
WAIT. I TAKE IT BACK!
TOO LATE.

Artisticus Pretentious (The Common Artist) An artist is an individual who excels at any activity which is considered "art" (fig. 1). These activities can include Painting, Poetry, Sculpture, Bowling, Swearing, Drooling and essentially any field which is not "Sales" or "Comic Books." Most of these individuals fall into the trap of learning "skills." This immediately disqualifies them from the title of artist, and they become "hacks", or, if they're the loud-mouthed type, "art directors." A true artist should have no skills, and if possible the work should look as if it were done by a deranged toddler (fig.2).

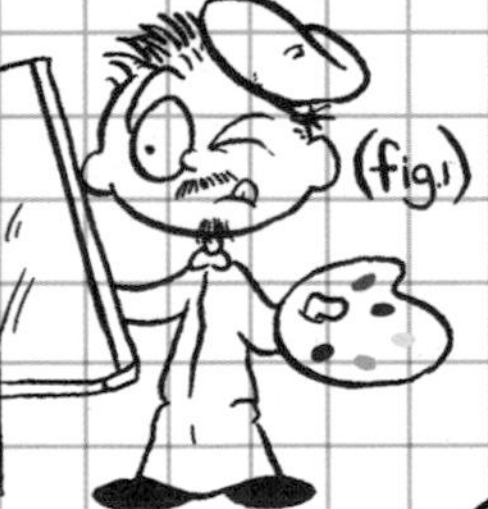
(fig.1)

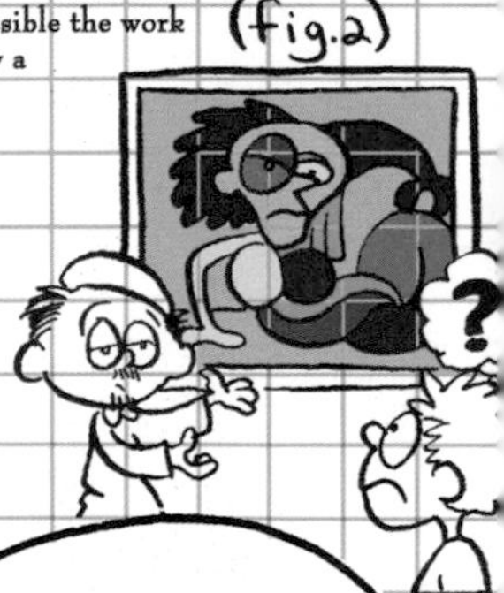
(fig.2)
?

When an individual has reached the level of Artist, one of two things can occur. If that person can go on to create work which is loved by the masses, and he or she reaps financial rewards from the work, then they become "sell-outs" (fig.3a). This group is easy to spot, as they are the only male artists ever to be seen with girls. Or, the artist might be lucky and receive no credit, money, success or attention, thereby guaranteeing themselves recognition as a "great artist" (fig3b). For these fortunate few, the only step left is to be declared a genius. This is easily accomplished by dying a stupid, preventable death, or severing a body part and sending it to a loved one (fig4).

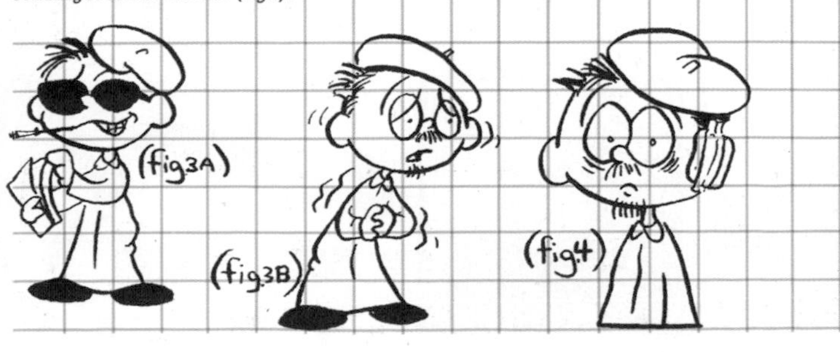
(fig3A)
(fig3B)
(fig4)

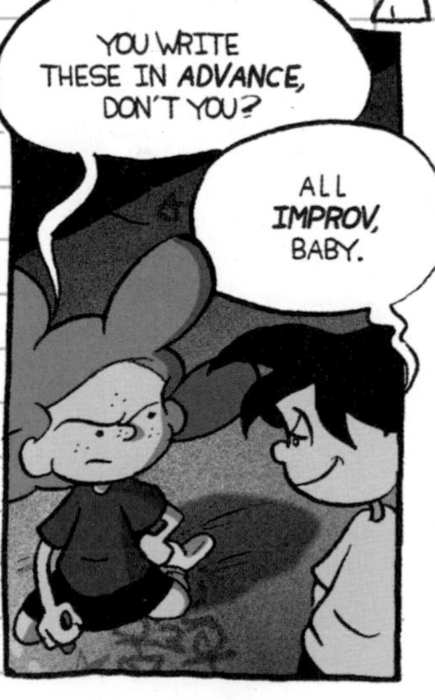
YOU WRITE THESE IN ADVANCE, DON'T YOU?
ALL IMPROV, BABY.

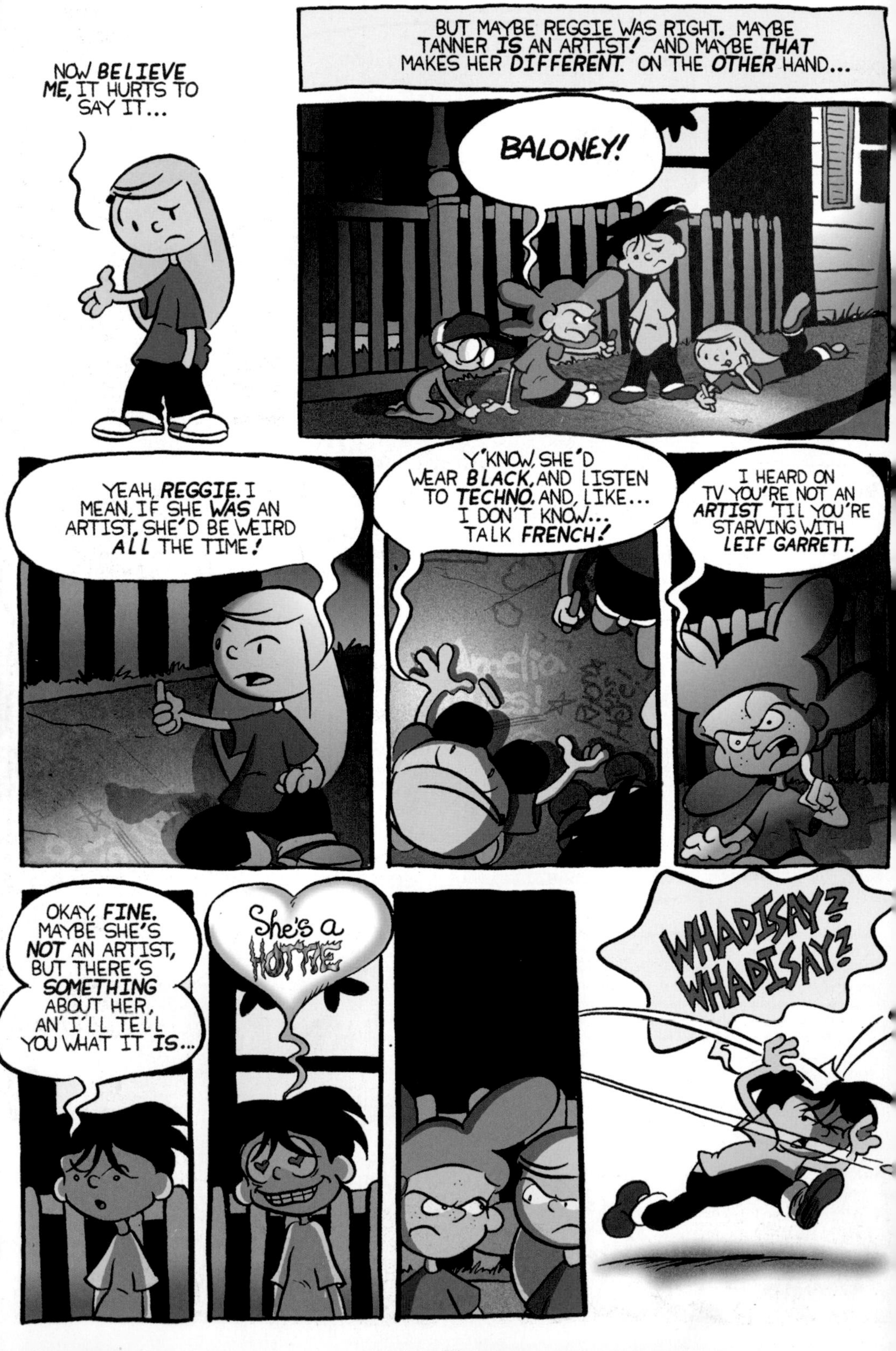

NOW BELIEVE ME, IT HURTS TO SAY IT...
BUT MAYBE REGGIE WAS RIGHT. MAYBE TANNER IS AN ARTIST! AND MAYBE THAT MAKES HER DIFFERENT. ON THE OTHER HAND...
BALONEY!
YEAH, REGGIE. I MEAN, IF SHE WAS AN ARTIST, SHE'D BE WEIRD ALL THE TIME!
Y'KNOW, SHE'D WEAR BLACK, AND LISTEN TO TECHNO. AND, LIKE... I DON'T KNOW... TALK FRENCH!
I HEARD ON TV YOU'RE NOT AN ARTIST 'TIL YOU'RE STARVING WITH LEIF GARRETT.
OKAY, FINE. MAYBE SHE'S NOT AN ARTIST, BUT THERE'S SOMETHING ABOUT HER, AN' I'LL TELL YOU WHAT IT IS...
She's a HOTTIE
WHADISAY? WHADISAY?

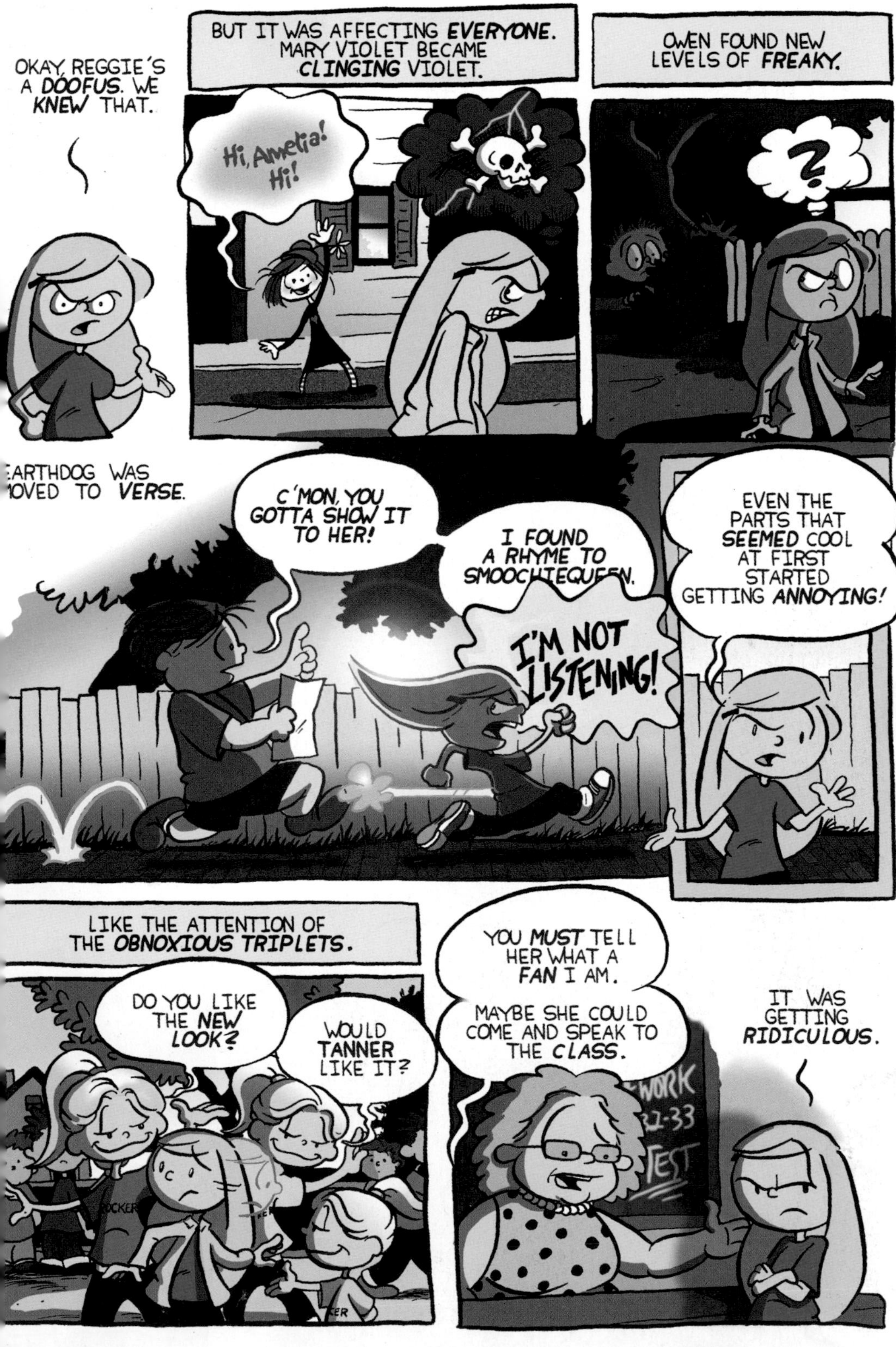

OKAY, REGGIE'S A DOOFUS. WE KNEW THAT.
BUT IT WAS AFFECTING EVERYONE. MARY VIOLET BECAME CLINGING VIOLET.
Hi, Amelia! Hi!
OWEN FOUND NEW LEVELS OF FREAKY.
?
EARTHDOG WAS MOVED TO VERSE.
C'MON, YOU GOTTA SHOW IT TO HER!
I FOUND A RHYME TO SMOOCHIEQUEEN.
I'M NOT LISTENING!
EVEN THE PARTS THAT SEEMED COOL AT FIRST STARTED GETTING ANNOYING!
LIKE THE ATTENTION OF THE OBNOXIOUS TRIPLETS.
DO YOU LIKE THE NEW LOOK?
WOULD TANNER LIKE IT?
YOU MUST TELL HER WHAT A FAN I AM.
MAYBE SHE COULD COME AND SPEAK TO THE CLASS.
IT WAS GETTING RIDICULOUS.

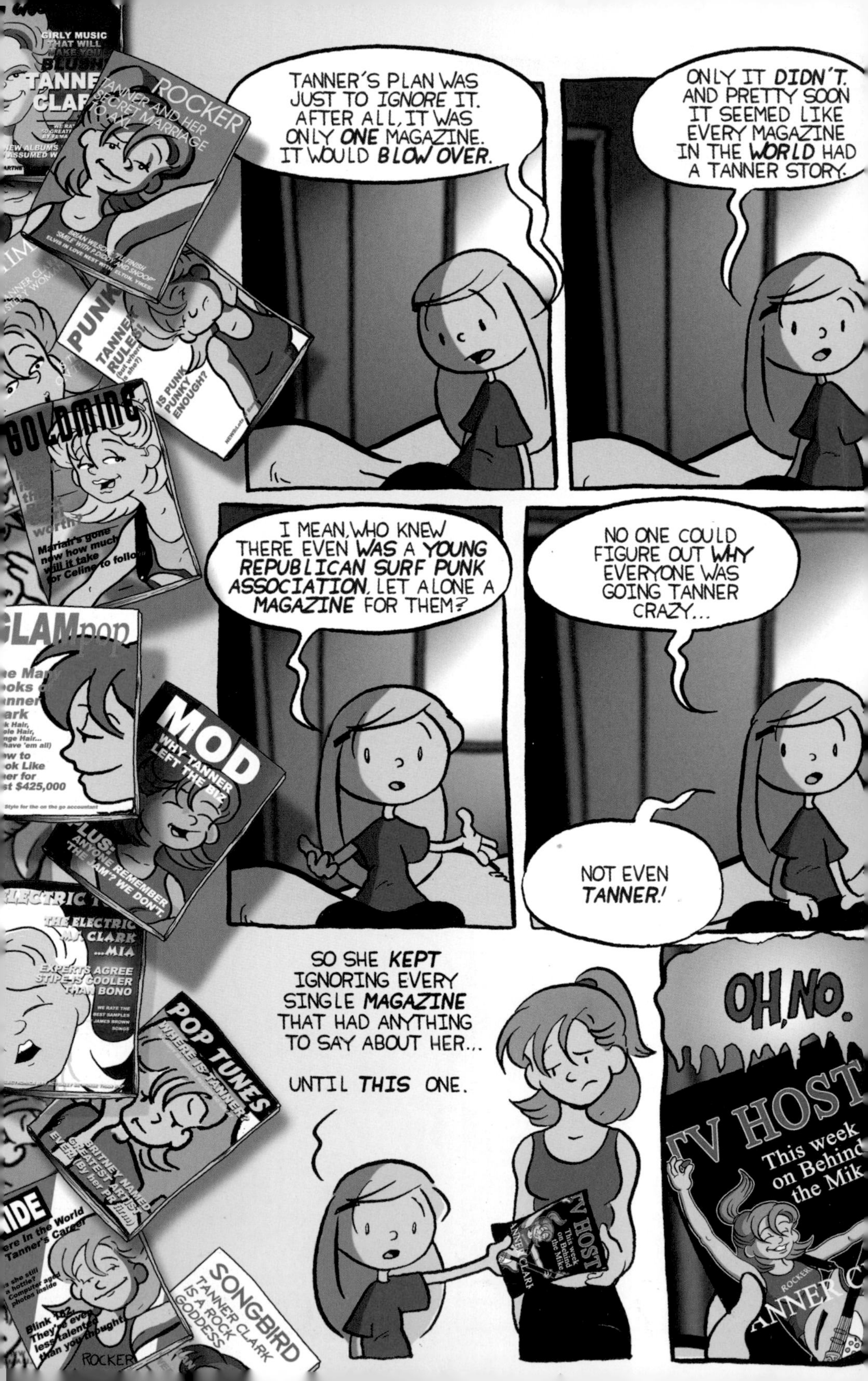
TANNER'S PLAN WAS JUST TO IGNORE IT. AFTER ALL, IT WAS ONLY ONE MAGAZINE. IT WOULD BLOW OVER.
ONLY IT DIDN'T. AND PRETTY SOON IT SEEMED LIKE EVERY MAGAZINE IN THE WORLD HAD A TANNER STORY.
I MEAN, WHO KNEW THERE EVEN WAS A YOUNG REPUBLICAN SURF PUNK ASSOCIATION, LET ALONE A MAGAZINE FOR THEM?
NO ONE COULD FIGURE OUT WHY EVERYONE WAS GOING TANNER CRAZY...
NOT EVEN TANNER!
SO SHE KEPT IGNORING EVERY SINGLE MAGAZINE THAT HAD ANYTHING TO SAY ABOUT HER...
UNTIL THIS ONE.
OH, NO.
TV HOST
This week on Behind the Mike
ROCKER
TANNER AND HER SECRET MARRIAGE TO AXL
PUNK
TANNER RULES!
IS PUNK PUNKY ENOUGH?
GOLDMINE
GLAMpop
MOD
WHY TANNER LEFT THE BIZ
PLUS: ANYONE REMEMBER "THE JAM"? WE DON'T.
EXPERTS AGREE STIPE IS COOLER THAN BONO
POP TUNES
WHERE IS TANNER?
SONGBIRD
TANNER CLARK IS A ROCK GODDESS

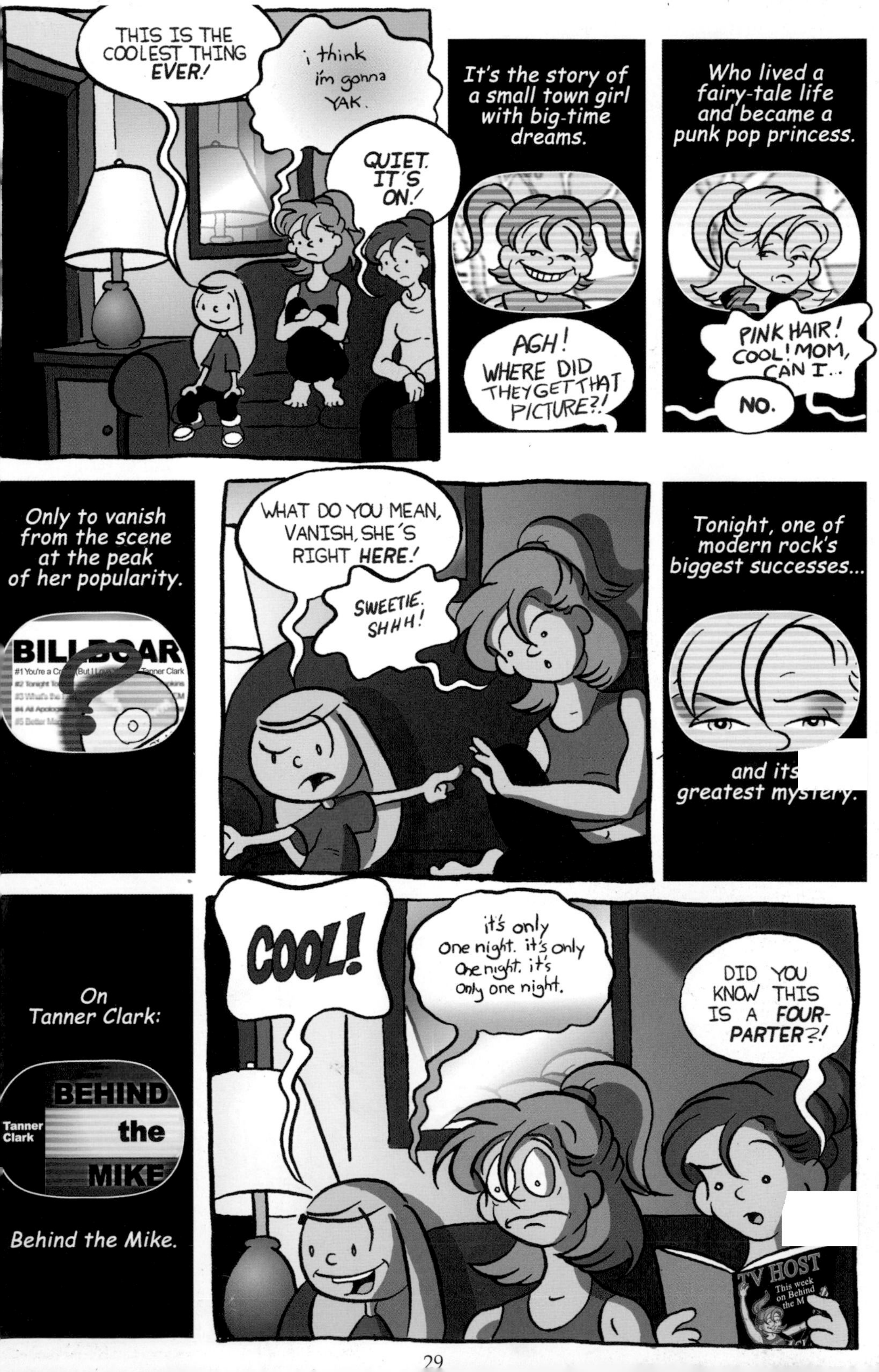
THIS IS THE COOLEST THING EVER!
i think i'm gonna YAK.
QUIET. IT'S ON!
It's the story of a small town girl with big-time dreams.
AGH! WHERE DID THEY GET THAT PICTURE?!
Who lived a fairy-tale life and became a punk pop princess.
PINK HAIR! COOL! MOM, CAN I...
NO.
Only to vanish from the scene at the peak of her popularity.
WHAT DO YOU MEAN, VANISH, SHE'S RIGHT HERE!
SWEETIE. SHHH!
Tonight, one of modern rock's biggest successes...
and its greatest mystery.
On Tanner Clark:
BEHIND the MIKE
Tanner Clark
Behind the Mike.
COOL!
it's only one night. it's only one night. it's only one night.
DID YOU KNOW THIS IS A FOUR-PARTER?!
TV HOST
This week on Behind the M

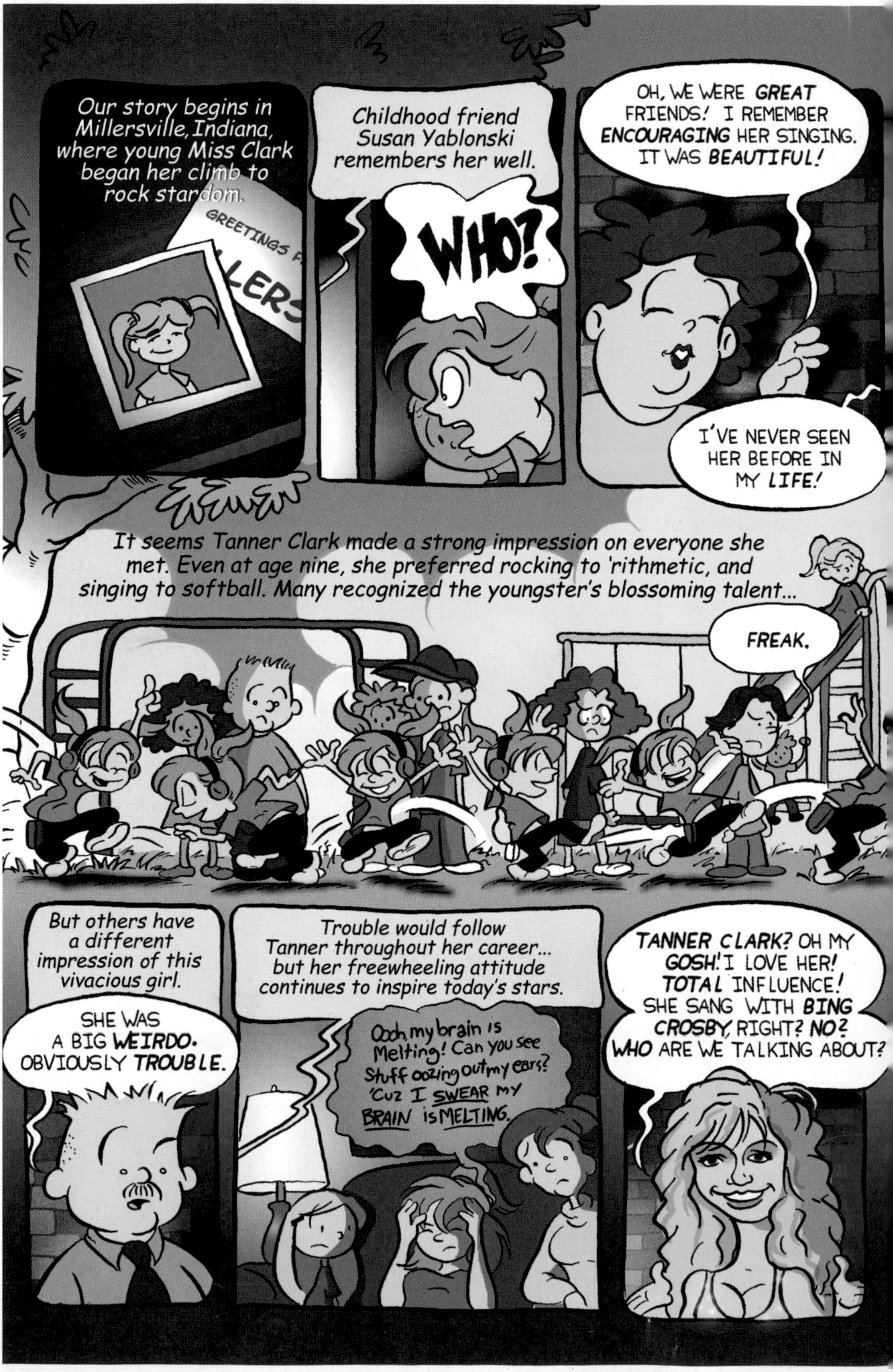
Our story begins in Millersville, Indiana, where young Miss Clark began her climb to rock stardom.
GREETINGS F
LERS
Childhood friend Susan Yablonski remembers her well.
WHO?
OH, WE WERE GREAT FRIENDS! I REMEMBER ENCOURAGING HER SINGING. IT WAS BEAUTIFUL!
I'VE NEVER SEEN HER BEFORE IN MY LIFE!
It seems Tanner Clark made a strong impression on everyone she met. Even at age nine, she preferred rocking to 'rithmetic, and singing to softball. Many recognized the youngster's blossoming talent...
FREAK.
But others have a different impression of this vivacious girl.
SHE WAS A BIG WEIRDO. OBVIOUSLY TROUBLE.
Trouble would follow Tanner throughout her career... but her freewheeling attitude continues to inspire today's stars.
Oooh, my brain is Melting! Can you see Stuff oozing out my ears? 'Cuz I SWEAR MY BRAIN is MELTING.
TANNER CLARK? OH MY GOSH! I LOVE HER! TOTAL INFLUENCE! SHE SANG WITH BING CROSBY, RIGHT? NO? WHO ARE WE TALKING ABOUT?

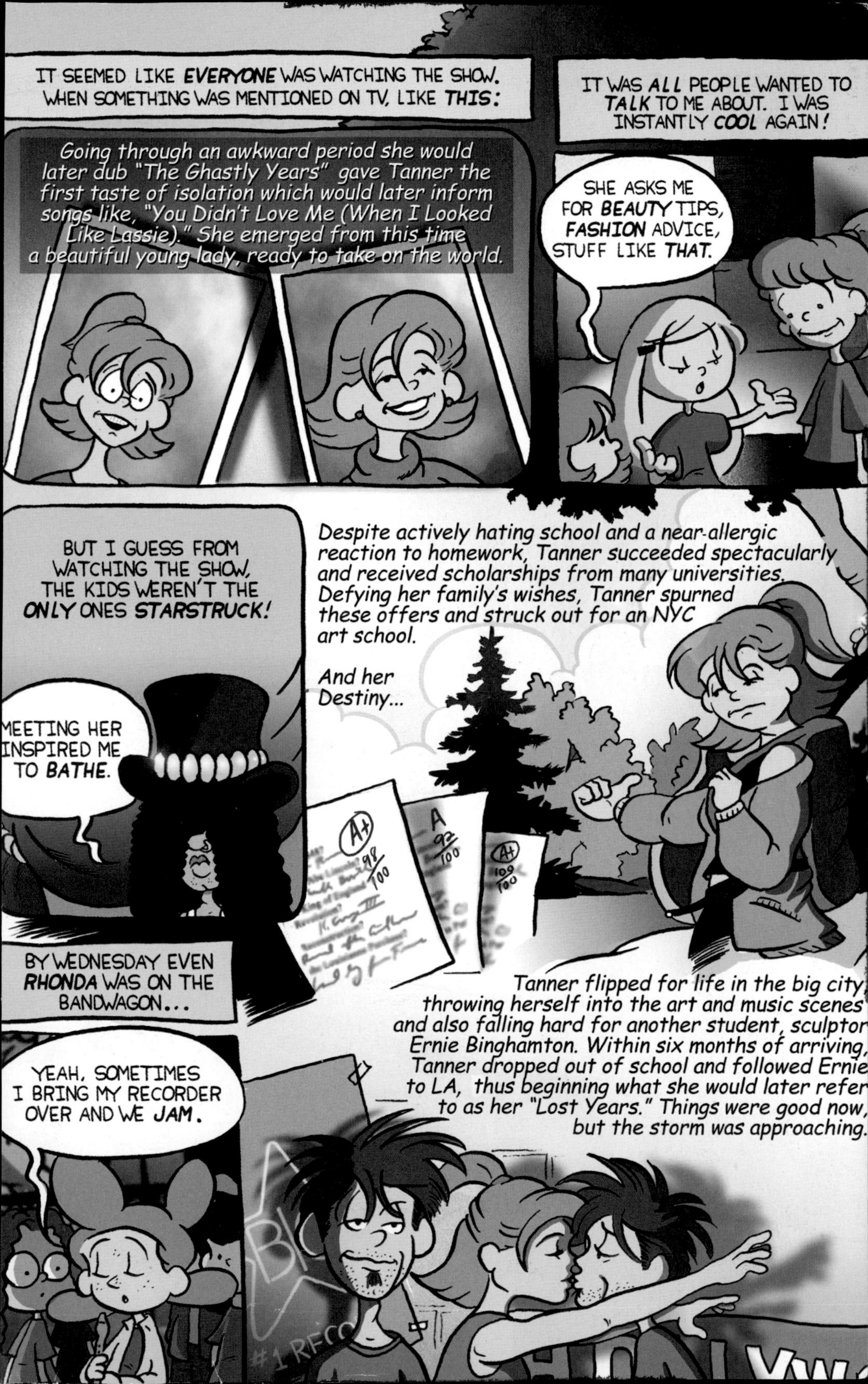
IT SEEMED LIKE EVERYONE WAS WATCHING THE SHOW. WHEN SOMETHING WAS MENTIONED ON TV, LIKE THIS:
Going through an awkward period she would later dub "The Ghastly Years" gave Tanner the first taste of isolation which would later inform songs like, "You Didn't Love Me (When I Looked Like Lassie)." She emerged from this time a beautiful young lady, ready to take on the world.
IT WAS ALL PEOPLE WANTED TO TALK TO ME ABOUT. I WAS INSTANTLY COOL AGAIN!
SHE ASKS ME FOR BEAUTY TIPS, FASHION ADVICE, STUFF LIKE THAT.
BUT I GUESS FROM WATCHING THE SHOW, THE KIDS WEREN'T THE ONLY ONES STARSTRUCK!
MEETING HER INSPIRED ME TO BATHE.
Despite actively hating school and a near-allergic reaction to homework, Tanner succeeded spectacularly and received scholarships from many universities. Defying her family's wishes, Tanner spurned these offers and struck out for an NYC art school.
And her Destiny...
BY WEDNESDAY EVEN RHONDA WAS ON THE BANDWAGON...
YEAH, SOMETIMES I BRING MY RECORDER OVER AND WE JAM.
Tanner flipped for life in the big city, throwing herself into the art and music scenes and also falling hard for another student, sculptor Ernie Binghamton. Within six months of arriving, Tanner dropped out of school and followed Ernie to LA, thus beginning what she would later refer to as her "Lost Years." Things were good now, but the storm was approaching.

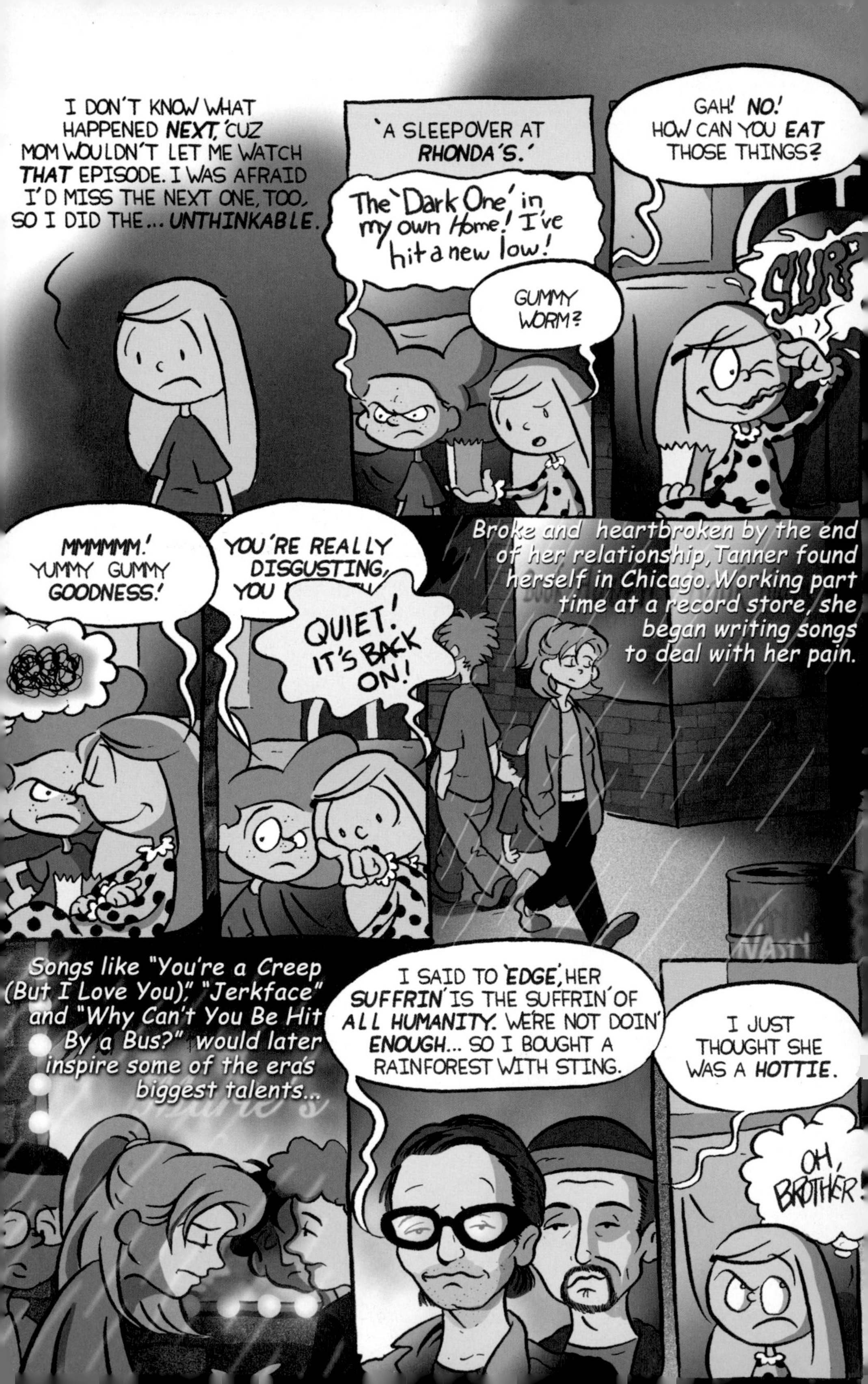

I DON'T KNOW WHAT HAPPENED **NEXT**, 'CUZ MOM WOULDN'T LET ME WATCH **THAT** EPISODE. I WAS AFRAID I'D MISS THE NEXT ONE, TOO, SO I DID THE... **UNTHINKABLE**.
'A SLEEPOVER AT **RHONDA'S**.'
The 'Dark One' in my own Home! I've hit a new low!
GUMMY WORM?
GAH! **NO!** HOW CAN YOU **EAT** THOSE THINGS?
SLURP
MMMMMM! YUMMY GUMMY **GOODNESS!**
YOU'RE REALLY DISGUSTING, YOU
QUIET! IT'S BACK ON!
Broke and heartbroken by the end of her relationship, Tanner found herself in Chicago. Working part time at a record store, she began writing songs to deal with her pain.
NASTY
Songs like "You're a Creep (But I Love You)," "Jerkface" and "Why Can't You Be Hit By a Bus?" would later inspire some of the era's biggest talents...
I SAID TO **'EDGE'**, HER **SUFFRIN'** IS THE SUFFRIN' OF **ALL HUMANITY**. WE'RE NOT DOIN' **ENOUGH**... SO I BOUGHT A RAINFOREST WITH STING.
I JUST THOUGHT SHE WAS A **HOTTIE**.
OH, BROTHER!

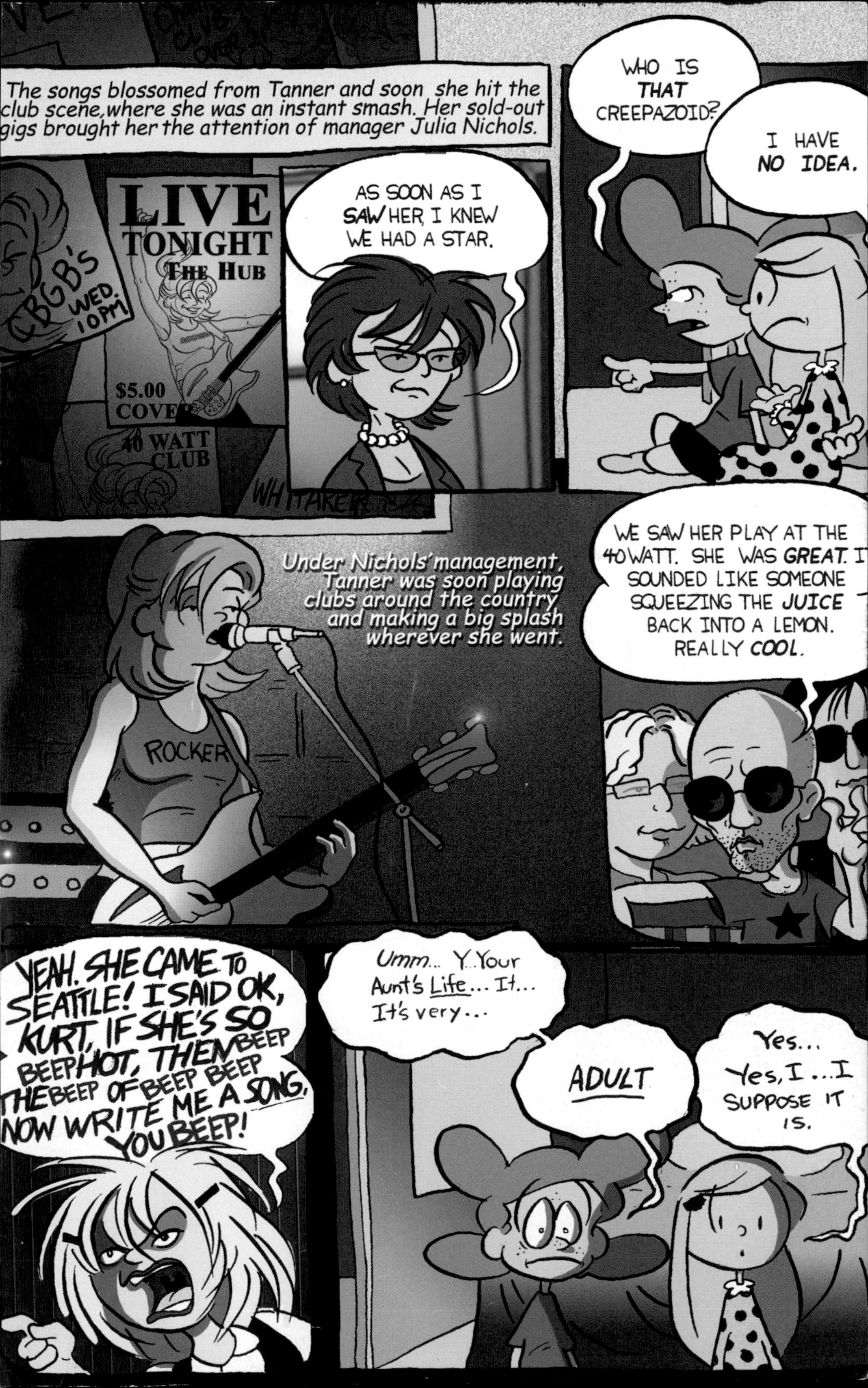
The songs blossomed from Tanner and soon she hit the club scene, where she was an instant smash. Her sold-out gigs brought her the attention of manager Julia Nichols.
LIVE TONIGHT THE HUB
CBGB's WED. 10PM
$5.00 COVER
40 WATT CLUB
AS SOON AS I SAW HER, I KNEW WE HAD A STAR.
WHO IS THAT CREEPAZOID?
I HAVE NO IDEA.
Under Nichols' management, Tanner was soon playing clubs around the country and making a big splash wherever she went.
ROCKER
WE SAW HER PLAY AT THE 40 WATT. SHE WAS GREAT. IT SOUNDED LIKE SOMEONE SQUEEZING THE JUICE BACK INTO A LEMON. REALLY COOL.
YEAH. SHE CAME TO SEATTLE! I SAID OK, KURT, IF SHE'S SO BEEP HOT, THEN BEEP THE BEEP OF BEEP BEEP NOW WRITE ME A SONG, YOU BEEP!
Umm... Y..Your Aunt's Life... It... It's very...
ADULT
Yes... Yes, I ...I SUPPOSE IT IS.

I GUESS MOM FIGURED THE LAST EPISODE WOULD BE *TAME*, SO SHE LET ME WATCH IT AT *HOME*. NOT THAT ANY OF US GOT TO *SEE* MUCH, ANYWAY.

Nichols was a master of promotion, and Tanner's debut single "Gabardine Prom Queen" was already in the top 20 when her album "Broken Record" hit the shelves. It looked like the beginning of a long pop reign, but then, just days after the release of "Broken Record", Tanner Clark cancelled her tour, stopped further recording, and vanished from the music scene entirely.

BROKEN RECORD

NIRVANA PEARL JAM SMASHING PUMPKINS
Rolling Stone

ALT-COUNTRY WITH
VICTORIA WILLIAMS
ALT-SIT-COM WITH
JERRY SEINFELD

BROKEN R

IT WAS A REAL *SHOCK*. I DIDN'T SEE IT COMING. NO ONE KNOWS *WHY* SHE DID WHAT SHE DID, BUT I *HOPE* TO *WORK* WITH HER AGAIN.

YOU DO TOO KNOW WHY, YOU... YOU... YOU... *NERDYBUTTBRAINFACE!*

˃SIGH˂ YA KNOW, I COULD USE BETTER *WORDS* IF *YOU* WEREN'T HERE.

SORRY.

Even though her time in the spotlight was brief, her influence was strong, and her peers remember her fondly.

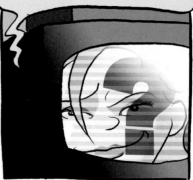

THE LAST TIME I SAW HER, SHE SAID, 'ALANIS, IN YOUR NEXT VIDEO YOU SHOULD BE *NAKED*.' I REALIZE *NOW* SHE WAS KIDDING.

Oh, of *COURSE* I was kidding, you *DUMB*... OOOOOH!

˃ *CLICK* ˂

I WENT UP TO BED AND LAY THERE FOR A WHILE LISTENING TO TANNER USE WORDS LESS *CREATIVE* THAN 'NERDYBUTTBRAINFACE.'

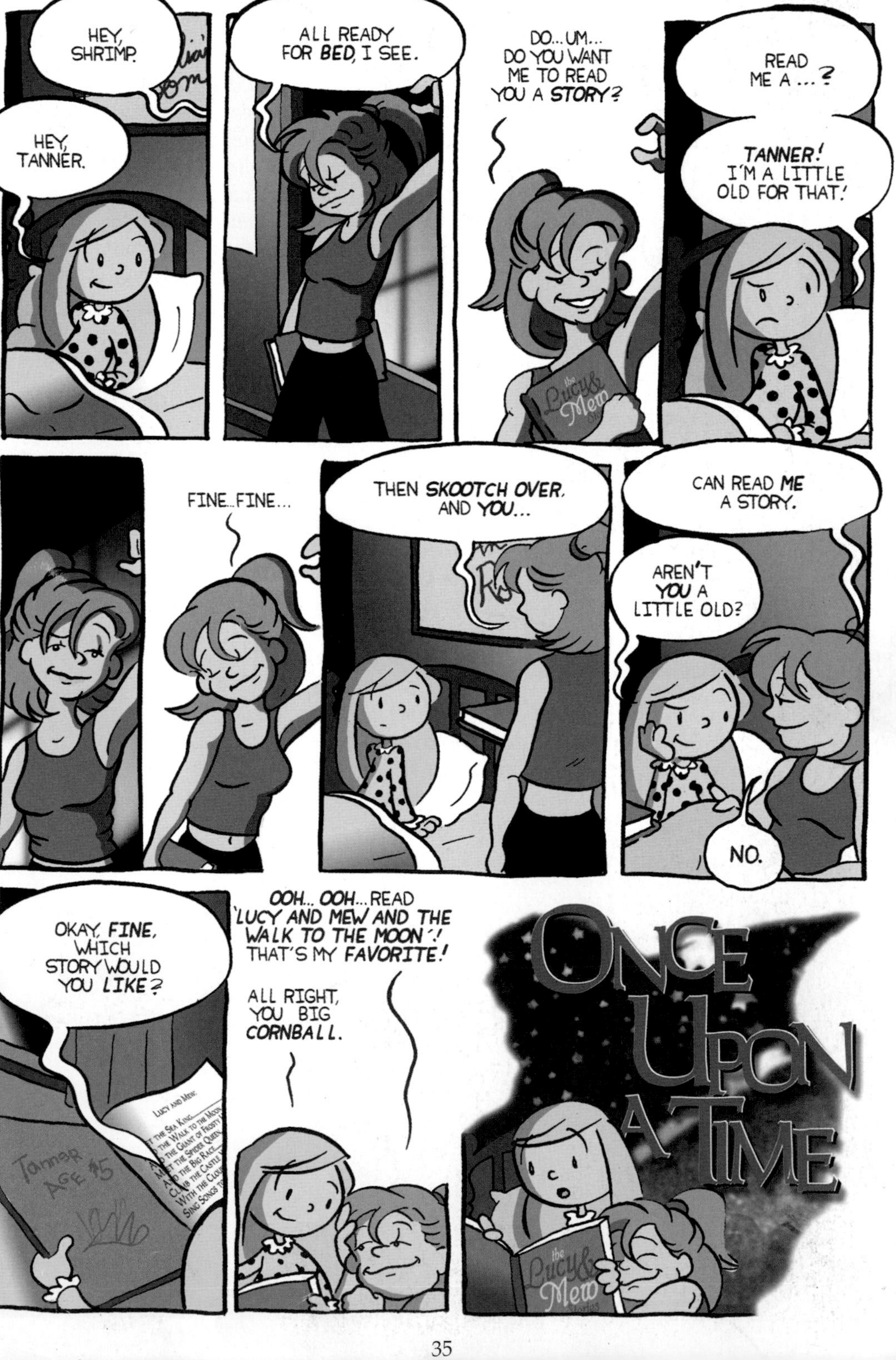
HEY, SHRIMP.
HEY, TANNER.
ALL READY FOR BED, I SEE.
DO...UM... DO YOU WANT ME TO READ YOU A STORY?
READ ME A ...?
TANNER! I'M A LITTLE OLD FOR THAT!
FINE...FINE...
THEN SKOOTCH OVER, AND YOU...
CAN READ ME A STORY.
AREN'T YOU A LITTLE OLD?
NO.
OKAY, FINE, WHICH STORY WOULD YOU LIKE?
OOH... OOH...READ 'LUCY AND MEW AND THE WALK TO THE MOON'! THAT'S MY FAVORITE!
ALL RIGHT, YOU BIG CORNBALL.
Tanner AGE 5
ONCE UPON A TIME

The Walk to the Moon

By Beth Ellen Welch

Once upon a time there was a poor young girl named Lucy who lived with a cat named Mew. Lucy and Mew lived in a very small house in a very small village in an enormous country which probably never existed, but which seemed quite nice. Lucy had no parents, and so she relied on Mew to care for her. This was not a problem, for Mew was a talented cat and earned more than many of the men in the village, and even as much as a few of the more prominent sheep. In exchange for her keep, Lucy kept the house tidy, the food and water dishes full, and the litter box clean. But Lucy was bored.

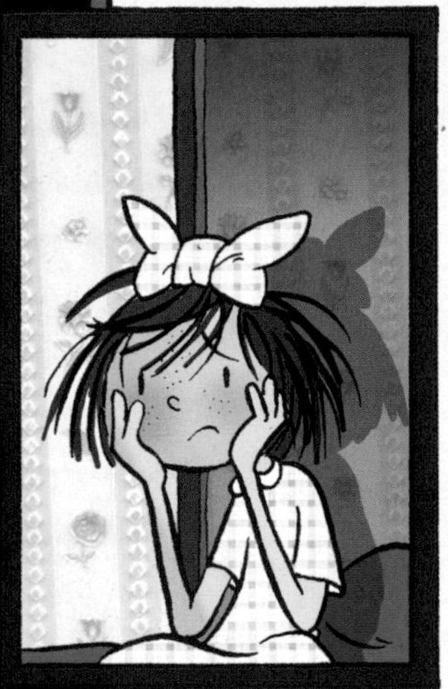

"There's nothing ever to do in this village," she complained to Mew. "I've heard other girls speak of villages with many dwellings under one roof, staircases that carry you magically from floor to floor, and merchants with goods from faraway lands... shops of all kinds selling fragrances, literature, garments, and equipment for sport, a common area where people may sample morsels and delicacies from all the world over. And outside, yet another dining hall, set under glorious, illuminated golden arches."

"My business dealings have taken me to such villages," said Mew. "The people seem no happier there than they do any place else on earth."

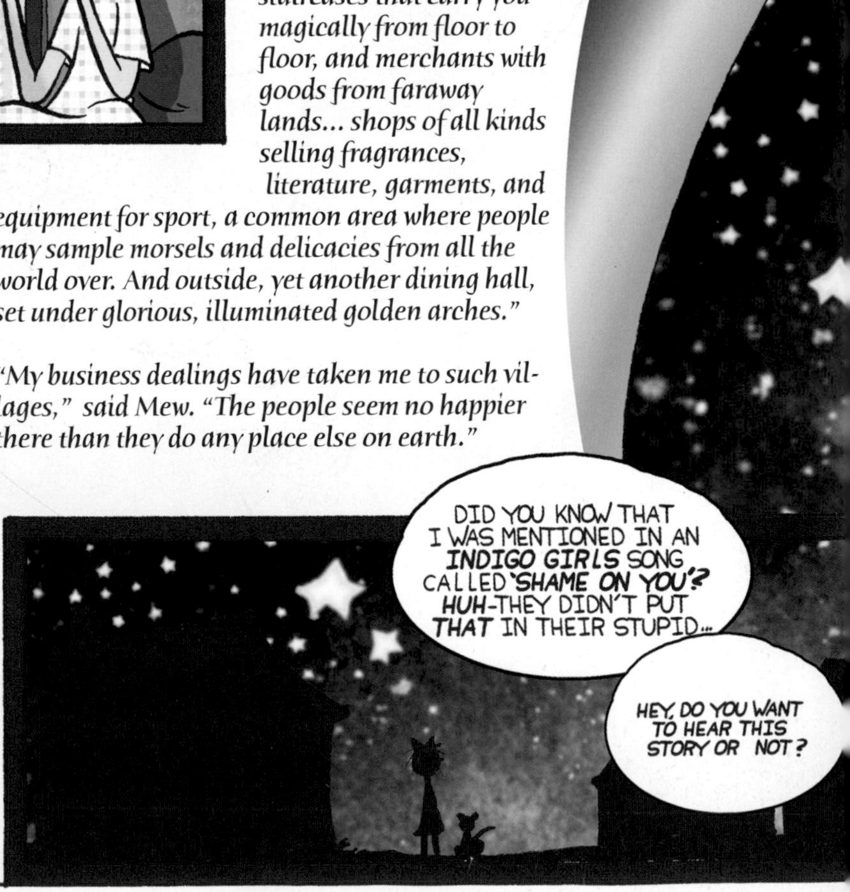
DID YOU KNOW THAT I WAS MENTIONED IN AN INDIGO GIRLS SONG CALLED 'SHAME ON YOU'? HUH-THEY DIDN'T PUT THAT IN THEIR STUPID...
HEY, DO YOU WANT TO HEAR THIS STORY OR NOT?

It was then that Lucy had a
brilliant idea.

"But what about off the Earth?" she cried.
"What about the village on the moon!" Mew
had to admit that he had never heard of such
villages, but still he was intrigued. "I imagine a cat
with my skills in accounting could make as good a living
on the moon as in this village," he said. And so Lucy and
Mew decided to walk to the moon.

The plan was simple: wait until the next rainbow appeared, walk to
the top, then jump the remaining distance to the moon. "A brilliant
plan," said Mew. "It's a wonder no one has thought of it before."

The two travelers took nothing with them save Lucy's umbrella and a large
roll of cash. Everything they needed, they reasoned, they would get in the
wondrous moon village.

The trip was longer than they expected, and Mew was very cross at Lucy
for not having thought to bring even a small can of tuna. Lucy's legs got
tired, but she sustained herself by thinking of the wonders the moon
villages were sure to contain.

Finally, the top of the rainbow was reached. The
leap was taken, and Lucy and Mew landed on
the moon. They were so happy to have
arrived that they danced as only an
orphan girl and her benefactor cat
can dance.

Unfortunately, after celebrating,
they realized there was not a
village in sight. "I'm sure they
are here," said Lucy. "We
just need to explore a bit."

But after hours and days and weeks of exploring, all Lucy and Mew had found were some flags, a sculpture, and a carriage (but no horse).

This is terrible! cried Lucy. We're completely alone!

We're never alone if we have each other, said Mew.

Oh, shut up, said Lucy.

With nothing to do but sit on the rim of a crater and stare at the Earth, Lucy and Mew both became melancholy.

"I miss having a home to clean and dishes to fill, and , well...maybe not the litterbox," said Lucy.

"I'm just glad that cheese thing turned out to be true," said Mew. "Otherwise we would have starved."

Lucy decided that enough was enough, and, grabbing Mew with one hand and her umbrella with the other, she leapt off the edge of the moon.

Lucy opened her umbrella and used it to slow their fall, so they drifted down to earth in just a little under four days.

They landed back in the square of the very village they had left so long ago, and it seemed as if it had not changed at all.

"You know," Lucy said, "before we left, I wanted nothing more than to live the rest of my life on the moon, but now that we're back, I can't imagine why we ever left."

'THE END.'

HMMPH...THERE'S A 'TRUE THING ADULTS DON'T WANT *KIDS* TO KNOW.'

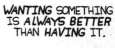

WANTING SOMETHING IS *ALWAYS BETTER* THAN *HAVING IT.*

REALLY? HMMMM...

UNEMPLOYMENT

THE McBRIDES

YEAH... I CAN SEE...

TANNER?

G'NIGHT.

'CLICK'

39

I COULDN'T STOP THINKING ABOUT THE **SHOW** AND WHY TANNER QUIT SINGING. IT WASN'T LIKE HER TO BE A **QUITTER!** SO THE NEXT DAY AFTER SCHOOL, I DECIDED TO TRY TO WEASEL SOME INFO OUT OF **MOM**.

I WAS **SURPRISED**, 'CUZ MOM SEEMED KINDA **HAPPY** TO TALK ABOUT IT. SHE TOLD ME THAT WHEN TANNER WAS OUT IN CALIFORNIA AND **LATER** WHEN SHE WAS ON TOUR, THAT THEY DIDN'T REALLY **TALK MUCH**. I GUESS NO ONE THOUGHT TANNER SHOULD BE DOING WHAT SHE WAS DOING, 'CUZ SHE WAS SO SMART AND ALL.

(**PLUS** NO ONE **LIKED** THAT ERNIE CREEP.)

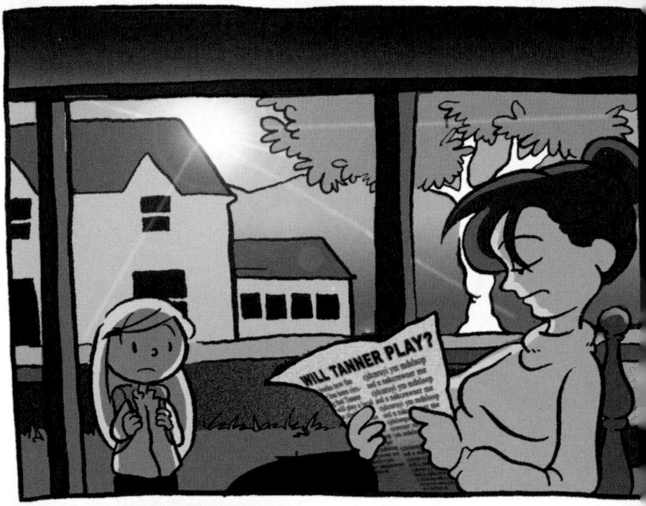
WILL TANNER PLAY?

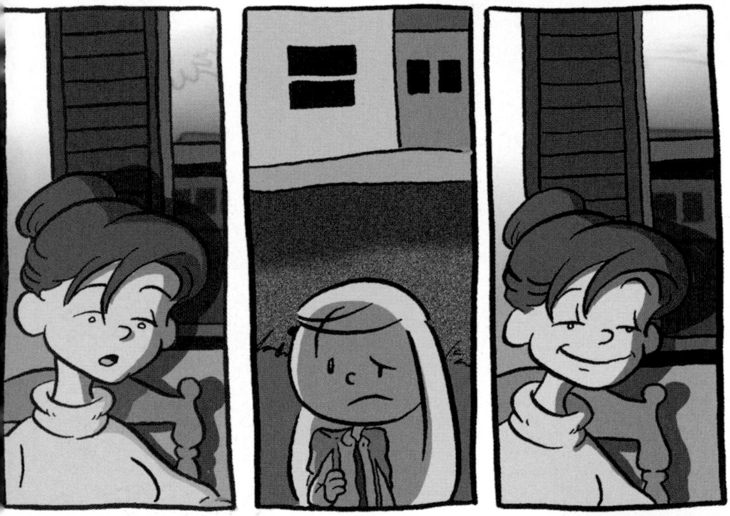

I DON'T THINK MOM HAD ANY **REAL** IDEA WHY TANNER QUIT SINGING. WHEN I **ASKED** HER ABOUT IT, ALL SHE SAID WAS THAT TANNER WAS A VERY **HONEST** PERSON, AND THAT NOT ALL THE PEOPLE SHE **DEALT** WITH WERE AS HONEST AS **SHE** IS.

MOM ALSO SAID THAT SHE DIDN'T THINK TANNER REALIZED HOW BIG A **FAN** MY **MOM** WAS. SHE SAID **SHE** UNDERSTOOD WHY TANNER WAS A SINGER EVEN BETTER THAN TANNER **HERSELF** DID.

I DIDN'T REALLY UNDERSTAND WHAT SHE **MEANT**, BUT I THINK I DO **NOW**.

THEN MOM LET LOOSE WITH **THIS** BOMBSHELL: SHE HAD KEPT A COLLECTION OF **SOUVENIRS** FROM TANNER'S CAREER. MAGAZINES AND VIDEOS AND TAPES AND STUFF TANNER **HERSELF** PROBABLY DIDN'T EVEN REMEMBER. SHE SAID THAT EVEN THOUGH TANNER DIDN'T WANT TO LOOK AT THAT STUFF **NOW**, SHE WOULD **SOMEDAY**. AND THEN SHE'D REALIZE HOW **BIG A FAN** MY MOM HAD BEEN.

SHE SAID SHE HAD IT ALL IN A TRUNK IN THE **ATTIC**.

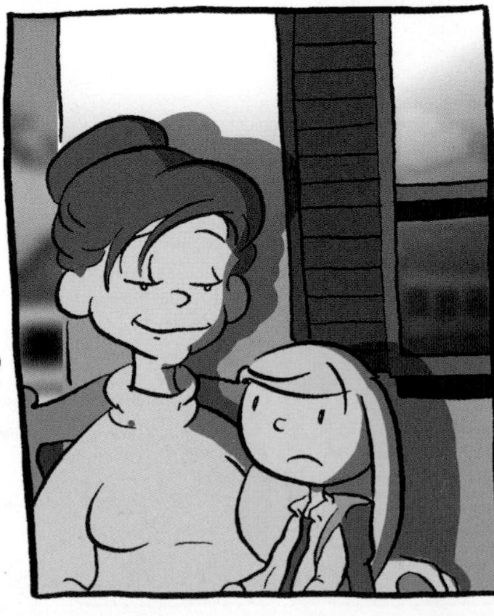

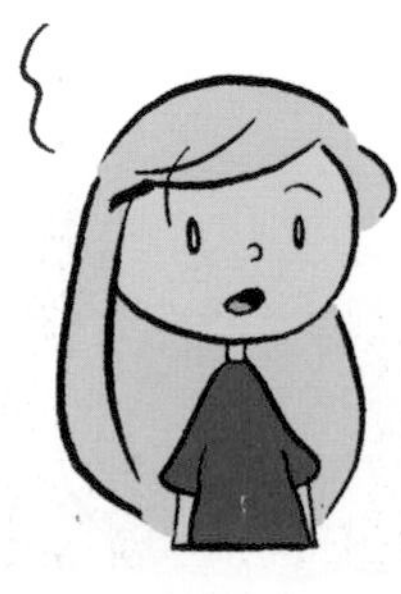
WELL, IF YOU WERE ME, WHAT WOULD YOU DO?

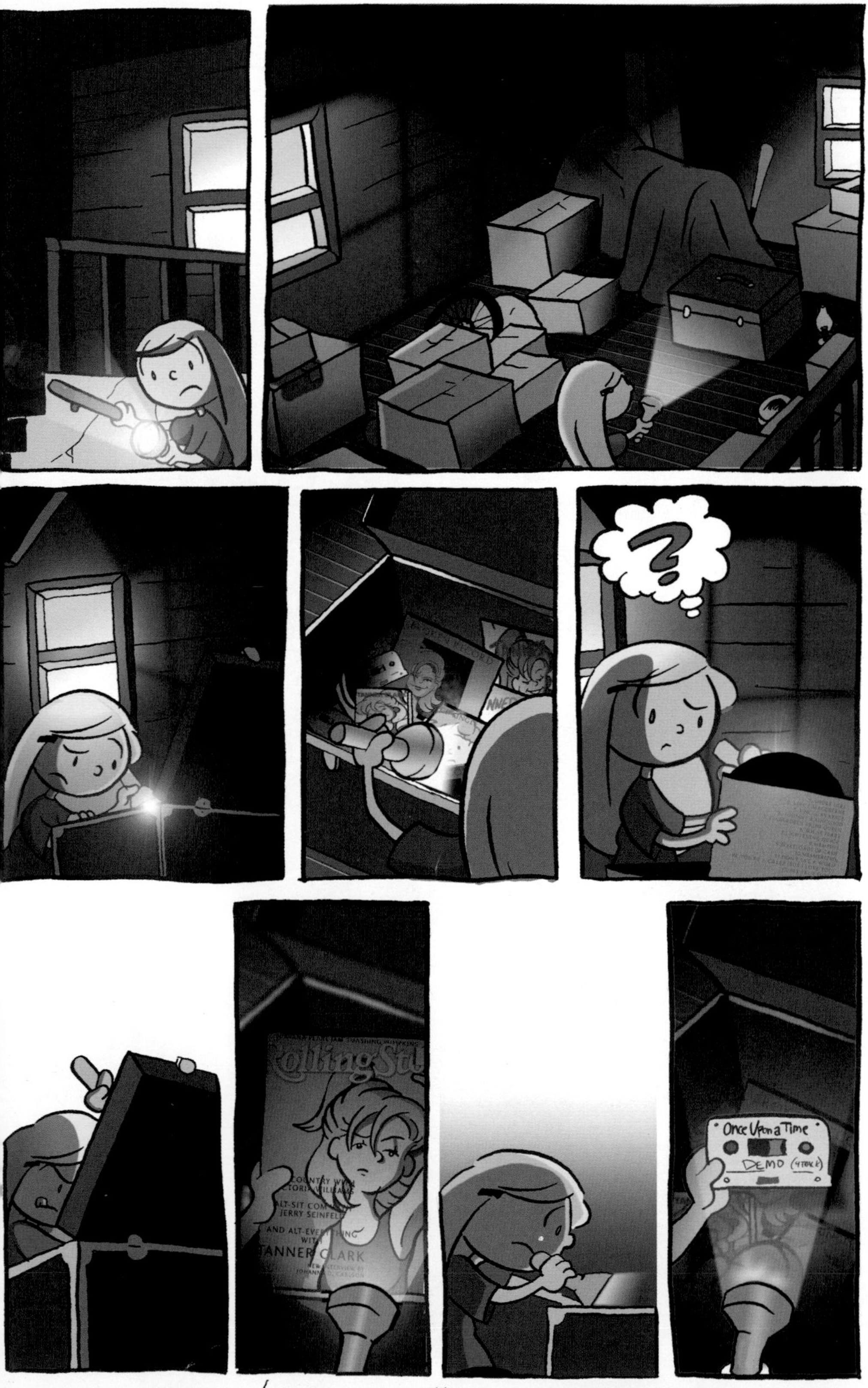
?
JERRY SEINFELD
TANNER CLARK
Once Upon a Time
DEMO

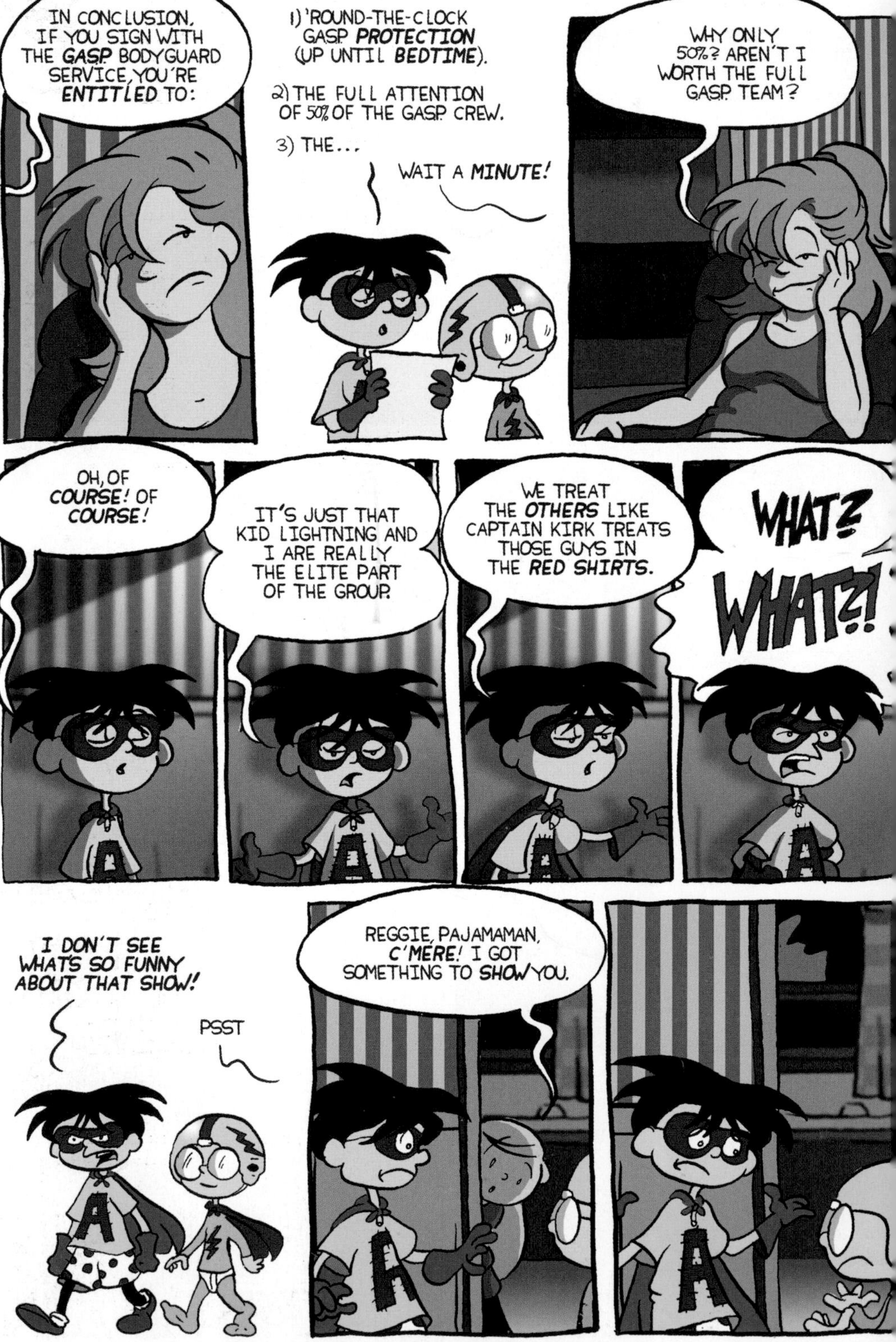

IN CONCLUSION, IF YOU SIGN WITH THE GASP BODYGUARD SERVICE, YOU'RE ENTITLED TO:
1) 'ROUND-THE-CLOCK GASP PROTECTION (UP UNTIL BEDTIME).
2) THE FULL ATTENTION OF 50% OF THE GASP CREW.
3) THE...
WAIT A MINUTE!
WHY ONLY 50%? AREN'T I WORTH THE FULL GASP TEAM?
OH, OF COURSE! OF COURSE!
IT'S JUST THAT KID LIGHTNING AND I ARE REALLY THE ELITE PART OF THE GROUP.
WE TREAT THE OTHERS LIKE CAPTAIN KIRK TREATS THOSE GUYS IN THE RED SHIRTS.
WHAT?
WHAT?!
I DON'T SEE WHAT'S SO FUNNY ABOUT THAT SHOW!
PSST
REGGIE, PAJAMAMAN, C'MERE! I GOT SOMETHING TO SHOW YOU.

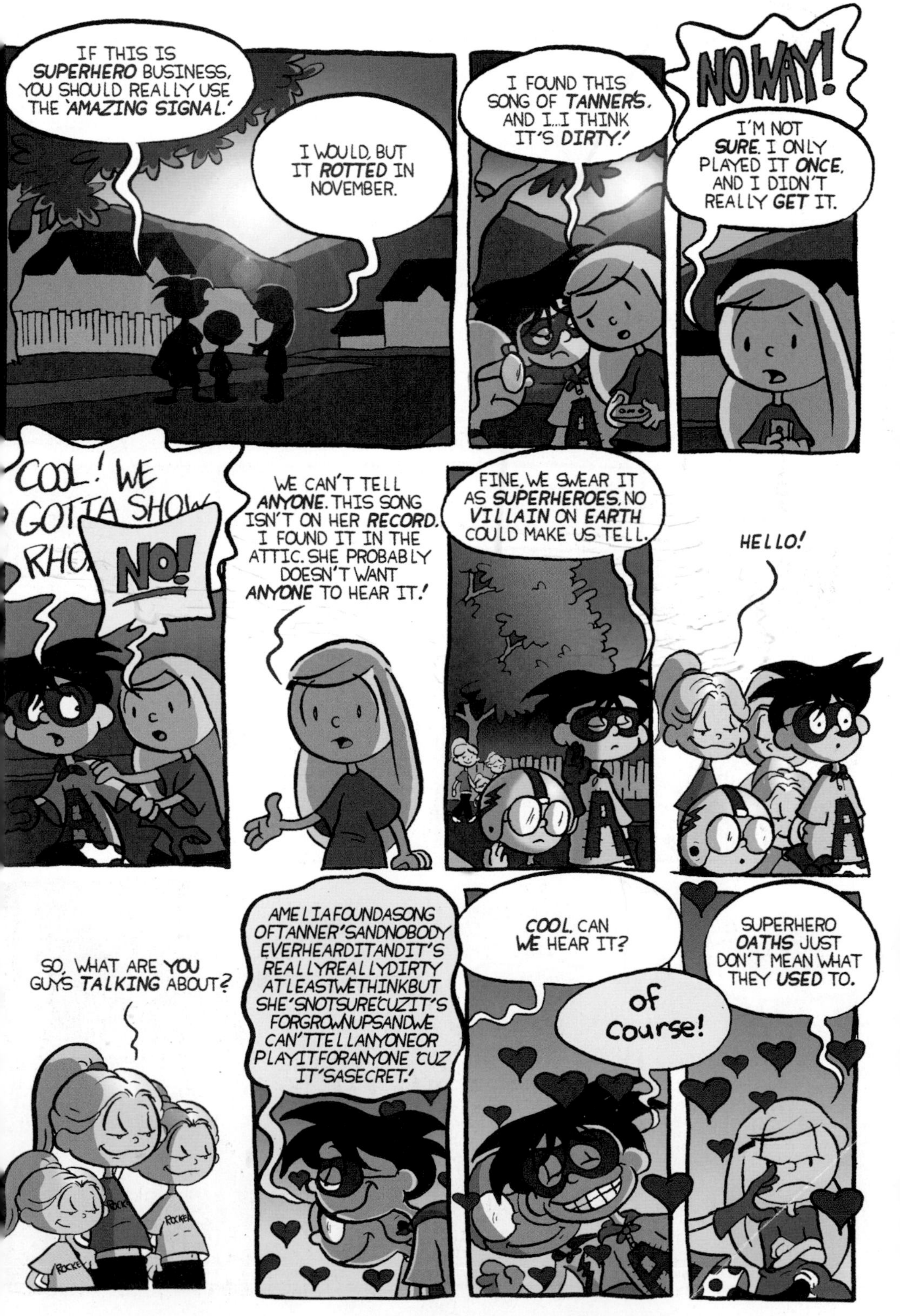
IF THIS IS SUPERHERO BUSINESS, YOU SHOULD REALLY USE THE 'AMAZING SIGNAL.'
I WOULD, BUT IT ROTTED IN NOVEMBER.
I FOUND THIS SONG OF TANNER'S, AND I...I THINK IT'S DIRTY!
NO WAY!
I'M NOT SURE. I ONLY PLAYED IT ONCE, AND I DIDN'T REALLY GET IT.
COOL! WE GOTTA SHOW
NO!
WE CAN'T TELL ANYONE. THIS SONG ISN'T ON HER RECORD. I FOUND IT IN THE ATTIC. SHE PROBABLY DOESN'T WANT ANYONE TO HEAR IT!
FINE, WE SWEAR IT AS SUPERHEROES. NO VILLAIN ON EARTH COULD MAKE US TELL.
HELLO!
SO, WHAT ARE YOU GUYS TALKING ABOUT?
AMELIAFOUNDASONG OFTANNER'SANDNOBODY EVERHEARDITANDIT'S REALLYREALLYDIRTY ATLEASTWETHINKBUT SHE'SNOTSURE'CUZIT'S FORGROWNUPSANDWE CAN'TTELLANYONEOR PLAYITFORANYONE 'CUZ IT'SASECRET!
COOL. CAN WE HEAR IT?
of course!
SUPERHERO OATHS JUST DON'T MEAN WHAT THEY USED TO.

HMMM...
IT STARTED TO RAIN *AGAIN*. IT'S BEEN *DOING* THAT LATELY.

OH. SO ANYWAY... I WANTED TO *KILL* REGGIE.

I KNEW *THOSE THREE* WOULDN'T KEEP THEIR *TRAPS* SHUT!

AND SURE *ENOUGH*... BY SCHOOL *MONDAY*...

THE CAT WAS OUT OF THE BAG.

EVEN THOUGH ALMOST *NO ONE* HEARD THE SONG *THEMSELVES*...

DID YOU HEAR IT?

MAYBE. DID YOU?

IT DIDN'T STOP EVERYONE FROM *TALKING* ABOUT IT.

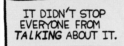

I DIDN'T HEAR IT, BUT I HEARD ABOUT IT.

DID YOU HEAR ABOUT IT?

I HEARD PEOPLE ARE TALKING.

AND EVERYONE WAS *SHOCKED* BY WHAT THEY *NEVER HEARD*.

I NEVER HEAR ANYTHING!

OF COURSE, WE *DID* STUPIDLY *PLAY* IT FOR *SOME* PEOPLE...

HOLEEEEE MOLEEEEE!

I ♥ TANNER!

AND EVERYONE HAD THE *SAME REACTION*.

Oh MY Oh MY Oh MY OO...

WELL, THERE WAS *ONE* STUPID EXCEPTION.

I Don't GET it!

OR *TWO*.

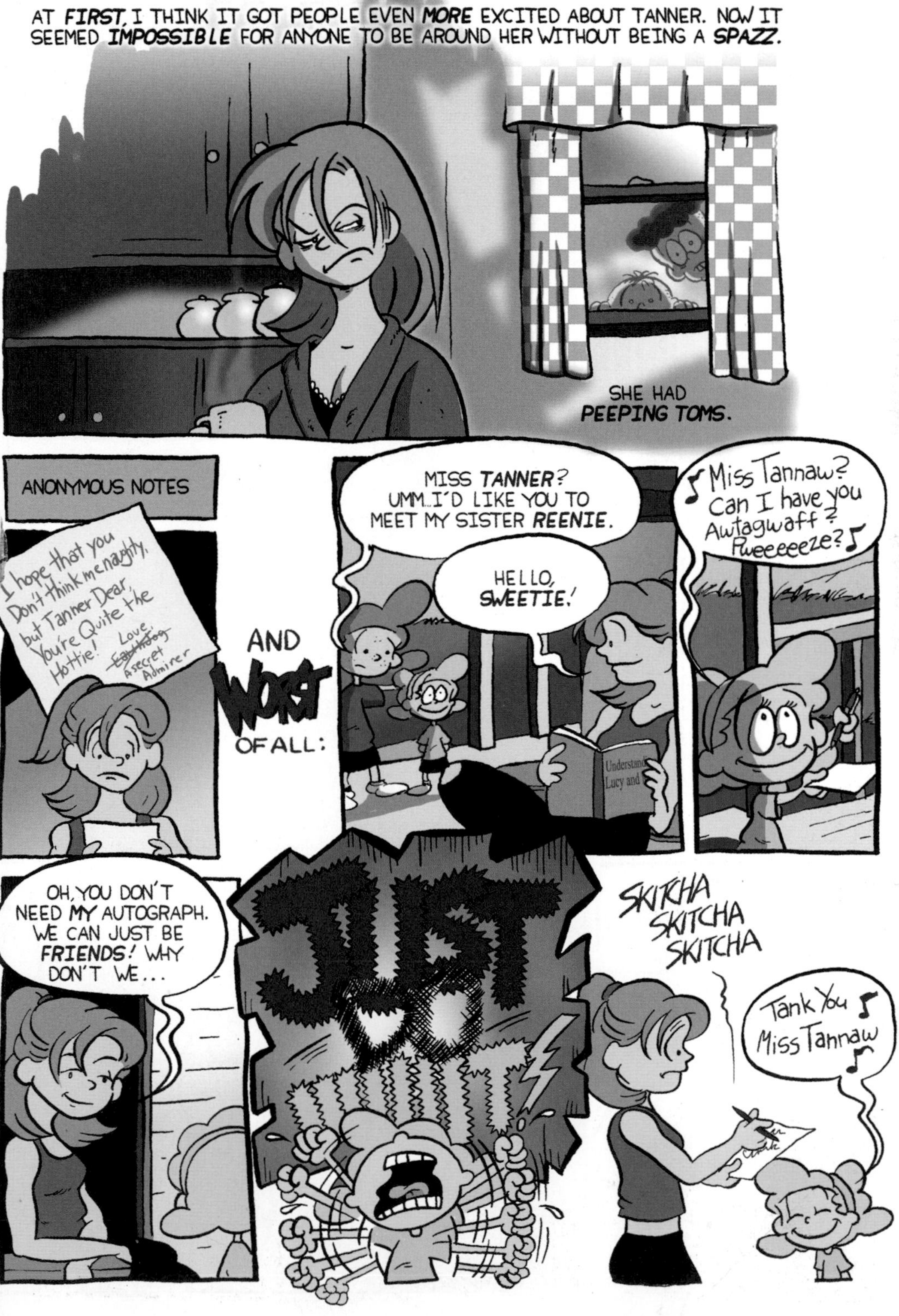

AT FIRST, I THINK IT GOT PEOPLE EVEN MORE EXCITED ABOUT TANNER. NOW IT SEEMED IMPOSSIBLE FOR ANYONE TO BE AROUND HER WITHOUT BEING A SPAZZ.
SHE HAD PEEPING TOMS.
ANONYMOUS NOTES
I hope that you Don't think me naughty, but Tanner Dear, You're Quite the Hottie! Love, A secret Admirer
AND WORST OF ALL:
MISS TANNER? UMM...I'D LIKE YOU TO MEET MY SISTER REENIE.
HELLO, SWEETIE!
Understand Lucy and
Miss Tannaw? Can I have you Awtagwaff? Pweeeeeze?
OH, YOU DON'T NEED MY AUTOGRAPH. WE CAN JUST BE FRIENDS! WHY DON'T WE...
JUST
SKITCHA SKITCHA SKITCHA
Tank You Miss Tannaw

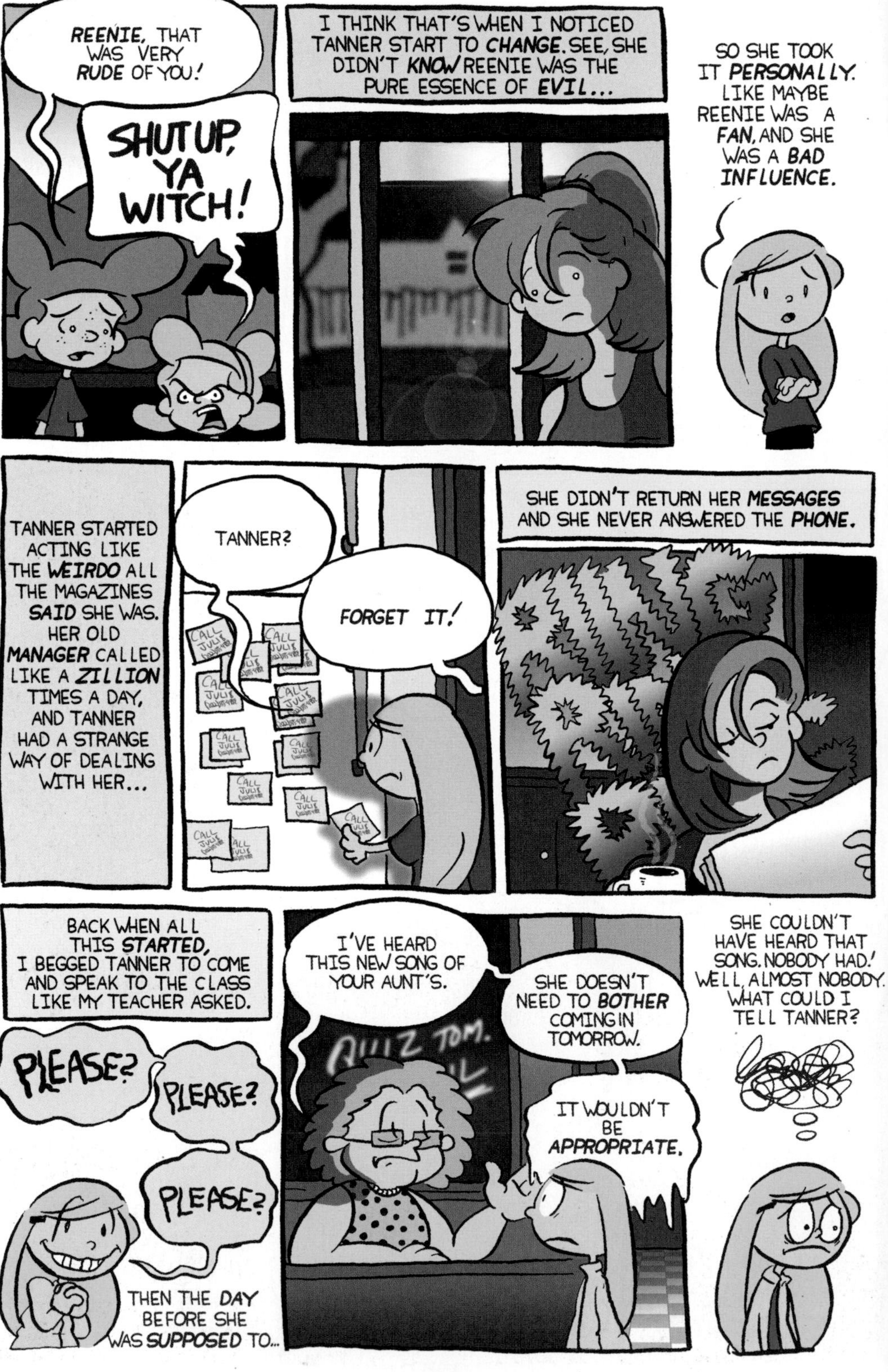
REENIE, THAT WAS VERY RUDE OF YOU!
SHUT UP, YA WITCH!
I THINK THAT'S WHEN I NOTICED TANNER START TO CHANGE. SEE, SHE DIDN'T KNOW REENIE WAS THE PURE ESSENCE OF EVIL...
SO SHE TOOK IT PERSONALLY. LIKE MAYBE REENIE WAS A FAN, AND SHE WAS A BAD INFLUENCE.
TANNER STARTED ACTING LIKE THE WEIRDO ALL THE MAGAZINES SAID SHE WAS. HER OLD MANAGER CALLED LIKE A ZILLION TIMES A DAY, AND TANNER HAD A STRANGE WAY OF DEALING WITH HER...
TANNER?
FORGET IT!
CALL JULIS
SHE DIDN'T RETURN HER MESSAGES AND SHE NEVER ANSWERED THE PHONE.
BACK WHEN ALL THIS STARTED, I BEGGED TANNER TO COME AND SPEAK TO THE CLASS LIKE MY TEACHER ASKED.
PLEASE?
PLEASE?
PLEASE?
THEN THE DAY BEFORE SHE WAS SUPPOSED TO...
I'VE HEARD THIS NEW SONG OF YOUR AUNT'S.
SHE DOESN'T NEED TO BOTHER COMING IN TOMORROW.
IT WOULDN'T BE APPROPRIATE.
SHE COULDN'T HAVE HEARD THAT SONG. NOBODY HAD! WELL, ALMOST NOBODY. WHAT COULD I TELL TANNER?

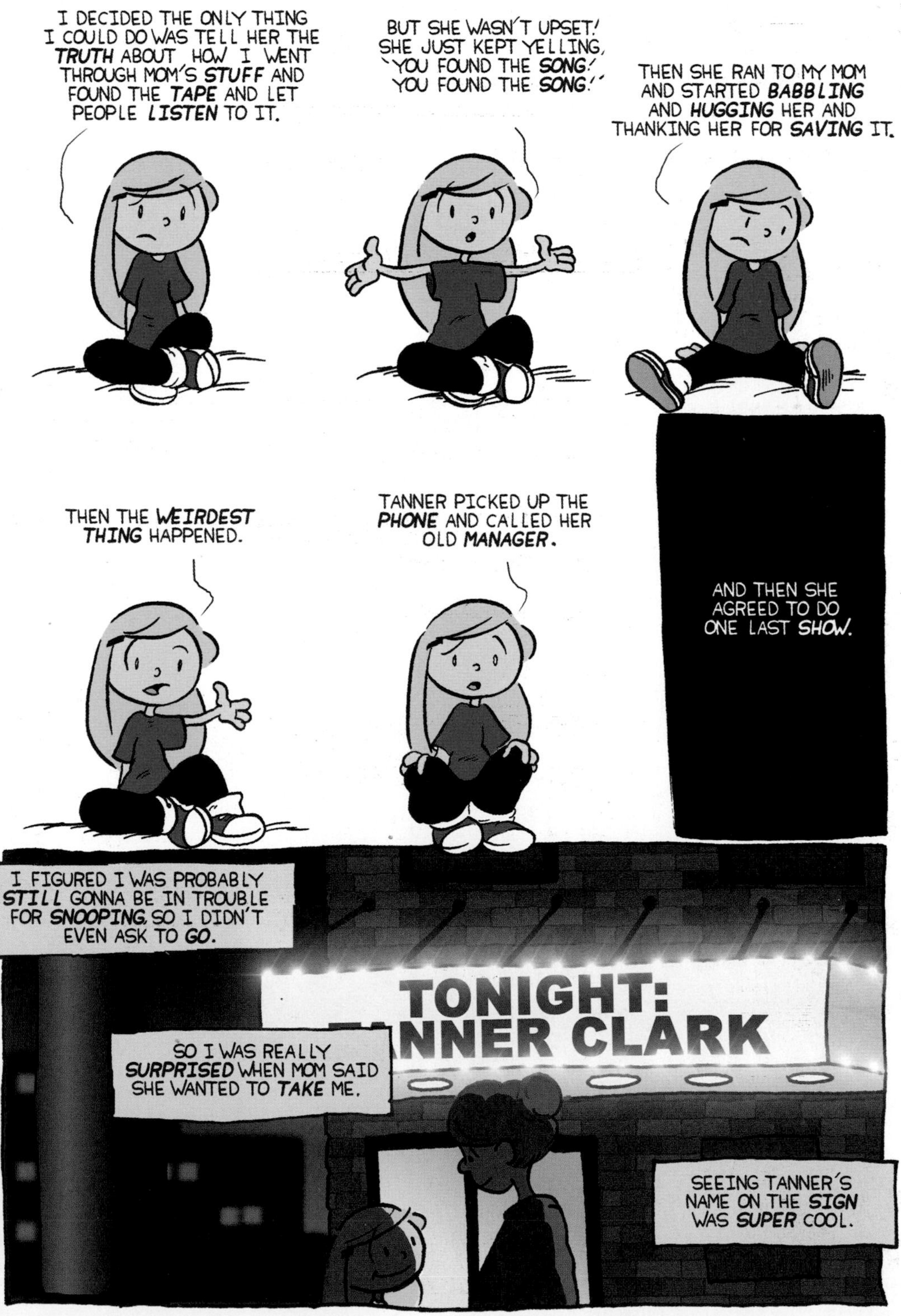
I DECIDED THE ONLY THING I COULD DO WAS TELL HER THE TRUTH ABOUT HOW I WENT THROUGH MOM'S STUFF AND FOUND THE TAPE AND LET PEOPLE LISTEN TO IT.
BUT SHE WASN'T UPSET! SHE JUST KEPT YELLING, "YOU FOUND THE SONG! YOU FOUND THE SONG!"
THEN SHE RAN TO MY MOM AND STARTED BABBLING AND HUGGING HER AND THANKING HER FOR SAVING IT.
THEN THE WEIRDEST THING HAPPENED.
TANNER PICKED UP THE PHONE AND CALLED HER OLD MANAGER.
AND THEN SHE AGREED TO DO ONE LAST SHOW.
I FIGURED I WAS PROBABLY STILL GONNA BE IN TROUBLE FOR SNOOPING, SO I DIDN'T EVEN ASK TO GO.
TONIGHT:
ANNER CLARK
SO I WAS REALLY SURPRISED WHEN MOM SAID SHE WANTED TO TAKE ME.
SEEING TANNER'S NAME ON THE SIGN WAS SUPER COOL.

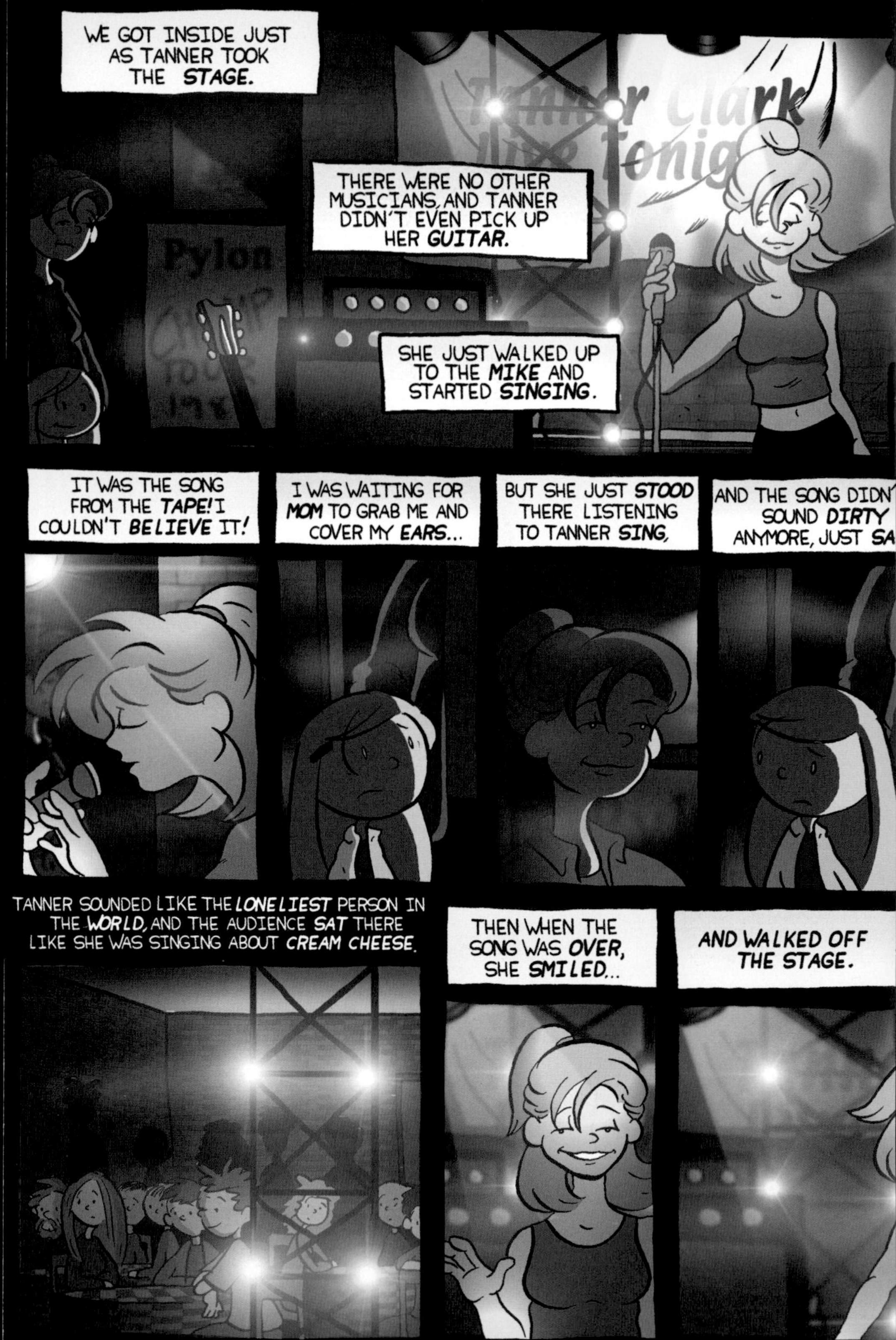
WE GOT INSIDE JUST AS TANNER TOOK THE STAGE.
Tanner Clark Live Tonig
Pylon
THERE WERE NO OTHER MUSICIANS, AND TANNER DIDN'T EVEN PICK UP HER GUITAR.
SHE JUST WALKED UP TO THE MIKE AND STARTED SINGING.
IT WAS THE SONG FROM THE TAPE! I COULDN'T BELIEVE IT!
I WAS WAITING FOR MOM TO GRAB ME AND COVER MY EARS...
BUT SHE JUST STOOD THERE LISTENING TO TANNER SING,
AND THE SONG DIDN'T SOUND DIRTY ANYMORE, JUST SA
TANNER SOUNDED LIKE THE LONELIEST PERSON IN THE WORLD, AND THE AUDIENCE SAT THERE LIKE SHE WAS SINGING ABOUT CREAM CHEESE.
THEN WHEN THE SONG WAS OVER, SHE SMILED...
AND WALKED OFF THE STAGE.

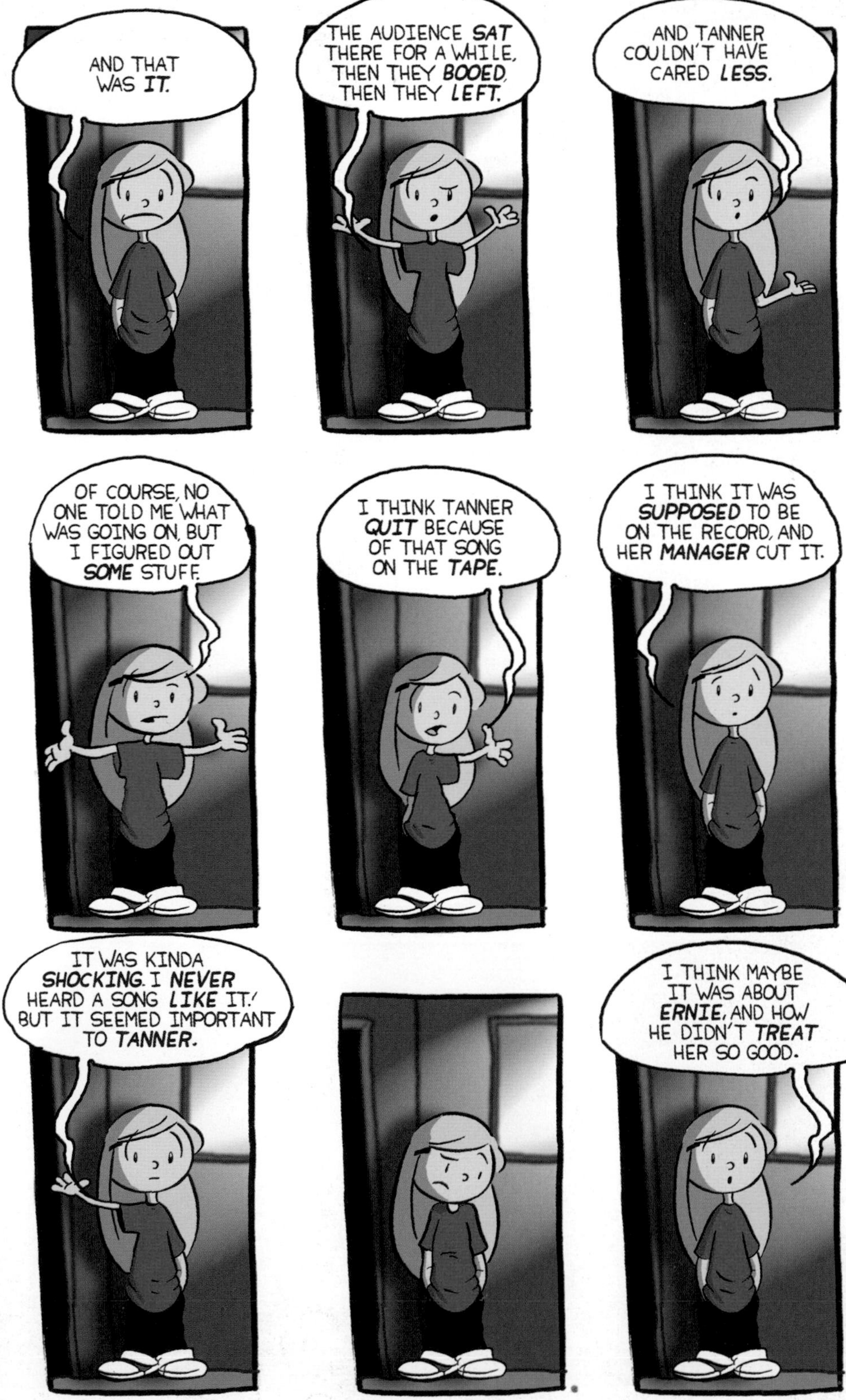

AND THAT WAS IT.
THE AUDIENCE SAT THERE FOR A WHILE, THEN THEY BOOED, THEN THEY LEFT.
AND TANNER COULDN'T HAVE CARED LESS.
OF COURSE, NO ONE TOLD ME WHAT WAS GOING ON, BUT I FIGURED OUT SOME STUFF.
I THINK TANNER QUIT BECAUSE OF THAT SONG ON THE TAPE.
I THINK IT WAS SUPPOSED TO BE ON THE RECORD, AND HER MANAGER CUT IT.
IT WAS KINDA SHOCKING. I NEVER HEARD A SONG LIKE IT! BUT IT SEEMED IMPORTANT TO TANNER.
I THINK MAYBE IT WAS ABOUT ERNIE, AND HOW HE DIDN'T TREAT HER SO GOOD.

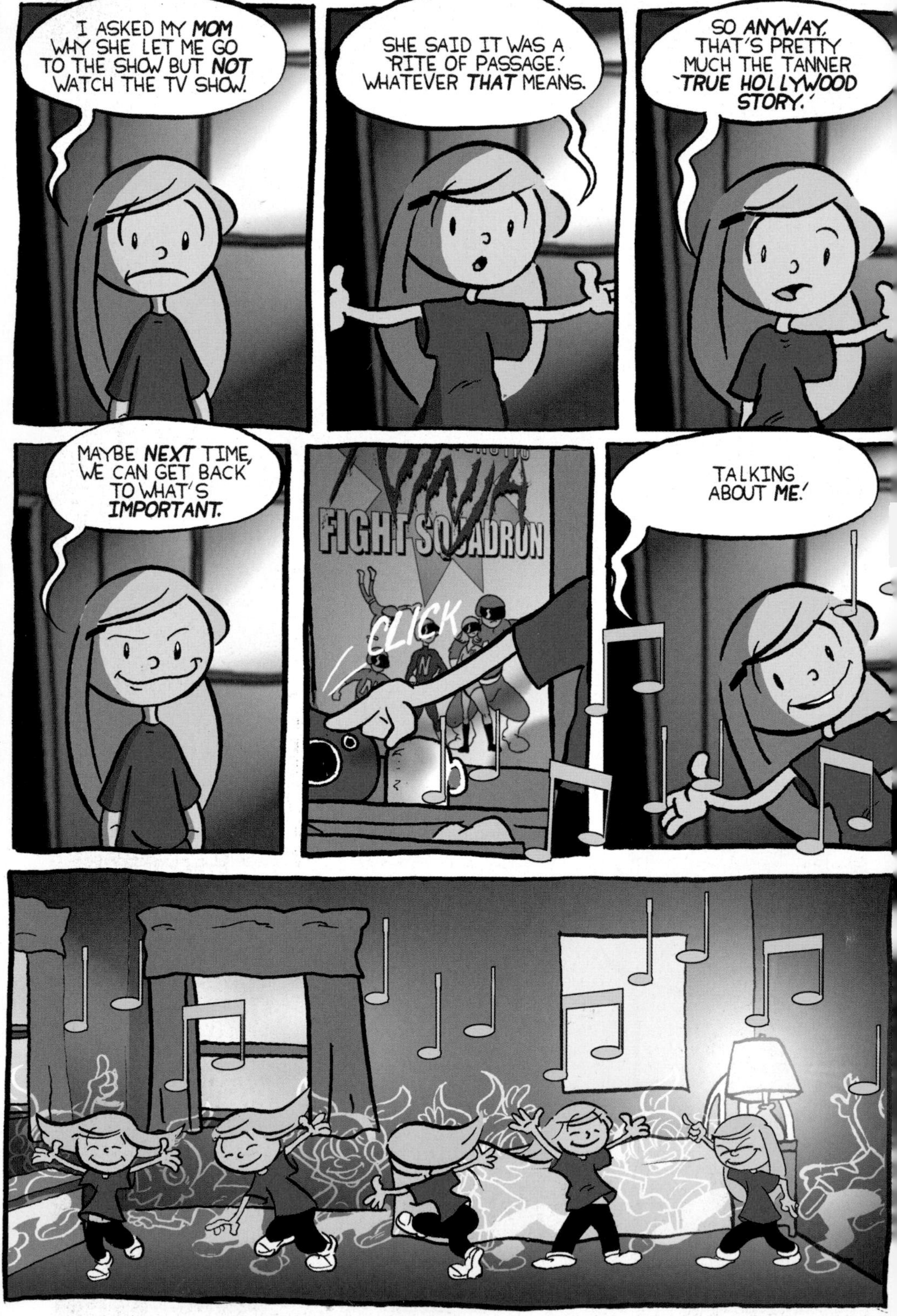
I ASKED MY MOM WHY SHE LET ME GO TO THE SHOW BUT NOT WATCH THE TV SHOW.
SHE SAID IT WAS A "RITE OF PASSAGE." WHATEVER THAT MEANS.
SO ANYWAY, THAT'S PRETTY MUCH THE TANNER "TRUE HOLLYWOOD STORY."
MAYBE NEXT TIME, WE CAN GET BACK TO WHAT'S IMPORTANT.
FIGHT SQUADRON
CLICK
TALKING ABOUT ME!

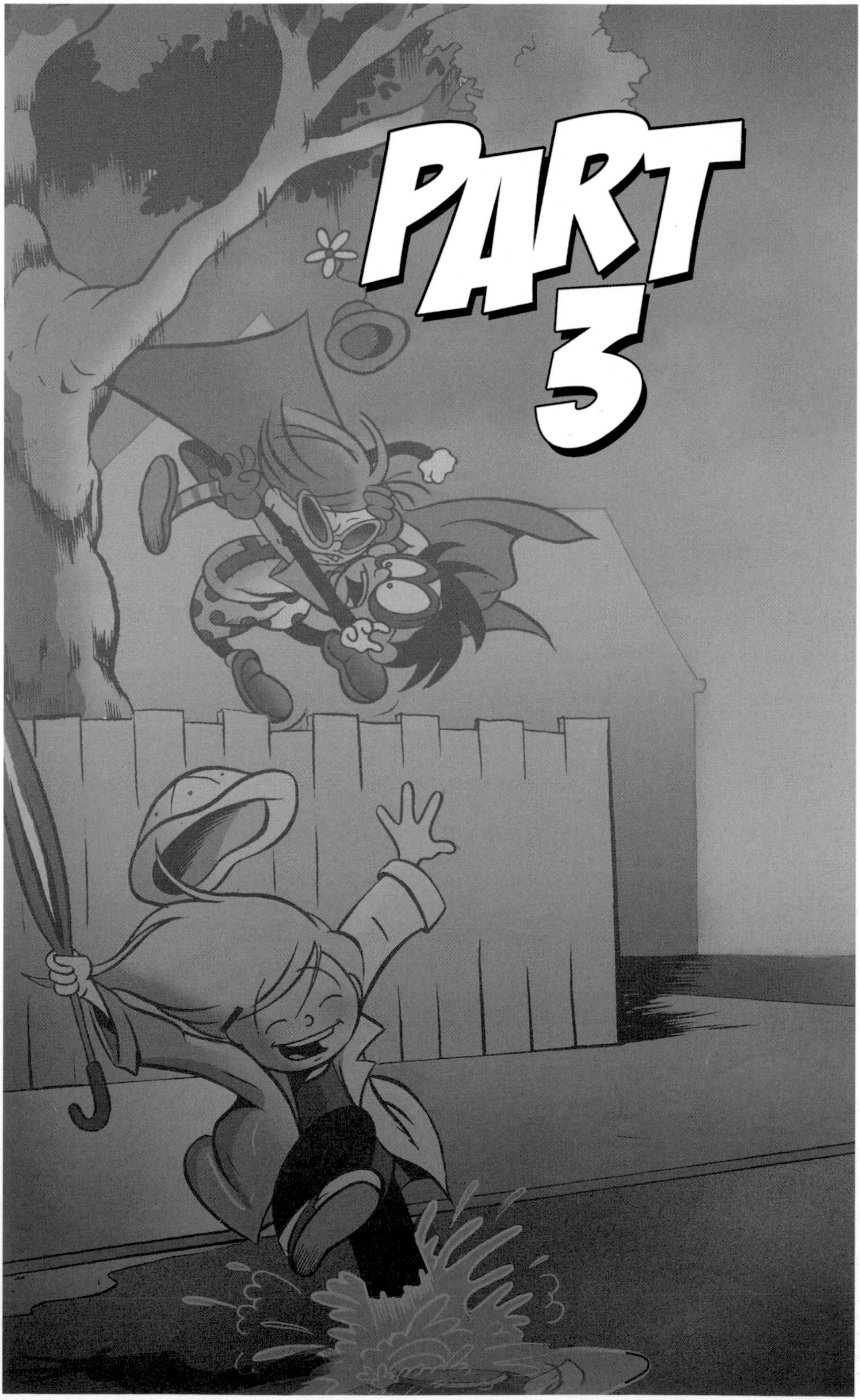
PART 3

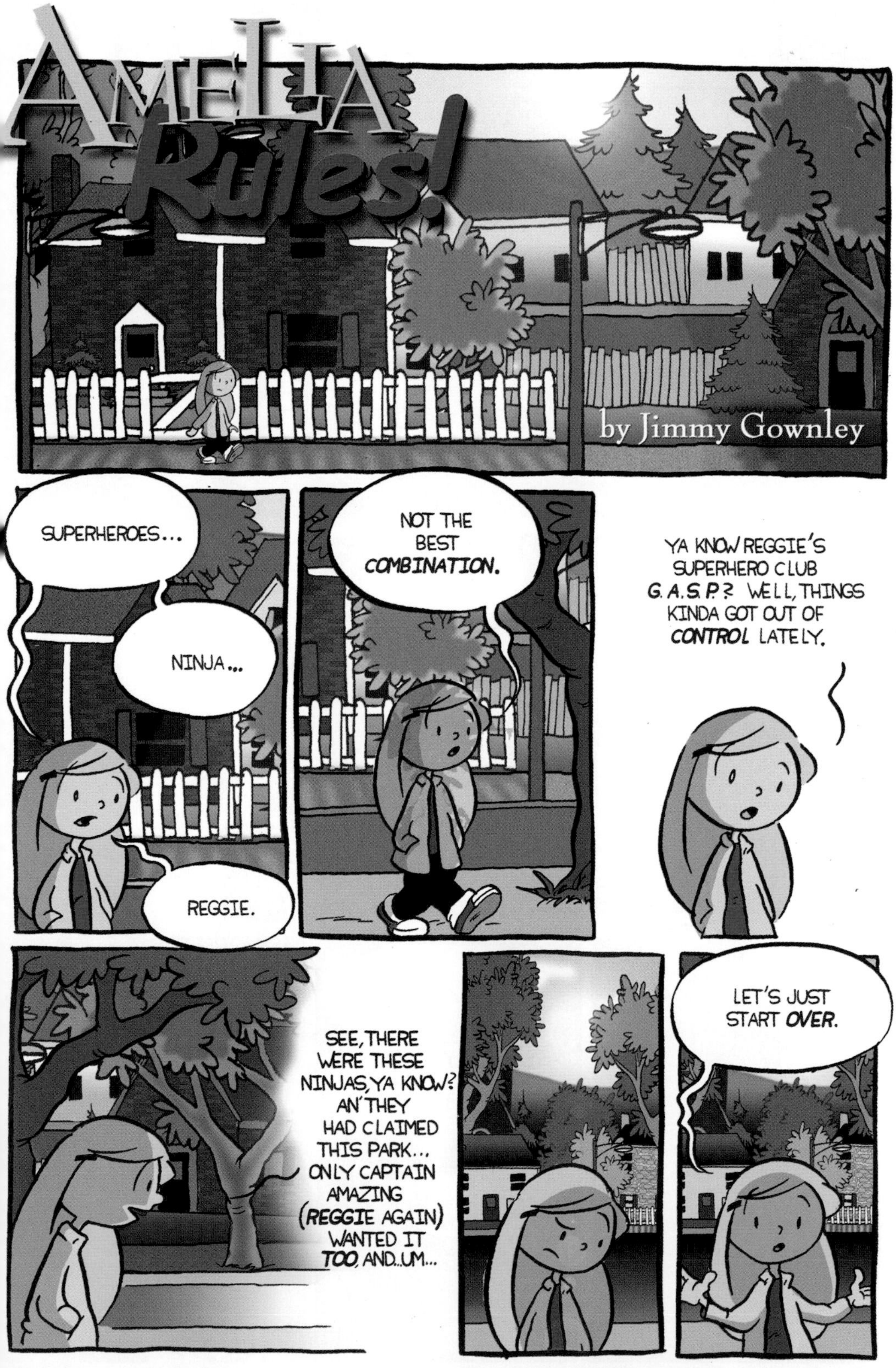
AMELIA Rules!
by Jimmy Gownley
SUPERHEROES...
NINJA...
REGGIE.
NOT THE BEST COMBINATION.
YA KNOW REGGIE'S SUPERHERO CLUB G.A.S.P.? WELL, THINGS KINDA GOT OUT OF CONTROL LATELY.
SEE, THERE WERE THESE NINJAS, YA KNOW? AN' THEY HAD CLAIMED THIS PARK... ONLY CAPTAIN AMAZING (REGGIE AGAIN) WANTED IT TOO, AND...UM...
LET'S JUST START OVER.

LIFE DURING WARTIME

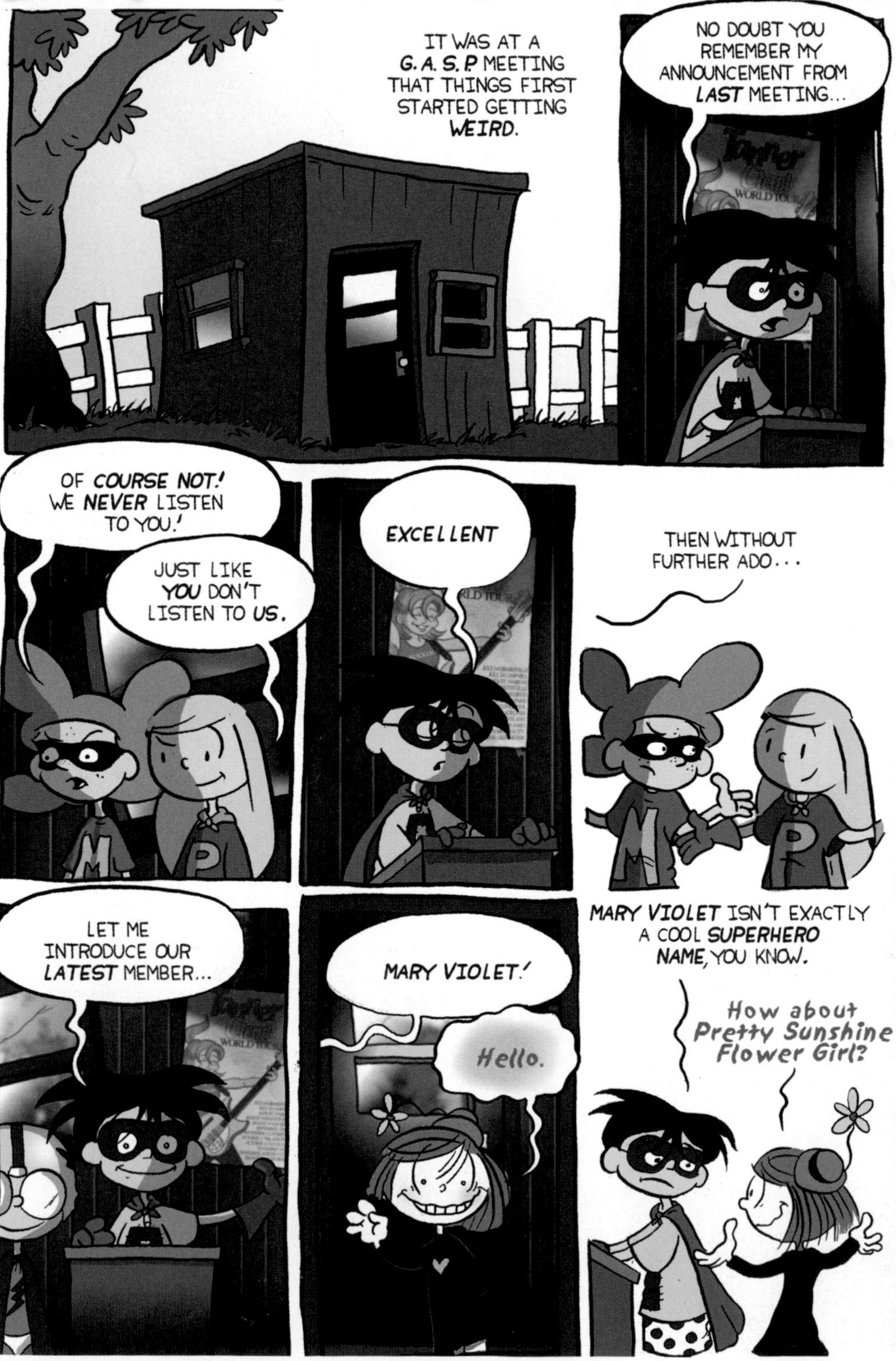

IT WAS AT A G.A.S.P. MEETING THAT THINGS FIRST STARTED GETTING WEIRD.
NO DOUBT YOU REMEMBER MY ANNOUNCEMENT FROM LAST MEETING...
OF COURSE NOT! WE NEVER LISTEN TO YOU!
JUST LIKE YOU DON'T LISTEN TO US.
EXCELLENT
THEN WITHOUT FURTHER ADO...
LET ME INTRODUCE OUR LATEST MEMBER...
MARY VIOLET!
Hello.
MARY VIOLET ISN'T EXACTLY A COOL SUPERHERO NAME, YOU KNOW.
How about Pretty Sunshine Flower Girl?

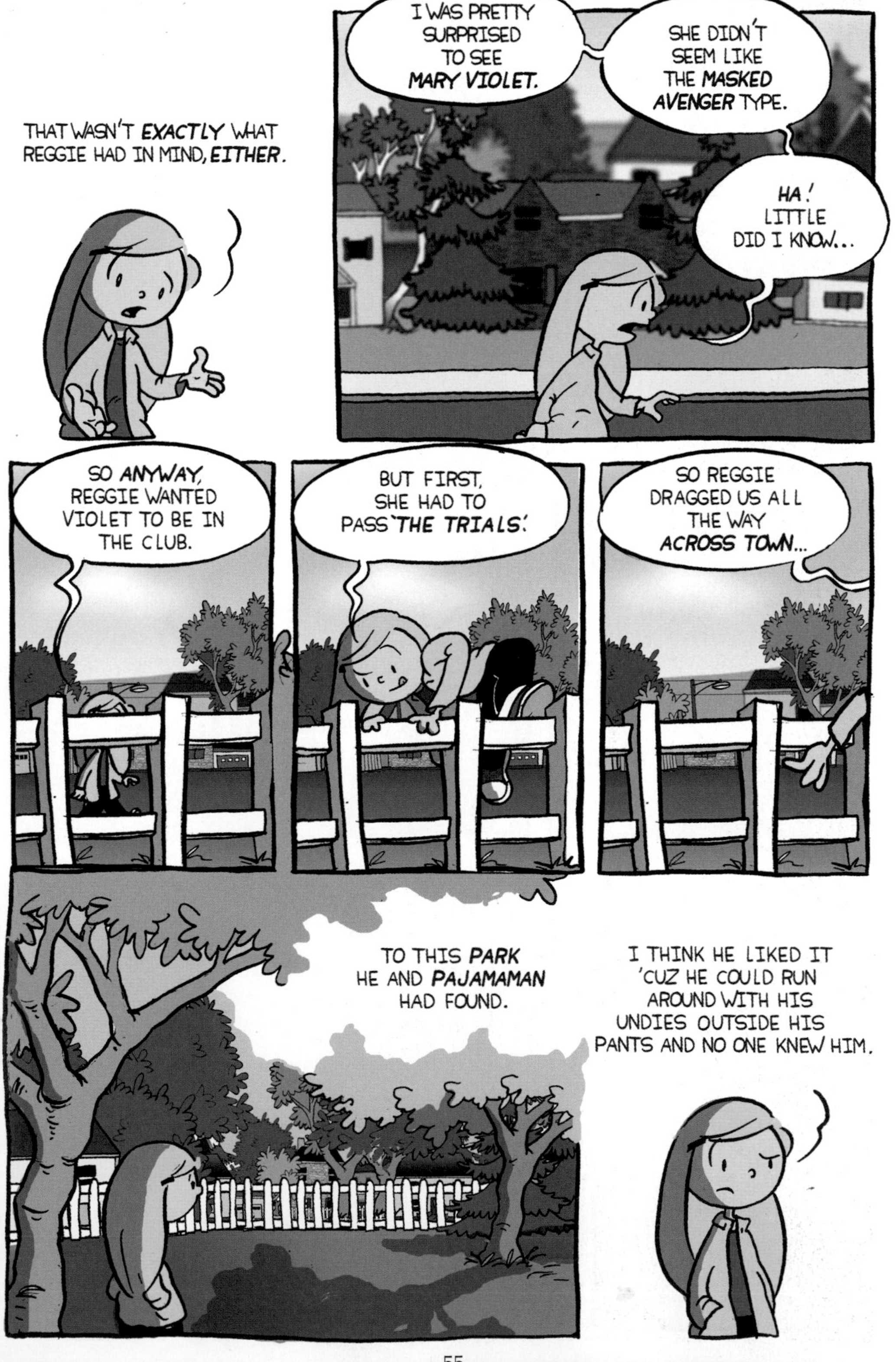
THAT WASN'T EXACTLY WHAT REGGIE HAD IN MIND, EITHER.
I WAS PRETTY SURPRISED TO SEE MARY VIOLET.
SHE DIDN'T SEEM LIKE THE MASKED AVENGER TYPE.
HA! LITTLE DID I KNOW...
SO ANYWAY, REGGIE WANTED VIOLET TO BE IN THE CLUB.
BUT FIRST, SHE HAD TO PASS "THE TRIALS."
SO REGGIE DRAGGED US ALL THE WAY ACROSS TOWN...
TO THIS PARK HE AND PAJAMAMAN HAD FOUND.
I THINK HE LIKED IT 'CUZ HE COULD RUN AROUND WITH HIS UNDIES OUTSIDE HIS PANTS AND NO ONE KNEW HIM.

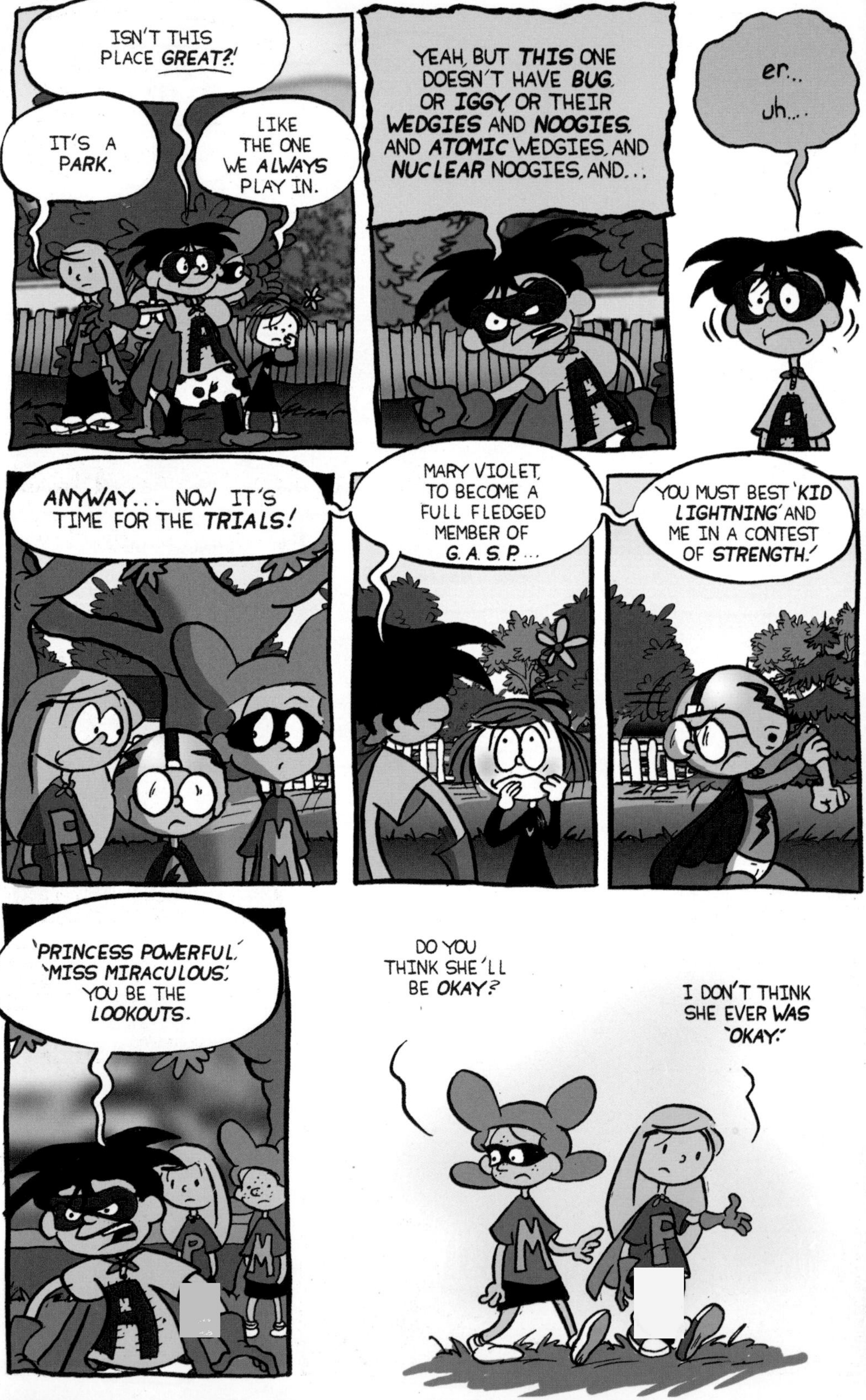
ISN'T THIS PLACE GREAT?!
IT'S A PARK.
LIKE THE ONE WE ALWAYS PLAY IN.
YEAH, BUT THIS ONE DOESN'T HAVE BUG, OR IGGY, OR THEIR WEDGIES AND NOOGIES, AND ATOMIC WEDGIES, AND NUCLEAR NOOGIES, AND...
er... uh...
ANYWAY... NOW IT'S TIME FOR THE TRIALS!
MARY VIOLET, TO BECOME A FULL FLEDGED MEMBER OF G.A.S.P...
YOU MUST BEST 'KID LIGHTNING' AND ME IN A CONTEST OF STRENGTH.'
'PRINCESS POWERFUL,' 'MISS MIRACULOUS,' YOU BE THE LOOKOUTS.
DO YOU THINK SHE'LL BE OKAY?
I DON'T THINK SHE EVER WAS "OKAY."

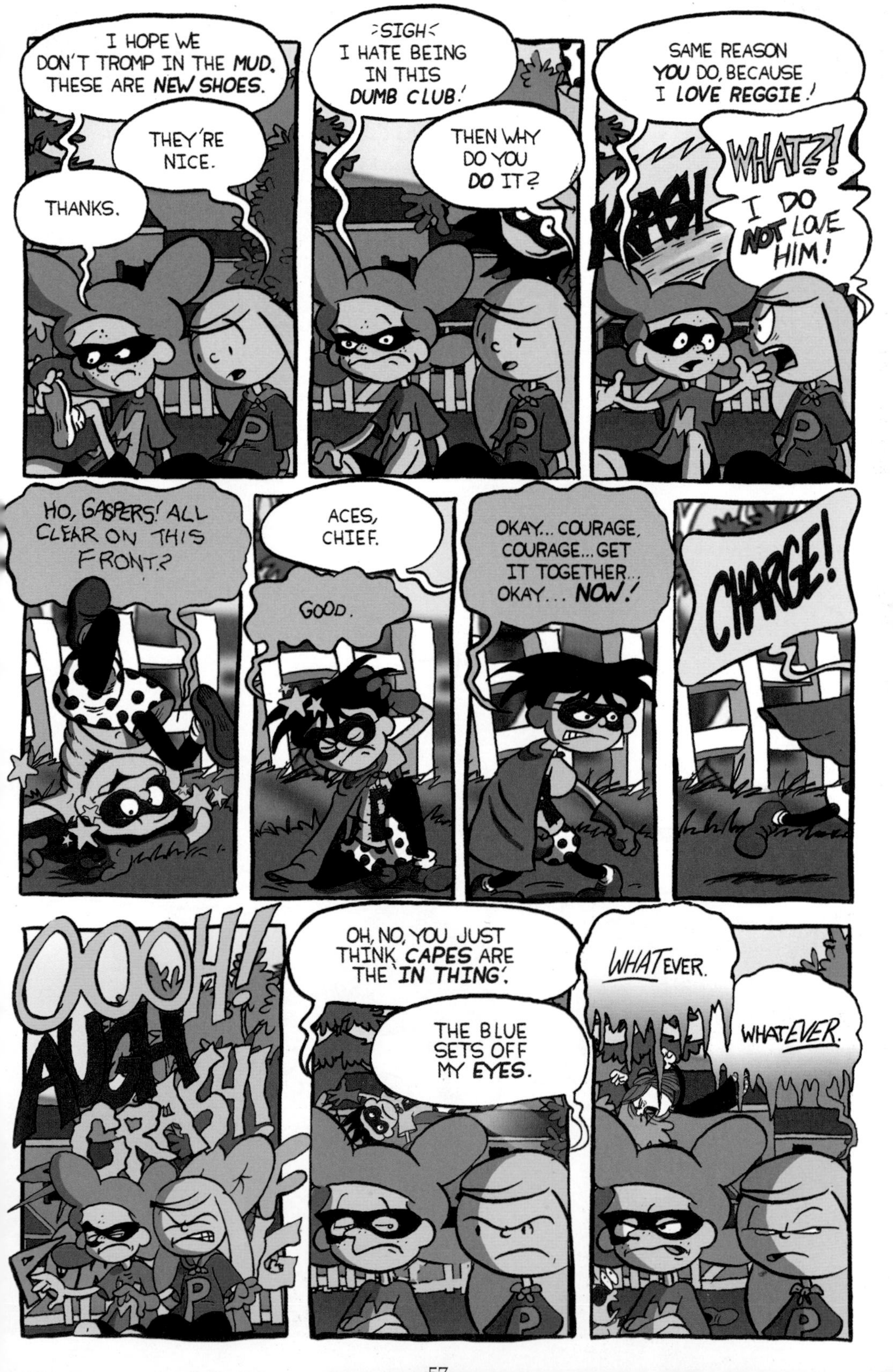
I HOPE WE DON'T TROMP IN THE MUD. THESE ARE NEW SHOES.
THEY'RE NICE.
THANKS.
>SIGH< I HATE BEING IN THIS DUMB CLUB!
THEN WHY DO YOU DO IT?
SAME REASON YOU DO, BECAUSE I LOVE REGGIE!
KRASH
WHAT?! I DO NOT LOVE HIM!
HO, GASPERS! ALL CLEAR ON THIS FRONT?
ACES, CHIEF.
GOOD.
OKAY... COURAGE, COURAGE... GET IT TOGETHER... OKAY... NOW!
CHARGE!
OOOH!
AUGH
CRASH!
OH, NO, YOU JUST THINK CAPES ARE THE 'IN THING'.
THE BLUE SETS OFF MY EYES.
WHATEVER.
WHATEVER.

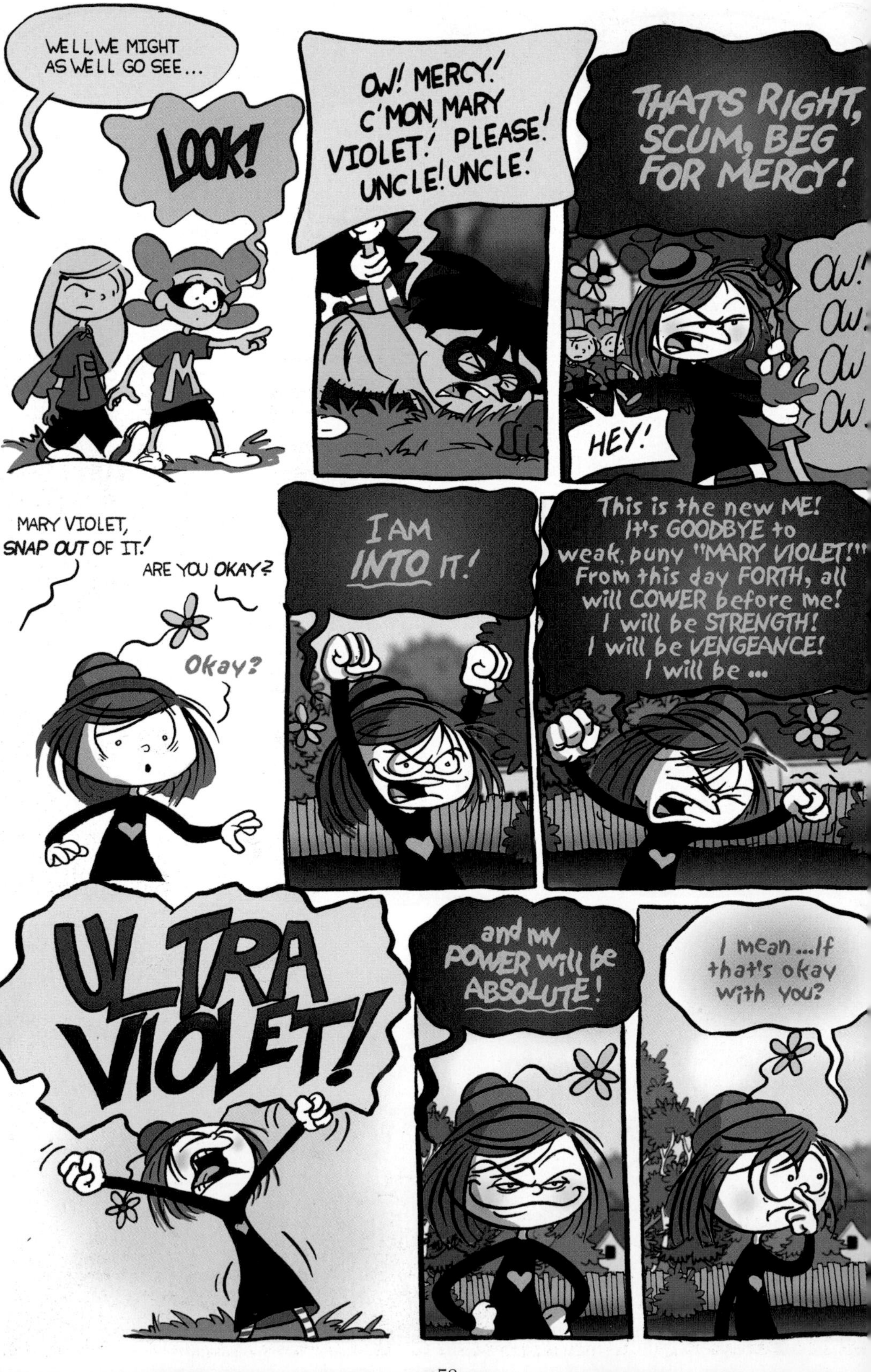
WELL, WE MIGHT AS WELL GO SEE...
LOOK!
OW! MERCY! C'MON, MARY VIOLET! PLEASE! UNCLE! UNCLE!
THAT'S RIGHT, SCUM, BEG FOR MERCY!
HEY!
MARY VIOLET, SNAP OUT OF IT!
ARE YOU OKAY?
Okay?
I AM INTO IT!
This is the new ME! It's GOODBYE to weak, puny "MARY VIOLET!" From this day FORTH, all will COWER before me! I will be STRENGTH! I will be VENGEANCE! I will be ...
ULTRA VIOLET!
and my POWER will be ABSOLUTE!
I mean ... If that's okay with you?

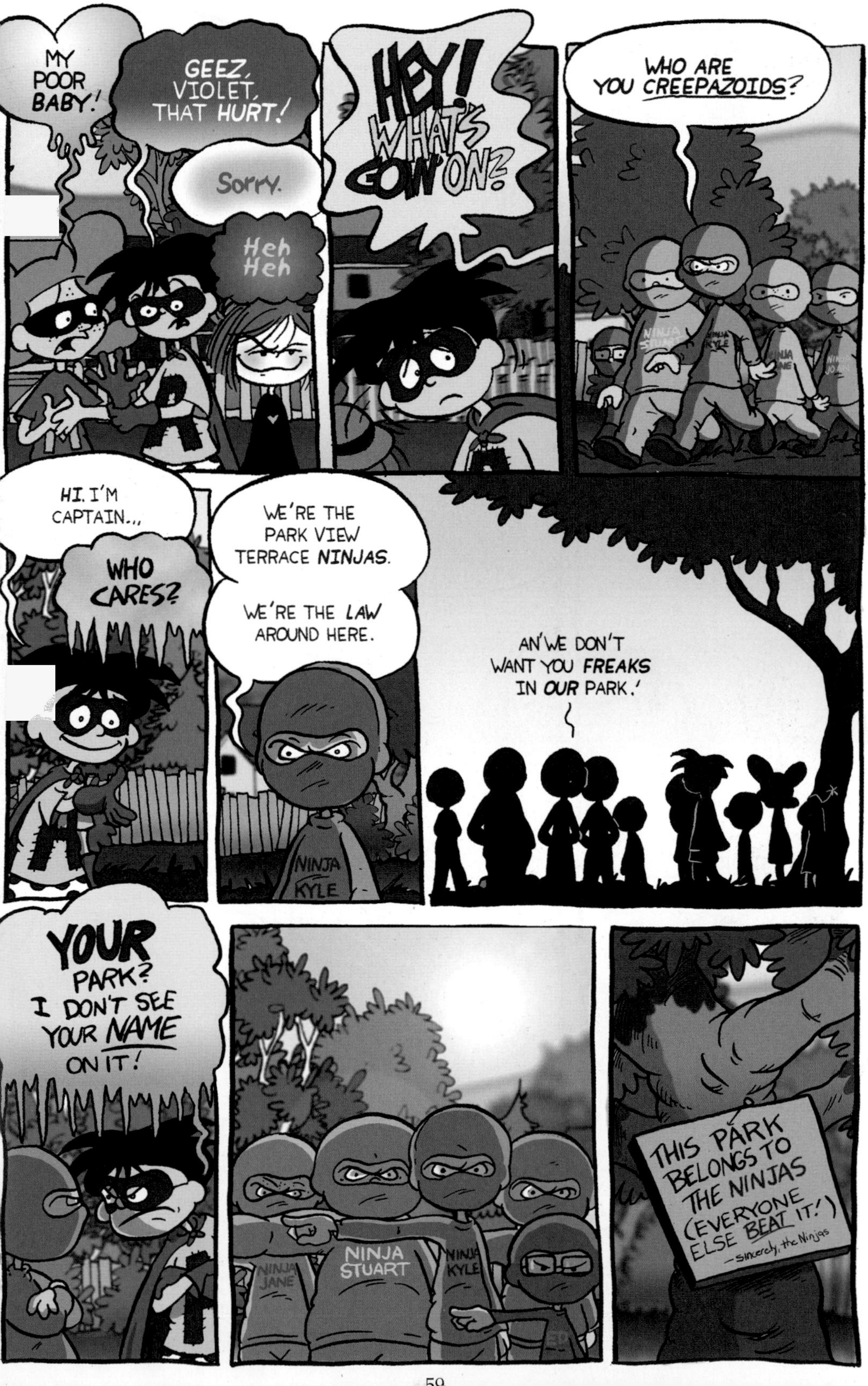
MY POOR BABY!
GEEZ, VIOLET, THAT HURT!
Sorry.
Heh Heh
HEY! WHAT'S GOIN' ON?
WHO ARE YOU CREEPAZOIDS?
NINJA STUART
NINJA KYLE
NINJA JANE
NINJA JOAN
HI. I'M CAPTAIN...
WHO CARES?
WE'RE THE PARK VIEW TERRACE NINJAS.
WE'RE THE LAW AROUND HERE.
NINJA KYLE
AN' WE DON'T WANT YOU FREAKS IN OUR PARK.
YOUR PARK? I DON'T SEE YOUR NAME ON IT!
NINJA JANE
NINJA STUART
NINJA KYLE
THIS PARK BELONGS TO THE NINJAS (EVERYONE ELSE BEAT IT!)
—sincerely, the Ninjas

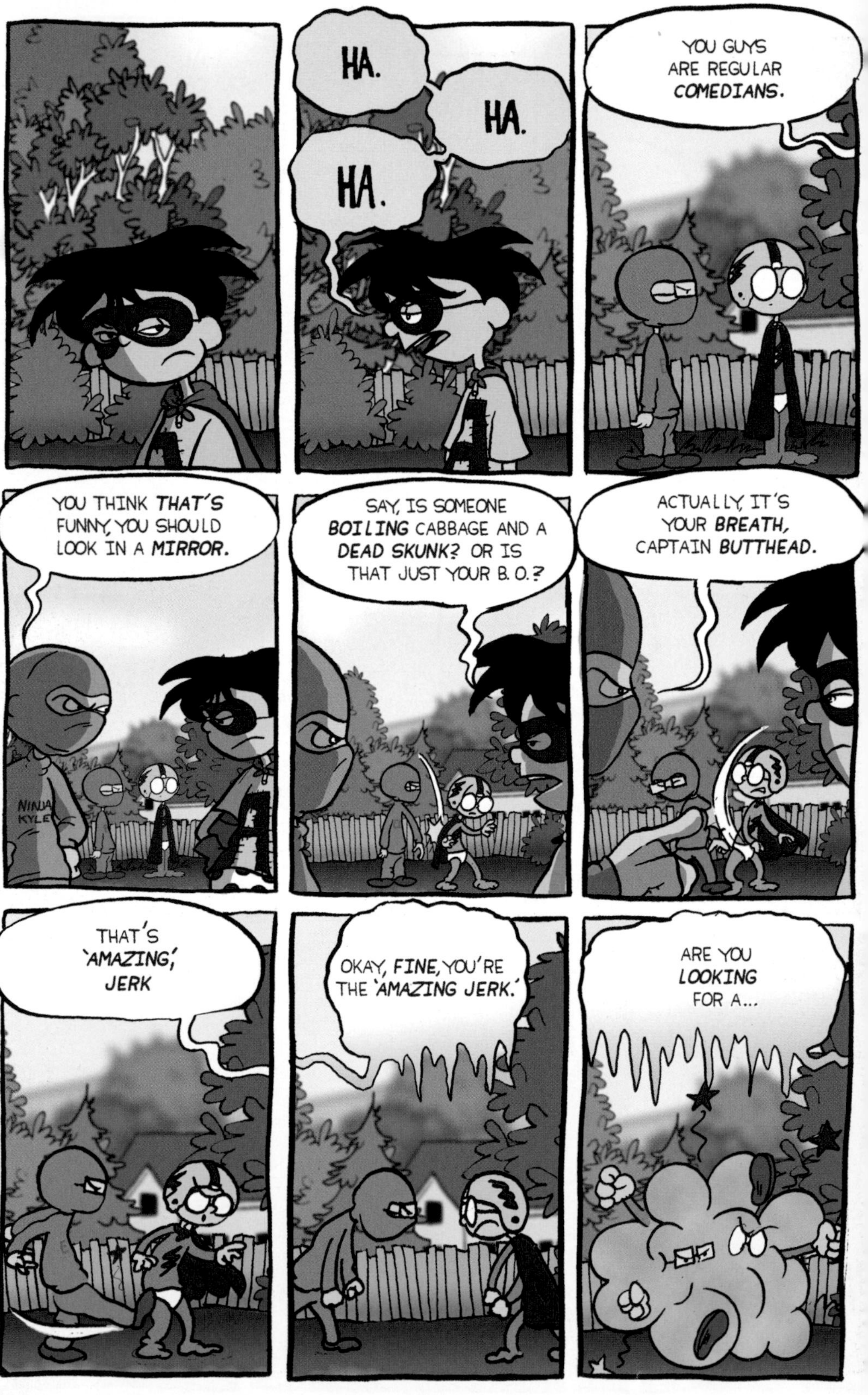
HA.
HA.
HA.
YOU GUYS ARE REGULAR COMEDIANS.
YOU THINK THAT'S FUNNY, YOU SHOULD LOOK IN A MIRROR.
NINJA KYLE
SAY, IS SOMEONE BOILING CABBAGE AND A DEAD SKUNK? OR IS THAT JUST YOUR B. O.?
ACTUALLY, IT'S YOUR BREATH, CAPTAIN BUTTHEAD.
THAT'S 'AMAZING,' JERK
OKAY, FINE, YOU'RE THE 'AMAZING JERK.'
ARE YOU LOOKING FOR A...

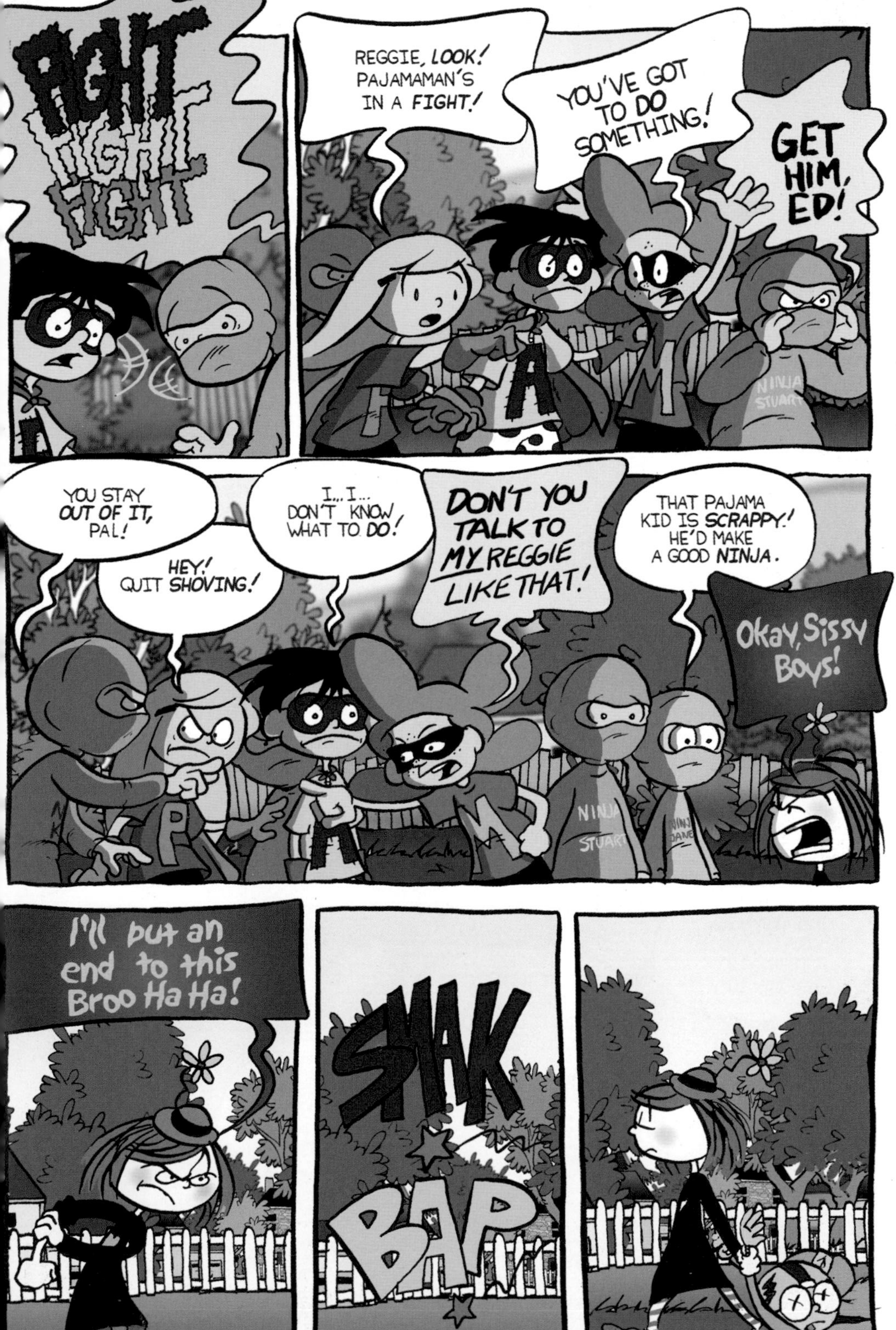
FIGHT FIGHT FIGHT
REGGIE, LOOK! PAJAMAMAN'S IN A FIGHT!
YOU'VE GOT TO DO SOMETHING!
GET HIM, ED!
NINJA STUART
YOU STAY OUT OF IT, PAL!
HEY! QUIT SHOVING!
I... I... DON'T KNOW WHAT TO DO!
DON'T YOU TALK TO MY REGGIE LIKE THAT!
THAT PAJAMA KID IS SCRAPPY! HE'D MAKE A GOOD NINJA.
Okay, Sissy Boys!
NINJA STUART
NINJA DANE
I'll put an end to this Broo Ha Ha!
SHAK
BAP

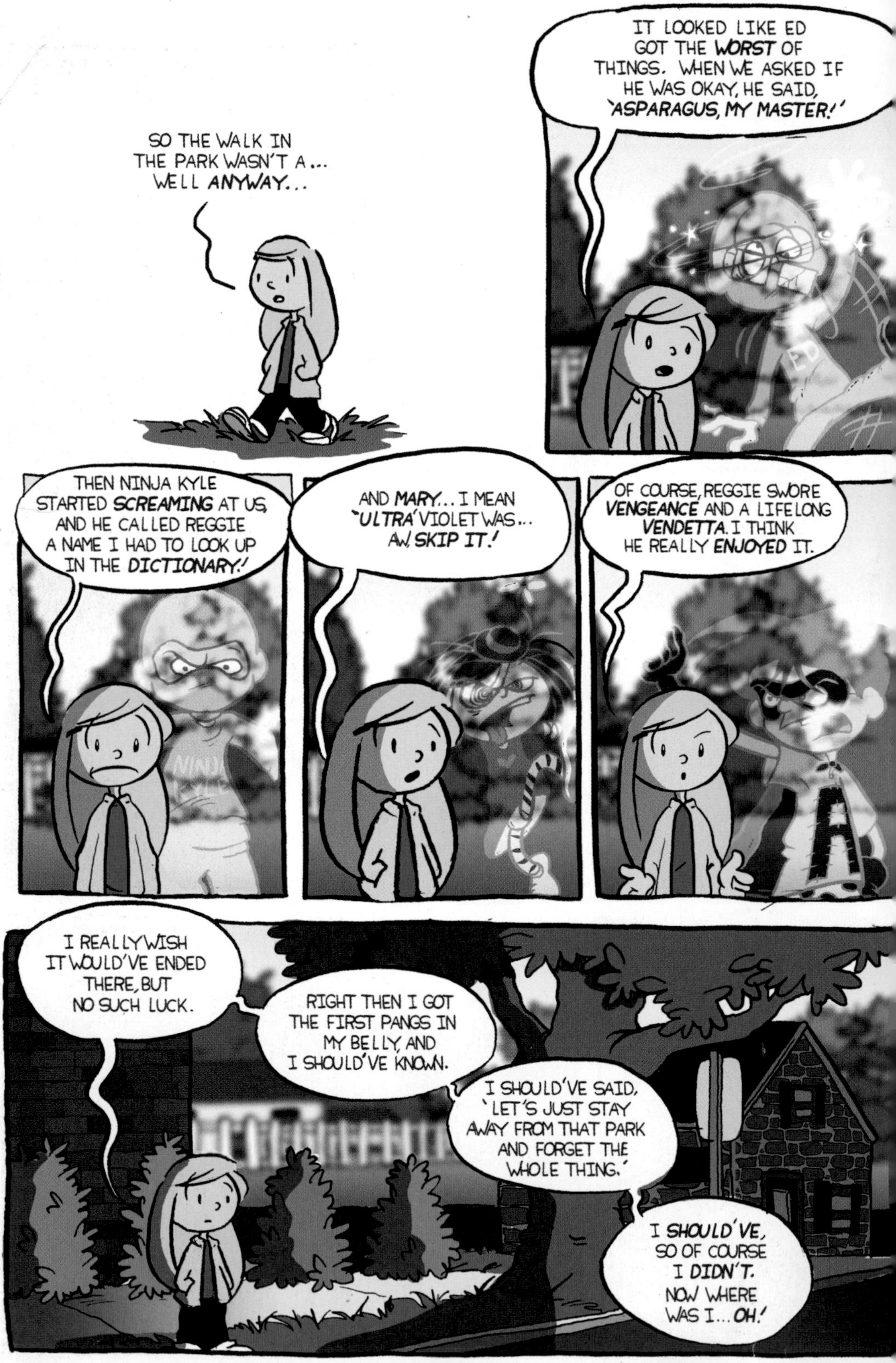
SO THE WALK IN THE PARK WASN'T A... WELL ANYWAY...
IT LOOKED LIKE ED GOT THE WORST OF THINGS. WHEN WE ASKED IF HE WAS OKAY, HE SAID, 'ASPARAGUS, MY MASTER!'
ED
THEN NINJA KYLE STARTED SCREAMING AT US, AND HE CALLED REGGIE A NAME I HAD TO LOOK UP IN THE DICTIONARY!
NINJA KYLE
AND MARY... I MEAN 'ULTRA' VIOLET WAS... AW, SKIP IT!
OF COURSE, REGGIE SWORE VENGEANCE AND A LIFELONG VENDETTA. I THINK HE REALLY ENJOYED IT.
I REALLY WISH IT WOULD'VE ENDED THERE, BUT NO SUCH LUCK.
RIGHT THEN I GOT THE FIRST PANGS IN MY BELLY, AND I SHOULD'VE KNOWN.
I SHOULD'VE SAID, 'LET'S JUST STAY AWAY FROM THAT PARK AND FORGET THE WHOLE THING.'
I SHOULD'VE, SO OF COURSE I DIDN'T. NOW WHERE WAS I... OH!

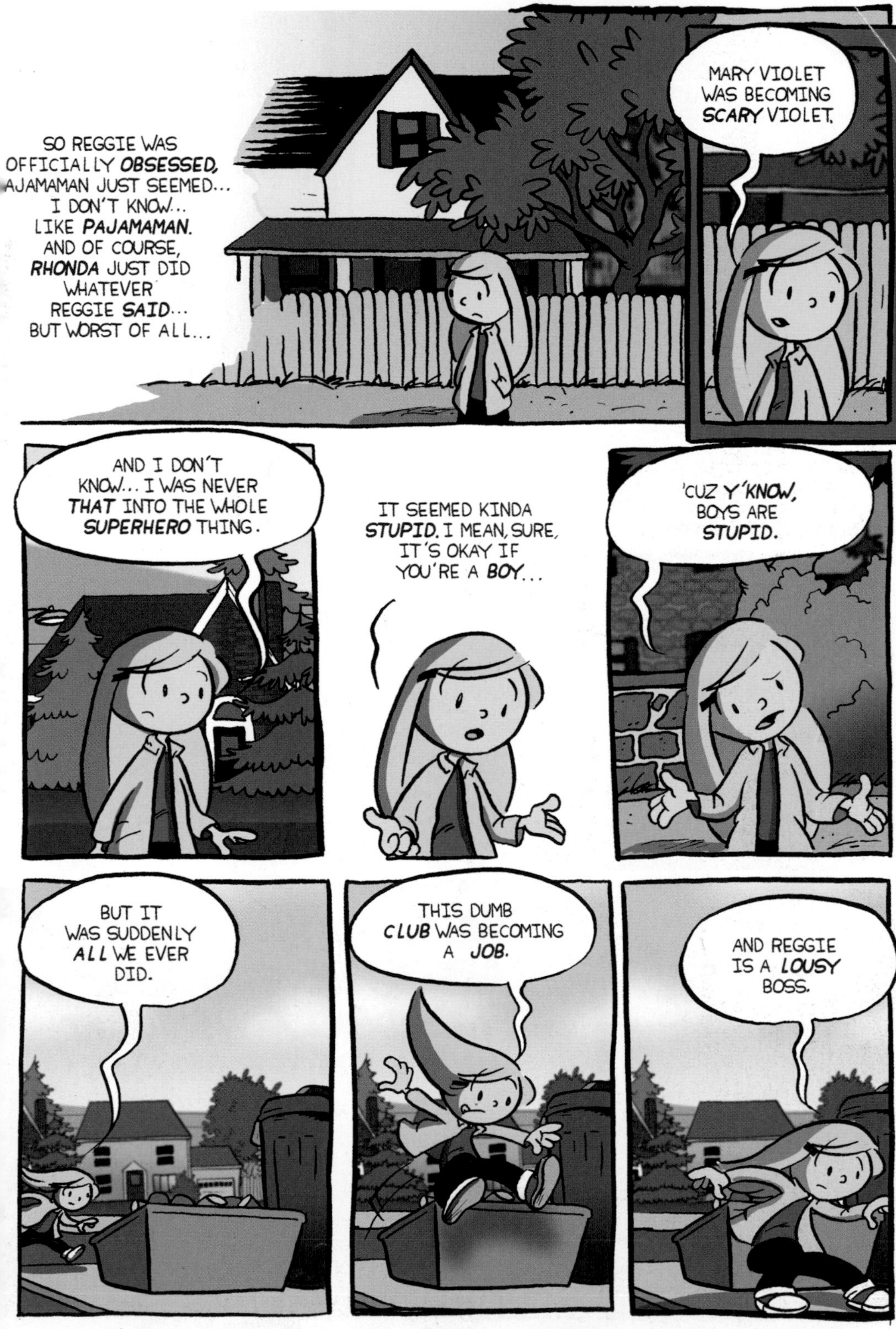
SO REGGIE WAS OFFICIALLY OBSESSED, AJAMAMAN JUST SEEMED... I DON'T KNOW... LIKE PAJAMAMAN. AND OF COURSE, RHONDA JUST DID WHATEVER REGGIE SAID... BUT WORST OF ALL...
MARY VIOLET WAS BECOMING SCARY VIOLET.
AND I DON'T KNOW... I WAS NEVER THAT INTO THE WHOLE SUPERHERO THING.
IT SEEMED KINDA STUPID. I MEAN, SURE, IT'S OKAY IF YOU'RE A BOY...
'CUZ Y'KNOW, BOYS ARE STUPID.
BUT IT WAS SUDDENLY ALL WE EVER DID.
THIS DUMB CLUB WAS BECOMING A JOB.
AND REGGIE IS A LOUSY BOSS.

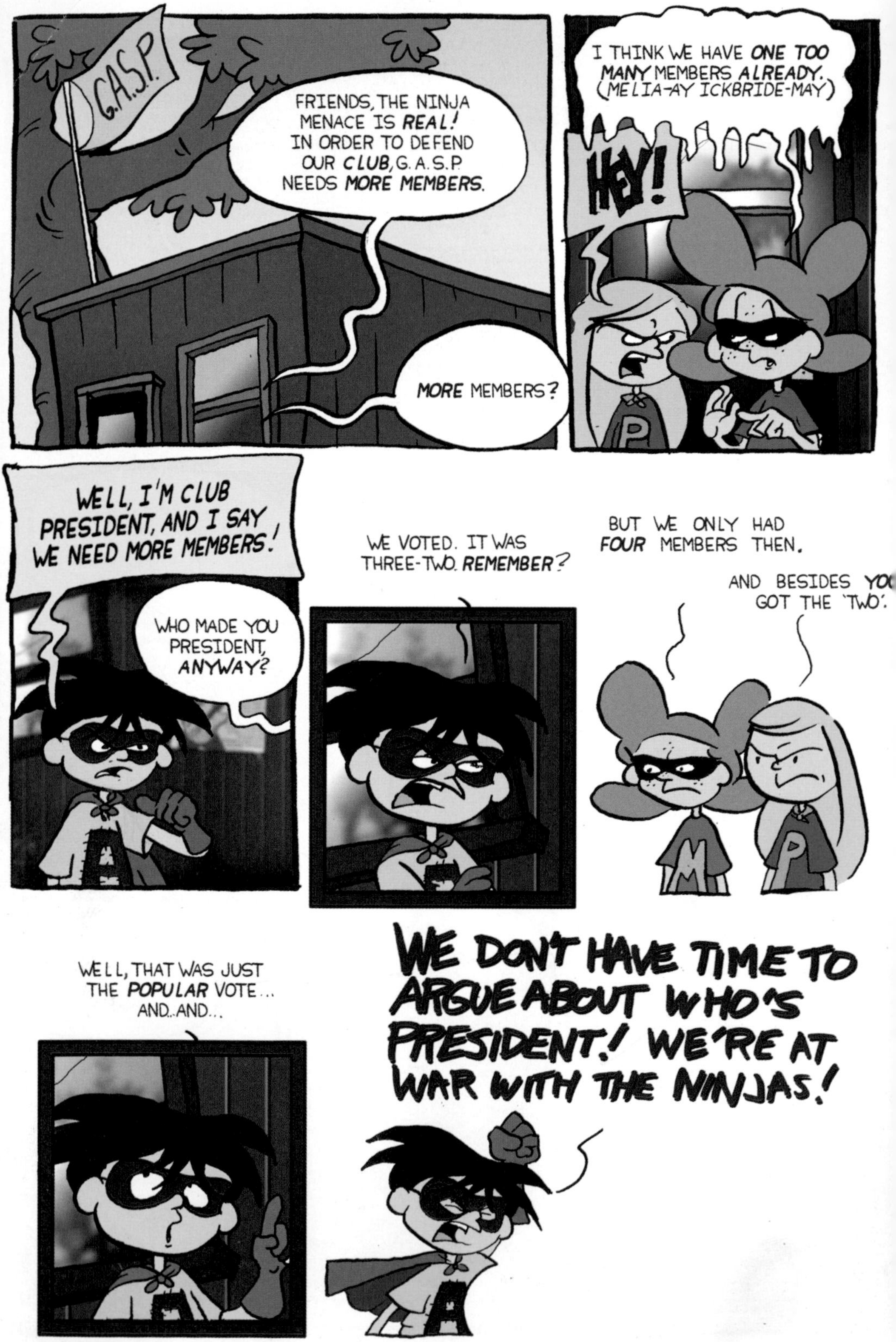
G.A.S.P.
FRIENDS, THE NINJA MENACE IS REAL! IN ORDER TO DEFEND OUR CLUB, G. A. S. P. NEEDS MORE MEMBERS.
MORE MEMBERS?
I THINK WE HAVE ONE TOO MANY MEMBERS ALREADY. (MELIA-AY ICKBRIDE-MAY)
HEY!
WELL, I'M CLUB PRESIDENT, AND I SAY WE NEED MORE MEMBERS!
WHO MADE YOU PRESIDENT, ANYWAY?
WE VOTED. IT WAS THREE-TWO. REMEMBER?
BUT WE ONLY HAD FOUR MEMBERS THEN.
AND BESIDES YOU GOT THE 'TWO'.
WELL, THAT WAS JUST THE POPULAR VOTE... AND..AND...
WE DON'T HAVE TIME TO ARGUE ABOUT WHO'S PRESIDENT! WE'RE AT WAR WITH THE NINJAS!

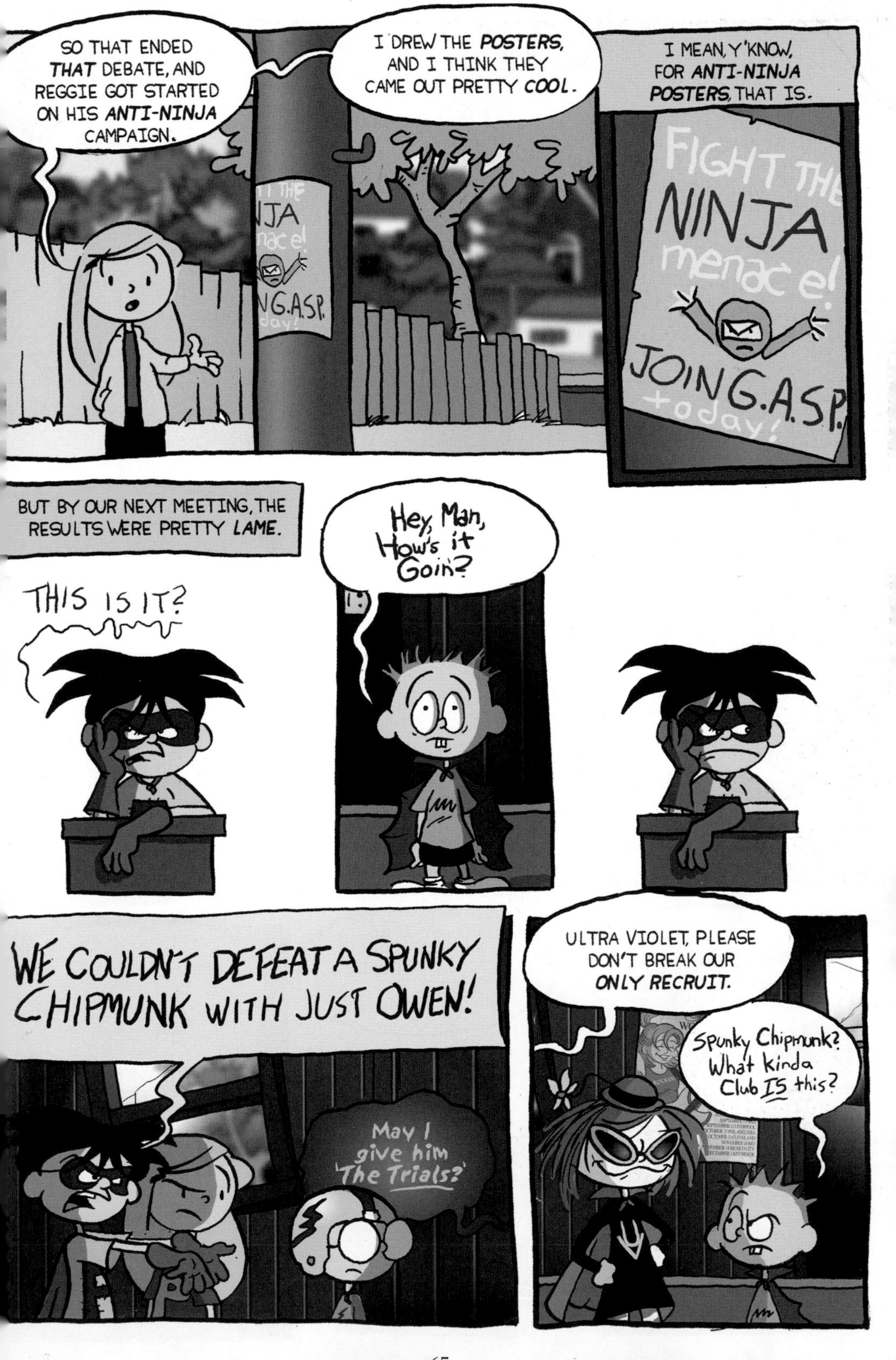
SO THAT ENDED THAT DEBATE, AND REGGIE GOT STARTED ON HIS ANTI-NINJA CAMPAIGN.
I DREW THE POSTERS, AND I THINK THEY CAME OUT PRETTY COOL.
I MEAN, Y'KNOW, FOR ANTI-NINJA POSTERS, THAT IS.
FIGHT THE NINJA menace! JOIN G.A.S.P. today!
BUT BY OUR NEXT MEETING, THE RESULTS WERE PRETTY LAME.
THIS IS IT?
Hey, Man, How's it Goin?
WE COULDN'T DEFEAT A SPUNKY CHIPMUNK WITH JUST OWEN!
May I give him 'The Trials?'
ULTRA VIOLET, PLEASE DON'T BREAK OUR ONLY RECRUIT.
Spunky Chipmunk? What kinda Club IS this?

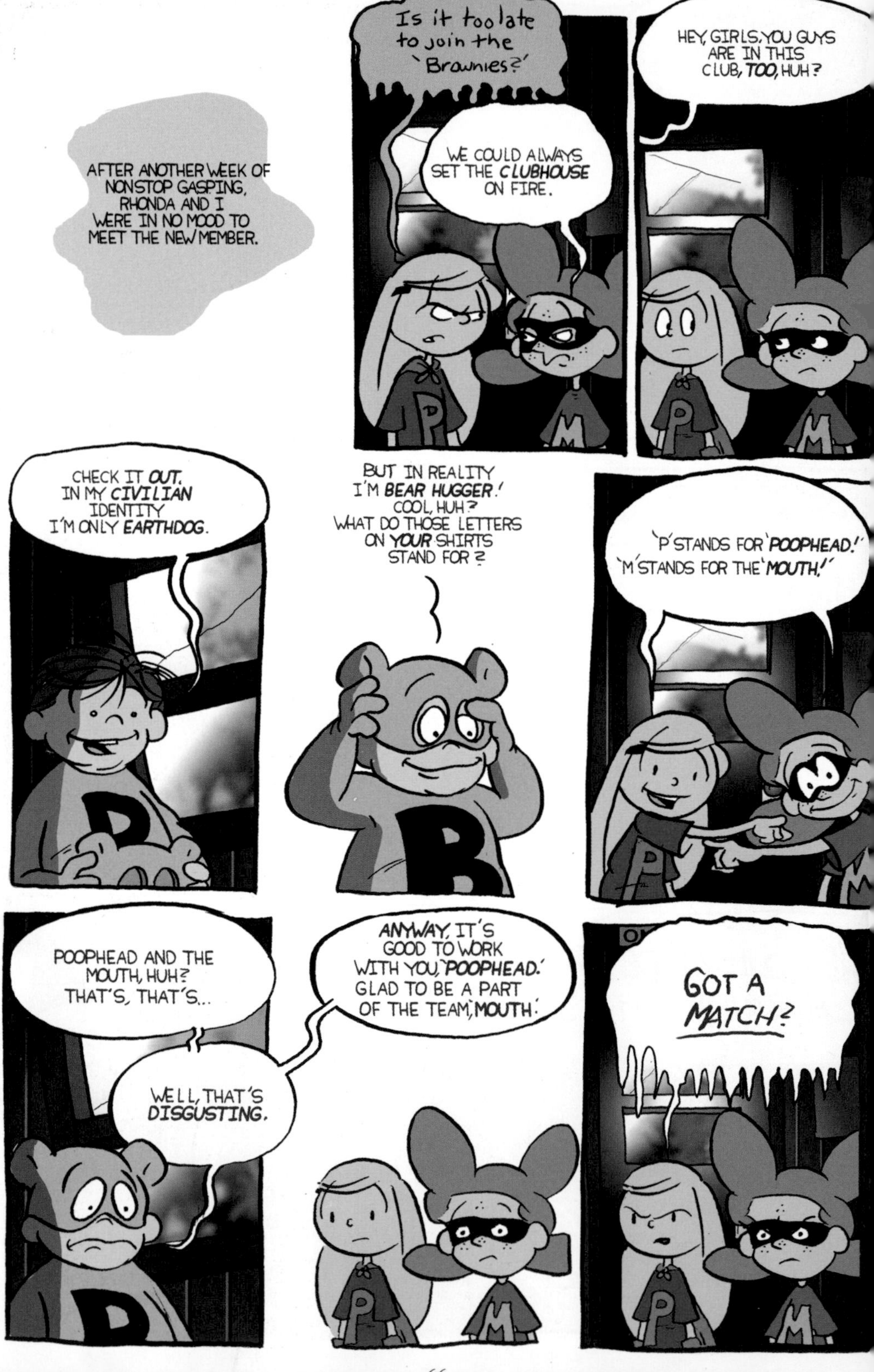
AFTER ANOTHER WEEK OF NONSTOP GASPING, RHONDA AND I WERE IN NO MOOD TO MEET THE NEW MEMBER.
Is it too late to join the 'Brownies?'
WE COULD ALWAYS SET THE CLUBHOUSE ON FIRE.
HEY, GIRLS, YOU GUYS ARE IN THIS CLUB, TOO, HUH?
CHECK IT OUT. IN MY CIVILIAN IDENTITY I'M ONLY EARTHDOG.
BUT IN REALITY I'M BEAR HUGGER! COOL, HUH? WHAT DO THOSE LETTERS ON YOUR SHIRTS STAND FOR?
'P' STANDS FOR 'POOPHEAD!'
'M' STANDS FOR THE 'MOUTH!'
POOPHEAD AND THE MOUTH, HUH? THAT'S, THAT'S...
WELL, THAT'S DISGUSTING.
ANYWAY, IT'S GOOD TO WORK WITH YOU, 'POOPHEAD.' GLAD TO BE A PART OF THE TEAM, 'MOUTH.'
GOT A MATCH?

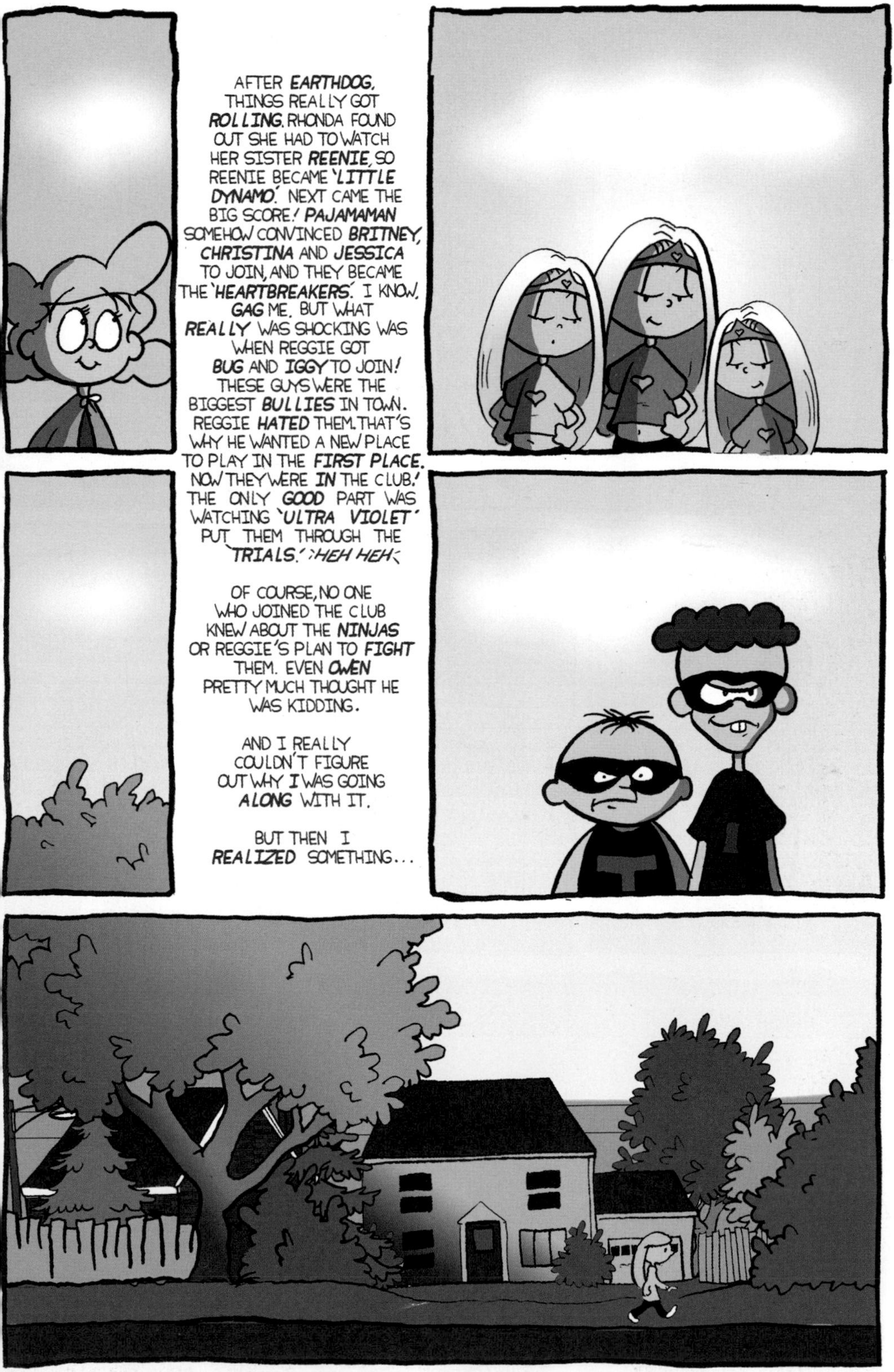
AFTER EARTHDOG, THINGS REALLY GOT ROLLING. RHONDA FOUND OUT SHE HAD TO WATCH HER SISTER REENIE, SO REENIE BECAME 'LITTLE DYNAMO'. NEXT CAME THE BIG SCORE! PAJAMAMAN SOMEHOW CONVINCED BRITNEY, CHRISTINA AND JESSICA TO JOIN, AND THEY BECAME THE 'HEARTBREAKERS'. I KNOW, GAG ME. BUT WHAT REALLY WAS SHOCKING WAS WHEN REGGIE GOT BUG AND IGGY TO JOIN! THESE GUYS WERE THE BIGGEST BULLIES IN TOWN. REGGIE HATED THEM. THAT'S WHY HE WANTED A NEW PLACE TO PLAY IN THE FIRST PLACE. NOW THEY WERE IN THE CLUB! THE ONLY GOOD PART WAS WATCHING 'ULTRA VIOLET' PUT THEM THROUGH THE 'TRIALS.' >HEH HEH<
OF COURSE, NO ONE WHO JOINED THE CLUB KNEW ABOUT THE NINJAS OR REGGIE'S PLAN TO FIGHT THEM. EVEN OWEN PRETTY MUCH THOUGHT HE WAS KIDDING.
AND I REALLY COULDN'T FIGURE OUT WHY I WAS GOING ALONG WITH IT.
BUT THEN I REALIZED SOMETHING...

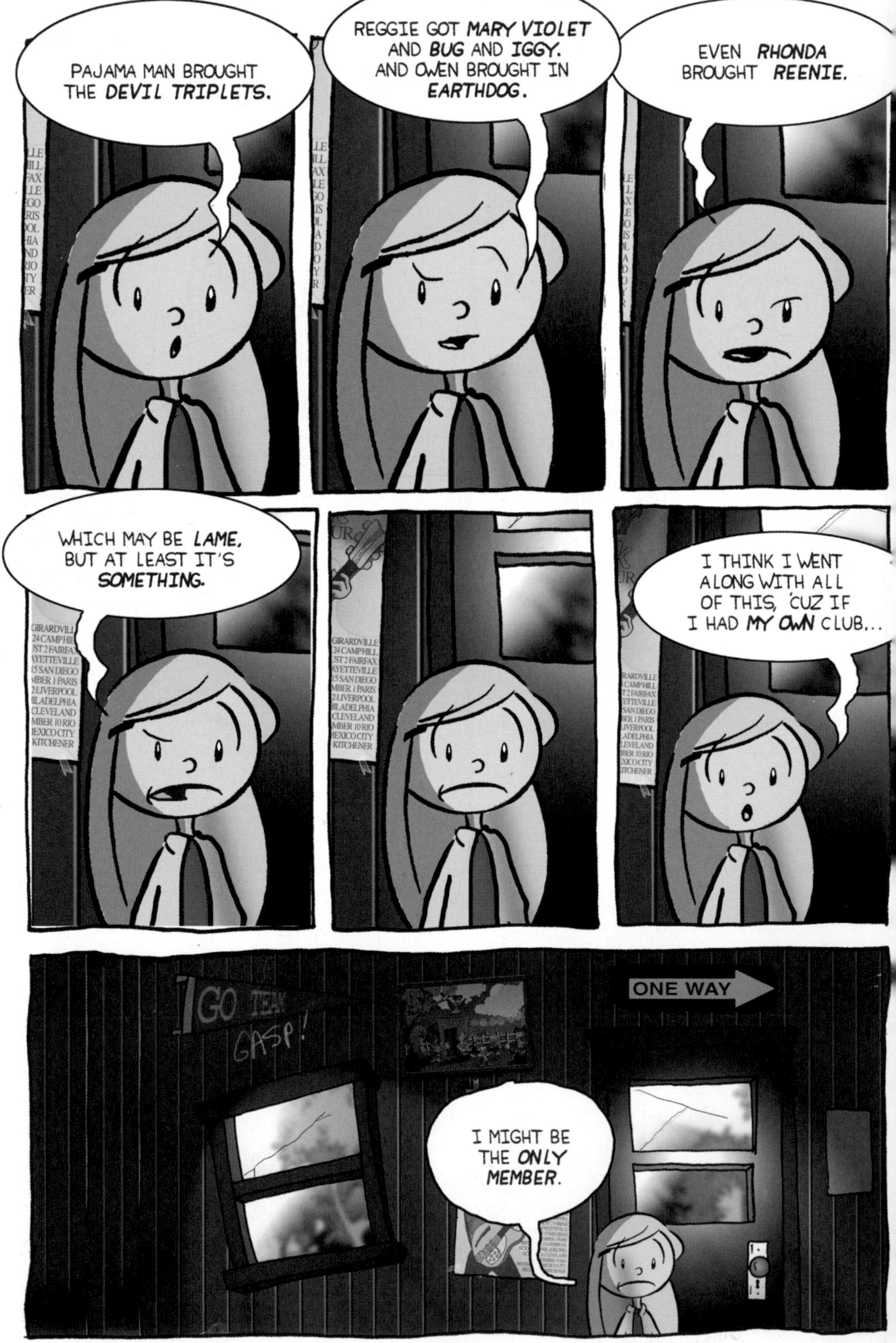
PAJAMA MAN BROUGHT THE DEVIL TRIPLETS.
REGGIE GOT MARY VIOLET AND BUG AND IGGY. AND OWEN BROUGHT IN EARTHDOG.
EVEN RHONDA BROUGHT REENIE.
WHICH MAY BE LAME, BUT AT LEAST IT'S SOMETHING.
I THINK I WENT ALONG WITH ALL OF THIS, 'CUZ IF I HAD MY OWN CLUB...
ONE WAY
GO TEAM
GASP!
I MIGHT BE THE ONLY MEMBER.

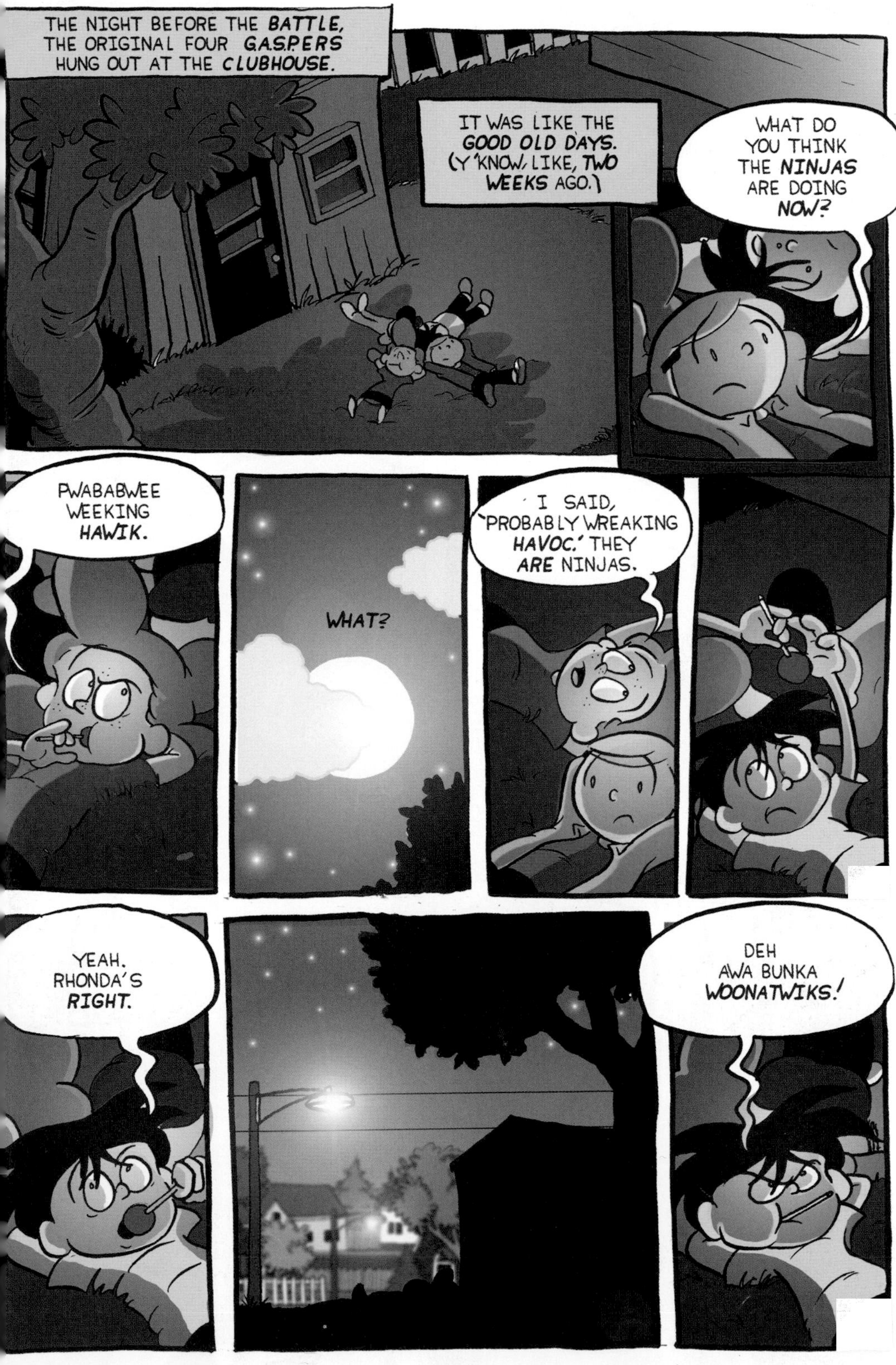
THE NIGHT BEFORE THE BATTLE, THE ORIGINAL FOUR GASPERS HUNG OUT AT THE CLUBHOUSE.
IT WAS LIKE THE GOOD OLD DAYS. (Y'KNOW, LIKE, TWO WEEKS AGO.)
WHAT DO YOU THINK THE NINJAS ARE DOING NOW?
PWABABWEE WEEKING HAWIK.
WHAT?
I SAID, 'PROBABLY WREAKING HAVOC.' THEY ARE NINJAS.
YEAH. RHONDA'S RIGHT.
DEH AWA BUNKA WOONATWIKS!

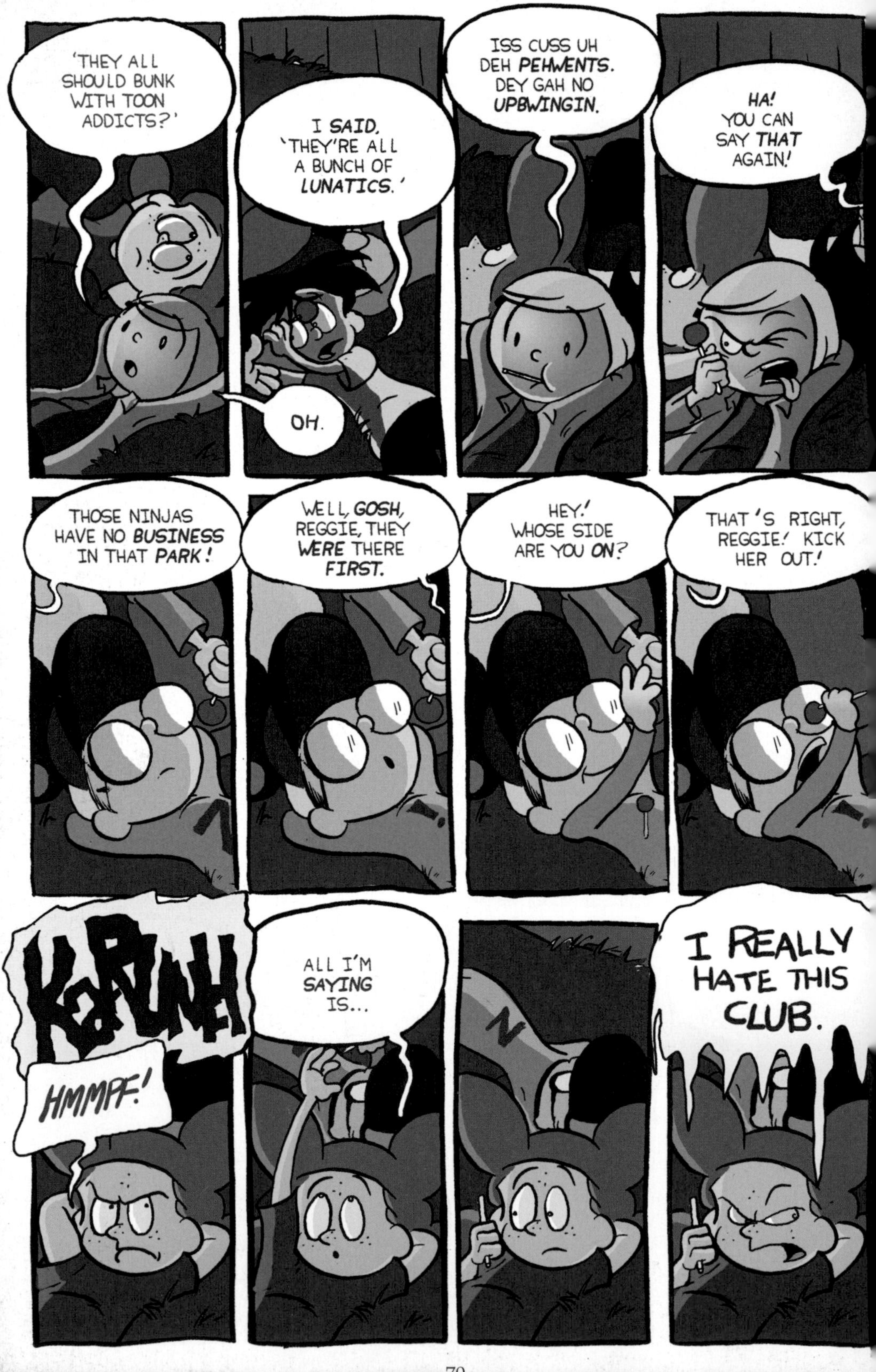
'THEY ALL SHOULD BUNK WITH TOON ADDICTS?'
I SAID, 'THEY'RE ALL A BUNCH OF LUNATICS.'
OH.
ISS CUSS UH DEH PEHWENTS. DEY GAH NO UPBWINGIN.
HA! YOU CAN SAY THAT AGAIN!
THOSE NINJAS HAVE NO BUSINESS IN THAT PARK!
WELL, GOSH, REGGIE, THEY WERE THERE FIRST.
HEY! WHOSE SIDE ARE YOU ON?
THAT'S RIGHT, REGGIE! KICK HER OUT!
KaRUNCH
HMMPF!
ALL I'M SAYING IS...
I REALLY HATE THIS CLUB.

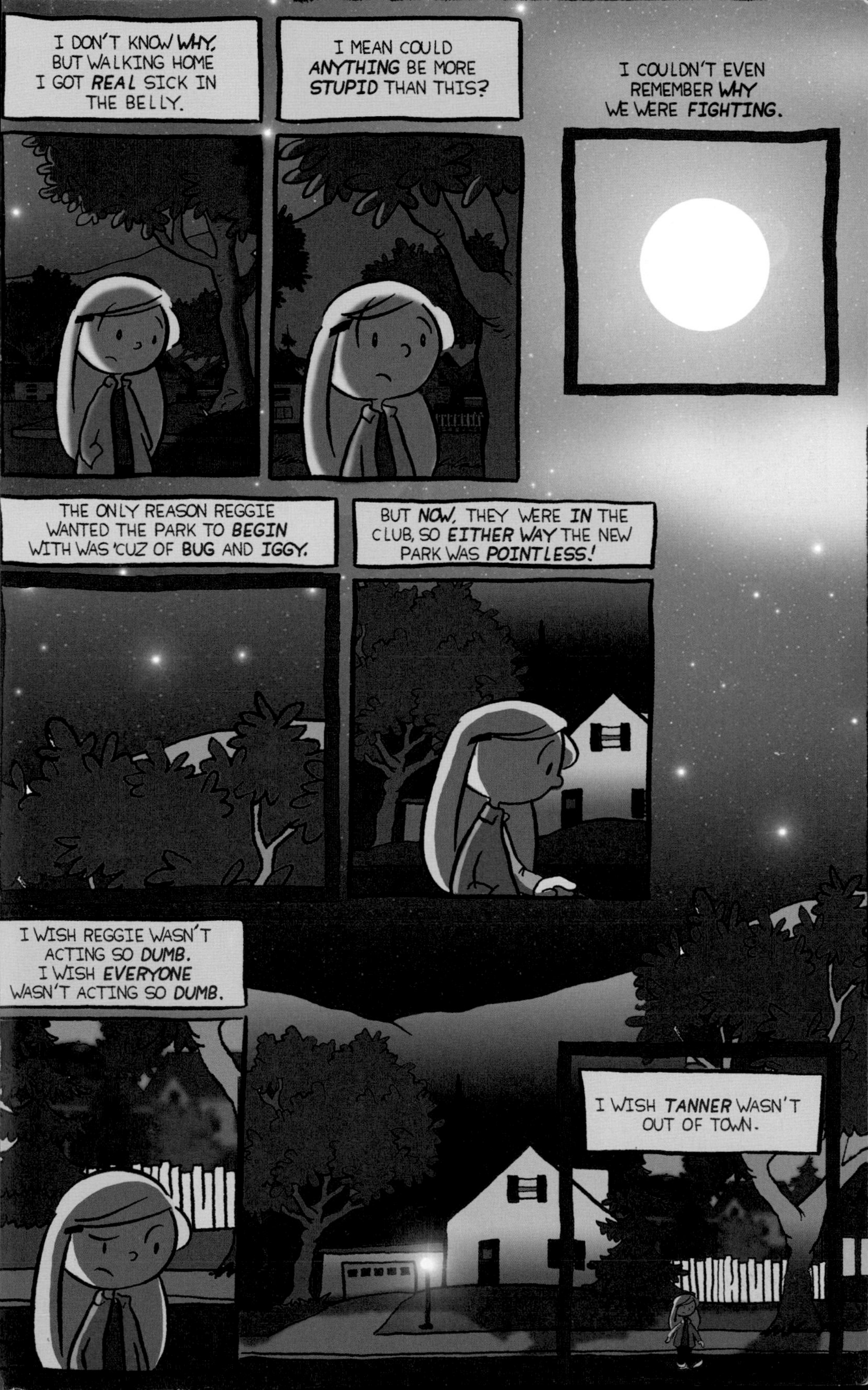
I DON'T KNOW WHY, BUT WALKING HOME I GOT REAL SICK IN THE BELLY.
I MEAN COULD ANYTHING BE MORE STUPID THAN THIS?
I COULDN'T EVEN REMEMBER WHY WE WERE FIGHTING.
THE ONLY REASON REGGIE WANTED THE PARK TO BEGIN WITH WAS 'CUZ OF BUG AND IGGY.
BUT NOW, THEY WERE IN THE CLUB, SO EITHER WAY THE NEW PARK WAS POINTLESS!
I WISH REGGIE WASN'T ACTING SO DUMB. I WISH EVERYONE WASN'T ACTING SO DUMB.
I WISH TANNER WASN'T OUT OF TOWN.

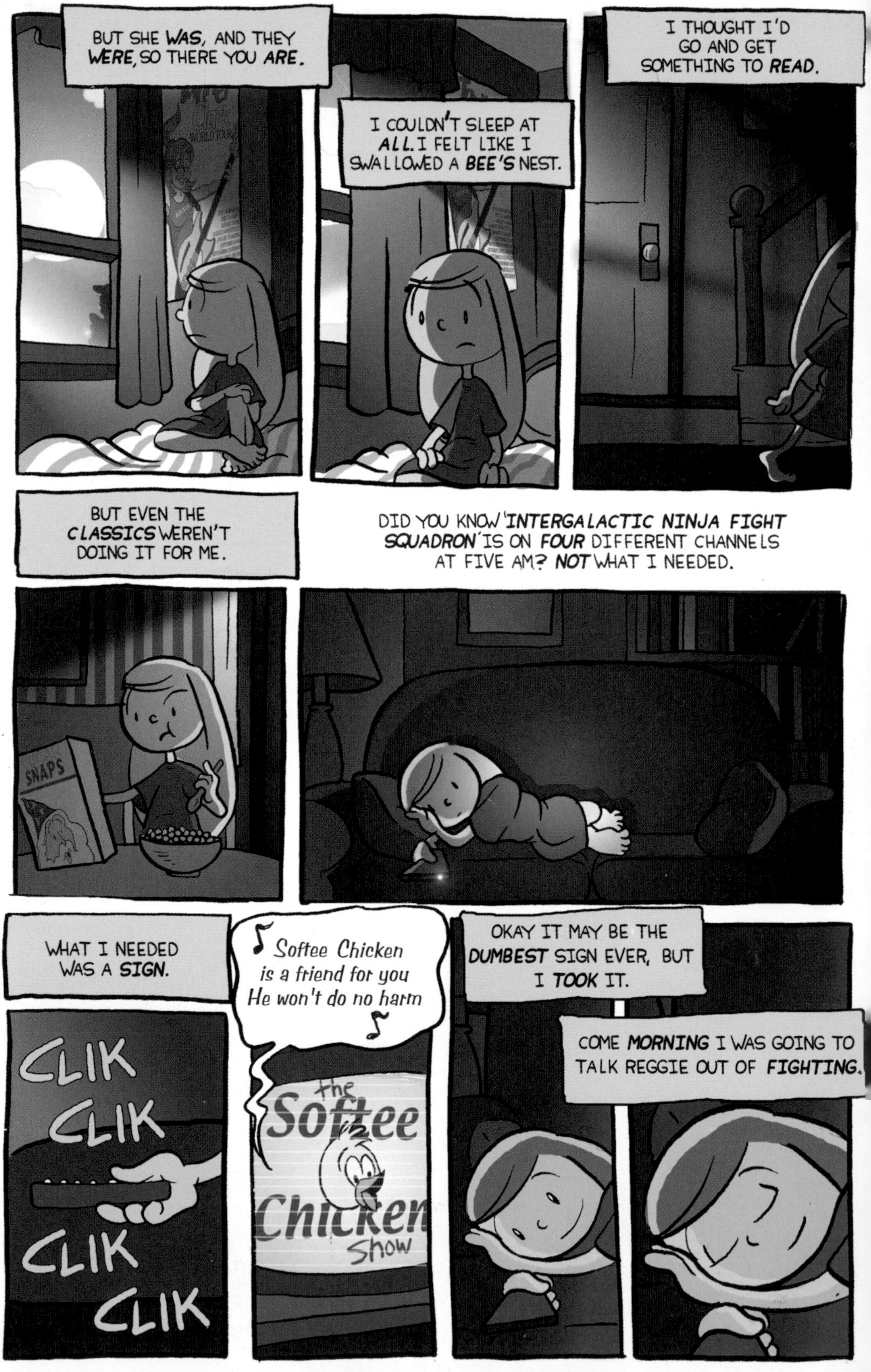

BUT SHE WAS, AND THEY WERE, SO THERE YOU ARE.
I COULDN'T SLEEP AT ALL. I FELT LIKE I SWALLOWED A BEE'S NEST.
I THOUGHT I'D GO AND GET SOMETHING TO READ.
BUT EVEN THE CLASSICS WEREN'T DOING IT FOR ME.
DID YOU KNOW 'INTERGALACTIC NINJA FIGHT SQUADRON' IS ON FOUR DIFFERENT CHANNELS AT FIVE AM? NOT WHAT I NEEDED.
SNAPS
WHAT I NEEDED WAS A SIGN.
Softee Chicken is a friend for you He won't do no harm
CLIK CLIK CLIK CLIK
the Softee Chicken show
OKAY IT MAY BE THE DUMBEST SIGN EVER, BUT I TOOK IT.
COME MORNING I WAS GOING TO TALK REGGIE OUT OF FIGHTING.

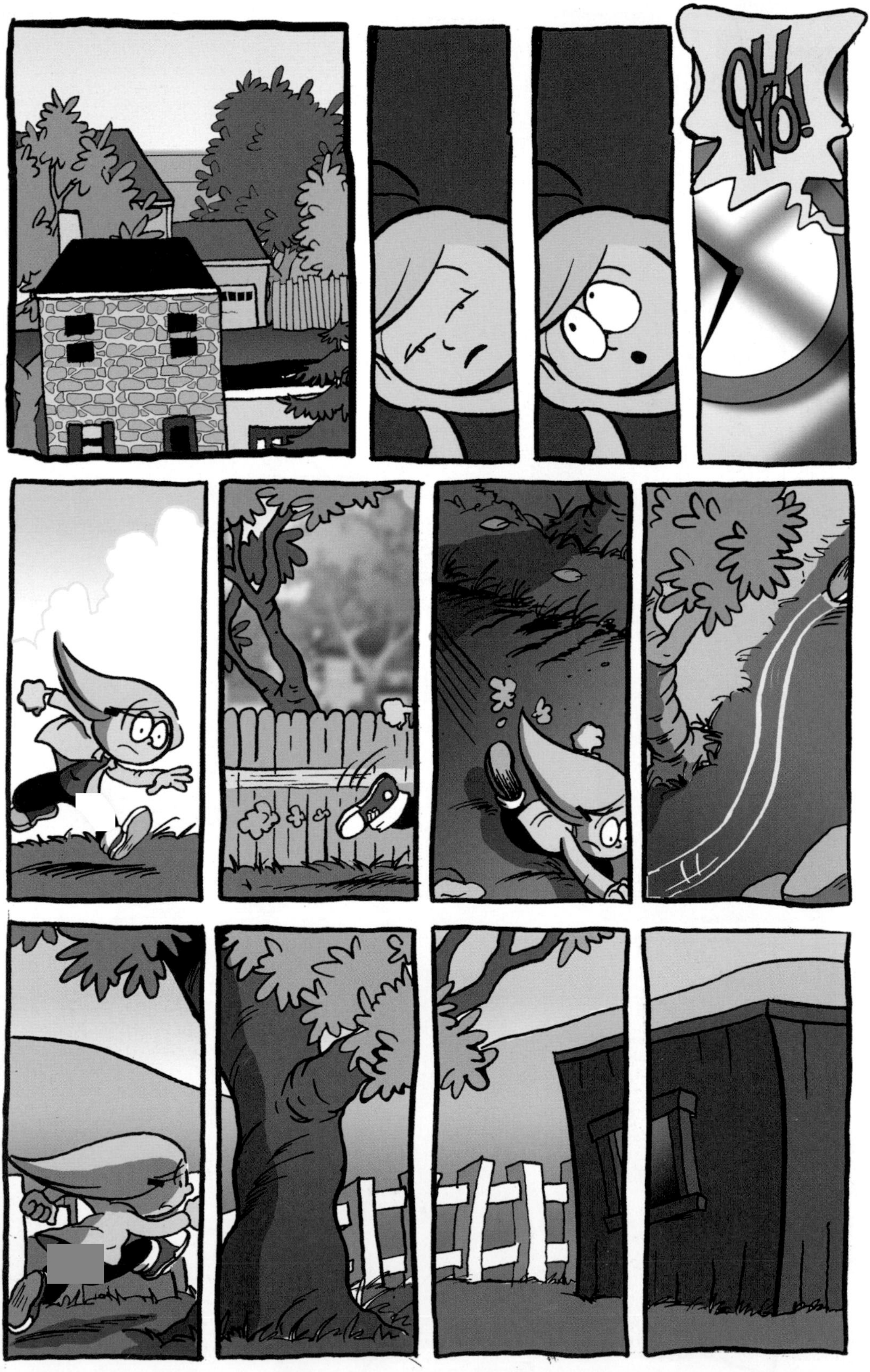
OH NO!

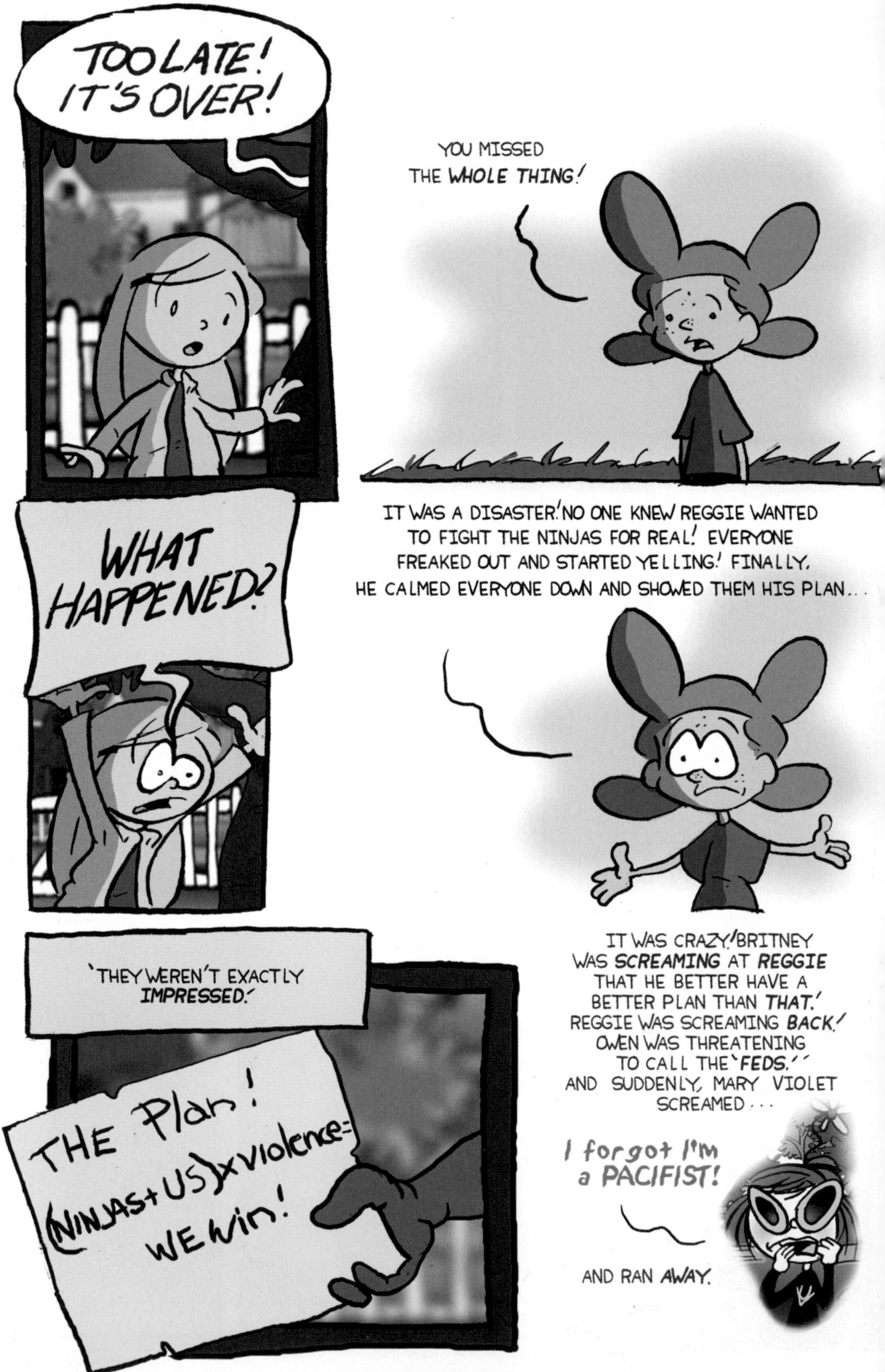

TOO LATE! IT'S OVER!
YOU MISSED THE WHOLE THING!
WHAT HAPPENED?
IT WAS A DISASTER! NO ONE KNEW REGGIE WANTED TO FIGHT THE NINJAS FOR REAL! EVERYONE FREAKED OUT AND STARTED YELLING! FINALLY, HE CALMED EVERYONE DOWN AND SHOWED THEM HIS PLAN...
"THEY WEREN'T EXACTLY IMPRESSED."
THE Plan! (NINJAS+US)x violence= WE Win!
IT WAS CRAZY! BRITNEY WAS SCREAMING AT REGGIE THAT HE BETTER HAVE A BETTER PLAN THAN THAT! REGGIE WAS SCREAMING BACK! OWEN WAS THREATENING TO CALL THE "FEDS." AND SUDDENLY, MARY VIOLET SCREAMED...
I forgot I'm a PACIFIST!
AND RAN AWAY.

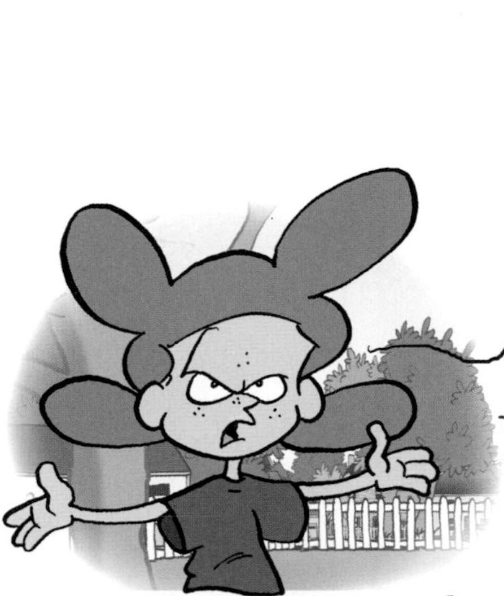

NO ONE KNEW WHAT WAS GOING ON, ***EVERYONE*** WAS FIGHTING!

THE WHOLE CLUB WAS FALLING ***APART***!

THEN REGGIE CLIMBED UP TO THE ***ROOF*** OF THE CLUBHOUSE AND STARTED TO GIVE THIS ***SPEECH***...

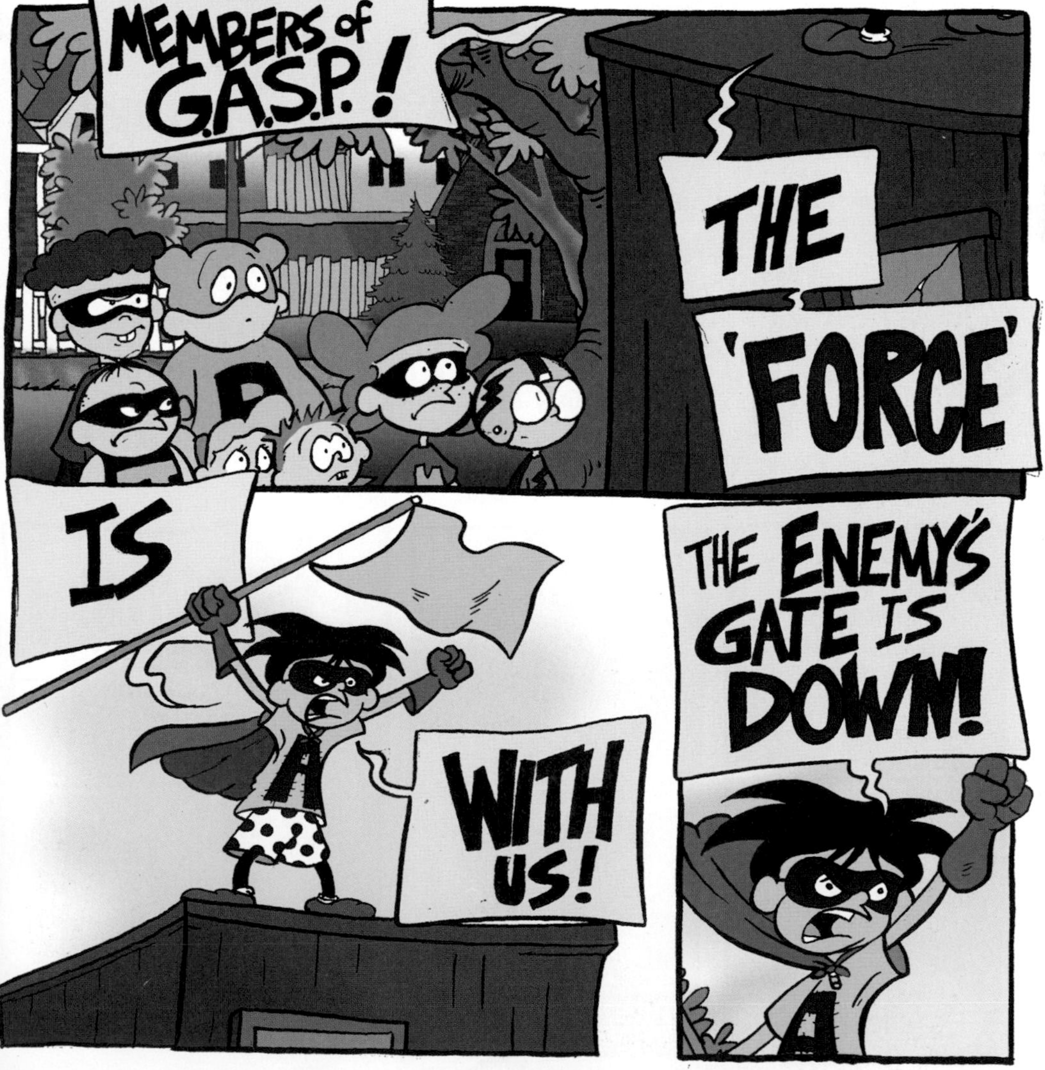
MEMBERS of G.A.S.P.!
THE
'FORCE'
IS
WITH US!
THE ENEMY'S GATE IS DOWN!

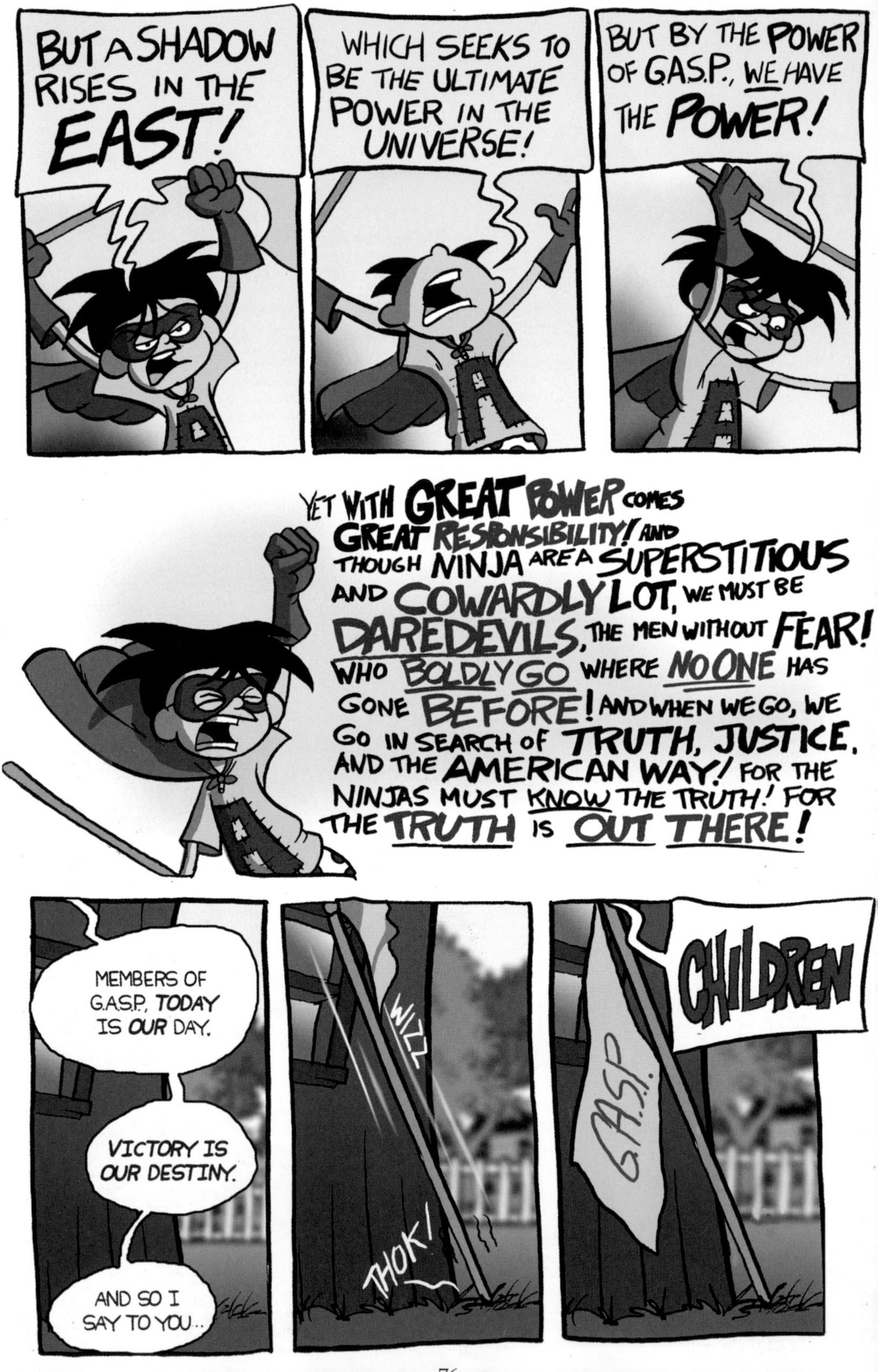
BUT A SHADOW RISES IN THE EAST!
WHICH SEEKS TO BE THE ULTIMATE POWER IN THE UNIVERSE!
BUT BY THE POWER OF G.A.S.P., WE HAVE THE POWER!
YET WITH GREAT POWER COMES GREAT RESPONSIBILITY! AND THOUGH NINJA ARE A SUPERSTITIOUS AND COWARDLY LOT, WE MUST BE DAREDEVILS, THE MEN WITHOUT FEAR! WHO BOLDLY GO WHERE NO ONE HAS GONE BEFORE! AND WHEN WE GO, WE GO IN SEARCH OF TRUTH, JUSTICE, AND THE AMERICAN WAY! FOR THE NINJAS MUST KNOW THE TRUTH! FOR THE TRUTH IS OUT THERE!
MEMBERS OF G.A.S.P., TODAY IS OUR DAY.
VICTORY IS OUR DESTINY.
AND SO I SAY TO YOU...
WIZZ
THOK!
G.A.S.P.
CHILDREN

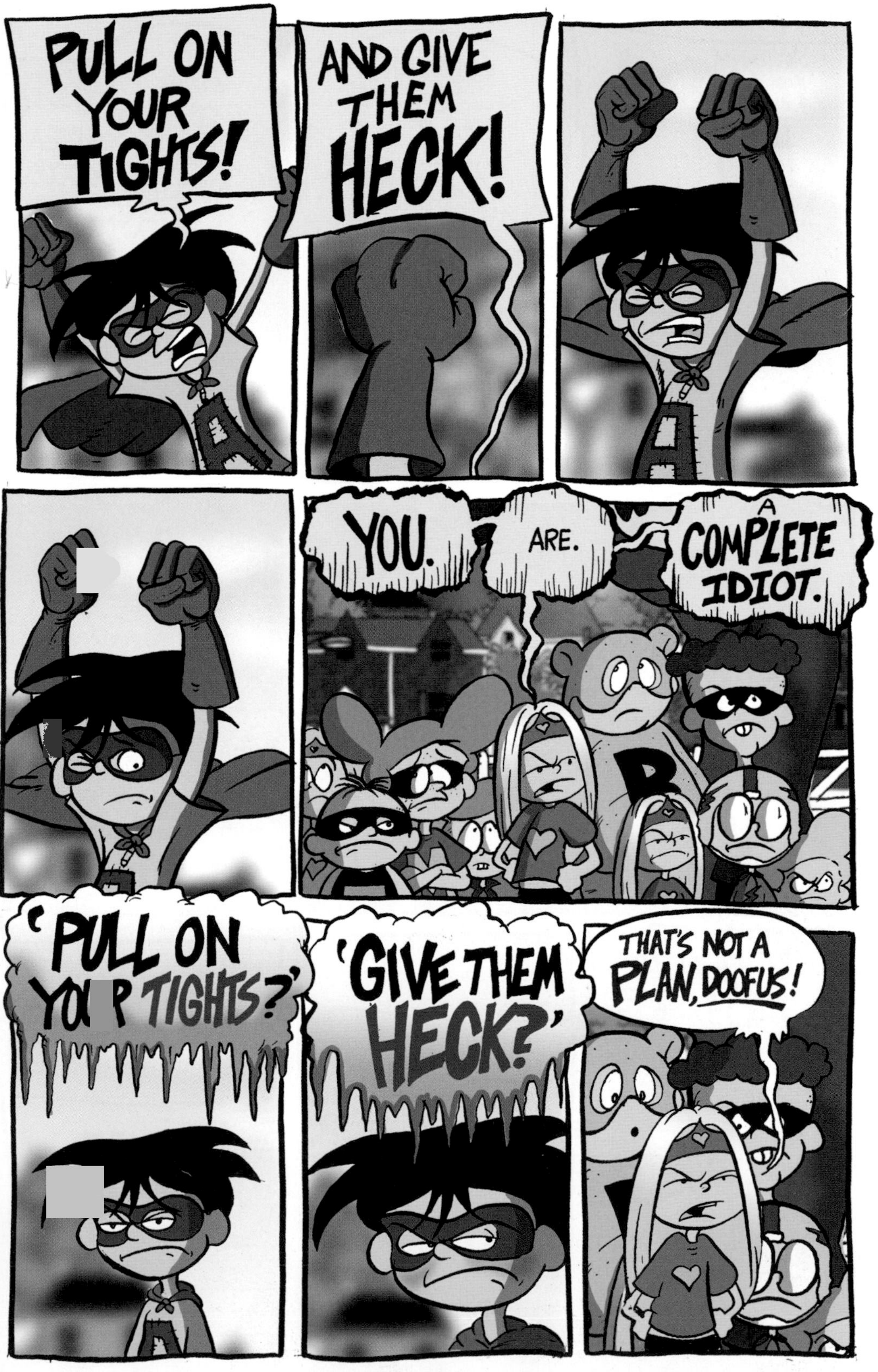
PULL ON YOUR TIGHTS!
AND GIVE THEM HECK!
YOU.
ARE.
A COMPLETE IDIOT.
'PULL ON YOUR TIGHTS?'
'GIVE THEM HECK?'
THAT'S NOT A PLAN, DOOFUS!

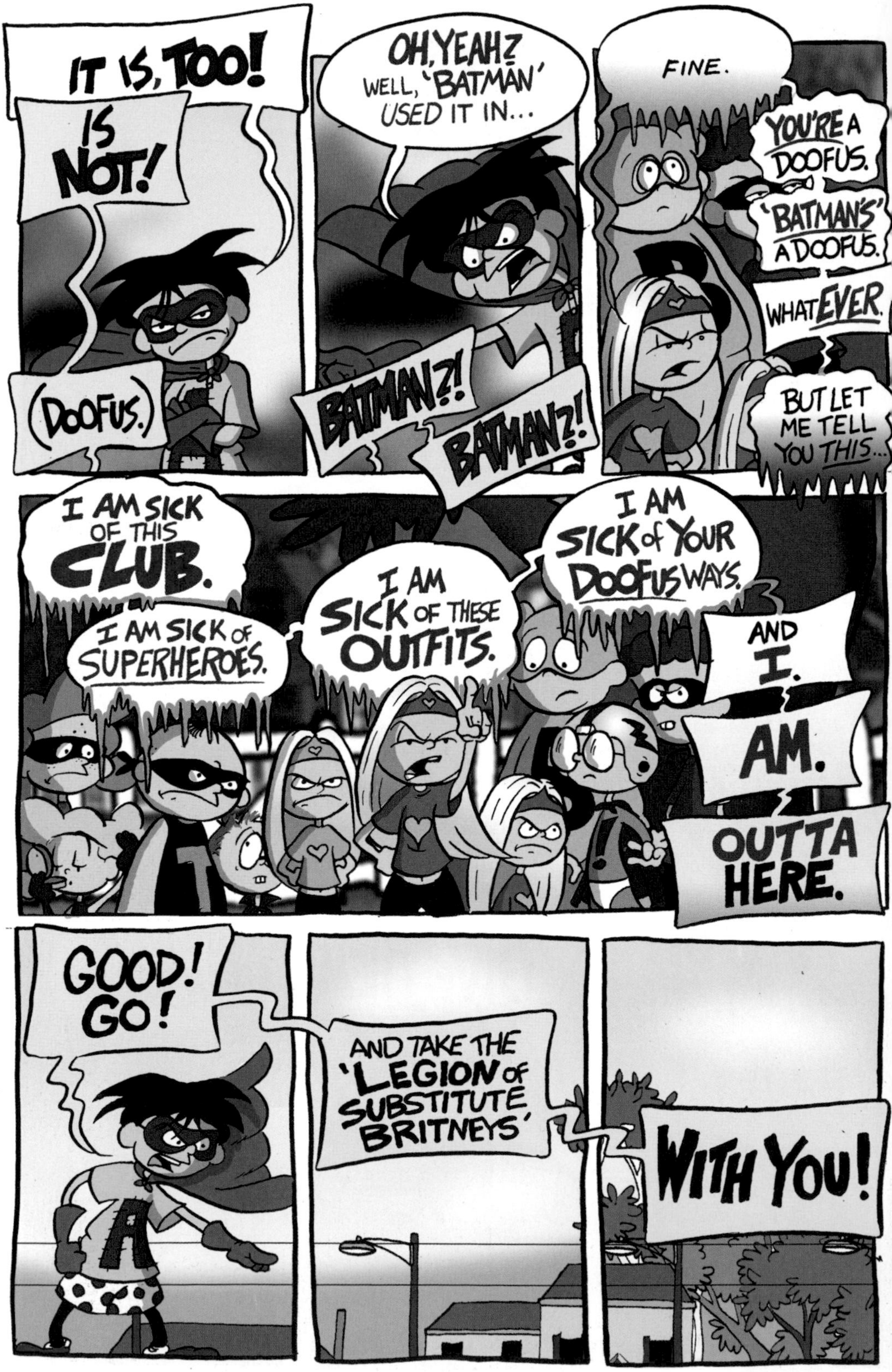
IT IS, TOO!
IS NOT!
(DOOFUS.)
OH, YEAH? WELL, 'BATMAN' USED IT IN...
BATMAN?!
BATMAN?!
FINE.
YOU'RE A DOOFUS.
'BATMAN'S' A DOOFUS.
WHATEVER.
BUT LET ME TELL YOU THIS...
I AM SICK OF THIS CLUB.
I AM SICK OF SUPERHEROES.
I AM SICK OF THESE OUTFITS.
I AM SICK OF YOUR DOOFUS WAYS.
AND I.
AM.
OUTTA HERE.
GOOD! GO!
AND TAKE THE 'LEGION OF SUBSTITUTE BRITNEYS'
WITH YOU!

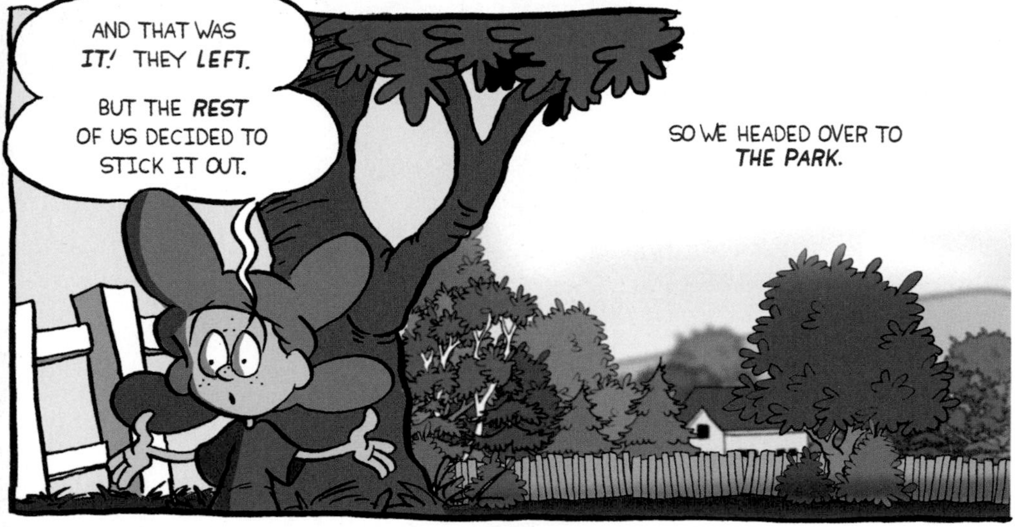
AND THAT WAS IT! THEY LEFT.
BUT THE REST OF US DECIDED TO STICK IT OUT.
SO WE HEADED OVER TO THE PARK.

THERE WAS **NO SIGN** OF THE NINJAS WHEN WE GOT THERE, SO WE DECIDED TO TRY AN **AMBUSH**.

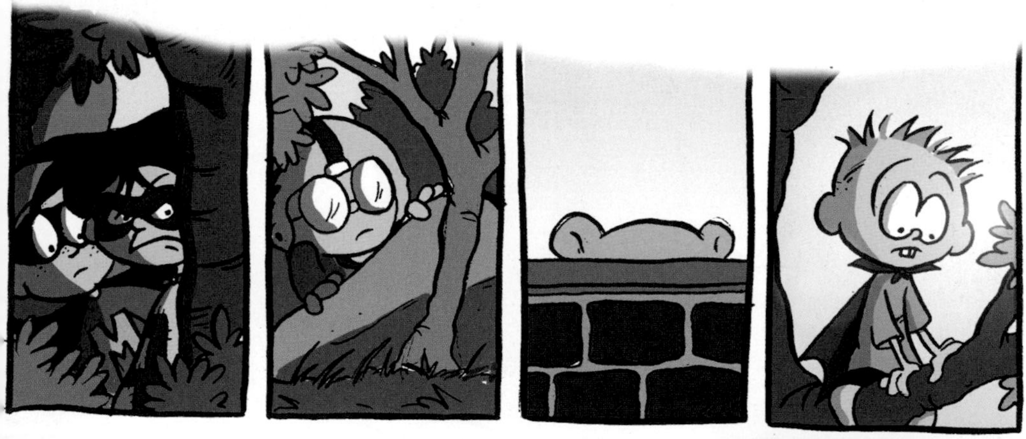

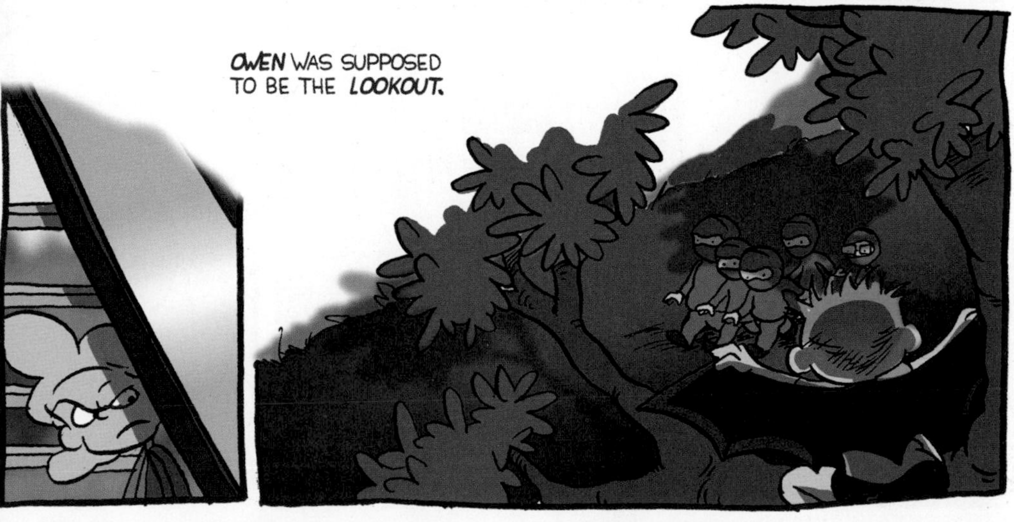
OWEN WAS SUPPOSED TO BE THE LOOKOUT.

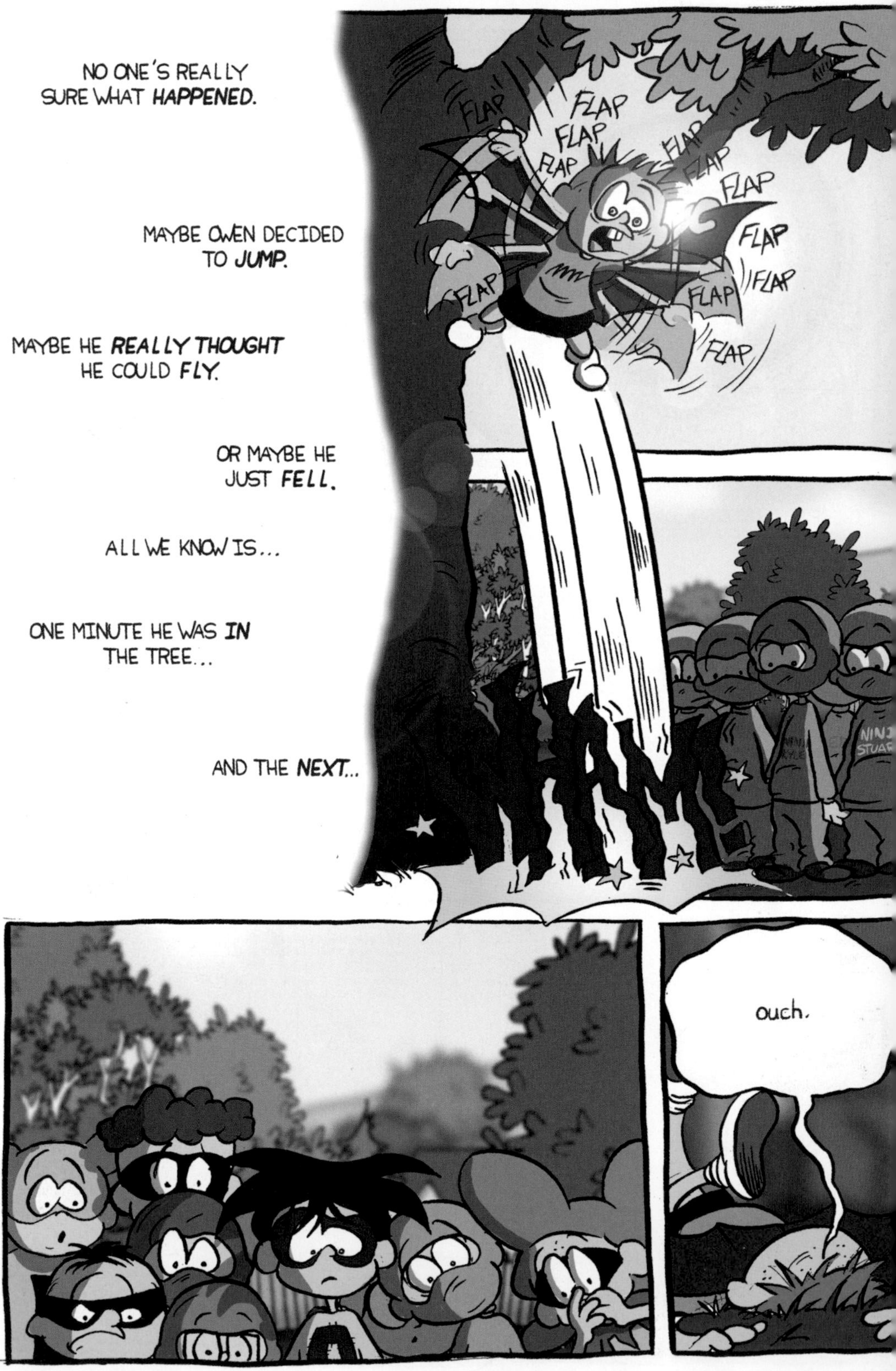
NO ONE'S REALLY SURE WHAT **HAPPENED.**
FLAP FLAP FLAP FLAP FLAP FLAP FLAP FLAP FLAP FLAP FLAP FLAP
MAYBE OWEN DECIDED TO **JUMP.**
MAYBE HE **REALLY THOUGHT** HE COULD **FLY.**
OR MAYBE HE JUST **FELL.**
ALL WE KNOW IS...
ONE MINUTE HE WAS **IN** THE TREE...
AND THE **NEXT...**
WHAM
ouch.

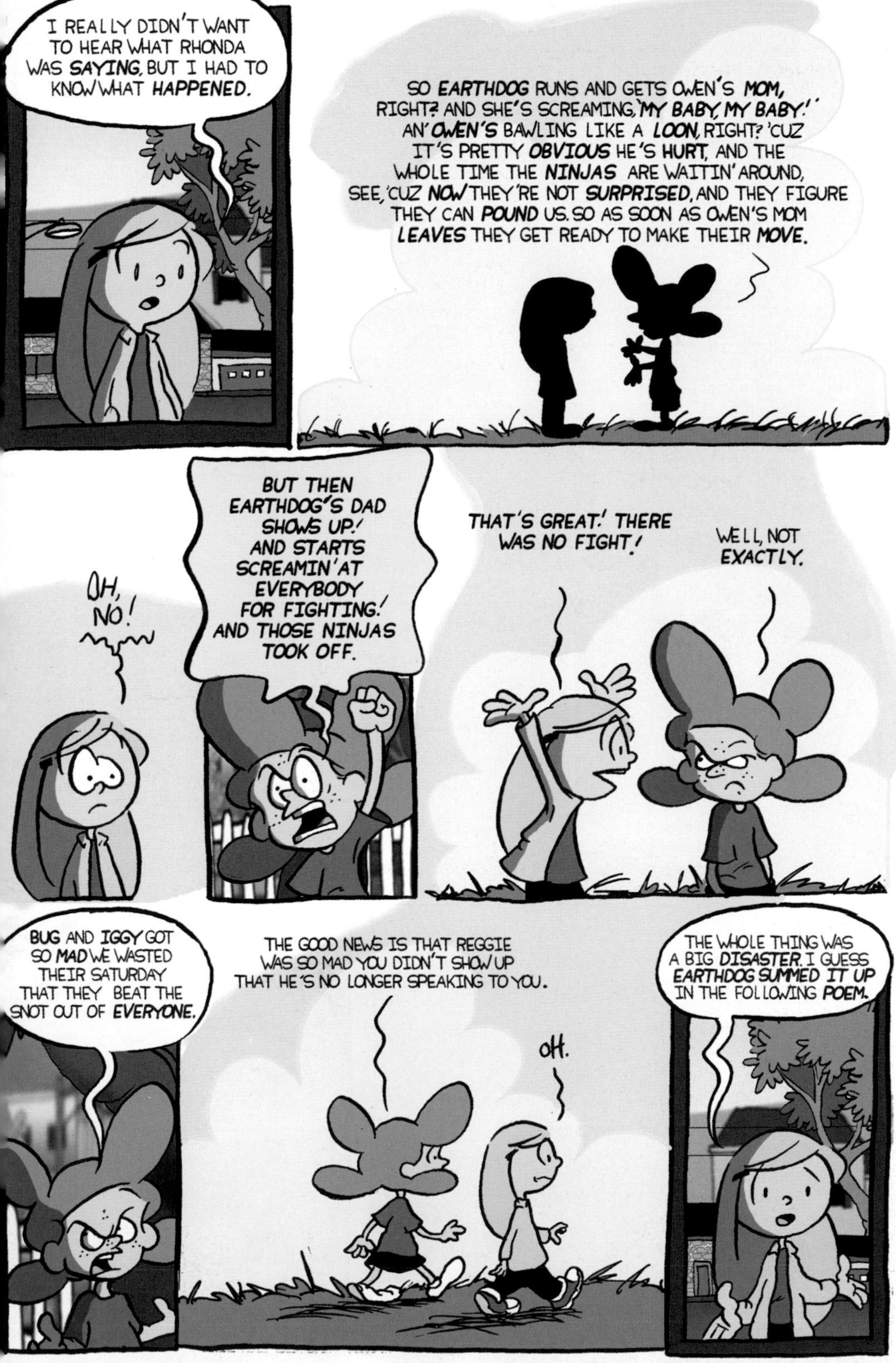
I REALLY DIDN'T WANT TO HEAR WHAT RHONDA WAS SAYING, BUT I HAD TO KNOW WHAT HAPPENED.
SO EARTHDOG RUNS AND GETS OWEN'S MOM, RIGHT? AND SHE'S SCREAMING, "MY BABY, MY BABY!" AN' OWEN'S BAWLING LIKE A LOON, RIGHT? 'CUZ IT'S PRETTY OBVIOUS HE'S HURT, AND THE WHOLE TIME THE NINJAS ARE WAITIN' AROUND, SEE, 'CUZ NOW THEY'RE NOT SURPRISED, AND THEY FIGURE THEY CAN POUND US. SO AS SOON AS OWEN'S MOM LEAVES THEY GET READY TO MAKE THEIR MOVE.
OH, NO!
BUT THEN EARTHDOG'S DAD SHOWS UP! AND STARTS SCREAMIN' AT EVERYBODY FOR FIGHTING! AND THOSE NINJAS TOOK OFF.
THAT'S GREAT! THERE WAS NO FIGHT!
WELL, NOT EXACTLY.
BUG AND IGGY GOT SO MAD WE WASTED THEIR SATURDAY THAT THEY BEAT THE SNOT OUT OF EVERYONE.
THE GOOD NEWS IS THAT REGGIE WAS SO MAD YOU DIDN'T SHOW UP THAT HE'S NO LONGER SPEAKING TO YOU.
OH.
THE WHOLE THING WAS A BIG DISASTER. I GUESS EARTHDOG SUMMED IT UP IN THE FOLLOWING POEM.

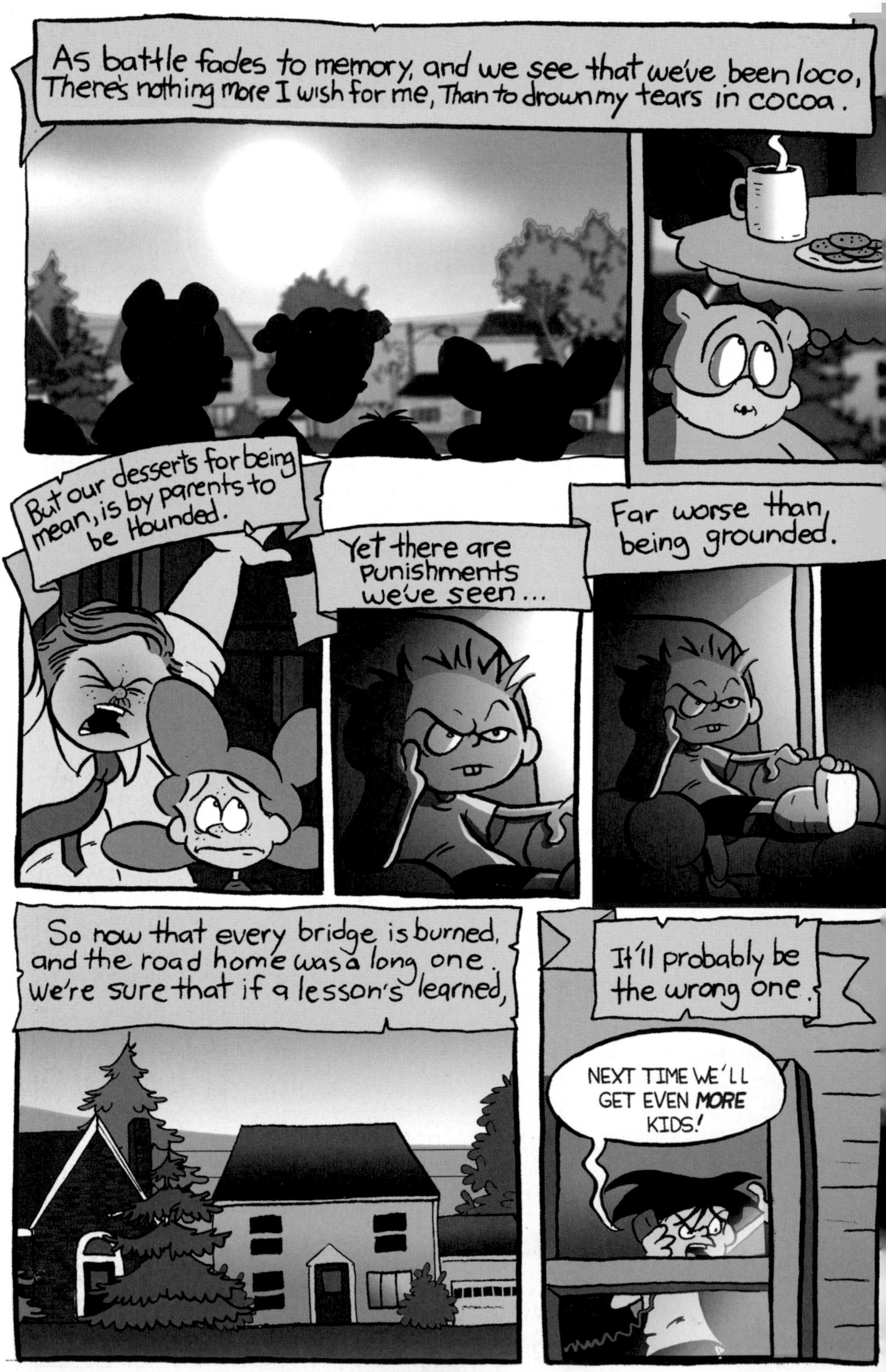
As battle fades to memory, and we see that we've been loco, There's nothing more I wish for me, Than to drown my tears in cocoa.
But our desserts for being mean, is by parents to be Hounded.
Yet there are punishments we've seen...
Far worse than being grounded.
So now that every bridge is burned, and the road home was a long one. we're sure that if a lesson's learned,
It'll probably be the wrong one.
NEXT TIME WE'LL GET EVEN *MORE* KIDS!

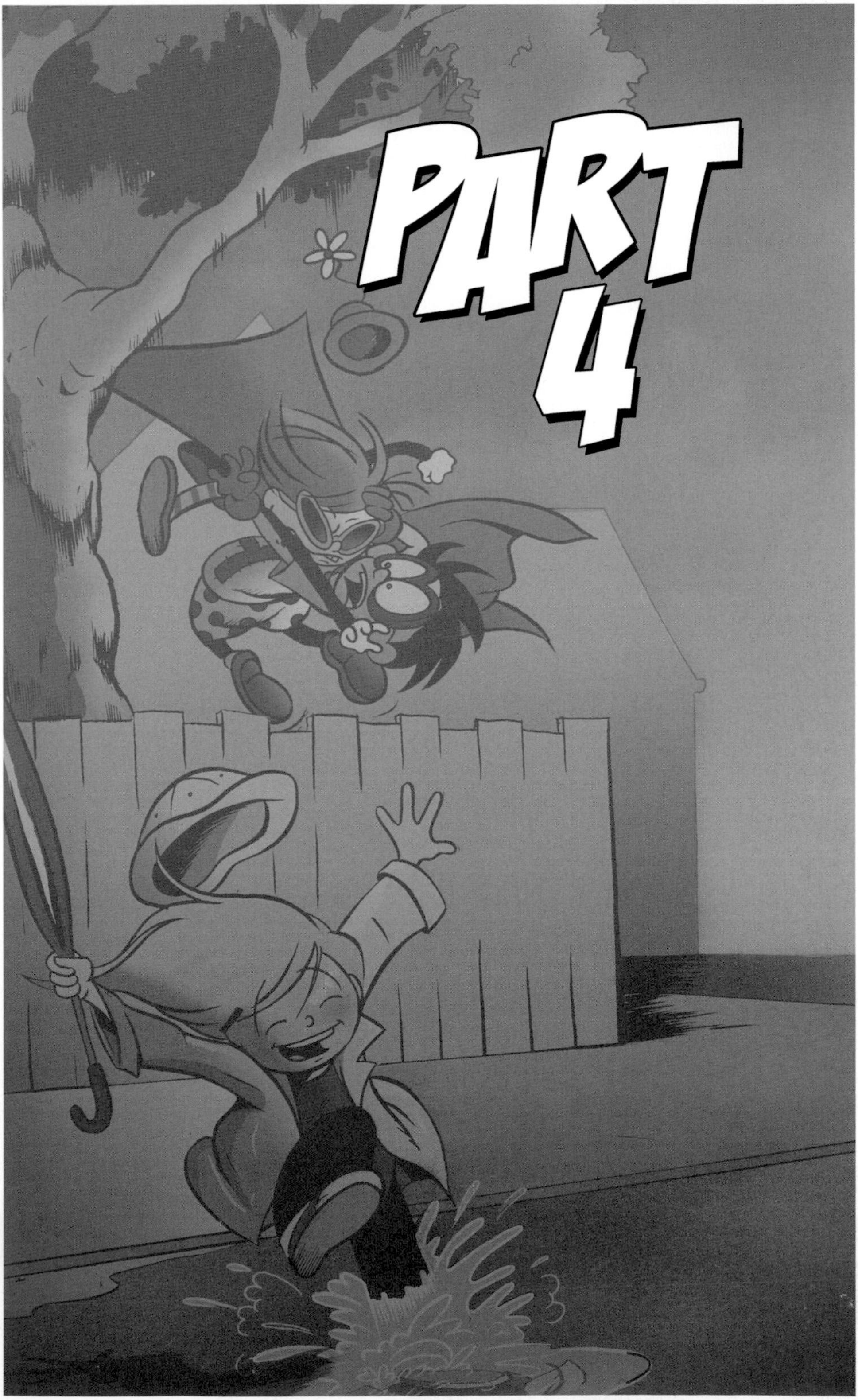
PART 4

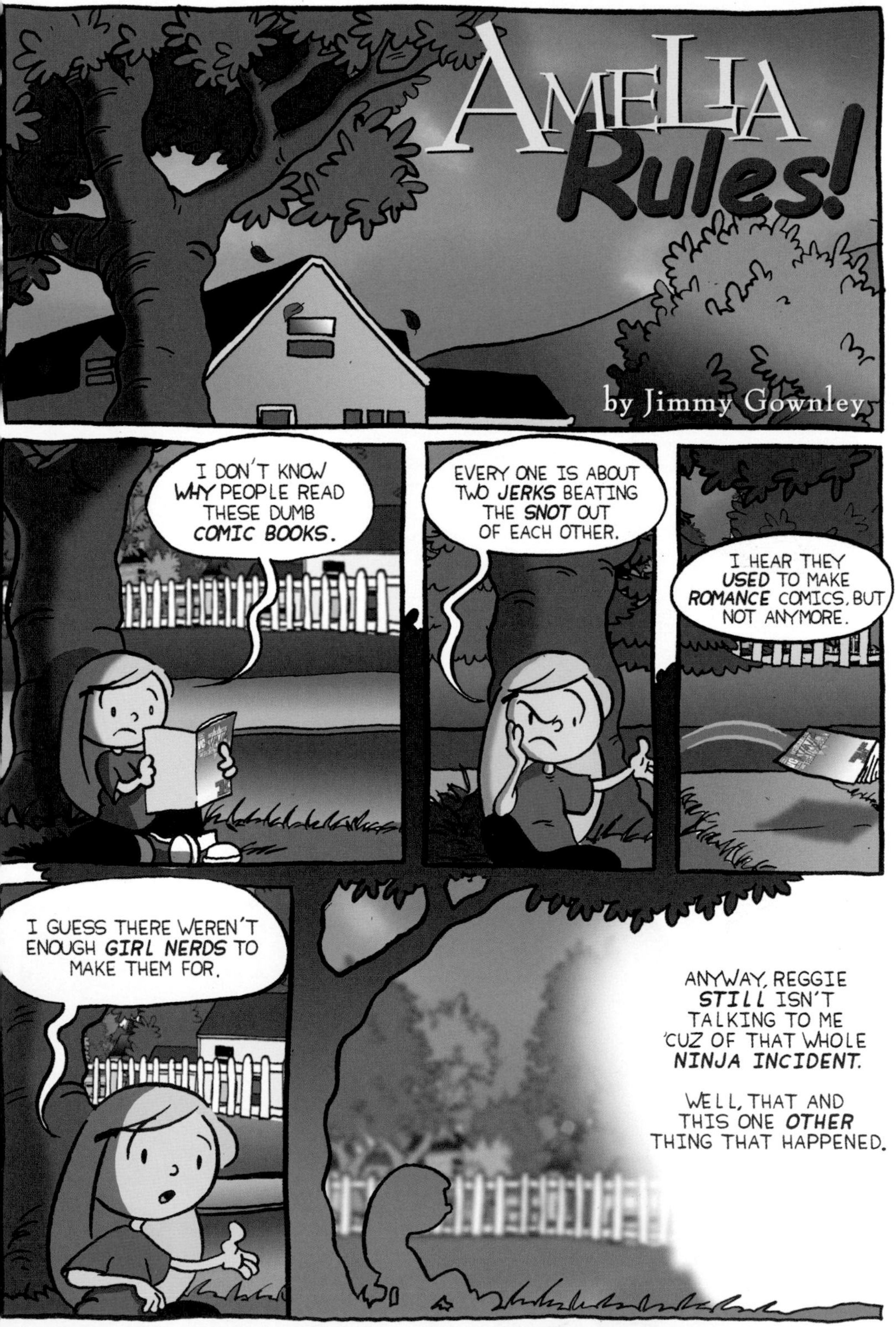
AMELIA Rules!
by Jimmy Gownley
I DON'T KNOW WHY PEOPLE READ THESE DUMB COMIC BOOKS.
EVERY ONE IS ABOUT TWO JERKS BEATING THE SNOT OUT OF EACH OTHER.
I HEAR THEY USED TO MAKE ROMANCE COMICS, BUT NOT ANYMORE.
I GUESS THERE WEREN'T ENOUGH GIRL NERDS TO MAKE THEM FOR.
ANYWAY, REGGIE STILL ISN'T TALKING TO ME 'CUZ OF THAT WHOLE NINJA INCIDENT.
WELL, THAT AND THIS ONE OTHER THING THAT HAPPENED.

HER THREE KISSES

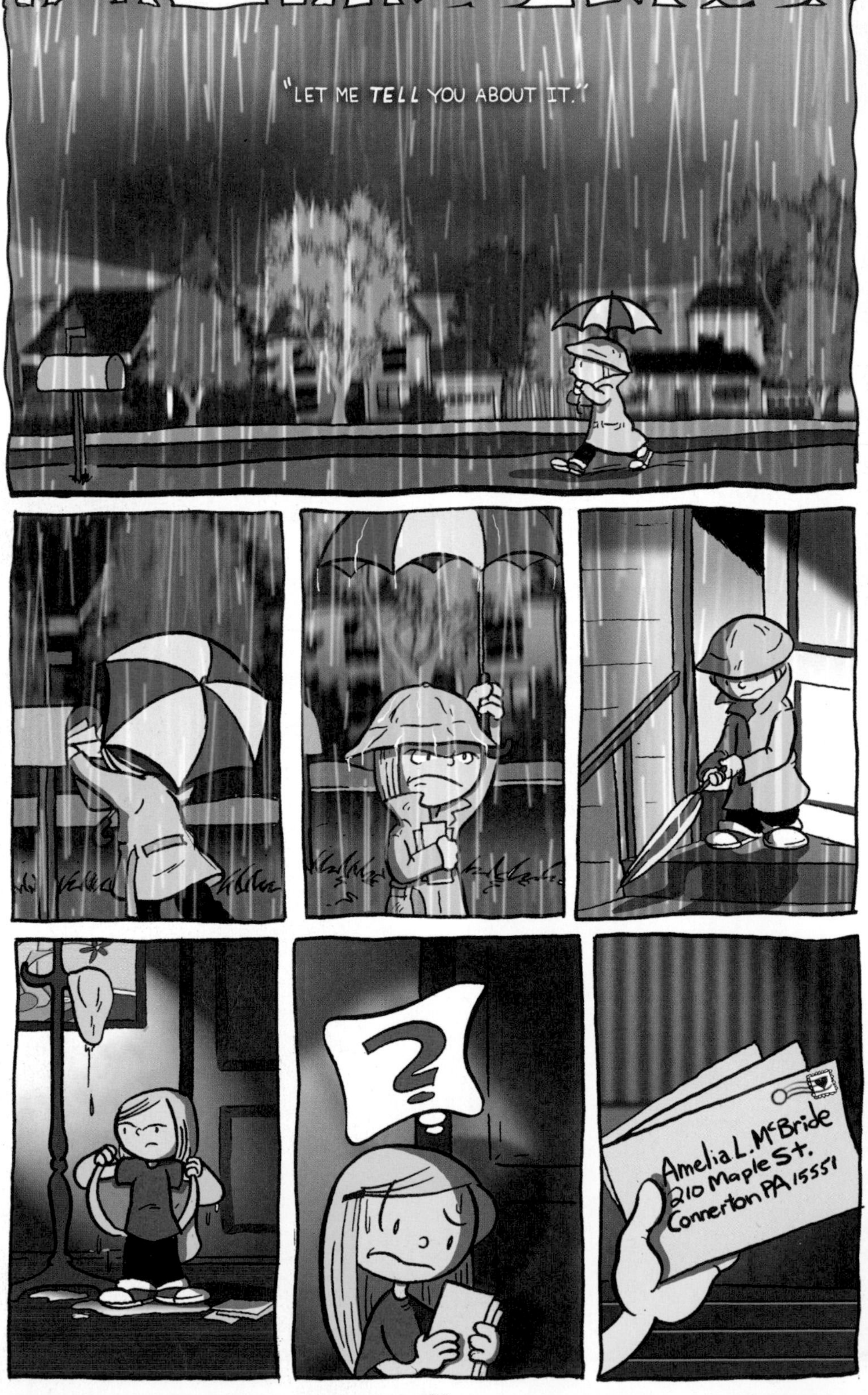
"LET ME TELL YOU ABOUT IT."
?
Amelia L. McBride
210 Maple St.
Connerton PA 15551

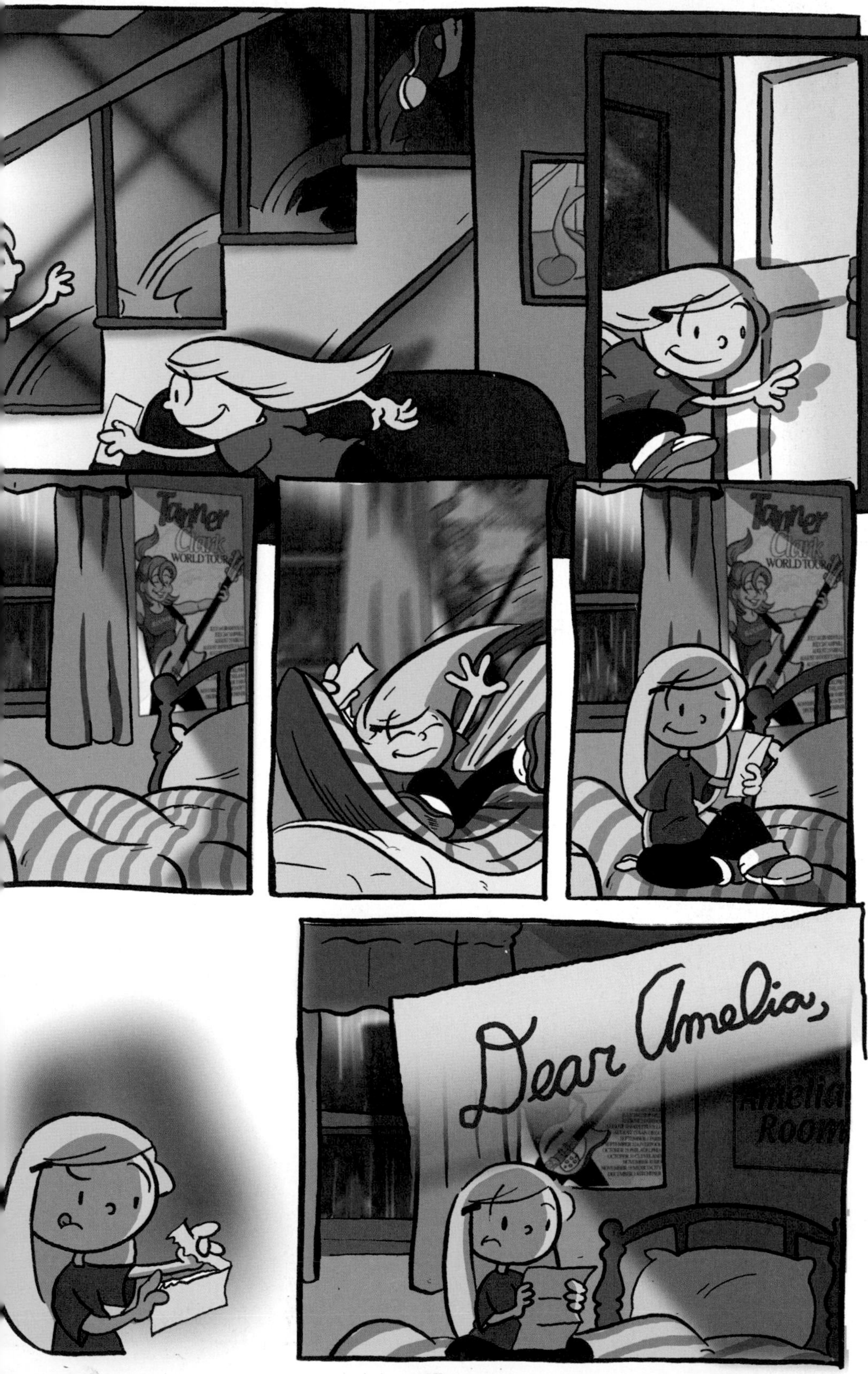
Tanner Clark WORLD TOUR
Tanner Clark WORLD TOUR
Dear Amelia,

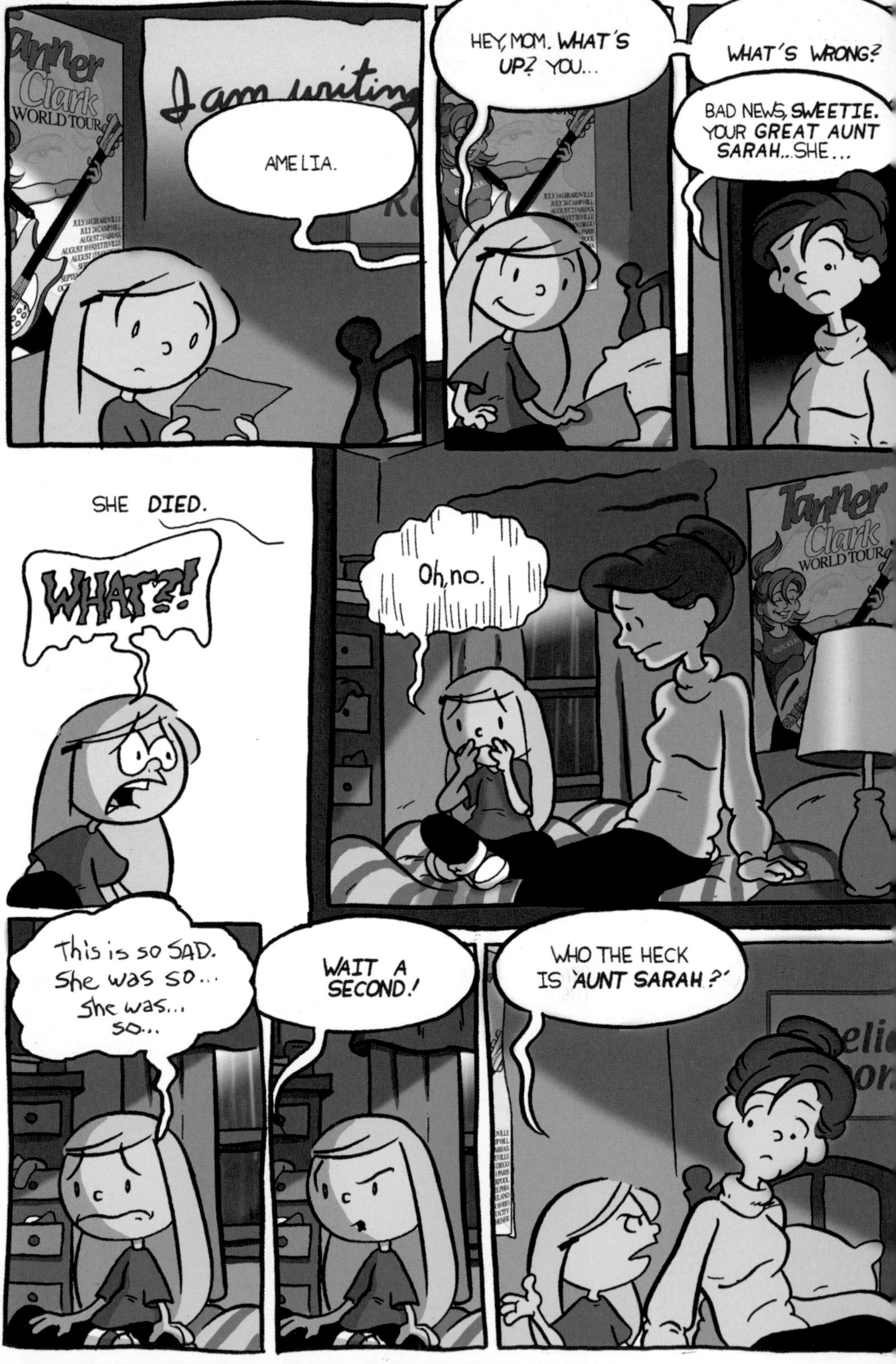
Tanner Clark WORLD TOUR
I am writing
AMELIA.
HEY, MOM. WHAT'S UP? YOU...
WHAT'S WRONG?
BAD NEWS, SWEETIE. YOUR GREAT AUNT SARAH... SHE...
SHE DIED.
WHAT?!
Oh, no.
Tanner Clark WORLD TOUR
This is so SAD. She was so... She was... so...
WAIT A SECOND!
WHO THE HECK IS 'AUNT SARAH?'

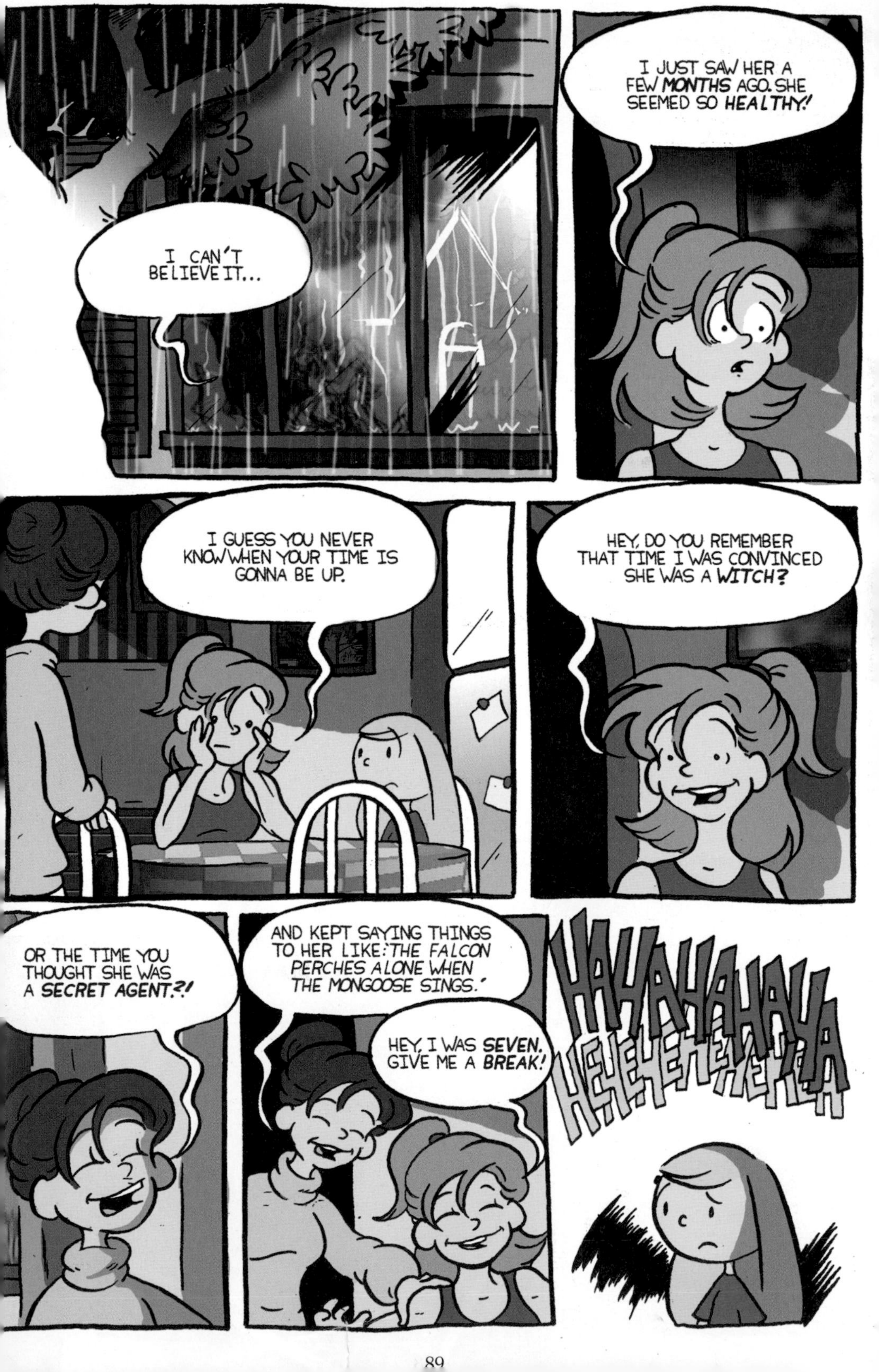
I CAN'T BELIEVE IT...
I JUST SAW HER A FEW MONTHS AGO. SHE SEEMED SO HEALTHY!
I GUESS YOU NEVER KNOW WHEN YOUR TIME IS GONNA BE UP.
HEY, DO YOU REMEMBER THAT TIME I WAS CONVINCED SHE WAS A WITCH?
OR THE TIME YOU THOUGHT SHE WAS A SECRET AGENT?!
AND KEPT SAYING THINGS TO HER LIKE: 'THE FALCON PERCHES ALONE WHEN THE MONGOOSE SINGS.'
HEY, I WAS SEVEN. GIVE ME A BREAK!
HAHAHAHAHAHA
HEHEHEHEHEHEHEHA

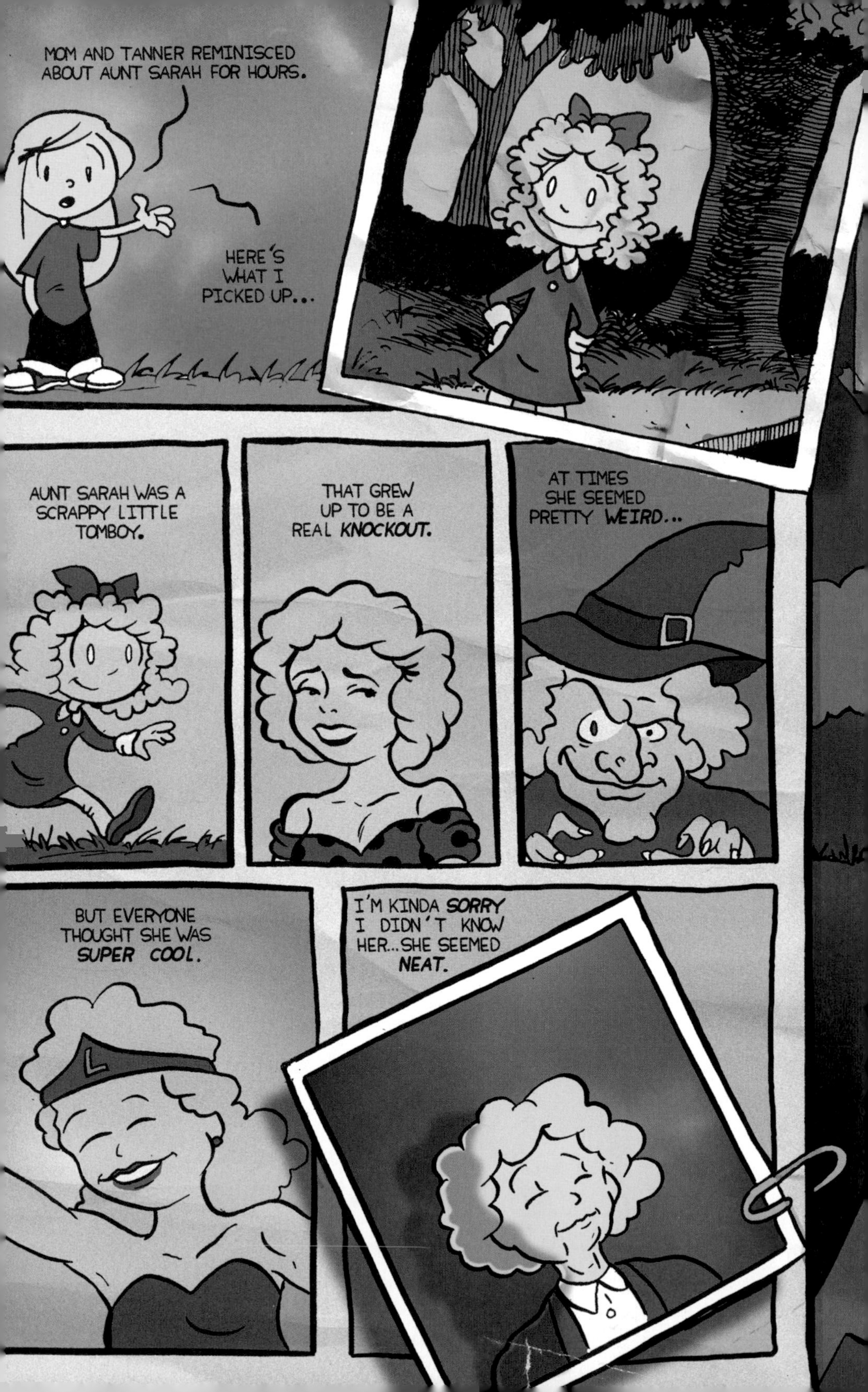
MOM AND TANNER REMINISCED ABOUT AUNT SARAH FOR HOURS.
HERE'S WHAT I PICKED UP...
AUNT SARAH WAS A SCRAPPY LITTLE TOMBOY.
THAT GREW UP TO BE A REAL **KNOCKOUT.**
AT TIMES SHE SEEMED PRETTY **WEIRD...**
BUT EVERYONE THOUGHT SHE WAS **SUPER COOL.**
I'M KINDA **SORRY** I DIDN'T KNOW HER...SHE SEEMED **NEAT.**

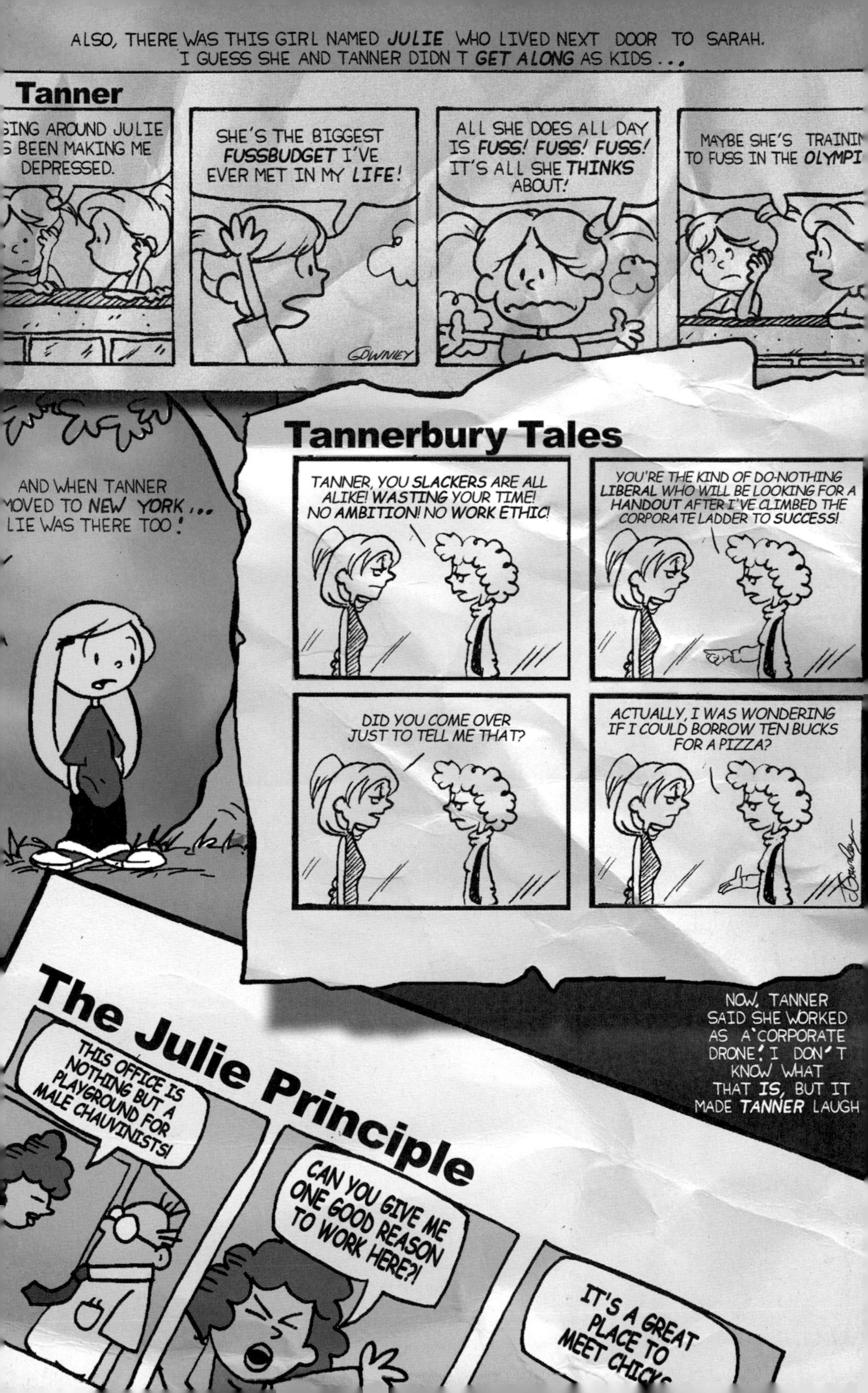
ALSO, THERE WAS THIS GIRL NAMED JULIE WHO LIVED NEXT DOOR TO SARAH.
I GUESS SHE AND TANNER DIDN'T GET ALONG AS KIDS...
Tanner
SING AROUND JULIE S BEEN MAKING ME DEPRESSED.
SHE'S THE BIGGEST FUSSBUDGET I'VE EVER MET IN MY LIFE!
ALL SHE DOES ALL DAY IS FUSS! FUSS! FUSS! IT'S ALL SHE THINKS ABOUT!
MAYBE SHE'S TRAININ TO FUSS IN THE OLYMPI
GDOWNEY
AND WHEN TANNER MOVED TO NEW YORK... LIE WAS THERE TOO!
Tannerbury Tales
TANNER, YOU SLACKERS ARE ALL ALIKE! WASTING YOUR TIME! NO AMBITION! NO WORK ETHIC!
YOU'RE THE KIND OF DO-NOTHING LIBERAL WHO WILL BE LOOKING FOR A HANDOUT AFTER I'VE CLIMBED THE CORPORATE LADDER TO SUCCESS!
DID YOU COME OVER JUST TO TELL ME THAT?
ACTUALLY, I WAS WONDERING IF I COULD BORROW TEN BUCKS FOR A PIZZA?
NOW, TANNER SAID SHE WORKED AS A CORPORATE DRONE! I DON'T KNOW WHAT THAT IS, BUT IT MADE TANNER LAUGH
The Julie Principle
THIS OFFICE IS NOTHING BUT A PLAYGROUND FOR MALE CHAUVINISTS!
CAN YOU GIVE ME ONE GOOD REASON TO WORK HERE?!
IT'S A GREAT PLACE TO MEET CHICKS

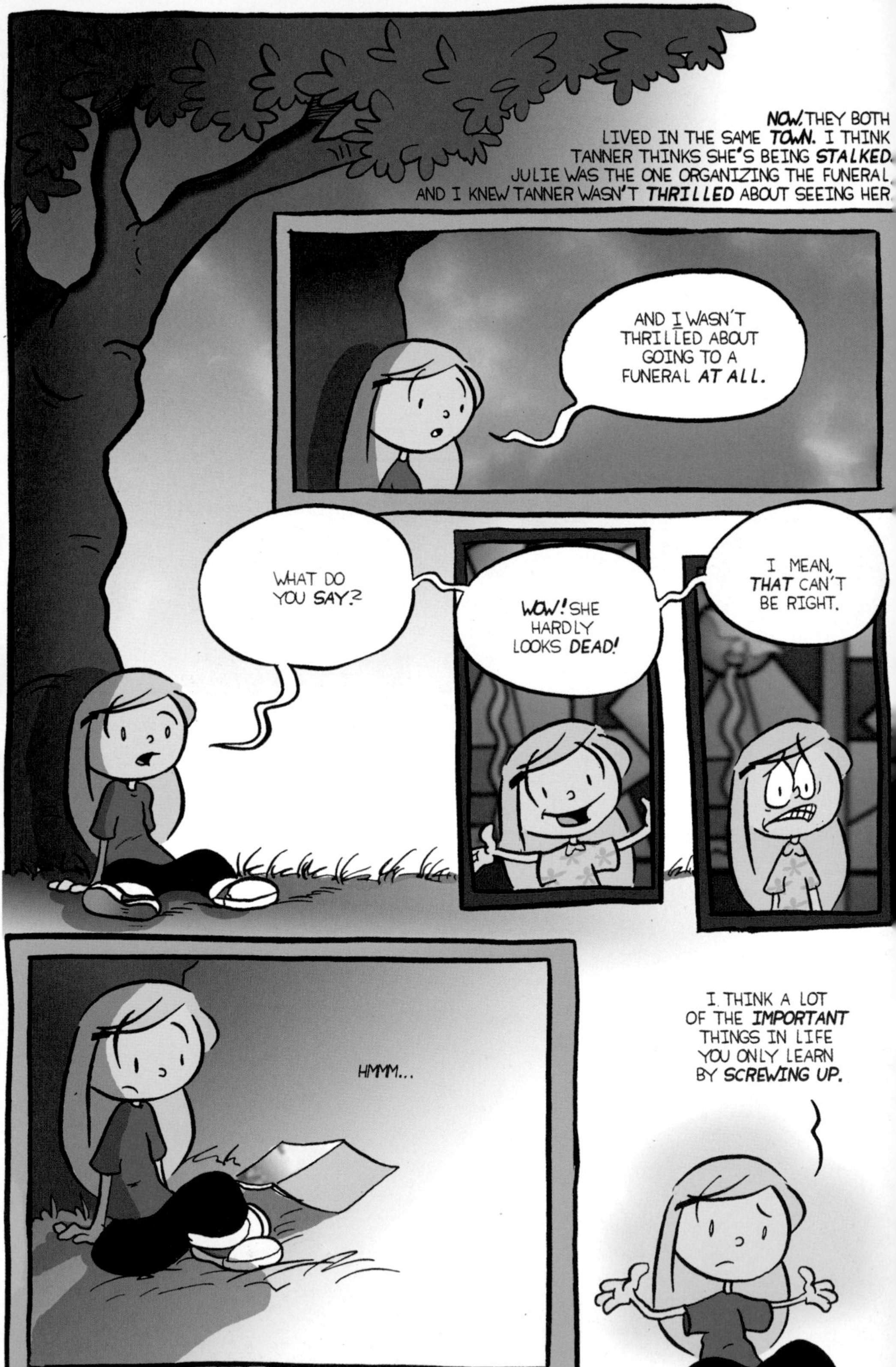
NOW, THEY BOTH LIVED IN THE SAME TOWN. I THINK TANNER THINKS SHE'S BEING STALKED. JULIE WAS THE ONE ORGANIZING THE FUNERAL, AND I KNEW TANNER WASN'T THRILLED ABOUT SEEING HER.
AND I WASN'T THRILLED ABOUT GOING TO A FUNERAL AT ALL.
WHAT DO YOU SAY?
WOW! SHE HARDLY LOOKS DEAD!
I MEAN, THAT CAN'T BE RIGHT.
HMMM...
I THINK A LOT OF THE IMPORTANT THINGS IN LIFE YOU ONLY LEARN BY SCREWING UP.

THERE WAS A LOT OF HUBBUB BEFORE WE LEFT FOR THE FUNERAL, LOTS OF CRYING AND PHONE CALLS.

AND TANNER MANAGED TO AVOID TALKING TO JULIE, WHO SEEMED TO CALL EVERY FIVE MINUTES.

ANYWAY..

IN ALL THE COMMOTION I ALMOST FORGOT ABOUT THE LETTER, BUT WHEN I READ IT, BOY DID I GET A SHOCK.

Dear Amelia,
I am writing because, although I have never met I have always felt a great fondness for you. Your mother was just a girl, we were very close, and I hoped it could be the same for us. I guess that isn't meant to be.
I have been thinking a lot about a suitable gift to leave for you, and decided what it should be. I know you will be at my house soon. Follow the directions on the back of this letter to find your surprise (It's always better when you have to work for something!)
I hope you like it. I believe it contains something magical that will sustain you for your whole life.
Love,
(GREAT) Aunt Sarah

WHY WOULD AUNT SARAH WRITE TO ME? WE NEVER EVEN MET! AND NOW SHE WAS DEAD!

THIS WAS TOO WEIRD.

BUT I DIDN'T HAVE MUCH TIME TO THINK ABOUT IT, 'CUZ BEFORE I KNEW IT...

WE WERE THERE...

THE HOUSE WHERE SARAH DIED.

93

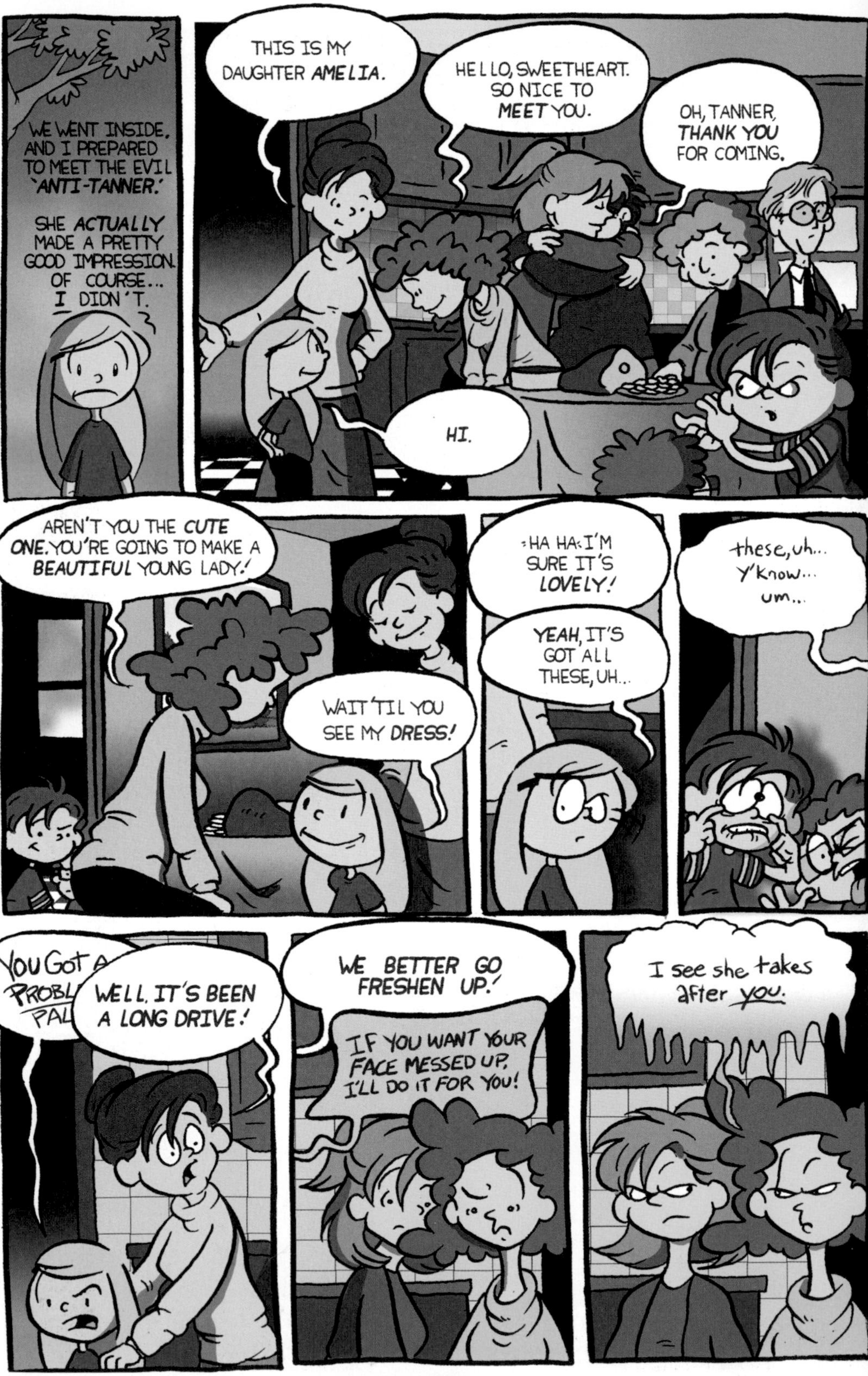
WE WENT INSIDE, AND I PREPARED TO MEET THE EVIL "ANTI-TANNER."
SHE ACTUALLY MADE A PRETTY GOOD IMPRESSION. OF COURSE... I DIDN'T.
THIS IS MY DAUGHTER AMELIA.
HELLO, SWEETHEART. SO NICE TO MEET YOU.
OH, TANNER, THANK YOU FOR COMING.
HI.
AREN'T YOU THE CUTE ONE. YOU'RE GOING TO MAKE A BEAUTIFUL YOUNG LADY!
WAIT 'TIL YOU SEE MY DRESS!
HA HA I'M SURE IT'S LOVELY!
YEAH, IT'S GOT ALL THESE, UH...
these, uh... y'know... um...
YOU GOT A PROBL PAL
WELL, IT'S BEEN A LONG DRIVE!
WE BETTER GO FRESHEN UP!
IF YOU WANT YOUR FACE MESSED UP, I'LL DO IT FOR YOU!
I see she takes after you.

I DON'T KNOW, I WAS ACTUALLY KINDA LOOKING FORWARD TO WEARING A **DRESS**. IT FELT KINDA **GROWN UP**, AND I THOUGHT I'D LOOK... DIFFERENT OR SOMETHING. IT TURNS OUT I JUST LOOK LIKE **ME**, ONLY **PINKER** AND WITH A BOW ON MY **BUTT**.

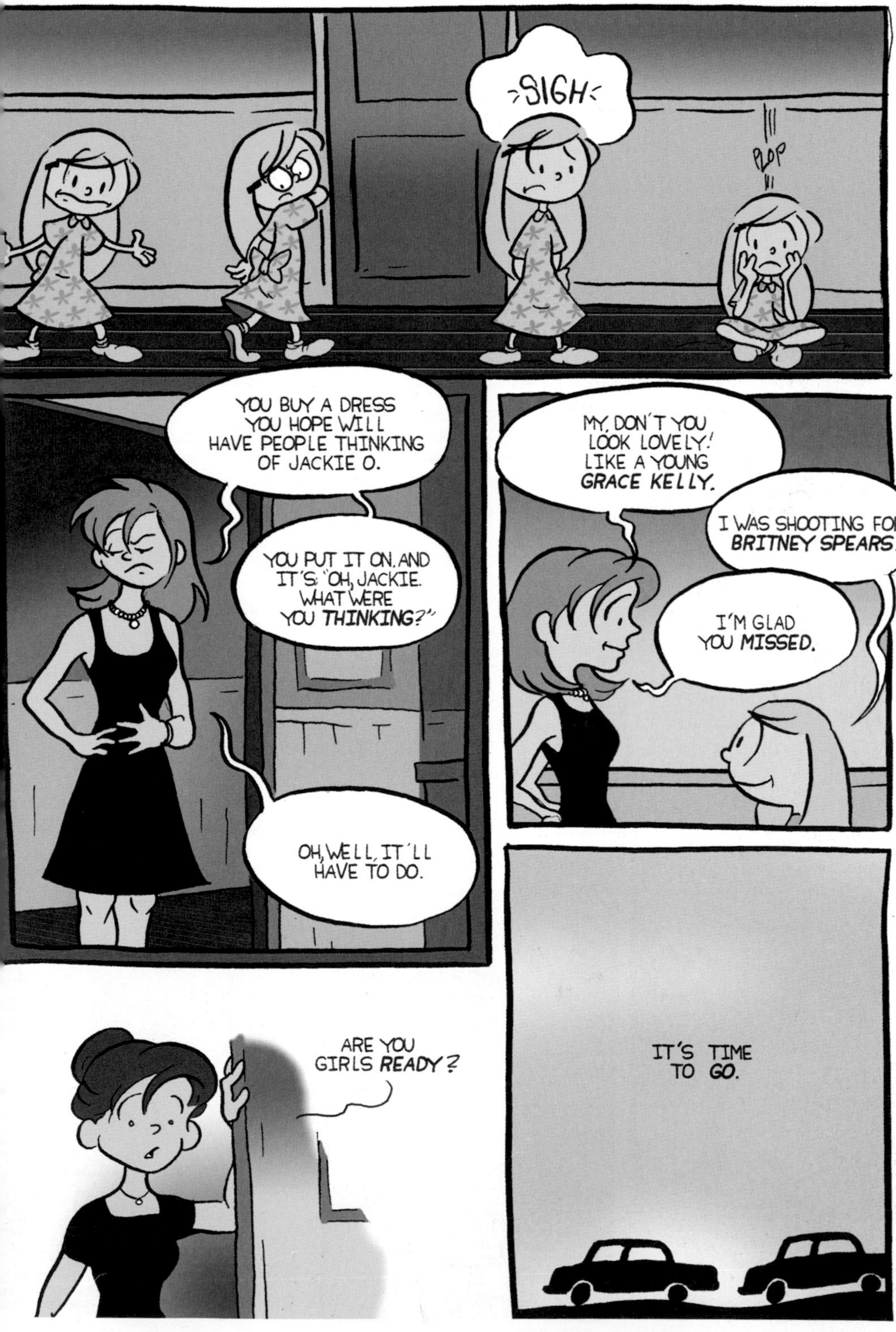

SIGH
PLOP
YOU BUY A DRESS YOU HOPE WILL HAVE PEOPLE THINKING OF JACKIE O.
YOU PUT IT ON. AND IT'S: "OH, JACKIE. WHAT WERE YOU THINKING?"
OH, WELL, IT'LL HAVE TO DO.
MY, DON'T YOU LOOK LOVELY! LIKE A YOUNG GRACE KELLY.
I WAS SHOOTING FOR BRITNEY SPEARS.
I'M GLAD YOU MISSED.
ARE YOU GIRLS READY?
IT'S TIME TO GO.

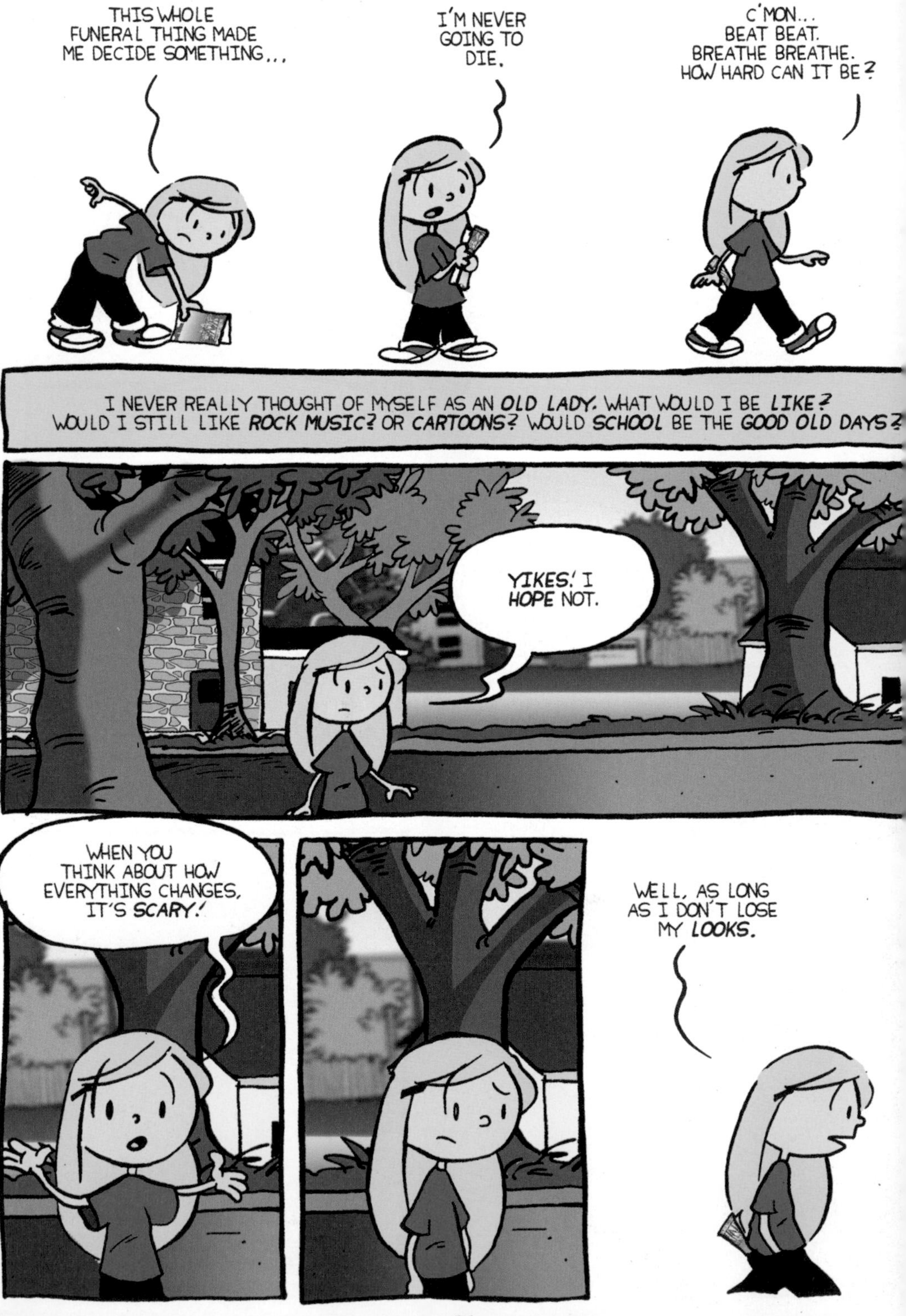
THIS WHOLE FUNERAL THING MADE ME DECIDE SOMETHING...
I'M NEVER GOING TO DIE.
C'MON... BEAT BEAT. BREATHE BREATHE. HOW HARD CAN IT BE?
I NEVER REALLY THOUGHT OF MYSELF AS AN OLD LADY. WHAT WOULD I BE LIKE? WOULD I STILL LIKE ROCK MUSIC? OR CARTOONS? WOULD SCHOOL BE THE GOOD OLD DAYS?
YIKES! I HOPE NOT.
WHEN YOU THINK ABOUT HOW EVERYTHING CHANGES, IT'S SCARY!
WELL, AS LONG AS I DON'T LOSE MY LOOKS.

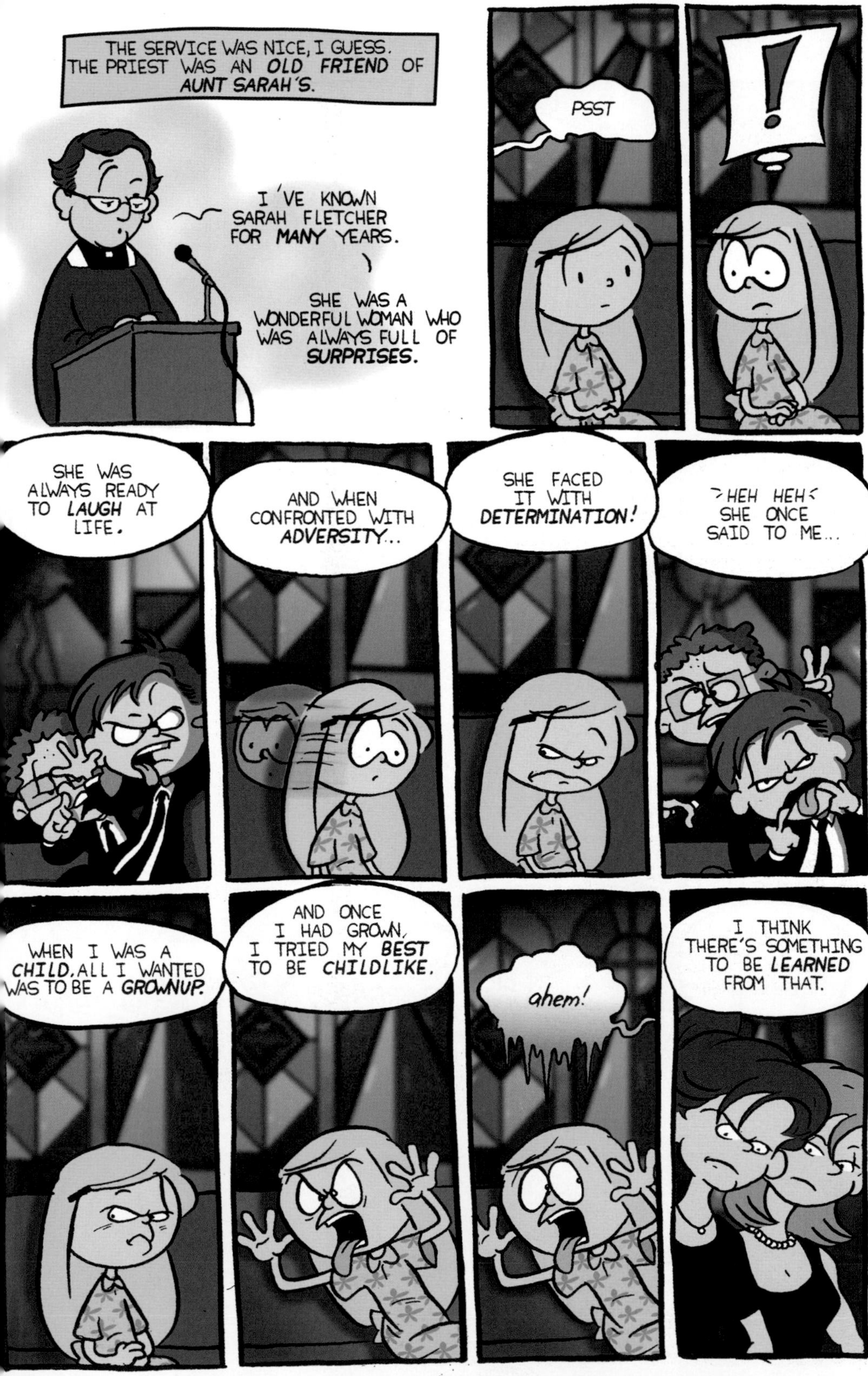
THE SERVICE WAS NICE, I GUESS. THE PRIEST WAS AN OLD FRIEND OF AUNT SARAH'S.
I'VE KNOWN SARAH FLETCHER FOR MANY YEARS.
SHE WAS A WONDERFUL WOMAN WHO WAS ALWAYS FULL OF SURPRISES.
PSST
!
SHE WAS ALWAYS READY TO LAUGH AT LIFE.
AND WHEN CONFRONTED WITH ADVERSITY...
SHE FACED IT WITH DETERMINATION!
HEH HEH SHE ONCE SAID TO ME...
WHEN I WAS A CHILD, ALL I WANTED WAS TO BE A GROWNUP.
AND ONCE I HAD GROWN, I TRIED MY BEST TO BE CHILDLIKE.
ahem!
I THINK THERE'S SOMETHING TO BE LEARNED FROM THAT.

AFTERWARDS, THERE WAS A RECEPTION AT THE HOUSE, BUT ALL *I* WANTED TO DO WAS GET ***CHANGED,*** AND ***GET AWAY.***

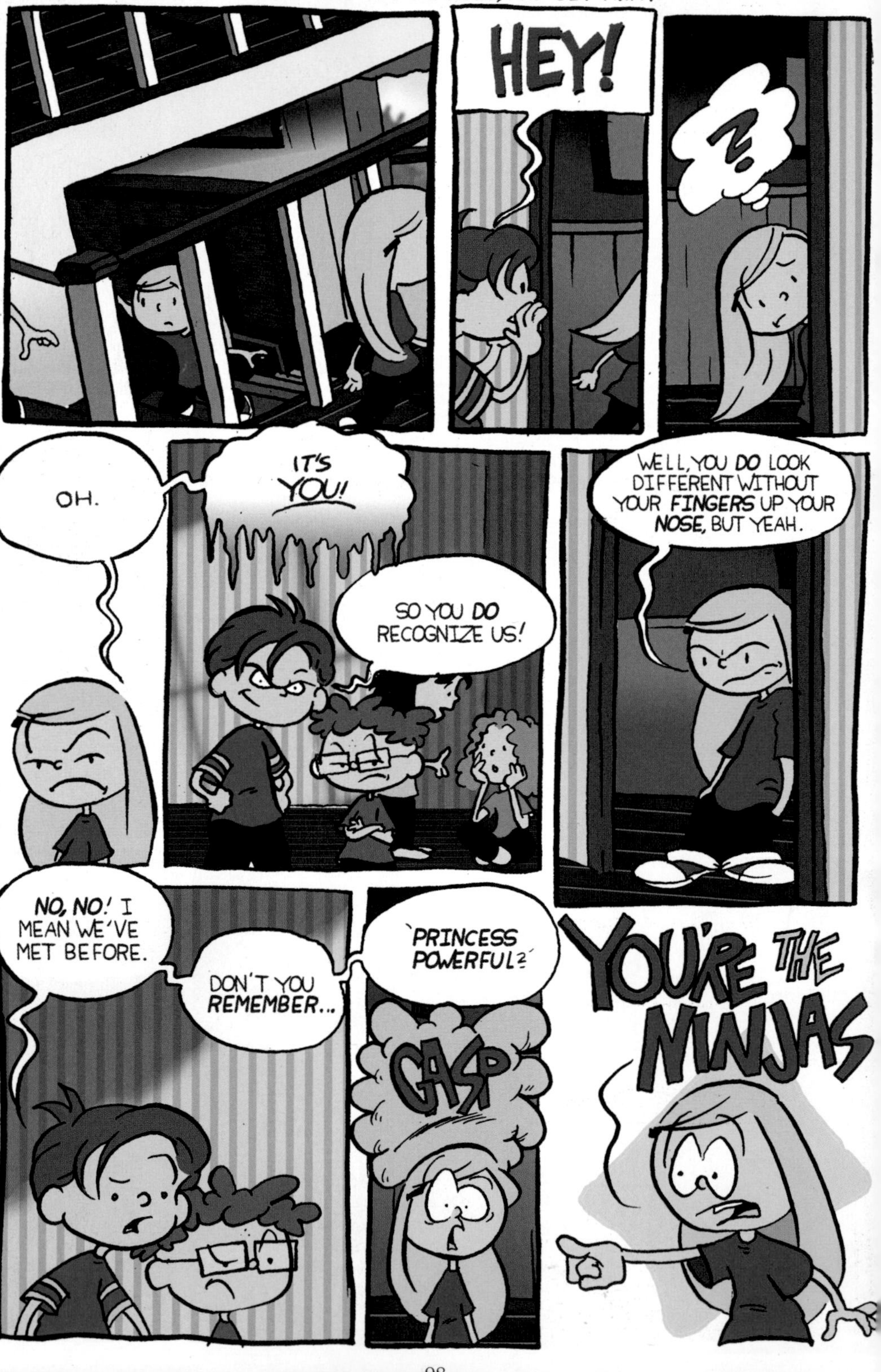
HEY!
?
OH.
IT'S YOU!
SO YOU DO RECOGNIZE US!
WELL, YOU DO LOOK DIFFERENT WITHOUT YOUR FINGERS UP YOUR NOSE, BUT YEAH.
NO, NO! I MEAN WE'VE MET BEFORE.
DON'T YOU REMEMBER...
'PRINCESS POWERFUL?'
GASP
YOU'RE THE NINJAS

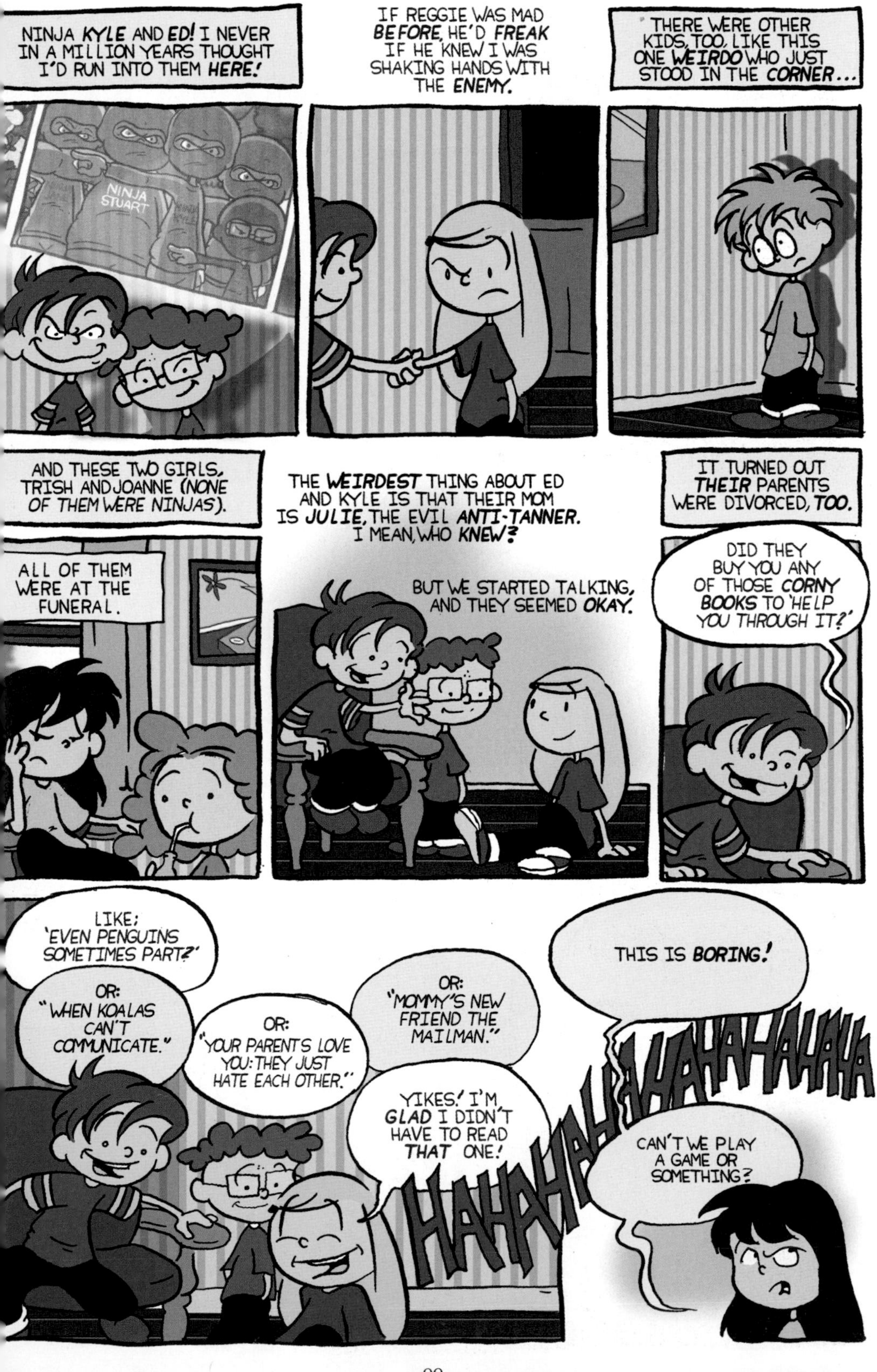

NINJA KYLE AND ED! I NEVER IN A MILLION YEARS THOUGHT I'D RUN INTO THEM HERE!
NINJA STUART
IF REGGIE WAS MAD BEFORE, HE'D FREAK IF HE KNEW I WAS SHAKING HANDS WITH THE ENEMY.
THERE WERE OTHER KIDS, TOO, LIKE THIS ONE WEIRDO WHO JUST STOOD IN THE CORNER...
AND THESE TWO GIRLS, TRISH AND JOANNE (NONE OF THEM WERE NINJAS).
ALL OF THEM WERE AT THE FUNERAL.
THE WEIRDEST THING ABOUT ED AND KYLE IS THAT THEIR MOM IS JULIE, THE EVIL ANTI-TANNER. I MEAN, WHO KNEW?
BUT WE STARTED TALKING, AND THEY SEEMED OKAY.
IT TURNED OUT THEIR PARENTS WERE DIVORCED, TOO.
DID THEY BUY YOU ANY OF THOSE CORNY BOOKS TO 'HELP YOU THROUGH IT?'
LIKE: 'EVEN PENGUINS SOMETIMES PART?'
OR: "WHEN KOALAS CAN'T COMMUNICATE."
OR: "YOUR PARENTS LOVE YOU: THEY JUST HATE EACH OTHER."
OR: "MOMMY'S NEW FRIEND THE MAILMAN."
YIKES! I'M GLAD I DIDN'T HAVE TO READ THAT ONE!
HAHAHAHAHAHAHAHAHAHAHA
THIS IS BORING!
CAN'T WE PLAY A GAME OR SOMETHING?

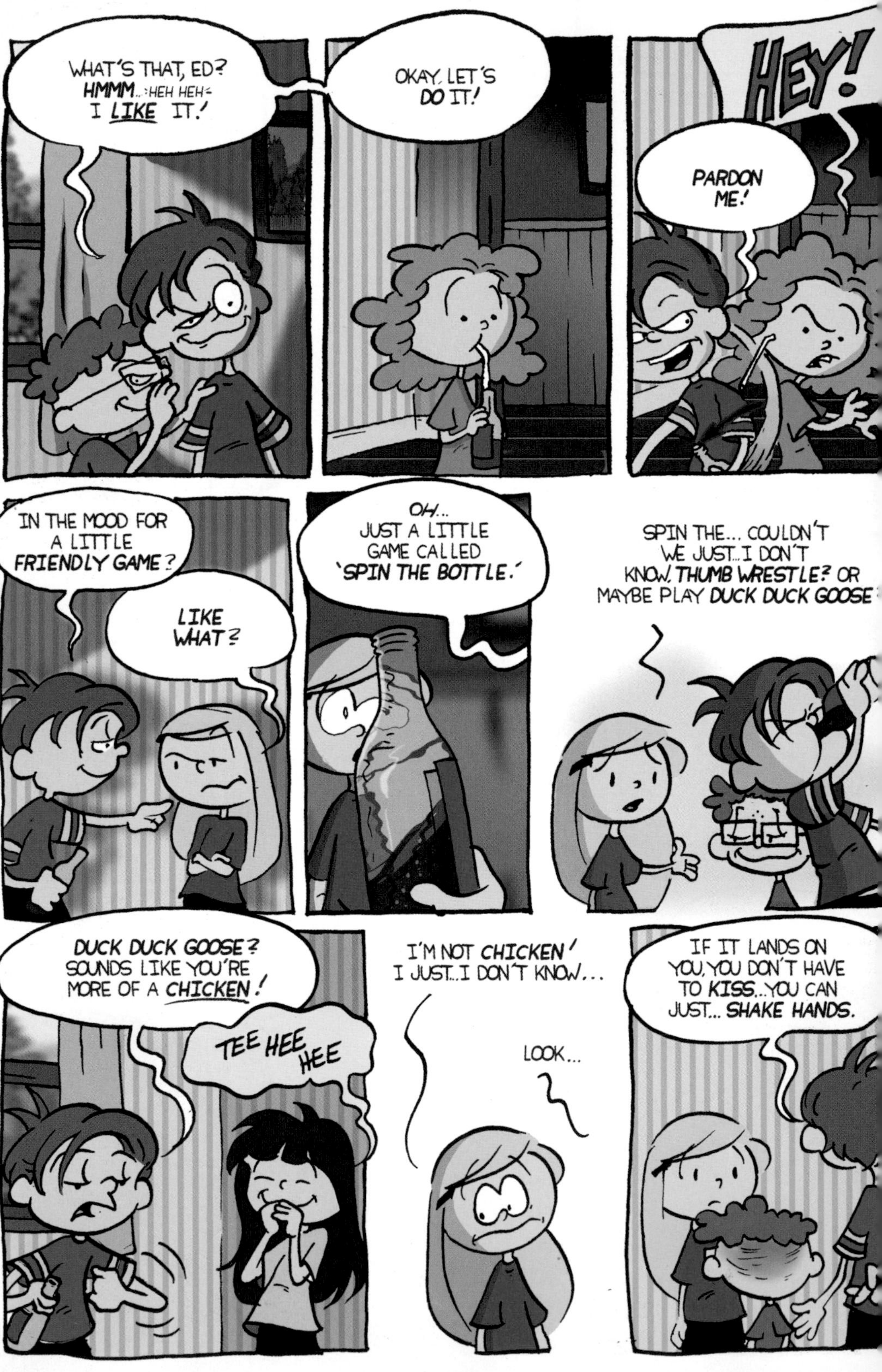

WHAT'S THAT, ED? HMMM... HEH HEH I LIKE IT!
OKAY, LET'S DO IT!
HEY!
PARDON ME!
IN THE MOOD FOR A LITTLE FRIENDLY GAME?
LIKE WHAT?
OH... JUST A LITTLE GAME CALLED 'SPIN THE BOTTLE.'
SPIN THE... COULDN'T WE JUST...I DON'T KNOW, THUMB WRESTLE? OR MAYBE PLAY DUCK DUCK GOOSE
DUCK DUCK GOOSE? SOUNDS LIKE YOU'RE MORE OF A CHICKEN!
TEE HEE HEE
I'M NOT CHICKEN! I JUST...I DON'T KNOW...
LOOK...
IF IT LANDS ON YOU, YOU DON'T HAVE TO KISS...YOU CAN JUST... SHAKE HANDS.

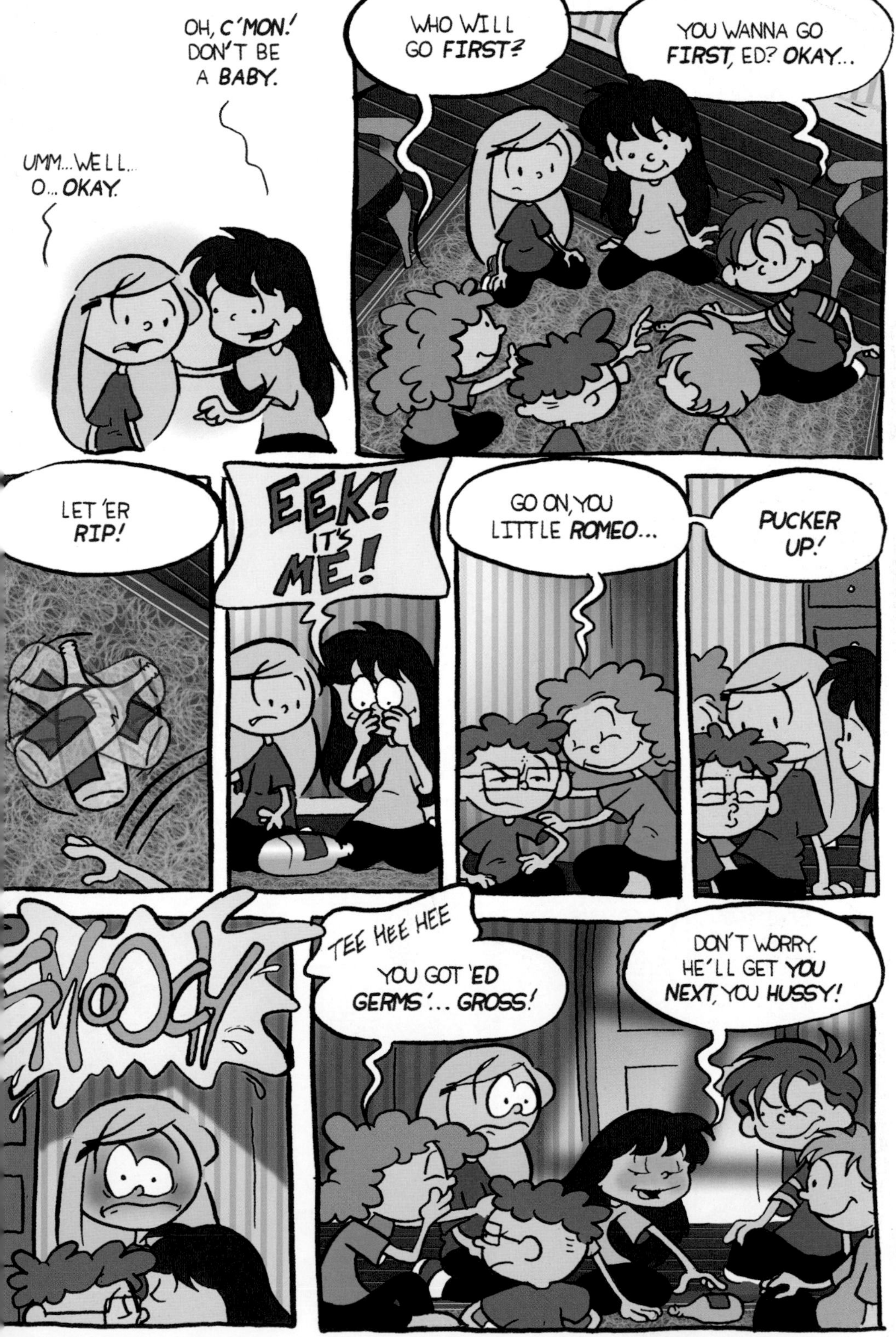
UMM... WELL... O... OKAY.
OH, C'MON! DON'T BE A BABY.
WHO WILL GO FIRST?
YOU WANNA GO FIRST, ED? OKAY...
LET 'ER RIP!
EEK! IT'S ME!
GO ON, YOU LITTLE ROMEO...
PUCKER UP!
SMOOCH
TEE HEE HEE
YOU GOT 'ED GERMS'... GROSS!
DON'T WORRY. HE'LL GET YOU NEXT, YOU HUSSY!

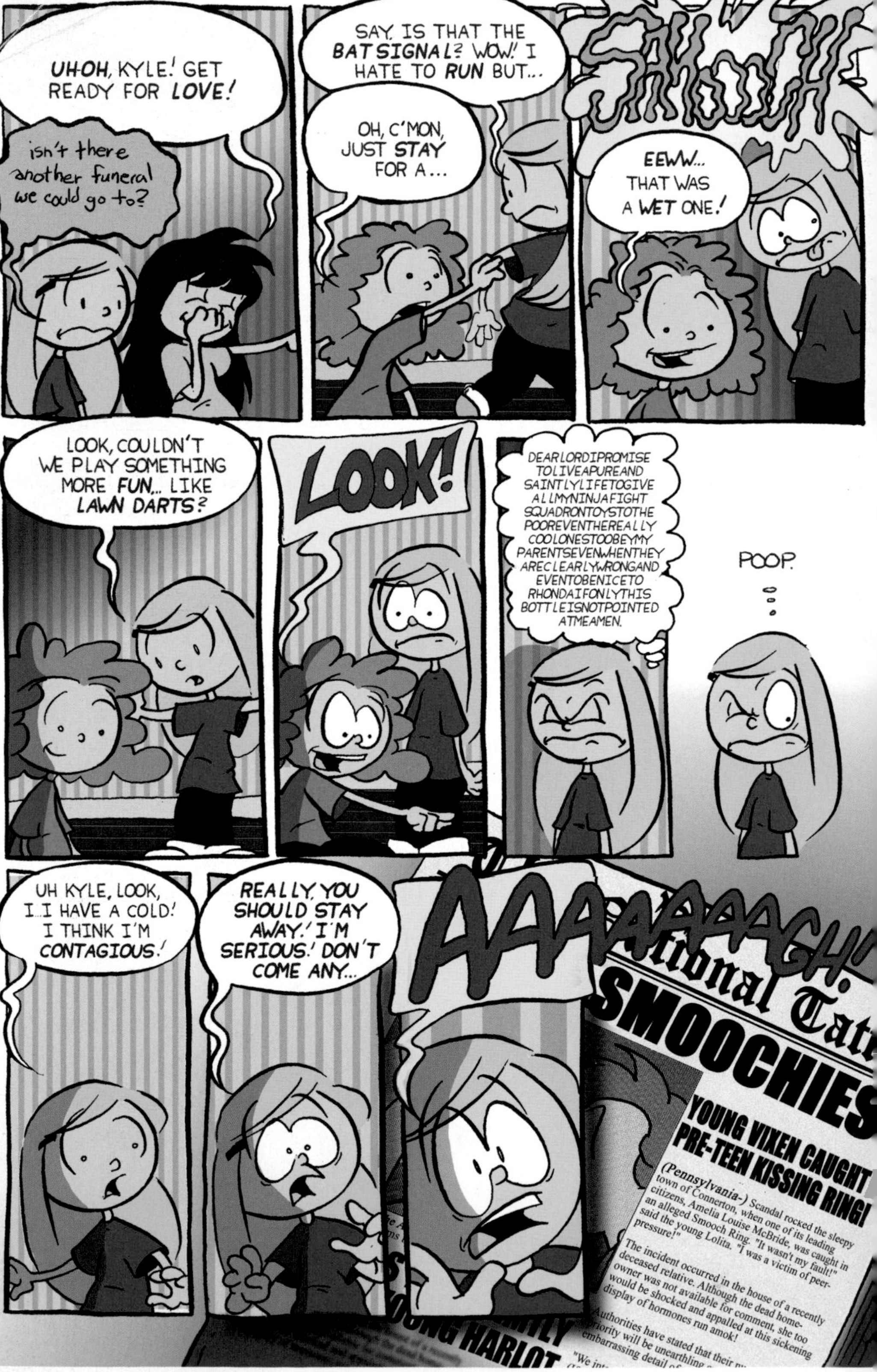

UH-OH, KYLE! GET READY FOR LOVE!
isn't there another funeral we could go to?
SAY, IS THAT THE BAT SIGNAL? WOW! I HATE TO RUN BUT...
OH, C'MON, JUST STAY FOR A...
SMOOCH!
EEWW... THAT WAS A WET ONE!
LOOK, COULDN'T WE PLAY SOMETHING MORE FUN... LIKE LAWN DARTS?
LOOK!
DEARLORDIPROMISE TOLIVEAPUREAND SAINTLYLIFETOGIVE ALLMYNINJAFIGHT SQUADRONTOYSTOTHE POOREVENTHEREALLY COOLONESTOOBEYMY PARENTSEVENWHENTHEY ARECLEARLYWRONGAND EVENTOBENICETO RHONDAIFONLYTHIS BOTTLEISNOTPOINTED ATMEAMEN.
POOP.
UH KYLE, LOOK, I...I HAVE A COLD! I THINK I'M CONTAGIOUS!
REALLY, YOU SHOULD STAY AWAY! I'M SERIOUS! DON'T COME ANY...
AAAAAAAAAGH!
SMOOCHIES
YOUNG VIXEN CAUGHT IN PRE-TEEN KISSING RING!
(Pennsylvania-) Scandal rocked the sleepy town of Connerton, when one of its leading citizens, Amelia Louise McBride, was caught in an alleged Smooch Ring. "It wasn't my fault!" said the young Lolita. "I was a victim of peer-pressure!"
The incident occurred in the house of a recently deceased relative. Although the dead home-owner was not available for comment, she too would be shocked and appalled at this sickening display of hormones run amok!
Authorities have stated that their priority will be unearthling embarrassing detail of
HARLOT

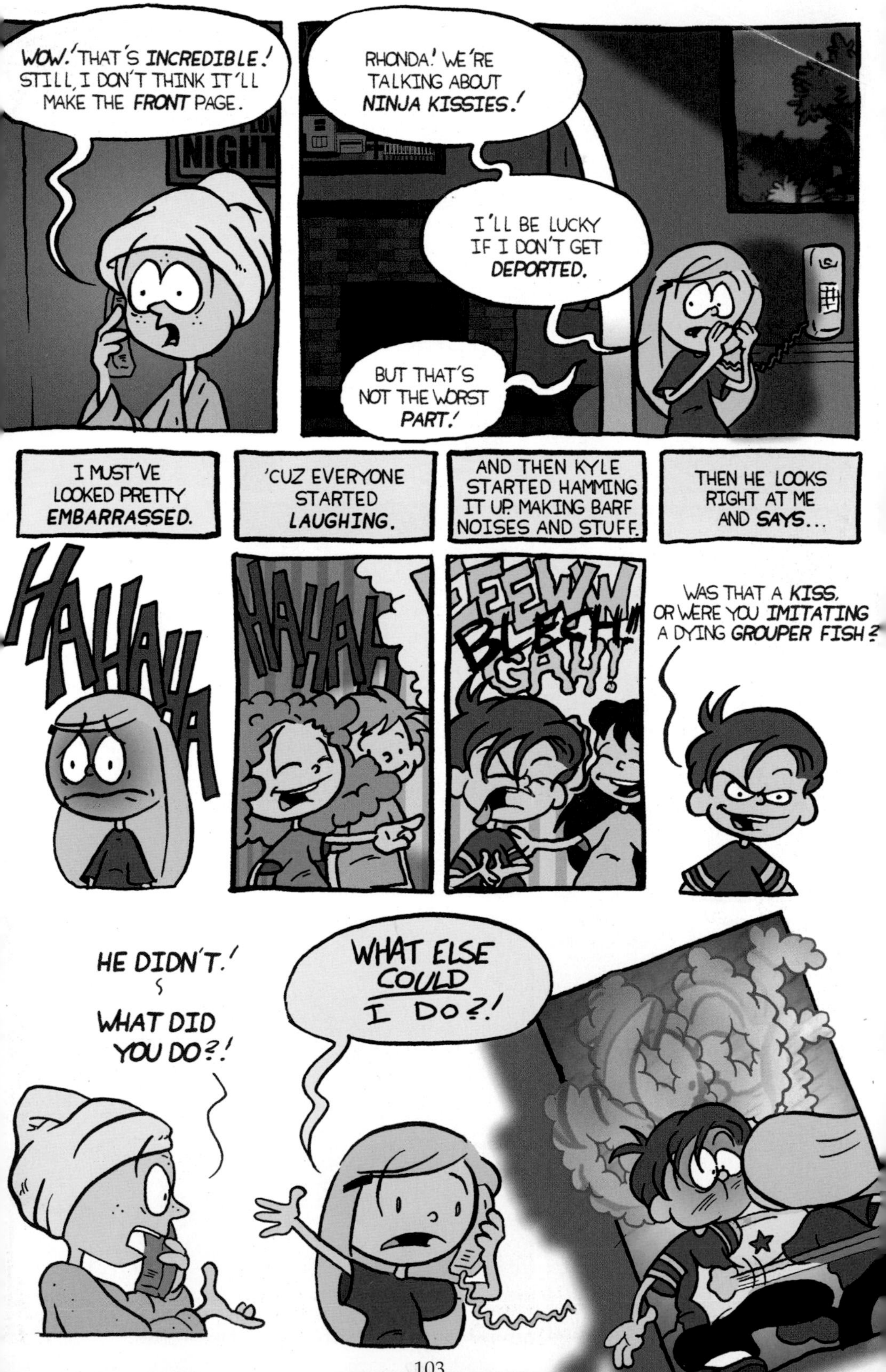
WOW.! THAT'S INCREDIBLE.! STILL, I DON'T THINK IT'LL MAKE THE FRONT PAGE.
RHONDA! WE'RE TALKING ABOUT NINJA KISSIES.!
I'LL BE LUCKY IF I DON'T GET DEPORTED.
BUT THAT'S NOT THE WORST PART.!
I MUST'VE LOOKED PRETTY EMBARRASSED.
'CUZ EVERYONE STARTED LAUGHING.
AND THEN KYLE STARTED HAMMING IT UP. MAKING BARF NOISES AND STUFF.
THEN HE LOOKS RIGHT AT ME AND SAYS...
HAHAHAHA
HAHAHA
EEEWW
BLEGH!!
GAH!
WAS THAT A KISS, OR WERE YOU IMITATING A DYING GROUPER FISH?
HE DIDN'T.!
WHAT DID YOU DO?!
WHAT ELSE COULD I DO?!

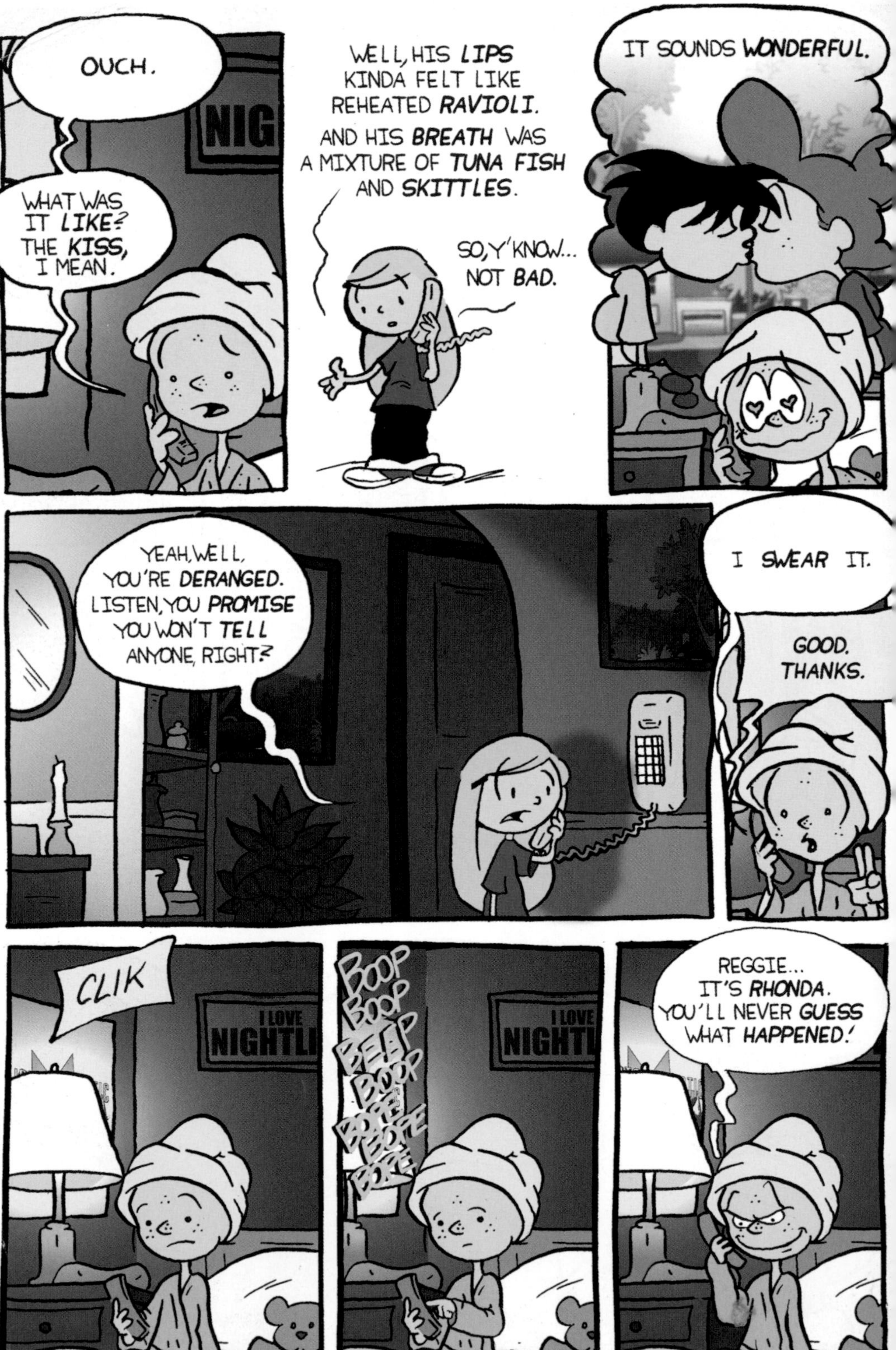
OUCH.
WHAT WAS IT LIKE? THE KISS, I MEAN.
WELL, HIS LIPS KINDA FELT LIKE REHEATED RAVIOLI. AND HIS BREATH WAS A MIXTURE OF TUNA FISH AND SKITTLES.
SO, Y'KNOW... NOT BAD.
IT SOUNDS WONDERFUL.
YEAH, WELL, YOU'RE DERANGED. LISTEN, YOU PROMISE YOU WON'T TELL ANYONE, RIGHT?
I SWEAR IT.
GOOD. THANKS.
CLIK
I LOVE NIGHTL
BOOP BOOP BEEP BOOP
REGGIE... IT'S RHONDA. YOU'LL NEVER GUESS WHAT HAPPENED!

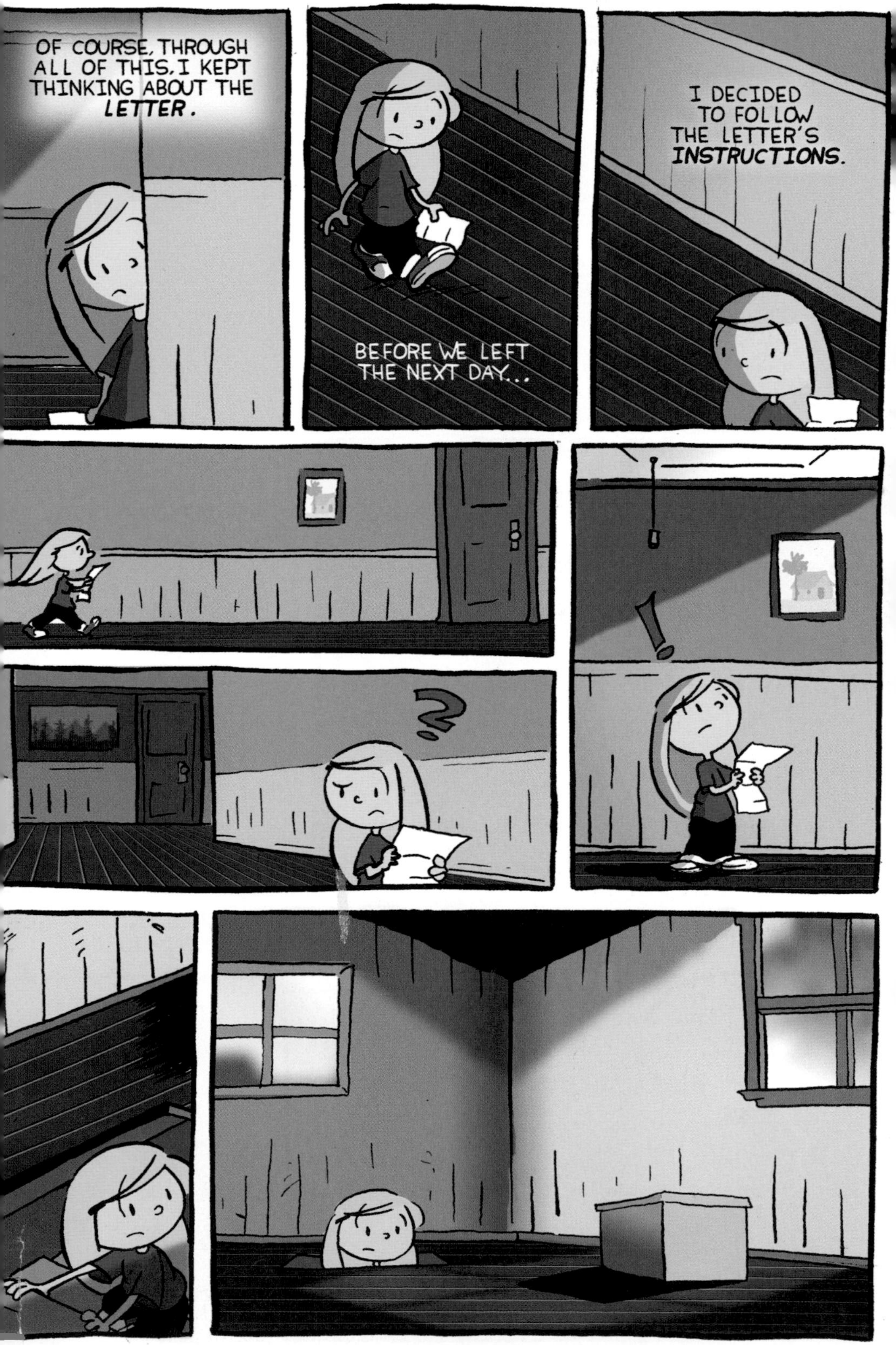
OF COURSE, THROUGH ALL OF THIS, I KEPT THINKING ABOUT THE LETTER.
BEFORE WE LEFT THE NEXT DAY...
I DECIDED TO FOLLOW THE LETTER'S INSTRUCTIONS.

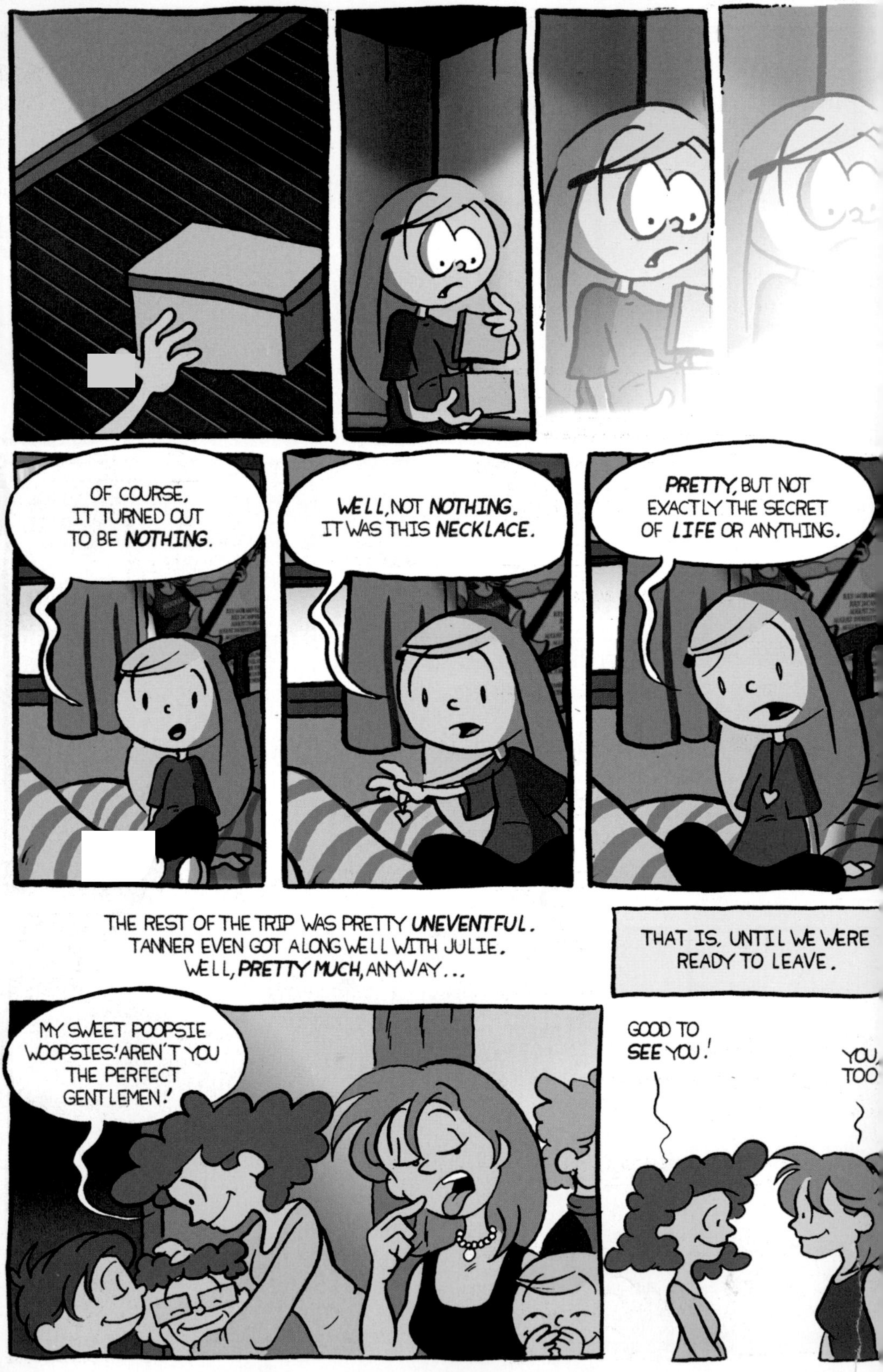
OF COURSE, IT TURNED OUT TO BE NOTHING.
WELL, NOT NOTHING. IT WAS THIS NECKLACE.
PRETTY, BUT NOT EXACTLY THE SECRET OF LIFE OR ANYTHING.
THE REST OF THE TRIP WAS PRETTY UNEVENTFUL. TANNER EVEN GOT ALONG WELL WITH JULIE. WELL, PRETTY MUCH, ANYWAY...
THAT IS, UNTIL WE WERE READY TO LEAVE.
MY SWEET POOPSIE WOOPSIES! AREN'T YOU THE PERFECT GENTLEMEN!
GOOD TO SEE YOU!
YOU, TOO

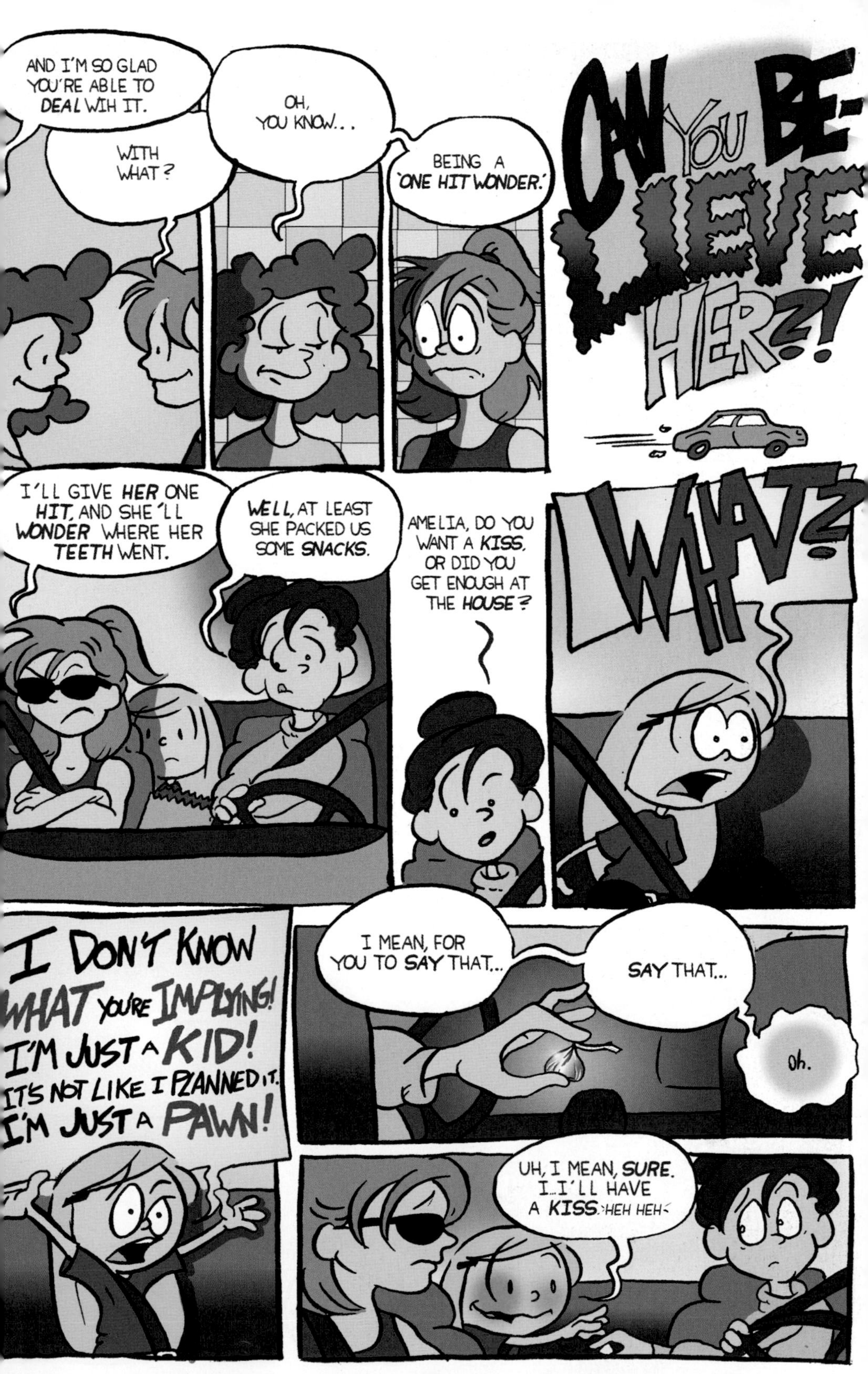
AND I'M SO GLAD YOU'RE ABLE TO DEAL WIH IT.
WITH WHAT?
OH, YOU KNOW...
BEING A 'ONE HIT WONDER.'
CAN YOU BE-LIEVE HER?!
I'LL GIVE HER ONE HIT, AND SHE'LL WONDER WHERE HER TEETH WENT.
WELL, AT LEAST SHE PACKED US SOME SNACKS.
AMELIA, DO YOU WANT A KISS, OR DID YOU GET ENOUGH AT THE HOUSE?
WHAT?
I DON'T KNOW WHAT YOU'RE IMPLYING! I'M JUST A KID! IT'S NOT LIKE I PLANNED IT. I'M JUST A PAWN!
I MEAN, FOR YOU TO SAY THAT...
SAY THAT...
Oh.
UH, I MEAN, SURE. I...I'LL HAVE A KISS. HEH HEH

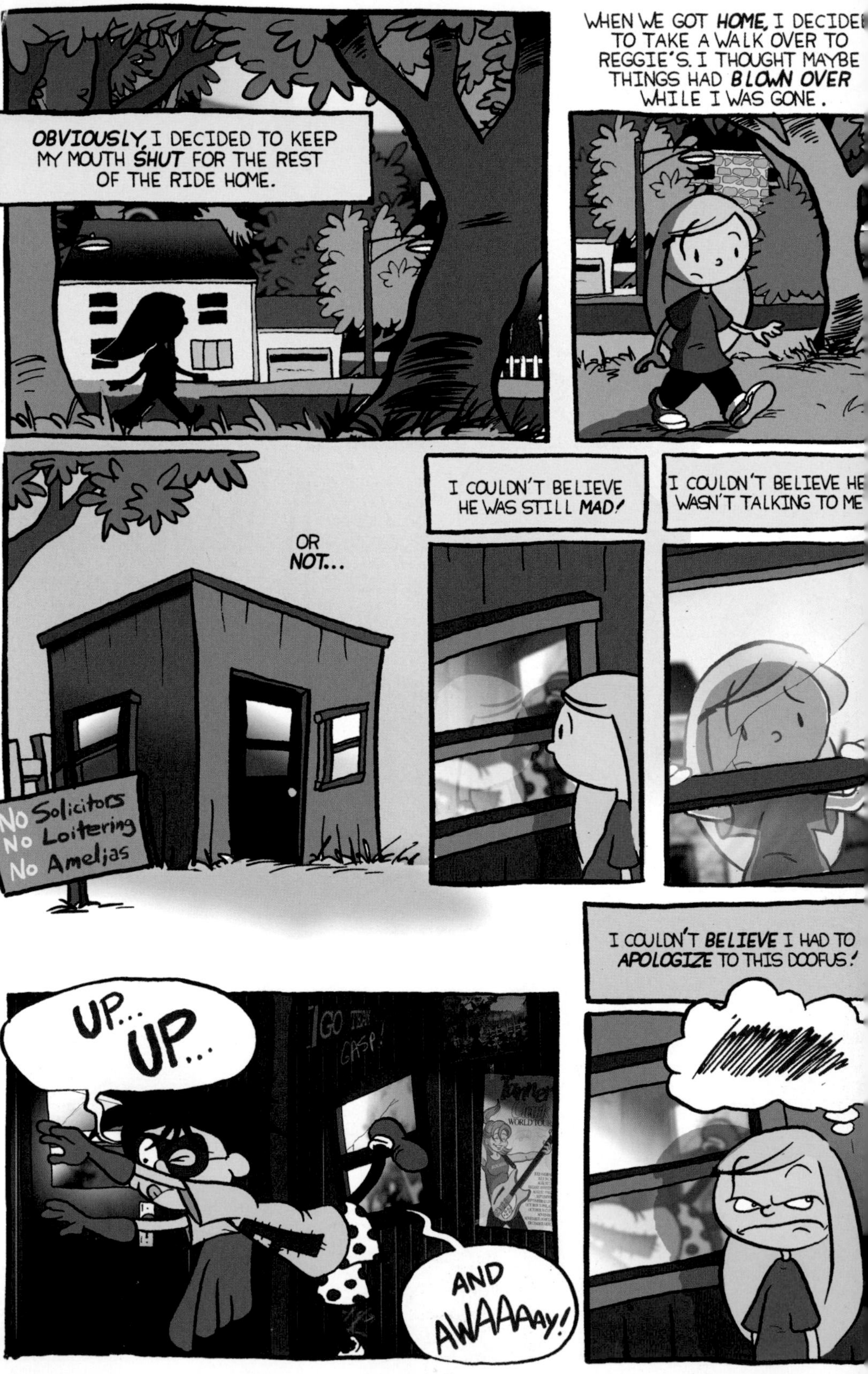

OBVIOUSLY, I DECIDED TO KEEP MY MOUTH SHUT FOR THE REST OF THE RIDE HOME.
WHEN WE GOT HOME, I DECIDED TO TAKE A WALK OVER TO REGGIE'S. I THOUGHT MAYBE THINGS HAD BLOWN OVER WHILE I WAS GONE.
OR NOT...
No Solicitors
No Loitering
No Amelias
I COULDN'T BELIEVE HE WAS STILL MAD!
I COULDN'T BELIEVE HE WASN'T TALKING TO ME
I COULDN'T BELIEVE I HAD TO APOLOGIZE TO THIS DOOFUS!
UP... UP...
AND AWAAAAAY!

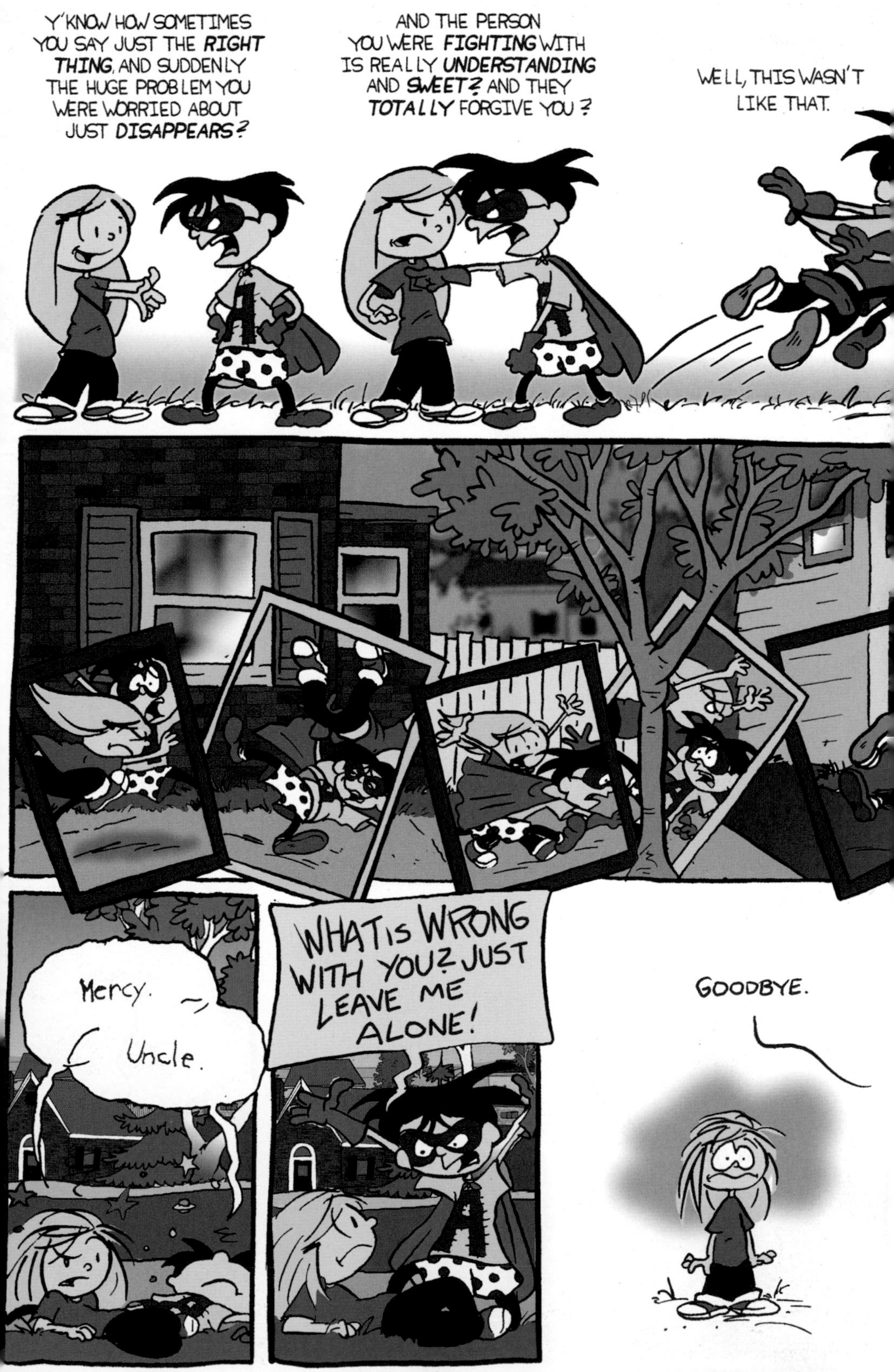
Y'KNOW HOW SOMETIMES YOU SAY JUST THE **RIGHT THING**, AND SUDDENLY THE HUGE PROBLEM YOU WERE WORRIED ABOUT JUST **DISAPPEARS**?
AND THE PERSON YOU WERE **FIGHTING** WITH IS REALLY **UNDERSTANDING** AND **SWEET**? AND THEY **TOTALLY** FORGIVE YOU?
WELL, THIS WASN'T LIKE THAT.
Mercy.
Uncle.
WHAT IS WRONG WITH YOU? JUST LEAVE ME ALONE!
GOODBYE.

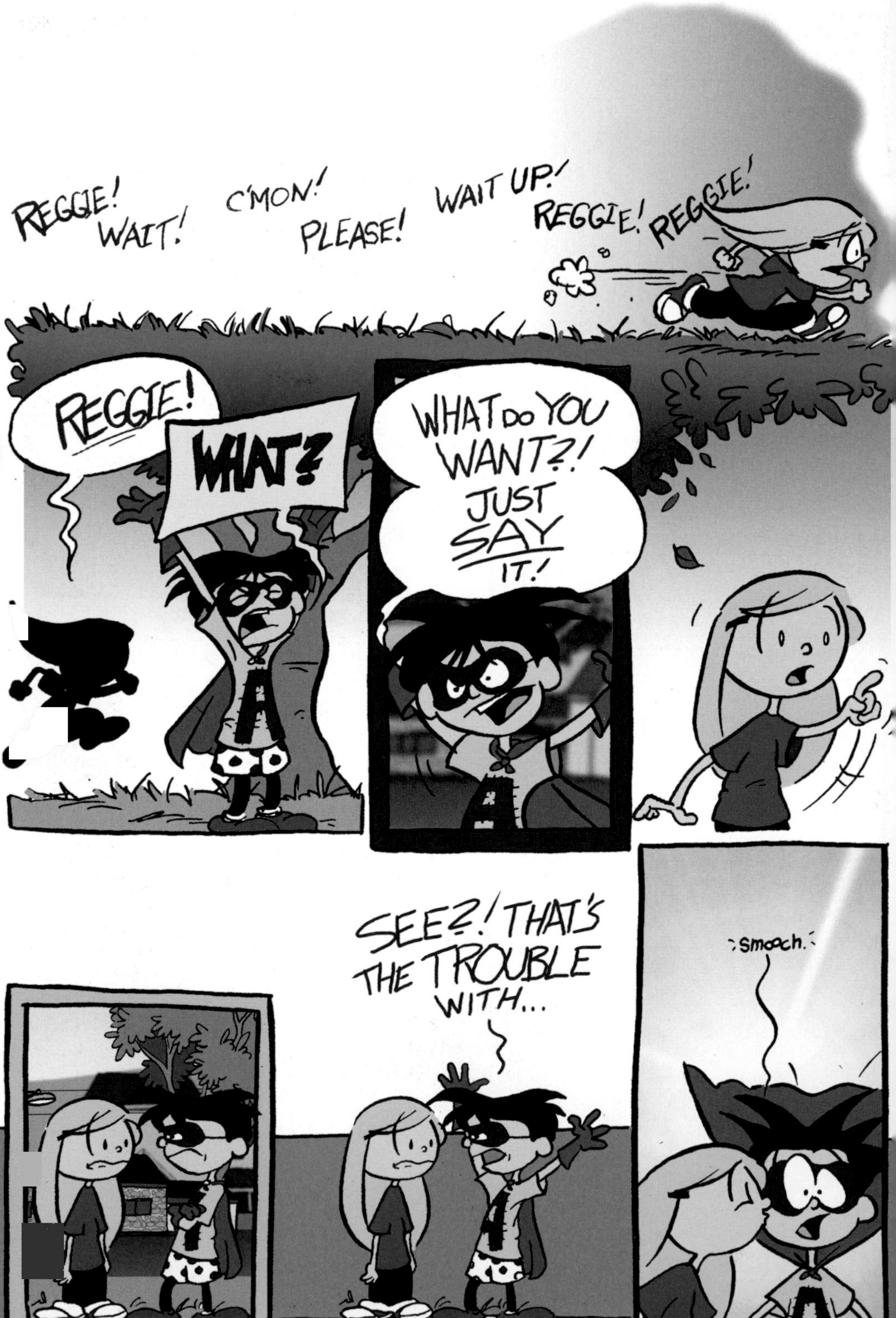
REGGIE!
WAIT!
C'MON!
PLEASE!
WAIT UP!
REGGIE!
REGGIE!
REGGIE!
WHAT?
WHAT DO YOU WANT?! JUST SAY IT!
SEE?! THAT'S THE TROUBLE WITH...
smooch.

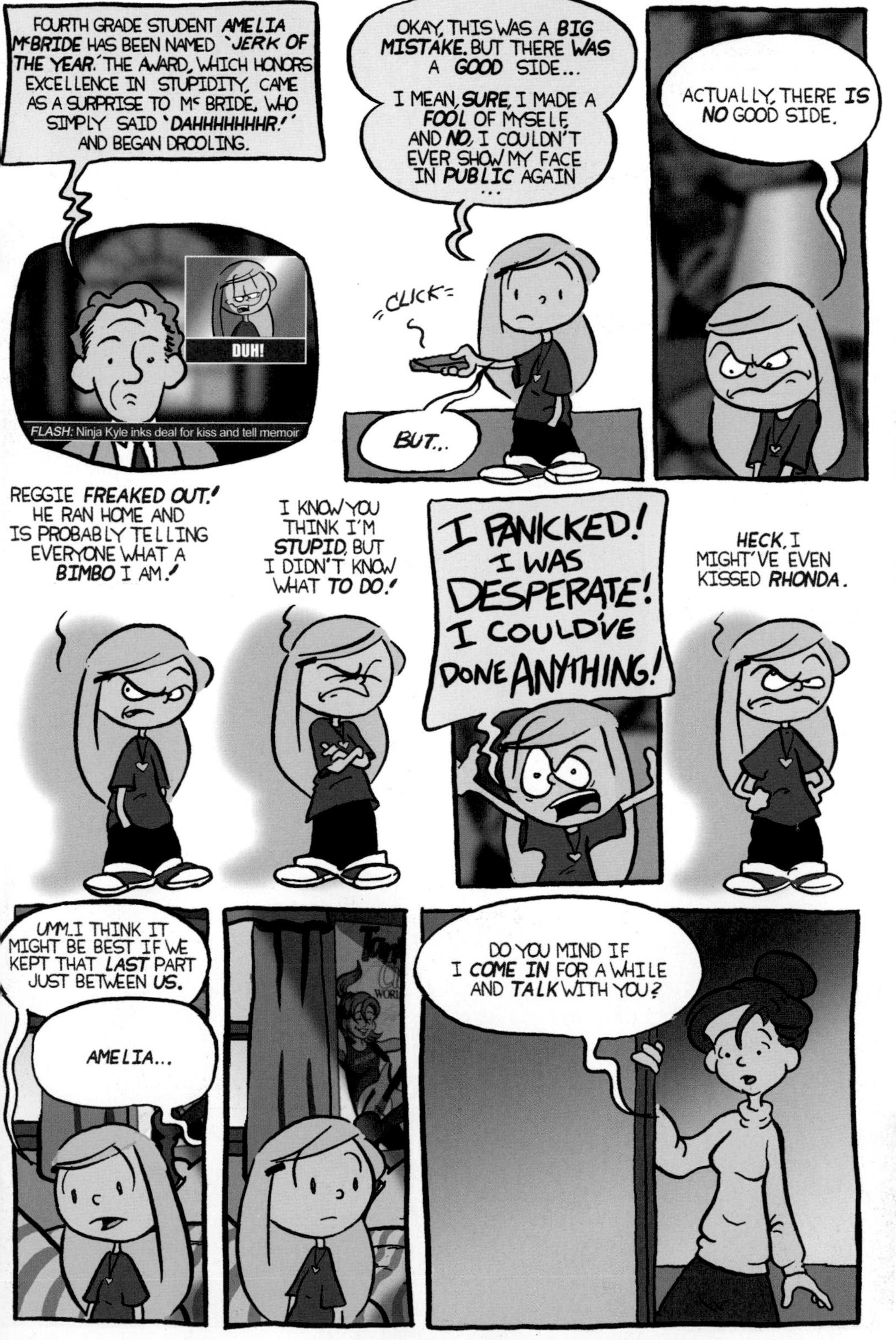
FOURTH GRADE STUDENT AMELIA McBRIDE HAS BEEN NAMED 'JERK OF THE YEAR.' THE AWARD, WHICH HONORS EXCELLENCE IN STUPIDITY, CAME AS A SURPRISE TO Mc BRIDE, WHO SIMPLY SAID 'DAHHHHHHHR!' AND BEGAN DROOLING.
DUH!
FLASH: Ninja Kyle inks deal for kiss and tell memoir
OKAY, THIS WAS A BIG MISTAKE. BUT THERE WAS A GOOD SIDE...
I MEAN, SURE, I MADE A FOOL OF MYSELF, AND NO, I COULDN'T EVER SHOW MY FACE IN PUBLIC AGAIN ...
CLICK
BUT...
ACTUALLY, THERE IS NO GOOD SIDE.
REGGIE FREAKED OUT! HE RAN HOME AND IS PROBABLY TELLING EVERYONE WHAT A BIMBO I AM!
I KNOW YOU THINK I'M STUPID, BUT I DIDN'T KNOW WHAT TO DO!
I PANICKED! I WAS DESPERATE! I COULD'VE DONE ANYTHING!
HECK, I MIGHT'VE EVEN KISSED RHONDA.
UMM..I THINK IT MIGHT BE BEST IF WE KEPT THAT LAST PART JUST BETWEEN US.
AMELIA...
DO YOU MIND IF I COME IN FOR A WHILE AND TALK WITH YOU?

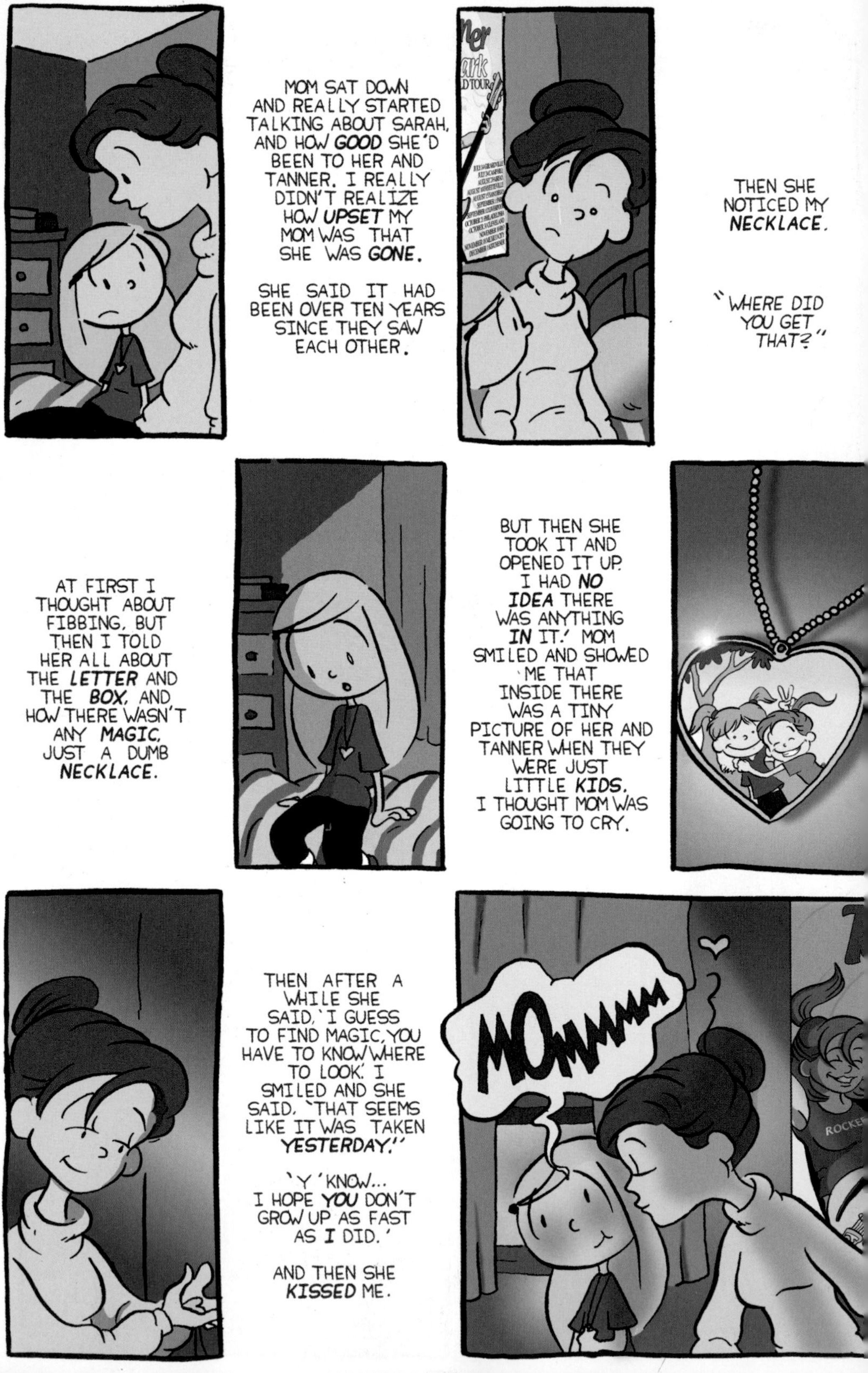
MOM SAT DOWN AND REALLY STARTED TALKING ABOUT SARAH, AND HOW GOOD SHE'D BEEN TO HER AND TANNER. I REALLY DIDN'T REALIZE HOW UPSET MY MOM WAS THAT SHE WAS GONE.
SHE SAID IT HAD BEEN OVER TEN YEARS SINCE THEY SAW EACH OTHER.
THEN SHE NOTICED MY NECKLACE.
"WHERE DID YOU GET THAT?"
AT FIRST I THOUGHT ABOUT FIBBING, BUT THEN I TOLD HER ALL ABOUT THE LETTER AND THE BOX, AND HOW THERE WASN'T ANY MAGIC, JUST A DUMB NECKLACE.
BUT THEN SHE TOOK IT AND OPENED IT UP. I HAD NO IDEA THERE WAS ANYTHING IN IT.' MOM SMILED AND SHOWED ME THAT INSIDE THERE WAS A TINY PICTURE OF HER AND TANNER WHEN THEY WERE JUST LITTLE KIDS. I THOUGHT MOM WAS GOING TO CRY.
THEN AFTER A WHILE SHE SAID, 'I GUESS TO FIND MAGIC, YOU HAVE TO KNOW WHERE TO LOOK.' I SMILED AND SHE SAID, 'THAT SEEMS LIKE IT WAS TAKEN YESTERDAY!'
'Y'KNOW... I HOPE YOU DON'T GROW UP AS FAST AS I DID.'
AND THEN SHE KISSED ME.
MOMMMM
ROCKER

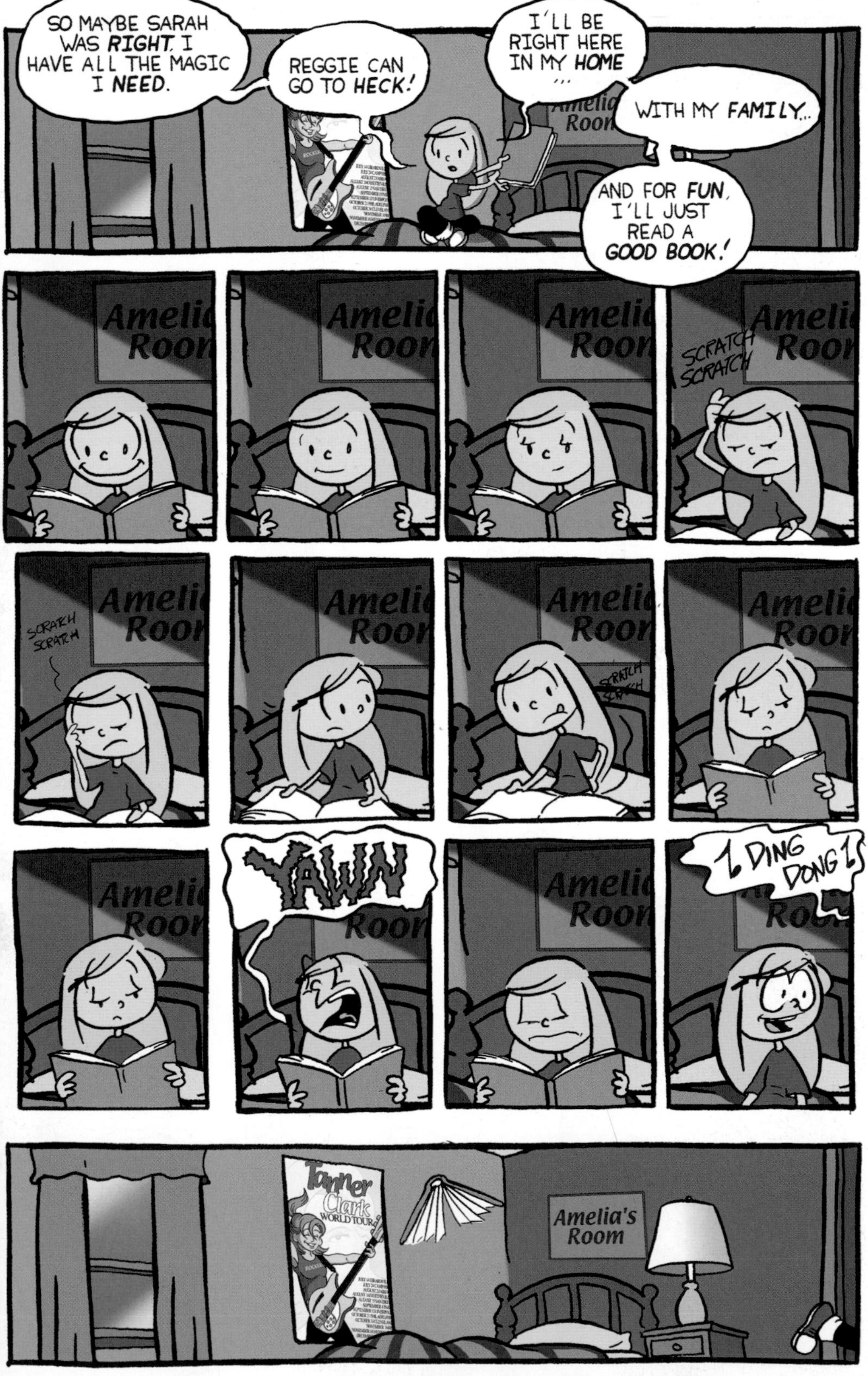
SO MAYBE SARAH WAS RIGHT. I HAVE ALL THE MAGIC I NEED.
REGGIE CAN GO TO HECK!
I'LL BE RIGHT HERE IN MY HOME...
WITH MY FAMILY...
AND FOR FUN, I'LL JUST READ A GOOD BOOK!
Amelia's Room
SCRATCH SCRATCH
SCRATCH SCRATCH
SCRATCH SCRATCH
YAWN
DING DONG
Tanner Clark WORLD TOUR
Amelia's Room

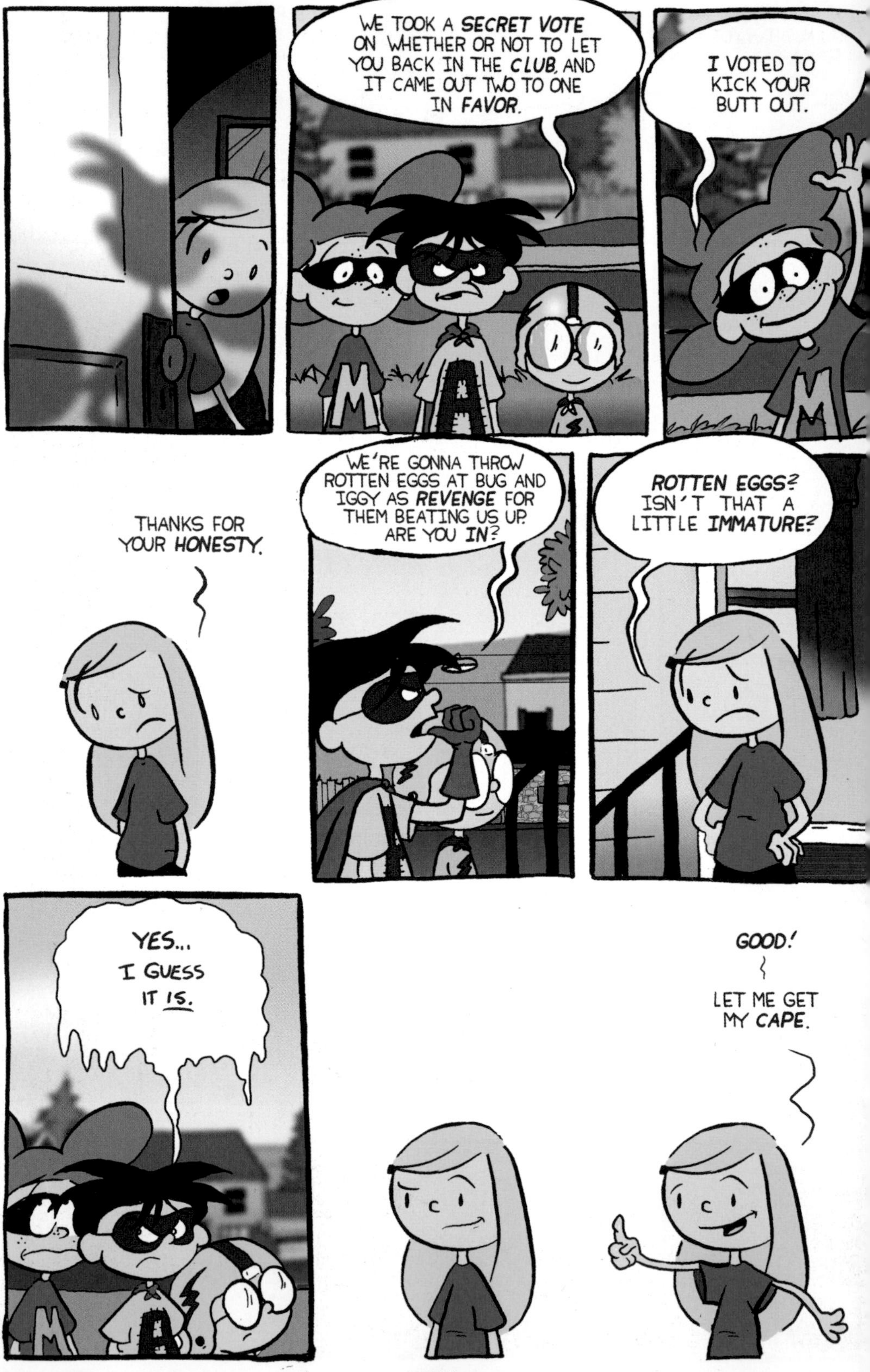
WE TOOK A SECRET VOTE ON WHETHER OR NOT TO LET YOU BACK IN THE CLUB, AND IT CAME OUT TWO TO ONE IN FAVOR.
I VOTED TO KICK YOUR BUTT OUT.
THANKS FOR YOUR HONESTY.
WE'RE GONNA THROW ROTTEN EGGS AT BUG AND IGGY AS REVENGE FOR THEM BEATING US UP. ARE YOU IN?
ROTTEN EGGS? ISN'T THAT A LITTLE IMMATURE?
YES... I GUESS IT IS.
GOOD!
LET ME GET MY CAPE.

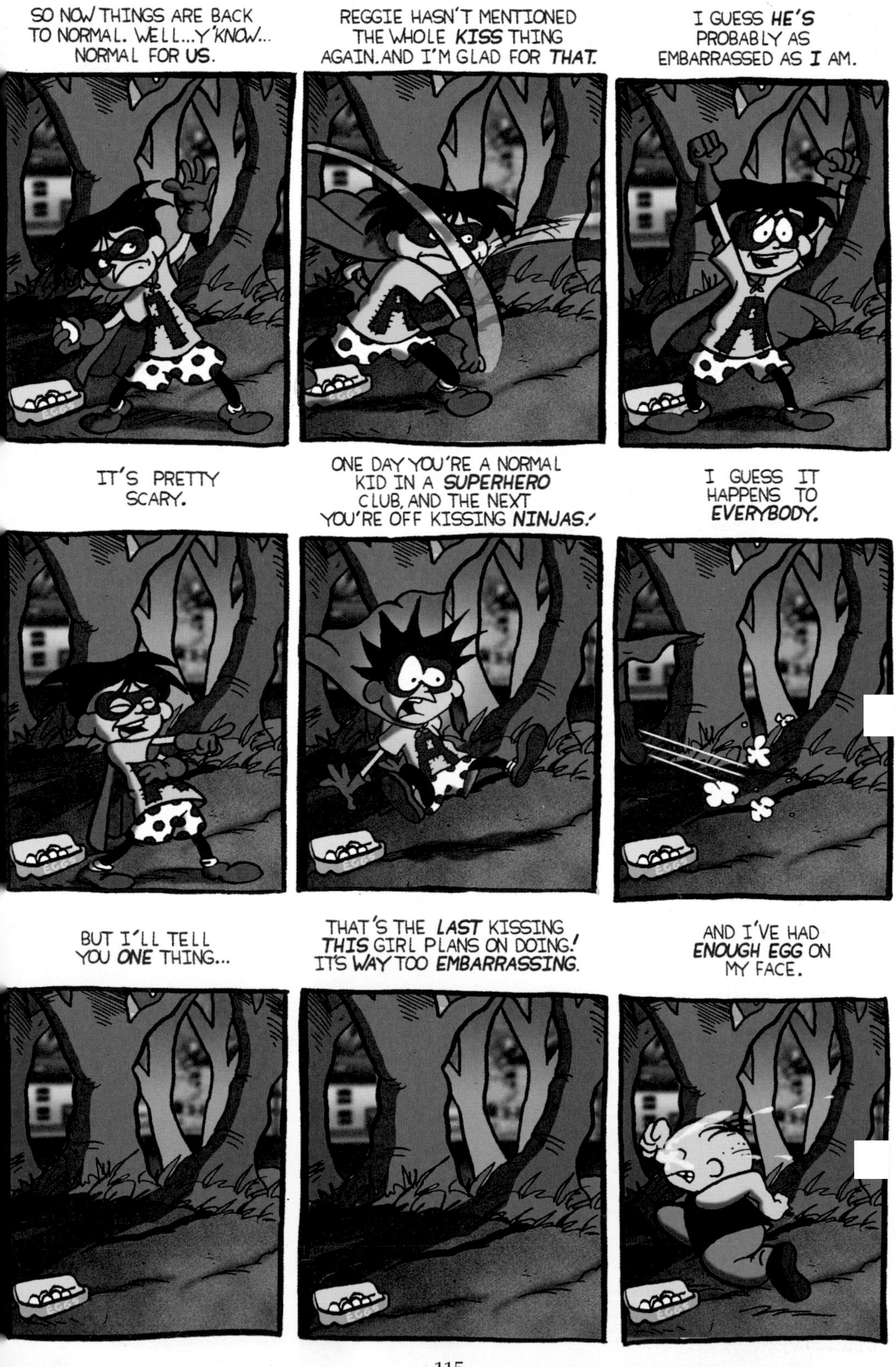
SO NOW THINGS ARE BACK TO NORMAL. WELL...Y'KNOW... NORMAL FOR US.
REGGIE HASN'T MENTIONED THE WHOLE KISS THING AGAIN. AND I'M GLAD FOR THAT.
I GUESS HE'S PROBABLY AS EMBARRASSED AS I AM.
IT'S PRETTY SCARY.
ONE DAY YOU'RE A NORMAL KID IN A SUPERHERO CLUB, AND THE NEXT YOU'RE OFF KISSING NINJAS!
I GUESS IT HAPPENS TO EVERYBODY.
BUT I'LL TELL YOU ONE THING...
THAT'S THE LAST KISSING THIS GIRL PLANS ON DOING! IT'S WAY TOO EMBARRASSING.
AND I'VE HAD ENOUGH EGG ON MY FACE.

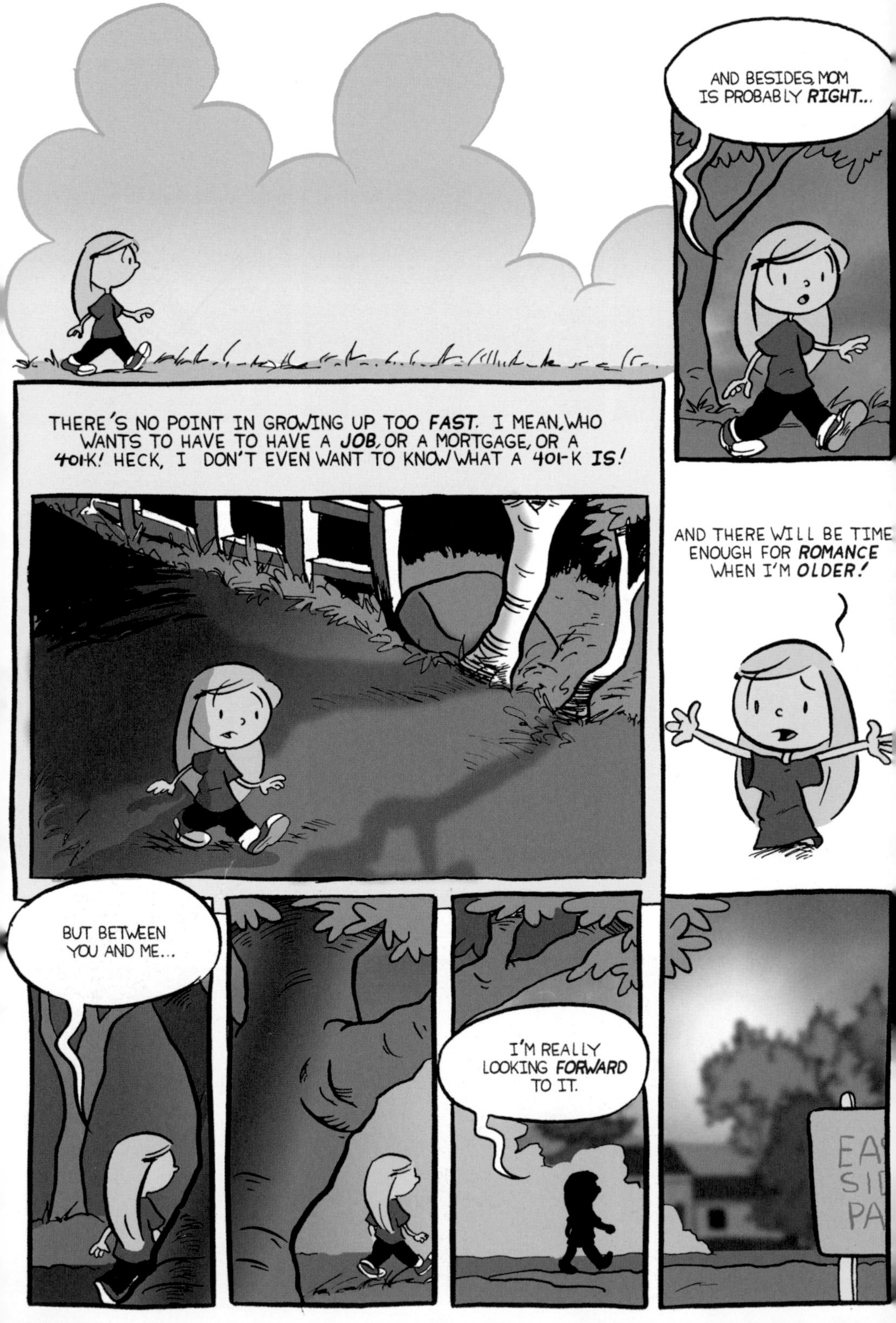
AND BESIDES, MOM IS PROBABLY RIGHT...
THERE'S NO POINT IN GROWING UP TOO FAST. I MEAN, WHO WANTS TO HAVE TO HAVE A JOB, OR A MORTGAGE, OR A 401-K! HECK, I DON'T EVEN WANT TO KNOW WHAT A 401-K IS!
AND THERE WILL BE TIME ENOUGH FOR ROMANCE WHEN I'M OLDER!
BUT BETWEEN YOU AND ME...
I'M REALLY LOOKING FORWARD TO IT.

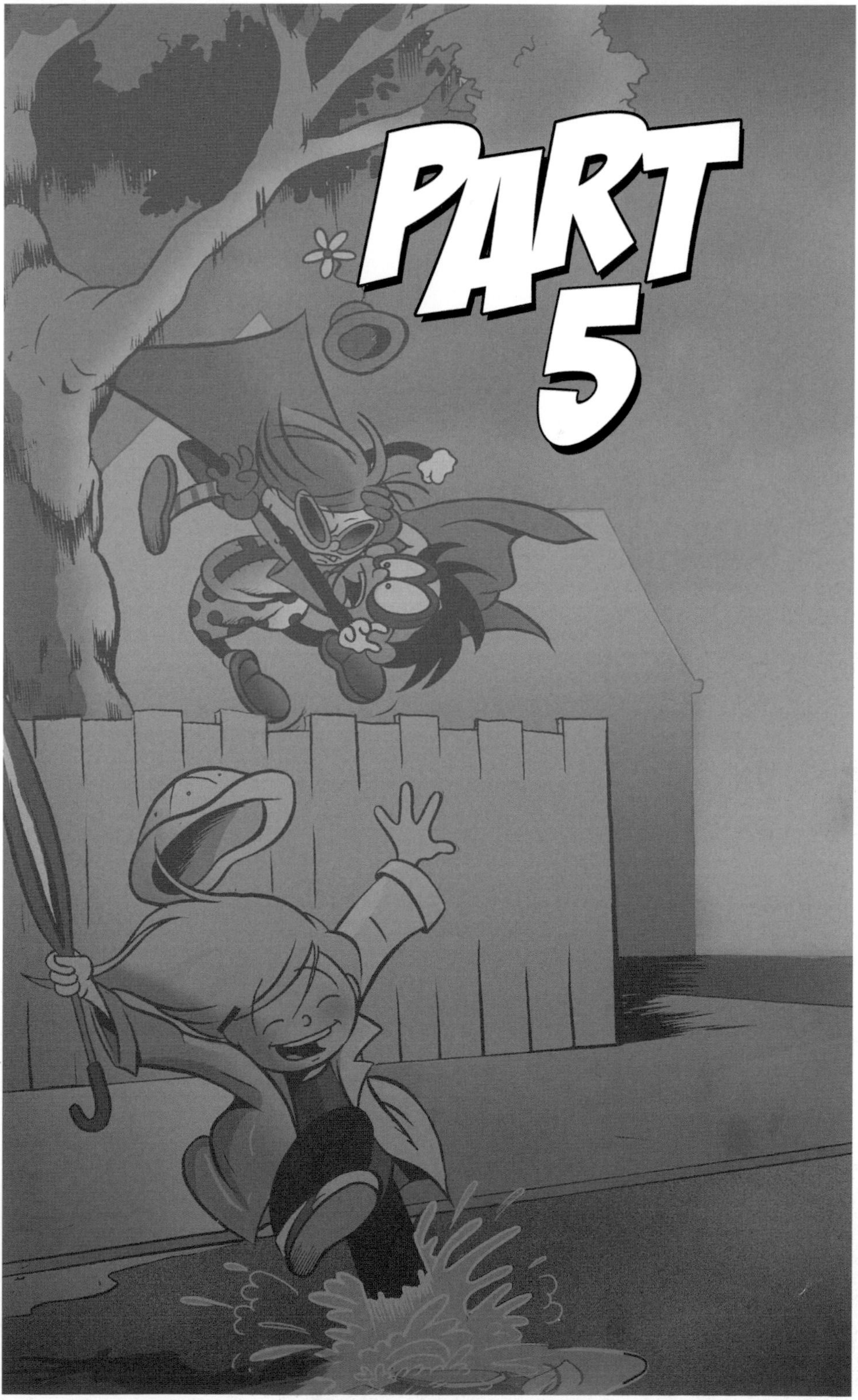
PART
5

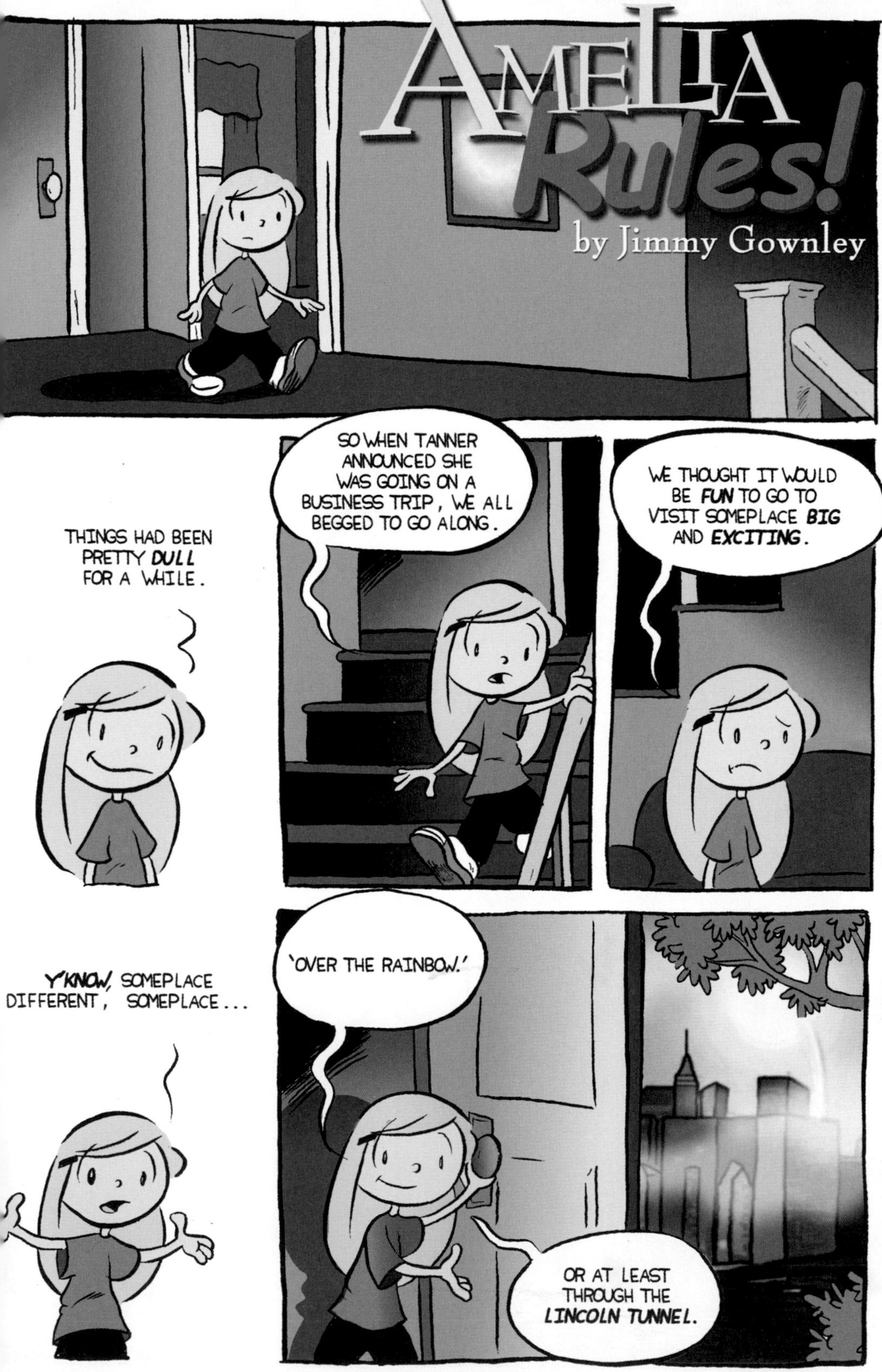
AMELIA Rules!
by Jimmy Gownley
THINGS HAD BEEN PRETTY DULL FOR A WHILE.
SO WHEN TANNER ANNOUNCED SHE WAS GOING ON A BUSINESS TRIP, WE ALL BEGGED TO GO ALONG.
WE THOUGHT IT WOULD BE FUN TO GO TO VISIT SOMEPLACE BIG AND EXCITING.
Y'KNOW, SOMEPLACE DIFFERENT, SOMEPLACE...
'OVER THE RAINBOW.'
OR AT LEAST THROUGH THE LINCOLN TUNNEL.

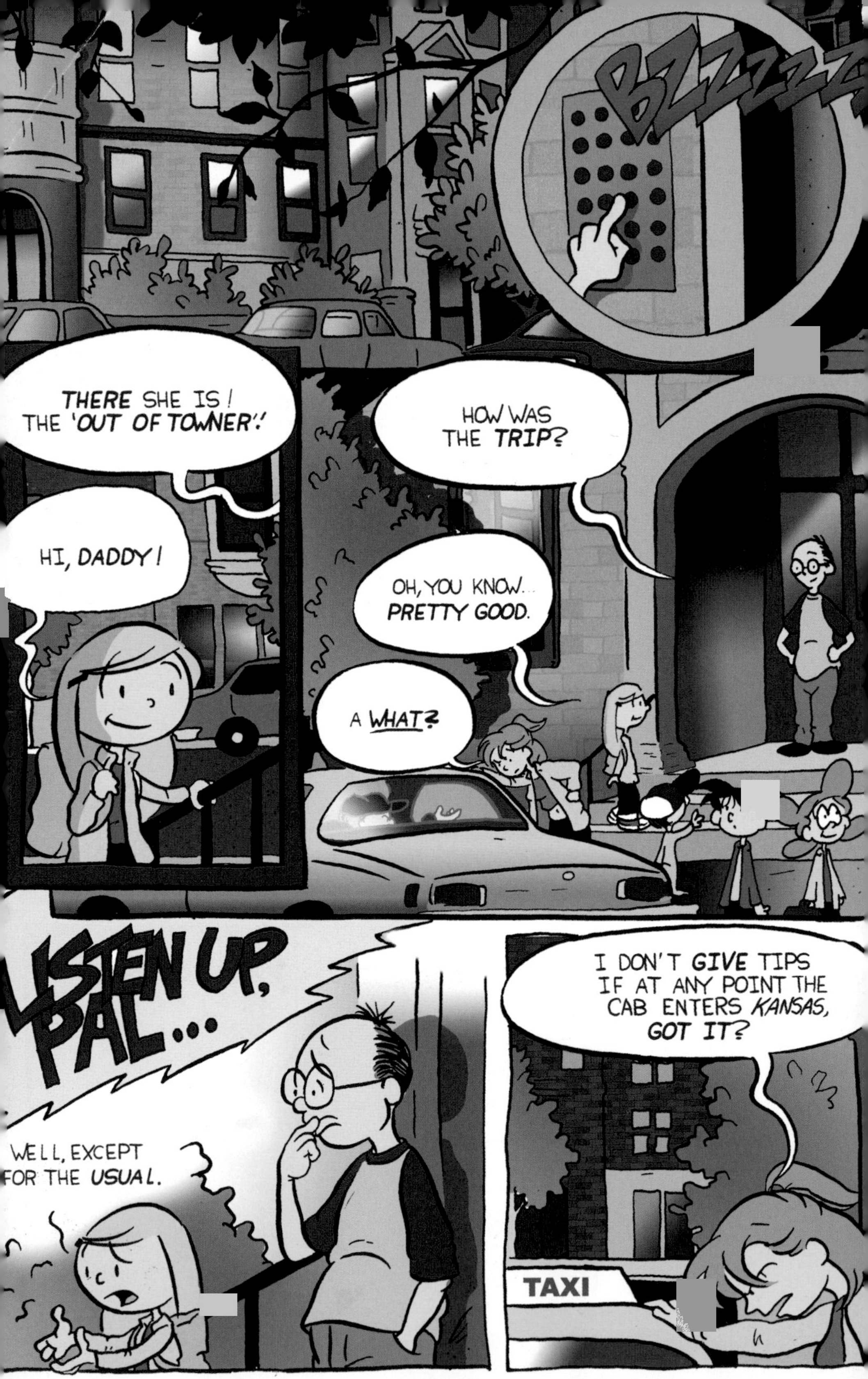
BZZZZZ
THERE SHE IS! THE 'OUT OF TOWNER'!
HOW WAS THE TRIP?
HI, DADDY!
OH, YOU KNOW... PRETTY GOOD.
A WHAT?
LISTEN UP, PAL...
WELL, EXCEPT FOR THE USUAL.
I DON'T GIVE TIPS IF AT ANY POINT THE CAB ENTERS KANSAS, GOT IT?
TAXI

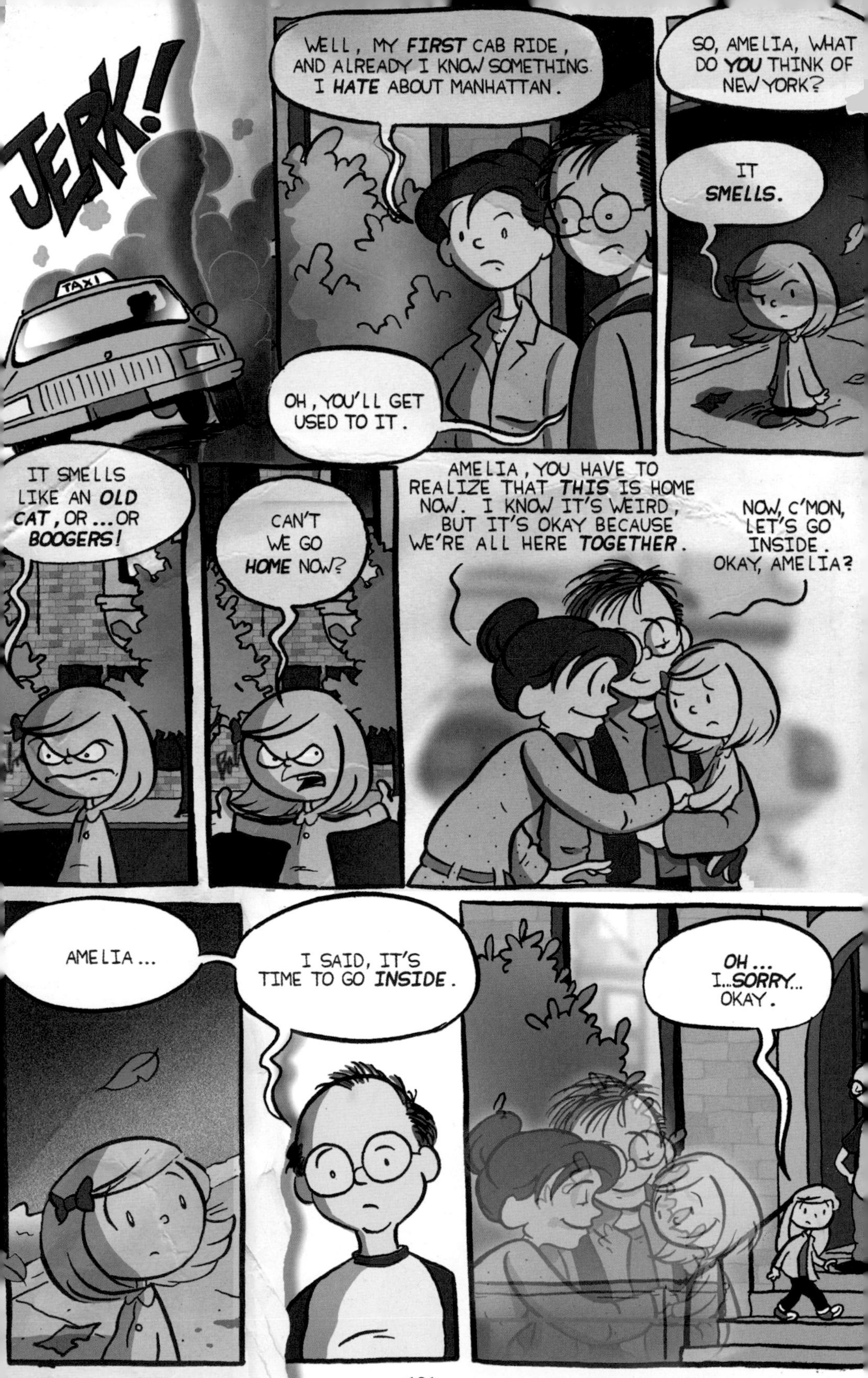
JERK!
TAXI
WELL, MY FIRST CAB RIDE, AND ALREADY I KNOW SOMETHING I HATE ABOUT MANHATTAN.
OH, YOU'LL GET USED TO IT.
SO, AMELIA, WHAT DO YOU THINK OF NEW YORK?
IT SMELLS.
IT SMELLS LIKE AN OLD CAT, OR ... OR BOOGERS!
CAN'T WE GO HOME NOW?
AMELIA, YOU HAVE TO REALIZE THAT THIS IS HOME NOW. I KNOW IT'S WEIRD, BUT IT'S OKAY BECAUSE WE'RE ALL HERE TOGETHER.
NOW, C'MON, LET'S GO INSIDE. OKAY, AMELIA?
AMELIA ...
I SAID, IT'S TIME TO GO INSIDE.
OH ... I...SORRY... OKAY.

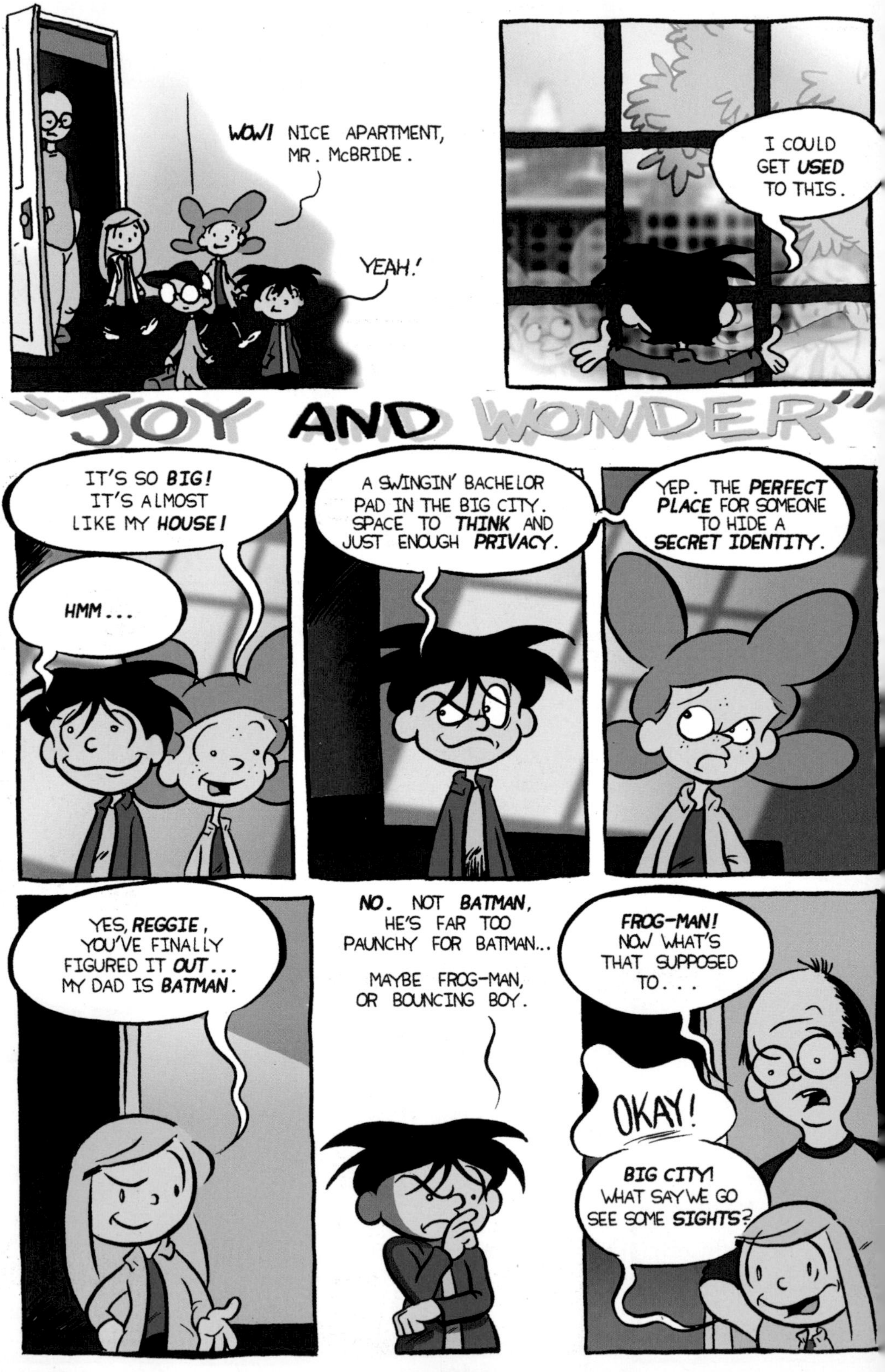
WOW! NICE APARTMENT, MR. McBRIDE.
YEAH!
I COULD GET USED TO THIS.
"JOY AND WONDER"
IT'S SO BIG! IT'S ALMOST LIKE MY HOUSE!
HMM...
A SWINGIN' BACHELOR PAD IN THE BIG CITY. SPACE TO THINK AND JUST ENOUGH PRIVACY.
YEP. THE PERFECT PLACE FOR SOMEONE TO HIDE A SECRET IDENTITY.
YES, REGGIE, YOU'VE FINALLY FIGURED IT OUT... MY DAD IS BATMAN.
NO. NOT BATMAN, HE'S FAR TOO PAUNCHY FOR BATMAN...
MAYBE FROG-MAN, OR BOUNCING BOY.
FROG-MAN! NOW WHAT'S THAT SUPPOSED TO...
OKAY!
BIG CITY! WHAT SAY WE GO SEE SOME SIGHTS?

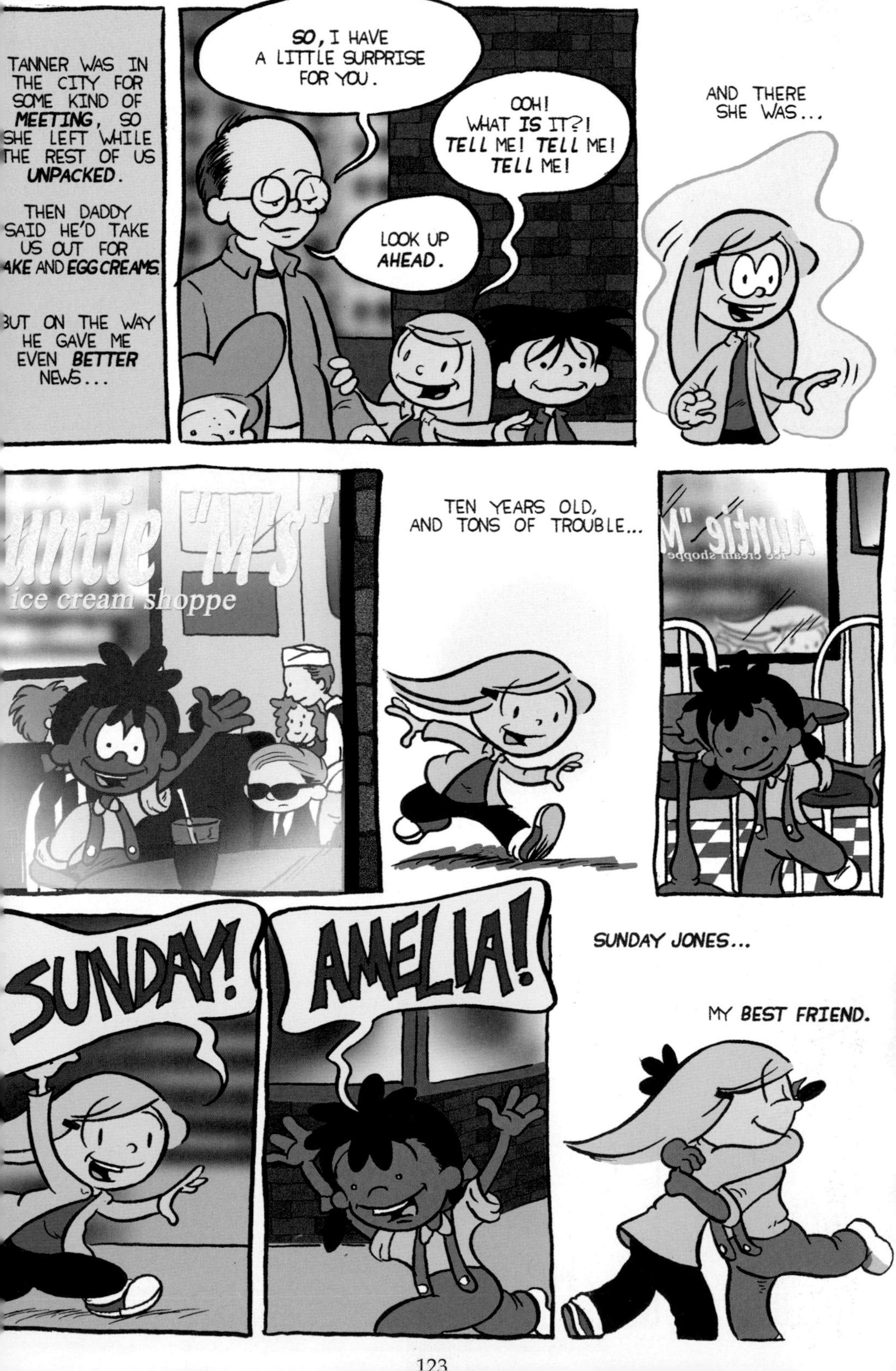

TANNER WAS IN THE CITY FOR SOME KIND OF MEETING, SO SHE LEFT WHILE THE REST OF US UNPACKED.
THEN DADDY SAID HE'D TAKE US OUT FOR AKE AND EGG CREAMS.
BUT ON THE WAY HE GAVE ME EVEN BETTER NEWS...
SO, I HAVE A LITTLE SURPRISE FOR YOU.
OOH! WHAT IS IT?! TELL ME! TELL ME! TELL ME!
LOOK UP AHEAD.
AND THERE SHE WAS...
untie "M's" ice cream shoppe
TEN YEARS OLD, AND TONS OF TROUBLE...
Auntie "M" ice cream shoppe
SUNDAY!
AMELIA!
SUNDAY JONES...
MY BEST FRIEND.

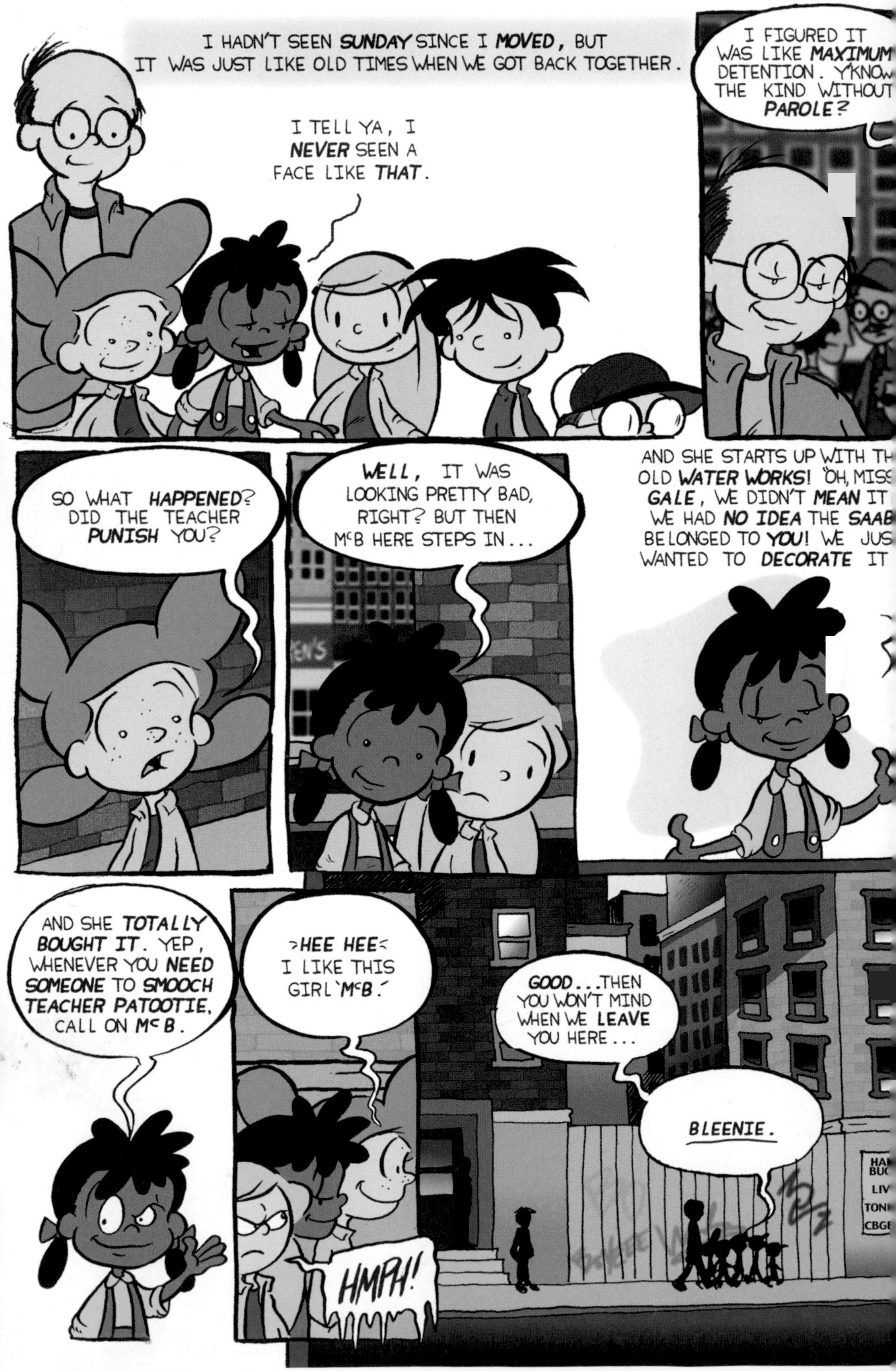
I HADN'T SEEN SUNDAY SINCE I MOVED, BUT IT WAS JUST LIKE OLD TIMES WHEN WE GOT BACK TOGETHER.
I TELL YA, I NEVER SEEN A FACE LIKE THAT.
I FIGURED IT WAS LIKE MAXIMUM DETENTION. Y'KNOW THE KIND WITHOUT PAROLE?
SO WHAT HAPPENED? DID THE TEACHER PUNISH YOU?
WELL, IT WAS LOOKING PRETTY BAD, RIGHT? BUT THEN M^cB HERE STEPS IN...
AND SHE STARTS UP WITH TH OLD WATER WORKS! "OH, MISS GALE, WE DIDN'T MEAN IT WE HAD NO IDEA THE SAAB BELONGED TO YOU! WE JUS WANTED TO DECORATE IT
AND SHE TOTALLY BOUGHT IT. YEP, WHENEVER YOU NEED SOMEONE TO SMOOCH TEACHER PATOOTIE, CALL ON M^cB.
>HEE HEE< I LIKE THIS GIRL 'M^cB.'
HMPH!
GOOD...THEN YOU WON'T MIND WHEN WE LEAVE YOU HERE...
BLEENIE.

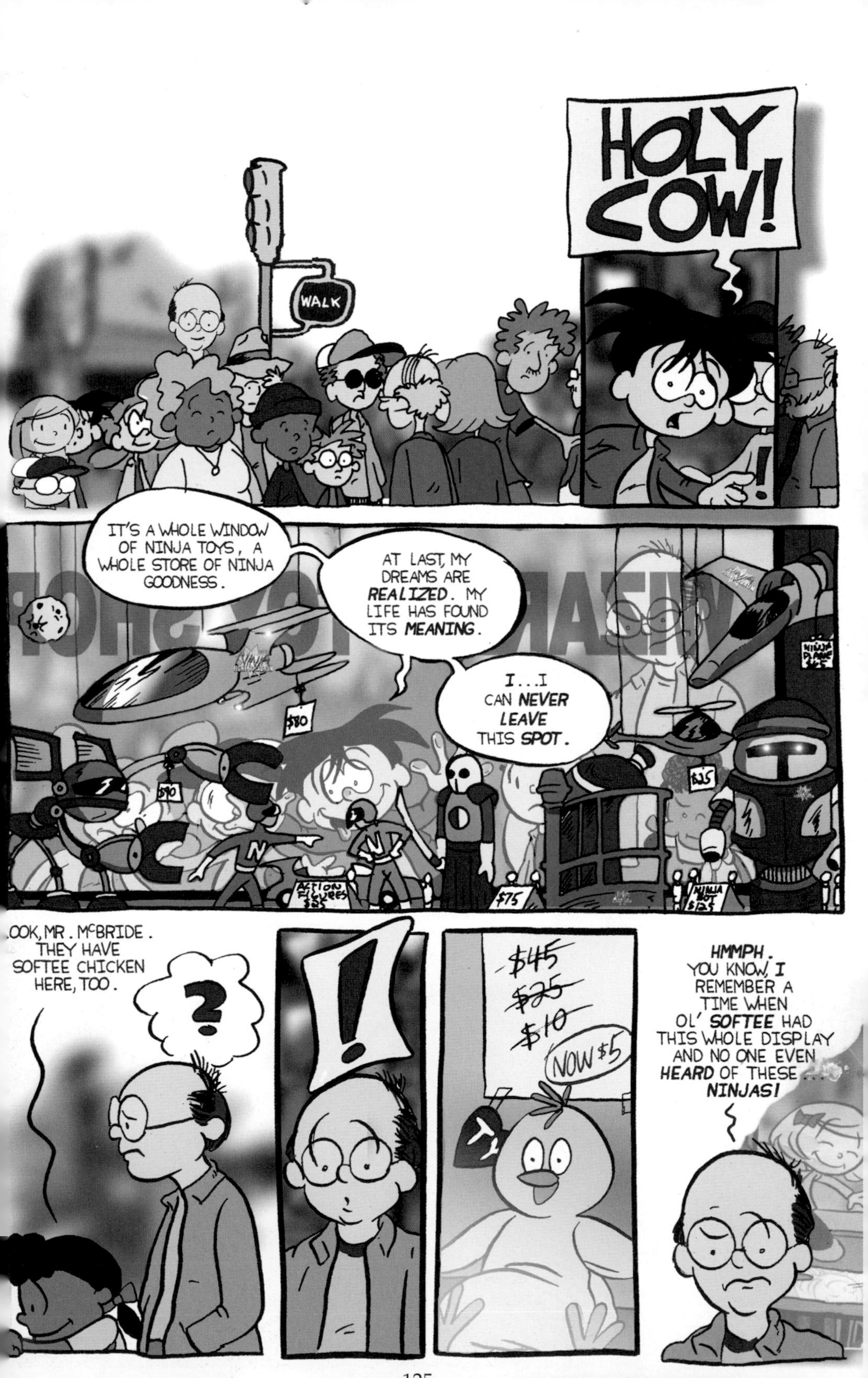
HOLY COW!
WALK
IT'S A WHOLE WINDOW OF NINJA TOYS, A WHOLE STORE OF NINJA GOODNESS.
AT LAST, MY DREAMS ARE REALIZED. MY LIFE HAS FOUND ITS MEANING.
I...I CAN NEVER LEAVE THIS SPOT.
$80
$90
$35
ACTION FIGURES $25
$75
NINJA BOT $125
NINJA PLANE $25
LOOK, MR. McBRIDE. THEY HAVE SOFTEE CHICKEN HERE, TOO.
?
!
$45
$25
$10
NOW $5
HMMPH. YOU KNOW, I REMEMBER A TIME WHEN OL' SOFTEE HAD THIS WHOLE DISPLAY AND NO ONE EVEN HEARD OF THESE... NINJAS!

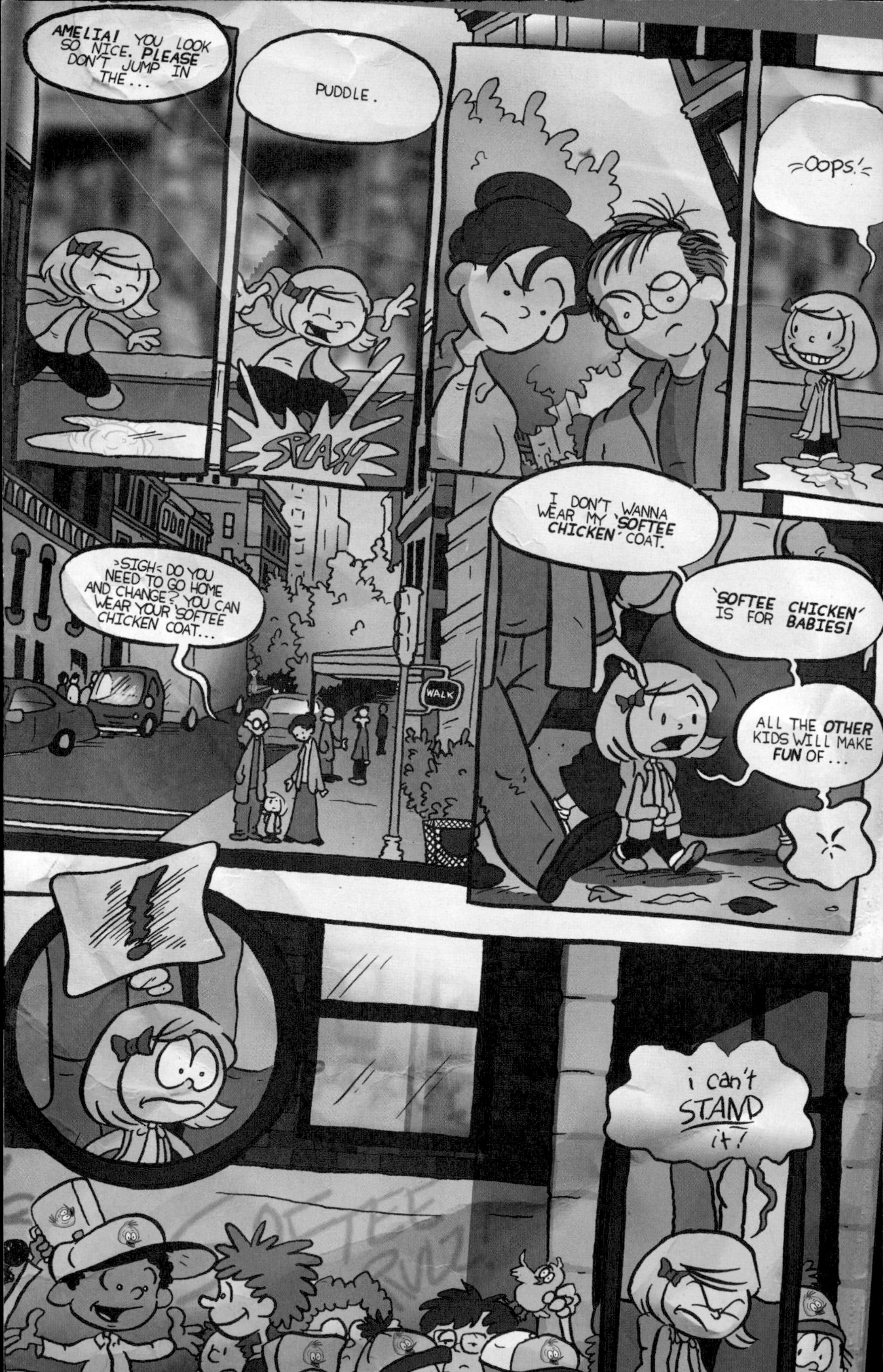
AMELIA! YOU LOOK SO NICE. PLEASE DON'T JUMP IN THE...
PUDDLE.
SPLASH
=OOPS!=
>SIGH< DO YOU NEED TO GO HOME AND CHANGE? YOU CAN WEAR YOUR 'SOFTEE CHICKEN' COAT...
WALK
I DON'T WANNA WEAR MY 'SOFTEE CHICKEN' COAT.
'SOFTEE CHICKEN' IS FOR BABIES!
ALL THE OTHER KIDS WILL MAKE FUN OF...
!
i can't STAND it!

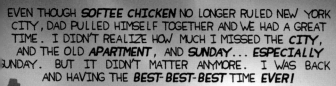

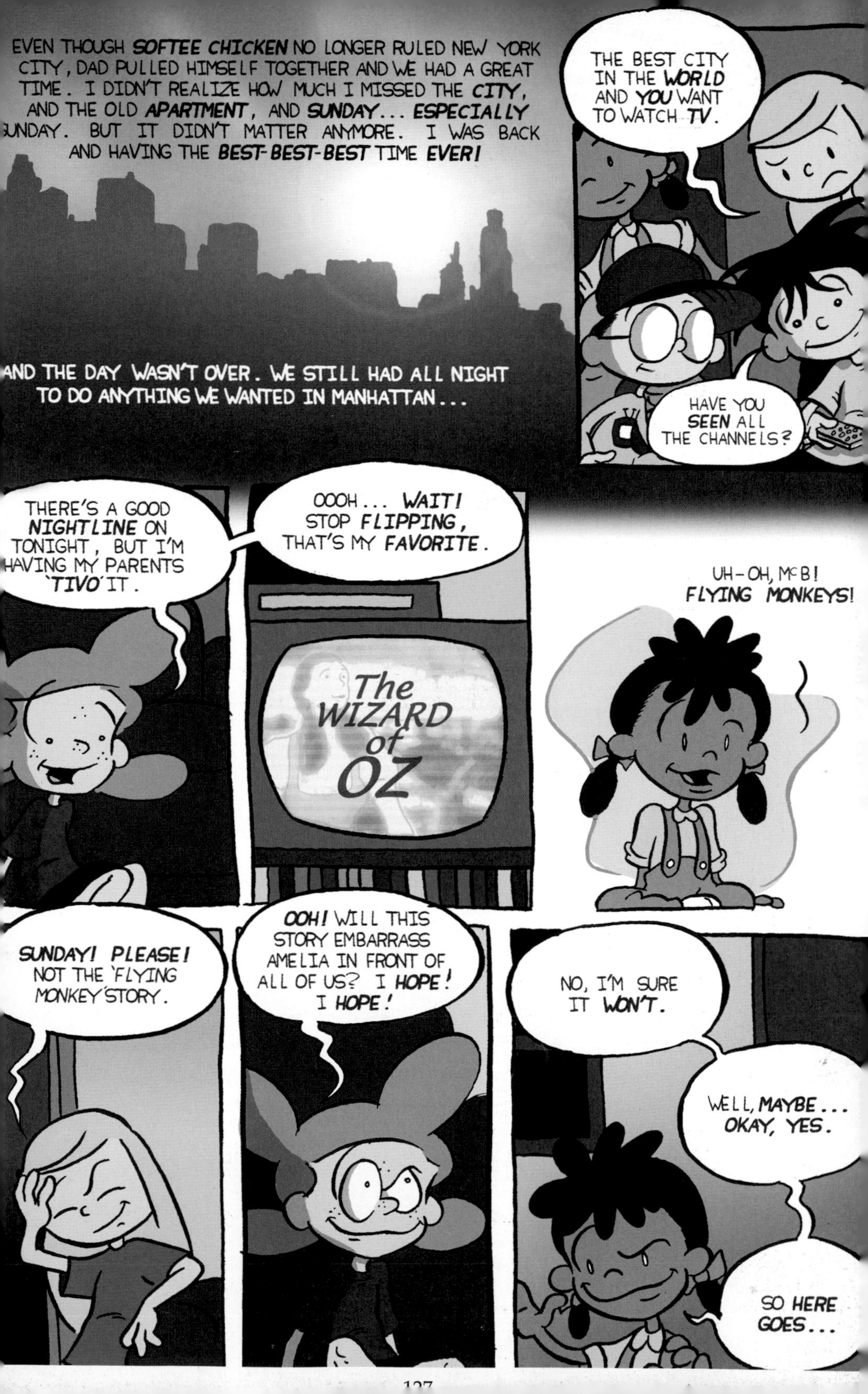

EVEN THOUGH **SOFTEE CHICKEN** NO LONGER RULED NEW YORK CITY, DAD PULLED HIMSELF TOGETHER AND WE HAD A GREAT TIME. I DIDN'T REALIZE HOW MUCH I MISSED THE **CITY**, AND THE OLD **APARTMENT**, AND **SUNDAY... ESPECIALLY** SUNDAY. BUT IT DIDN'T MATTER ANYMORE. I WAS BACK AND HAVING THE **BEST-BEST-BEST** TIME **EVER!**

THE BEST CITY IN THE **WORLD** AND **YOU** WANT TO WATCH **TV.**

HAVE YOU **SEEN** ALL THE CHANNELS?

AND THE DAY WASN'T OVER. WE STILL HAD ALL NIGHT TO DO ANYTHING WE WANTED IN MANHATTAN...

THERE'S A GOOD **NIGHTLINE** ON TONIGHT, BUT I'M HAVING MY PARENTS 'TIVO' IT.

OOOH... **WAIT!** STOP **FLIPPING,** THAT'S MY **FAVORITE.**

The WIZARD of OZ

UH-OH, MᶜB! **FLYING MONKEYS!**

SUNDAY! PLEASE! NOT THE 'FLYING MONKEY' STORY.

OOH! WILL THIS STORY EMBARRASS AMELIA IN FRONT OF ALL OF US? I **HOPE!** I **HOPE!**

NO, I'M SURE IT **WON'T.**

WELL, MAYBE... OKAY, YES.

SO **HERE** GOES...

It was back in first grade. See, by the time McB came to town, school had already been rolling for a while. And let's just say I had already made my rep. What I hadn't made was, y'know, any friends. And on top of that, we had this teacher, Miss Hamilton. She was a real witch, and she had it in for me BIG TIME.

And really, it was for no reason. I mean, sure... there were one or two little things, but the fire department was barely involved. And besides, they couldn't prove anyth....

uh... anyway...

So when Amelia joined the class, I barely even noticed. She was just this quiet, shy girl who kept to herself, and...

Rhonda?
Rhonda? What's so funny? Are you okay? Breathe, girl! ***BREATHE!***

So like I said, I pretty much ignored her. Then one day I noticed something.

If there was one person Miss Hamilton liked less than me, it was Amelia Louise McBride.

See, that's even what she called her... Amelia Louise... never just Amelia, she always stuck on Louise. Only it sounded like this...

Leweeeeeeeeeeez.

Like she just stepped in something nasty.

Rhonda, if you can't control the laughing, we'll have to ask you to leave.

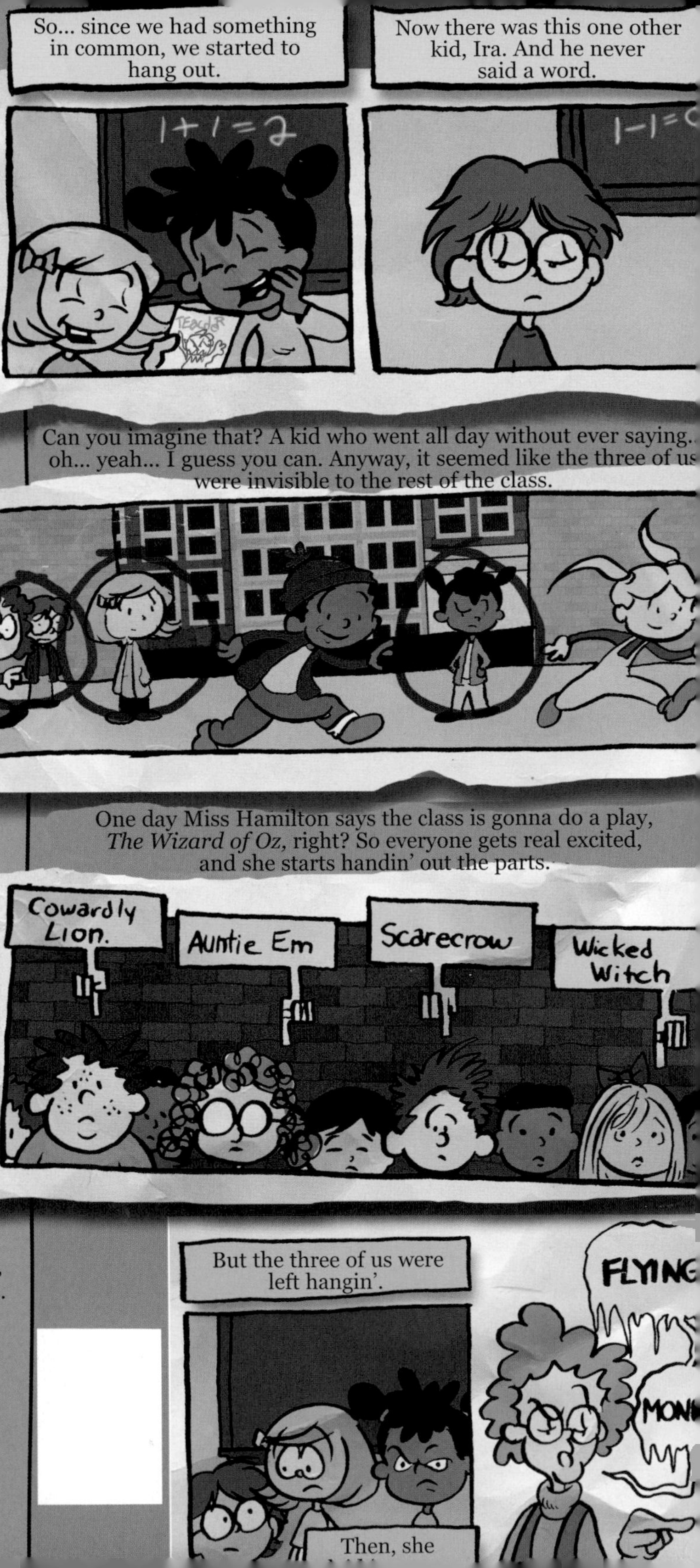

So... since we had something in common, we started to hang out.
Now there was this one other kid, Ira. And he never said a word.
1+1=2
Teacher
Can you imagine that? A kid who went all day without ever saying... oh... yeah... I guess you can. Anyway, it seemed like the three of us were invisible to the rest of the class.
One day Miss Hamilton says the class is gonna do a play, *The Wizard of Oz*, right? So everyone gets real excited, and she starts handin' out the parts.
Cowardly Lion.
Auntie Em
Scarecrow
Wicked Witch
But the three of us were left hangin'.
FLYING
Then, she

Not exactly a compliment, y'know? I mean, it's not like she picked her favorite students and said, "Ah, yes...you shall be my monkeys." It was more like, "Let's put these numbskulls where they can do the least amount of damage."

I think Mr. and Mrs. McBride felt bad for us. They invited us over a bunch of times so we could "rehearse" with Amelia. Not that there was much to rehearse. We pretty much just ran around the apartment going, "Eek! Eek!" But y'know, it was fun.

The best part was when Amelia's mom made us these way cool monkey costumes. They had wings and ears and big ol' monkey tails. We were stylin'! I think that's when we started getting into it. I came up with this name, "The Flying Monkey Society," and we ran around calling ourselves that. Whenever someone would ask what time it was, we'd yell, "IT'S MONKEY TIME!" (Well, me and McB would. Ira still wasn't talking) and then we'd jump around like rejects.

It must've looked like fun, 'cuz pretty soon everyone wanted to be a "Flying Monkey." Of course, we wouldn't let them. Heh, heh...It was pretty cool.

So anyway, the day of the big show finally comes, and everyone is freaking out. Even Miss Hamilton is kinda goin' wonky. And the more wonky she got, the more freaked out we got. It was a scene.

Then things really went downhill. First, the girl who was playing Dorothy forgot the words to "Over the Rainbow." Then the Tin Man got the hiccups, which wouldn't have been so bad if it didn't make Carlos, the kid playing the Scarecrow, laugh. He laughed so hard he fell off the stage. By the time we came on, it was a massacre. People were leaving. I'm pretty sure I even heard another teacher boo us.

So when we went out there, we froze. We didn't "Eek!" or flap our arms or nothing. It was gonna be the most disastrous part of the big disaster.
and then...
MY PEOPLE...
CITIZENS of OZ! YOUR DOOM is HERE!
FOR I AM IRA, THE FLYING MONKEY KING! ALL MUST KNEEL BEFORE ME, OR SUFFER MY WRATH. LOOK UPON THESE MERE MORTALS- REDUCED AS THEY ARE TO QUIVERING SHELLS OF THEIR FORMER SELVES! THESE FOOLS THOUGHT THEY WERE ON A QUEST, BUT IT WAS NOT SO! FOR THEY WERE, ALL OF THEM, MERE PAWNS OF IRA... SLAVES TO HIS WHIM! AND NOW SO ARE YOU.
FOR I AM...FEAR! I AM...VENGEANCE! I AM... IRA!
WHAT HE SAID.

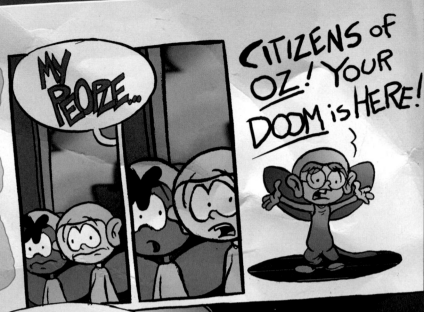

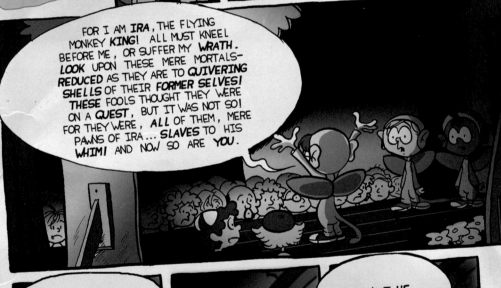

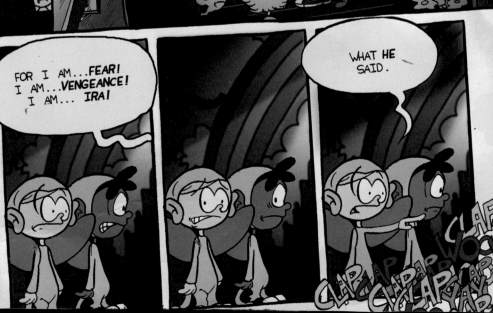

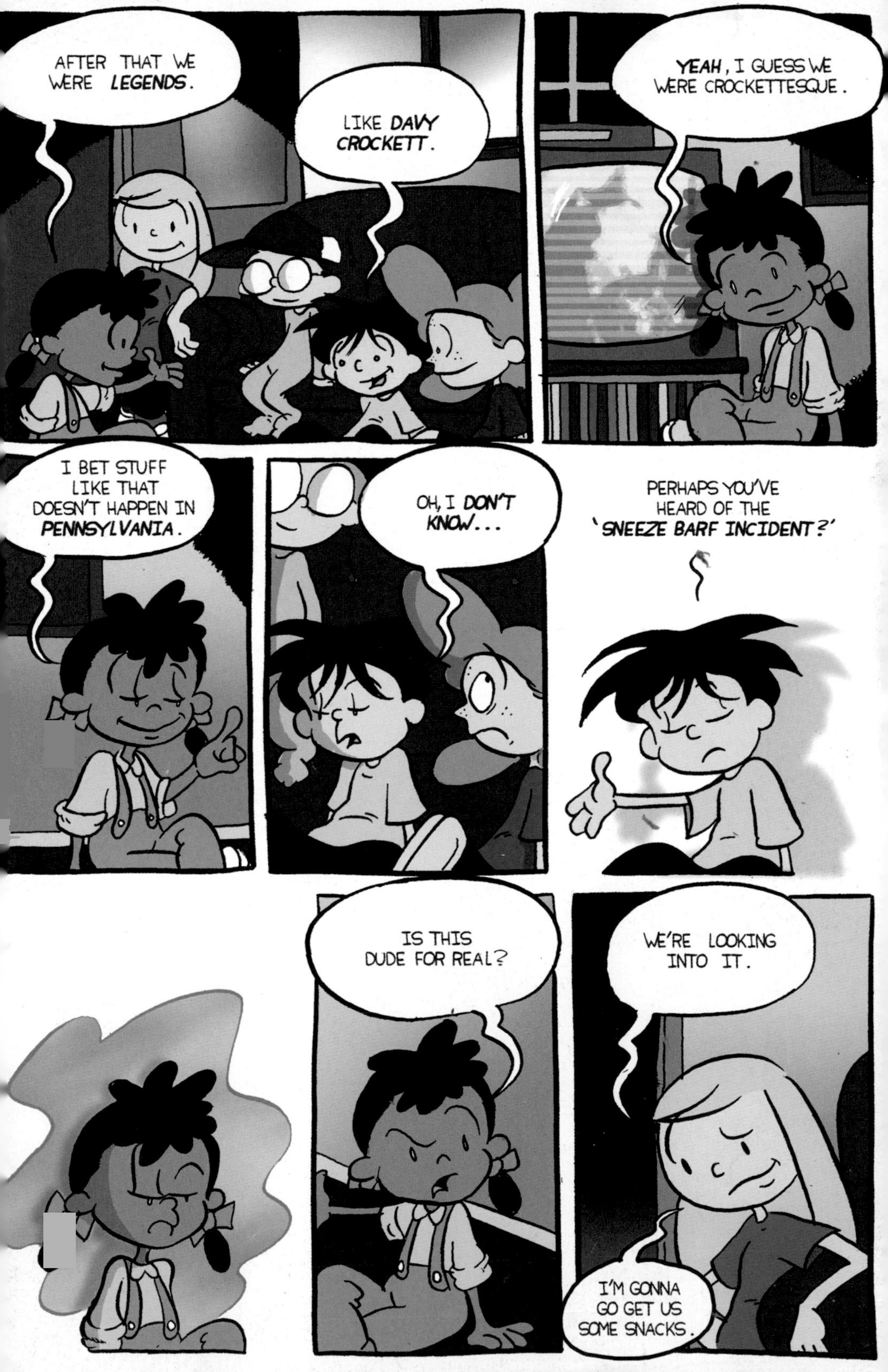

AFTER THAT WE WERE LEGENDS.
LIKE DAVY CROCKETT.
YEAH, I GUESS WE WERE CROCKETTESQUE.
I BET STUFF LIKE THAT DOESN'T HAPPEN IN PENNSYLVANIA.
OH, I DON'T KNOW...
PERHAPS YOU'VE HEARD OF THE 'SNEEZE BARF INCIDENT?'
IS THIS DUDE FOR REAL?
WE'RE LOOKING INTO IT.
I'M GONNA GO GET US SOME SNACKS.

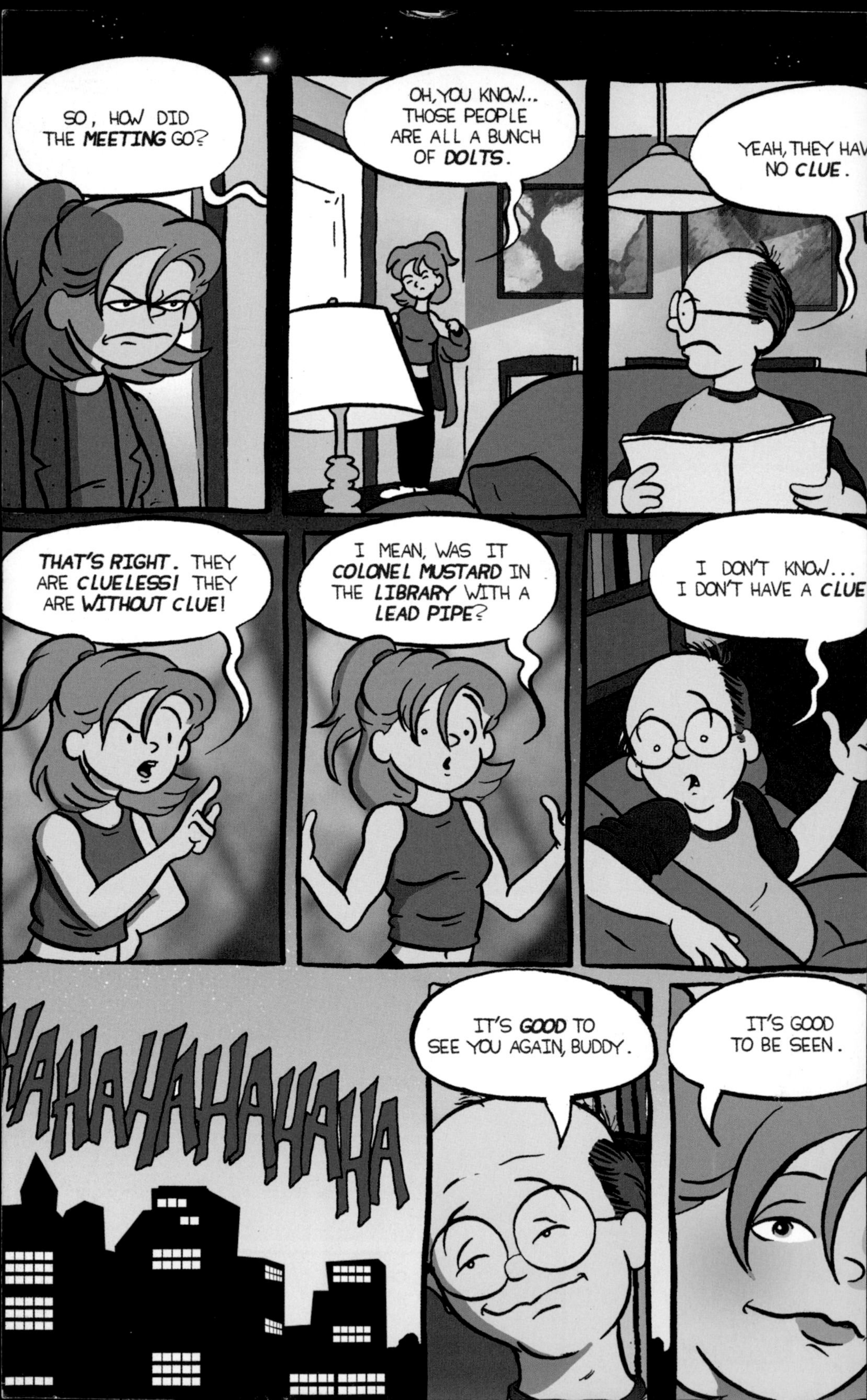
SO, HOW DID THE MEETING GO?
OH, YOU KNOW... THOSE PEOPLE ARE ALL A BUNCH OF DOLTS.
YEAH, THEY HAV NO CLUE.
THAT'S RIGHT. THEY ARE CLUELESS! THEY ARE WITHOUT CLUE!
I MEAN, WAS IT COLONEL MUSTARD IN THE LIBRARY WITH A LEAD PIPE?
I DON'T KNOW... I DON'T HAVE A CLUE
HAHAHAHAHAHAHA
IT'S GOOD TO SEE YOU AGAIN, BUDDY.
IT'S GOOD TO BE SEEN.

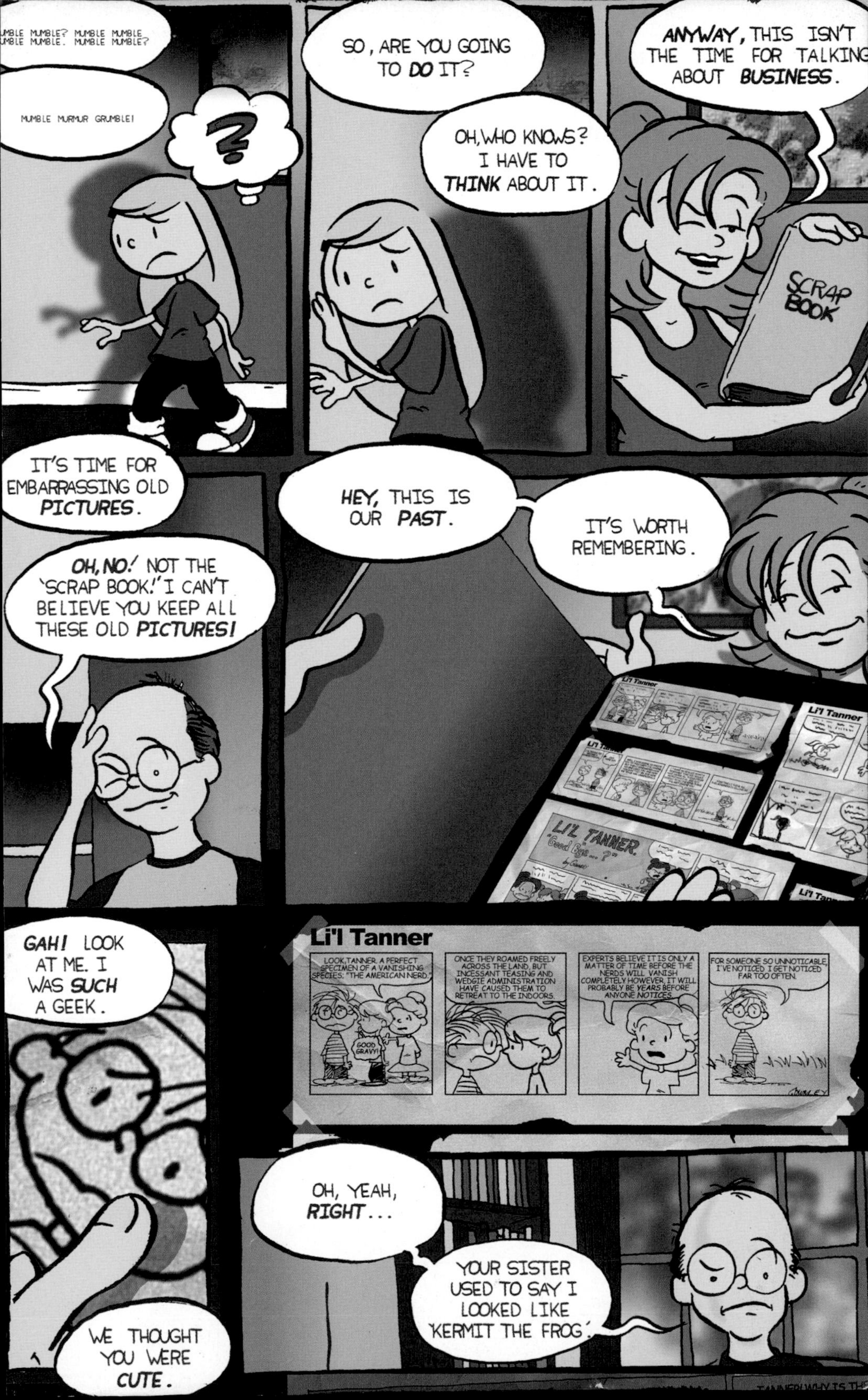
MBLE MUMBLE? MUMBLE MUMBLE MBLE MUMBLE. MUMBLE MUMBLE?
MUMBLE MURMUR GRUMBLE!
?
SO, ARE YOU GOING TO DO IT?
OH, WHO KNOWS? I HAVE TO THINK ABOUT IT.
ANYWAY, THIS ISN'T THE TIME FOR TALKING ABOUT BUSINESS.
SCRAP BOOK
IT'S TIME FOR EMBARRASSING OLD PICTURES.
OH, NO! NOT THE 'SCRAP BOOK!' I CAN'T BELIEVE YOU KEEP ALL THESE OLD PICTURES!
HEY, THIS IS OUR PAST.
IT'S WORTH REMEMBERING.
Li'l Tanner
LOOK, TANNER. A PERFECT SPECIMEN OF A VANISHING SPECIES: "THE AMERICAN NERD."
GOOD GRAVY!
ONCE THEY ROAMED FREELY ACROSS THE LAND, BUT INCESSANT TEASING AND WEDGIE ADMINISTRATION HAVE CAUSED THEM TO RETREAT TO THE INDOORS.
EXPERTS BELIEVE IT IS ONLY A MATTER OF TIME BEFORE THE NERDS WILL VANISH COMPLETELY. HOWEVER, IT WILL PROBABLY BE YEARS BEFORE ANYONE NOTICES.
FOR SOMEONE SO UNNOTICABLE, I'VE NOTICED I GET NOTICED FAR TOO OFTEN.
GAH! LOOK AT ME. I WAS SUCH A GEEK.
WE THOUGHT YOU WERE CUTE.
OH, YEAH, RIGHT...
YOUR SISTER USED TO SAY I LOOKED LIKE 'KERMIT THE FROG'.

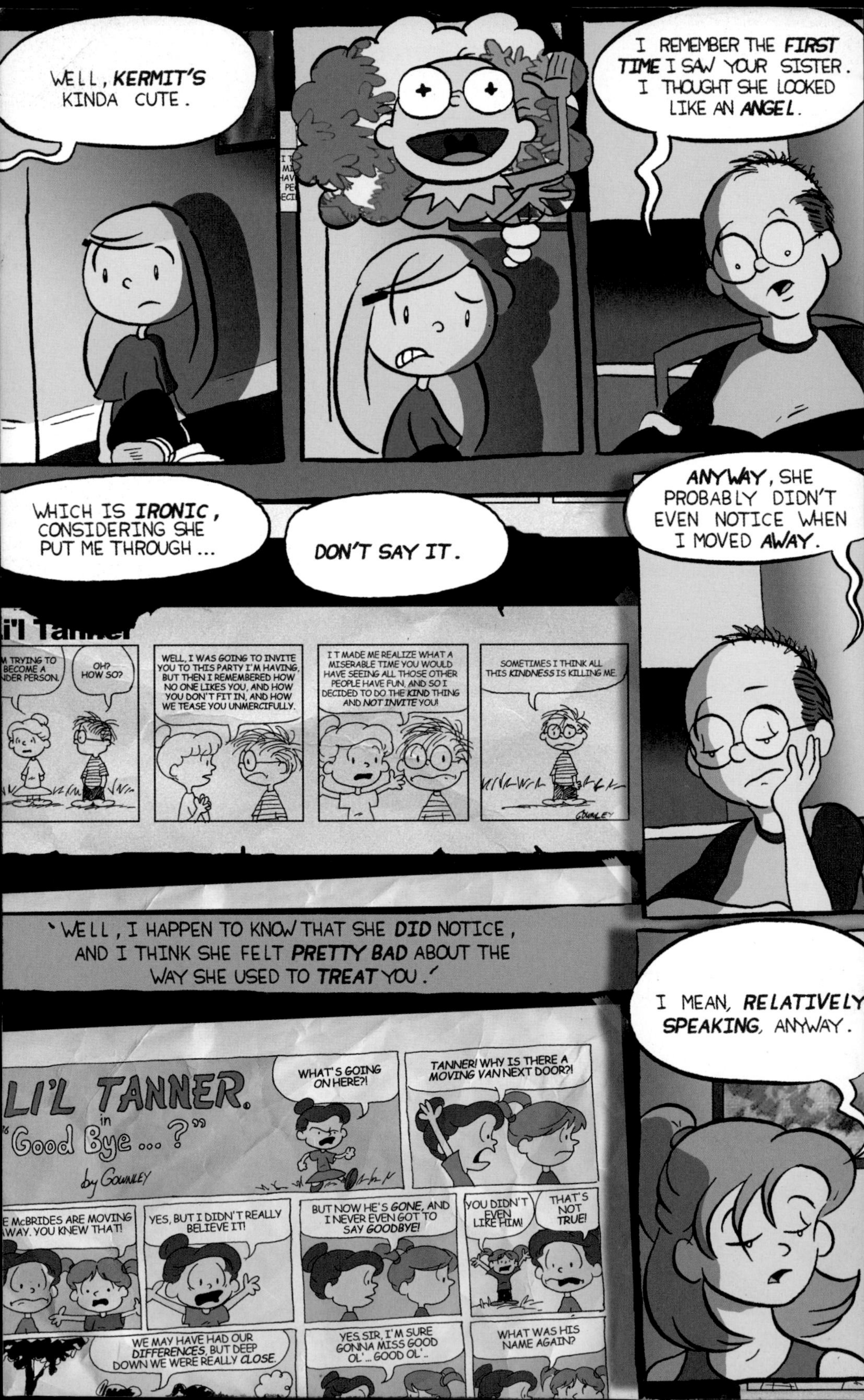

WELL, KERMIT'S KINDA CUTE.
I REMEMBER THE FIRST TIME I SAW YOUR SISTER. I THOUGHT SHE LOOKED LIKE AN ANGEL.
WHICH IS IRONIC, CONSIDERING SHE PUT ME THROUGH ...
DON'T SAY IT.
ANYWAY, SHE PROBABLY DIDN'T EVEN NOTICE WHEN I MOVED AWAY.
OH? HOW SO?
WELL, I WAS GOING TO INVITE YOU TO THIS PARTY I'M HAVING, BUT THEN I REMEMBERED HOW NO ONE LIKES YOU, AND HOW YOU DON'T FIT IN, AND HOW WE TEASE YOU UNMERCIFULLY.
IT MADE ME REALIZE WHAT A MISERABLE TIME YOU WOULD HAVE SEEING ALL THOSE OTHER PEOPLE HAVE FUN, AND SO I DECIDED TO DO THE KIND THING AND NOT INVITE YOU!
SOMETIMES I THINK ALL THIS KINDNESS IS KILLING ME.
GOWNLEY
'WELL, I HAPPEN TO KNOW THAT SHE DID NOTICE, AND I THINK SHE FELT PRETTY BAD ABOUT THE WAY SHE USED TO TREAT YOU.'
I MEAN, RELATIVELY SPEAKING, ANYWAY.
LI'L TANNER
in "Good Bye ... ?"
by GOWNLEY
WHAT'S GOING ON HERE?!
TANNER! WHY IS THERE A MOVING VAN NEXT DOOR?!
YES, BUT I DIDN'T REALLY BELIEVE IT!
BUT NOW HE'S GONE, AND I NEVER EVEN GOT TO SAY GOODBYE!
YOU DIDN'T EVEN LIKE HIM!
THAT'S NOT TRUE!
WE MAY HAVE HAD OUR DIFFERENCES, BUT DEEP DOWN WE WERE REALLY CLOSE.
YES SIR, I'M SURE GONNA MISS GOOD OL'... GOOD OL'..
WHAT WAS HIS NAME AGAIN?

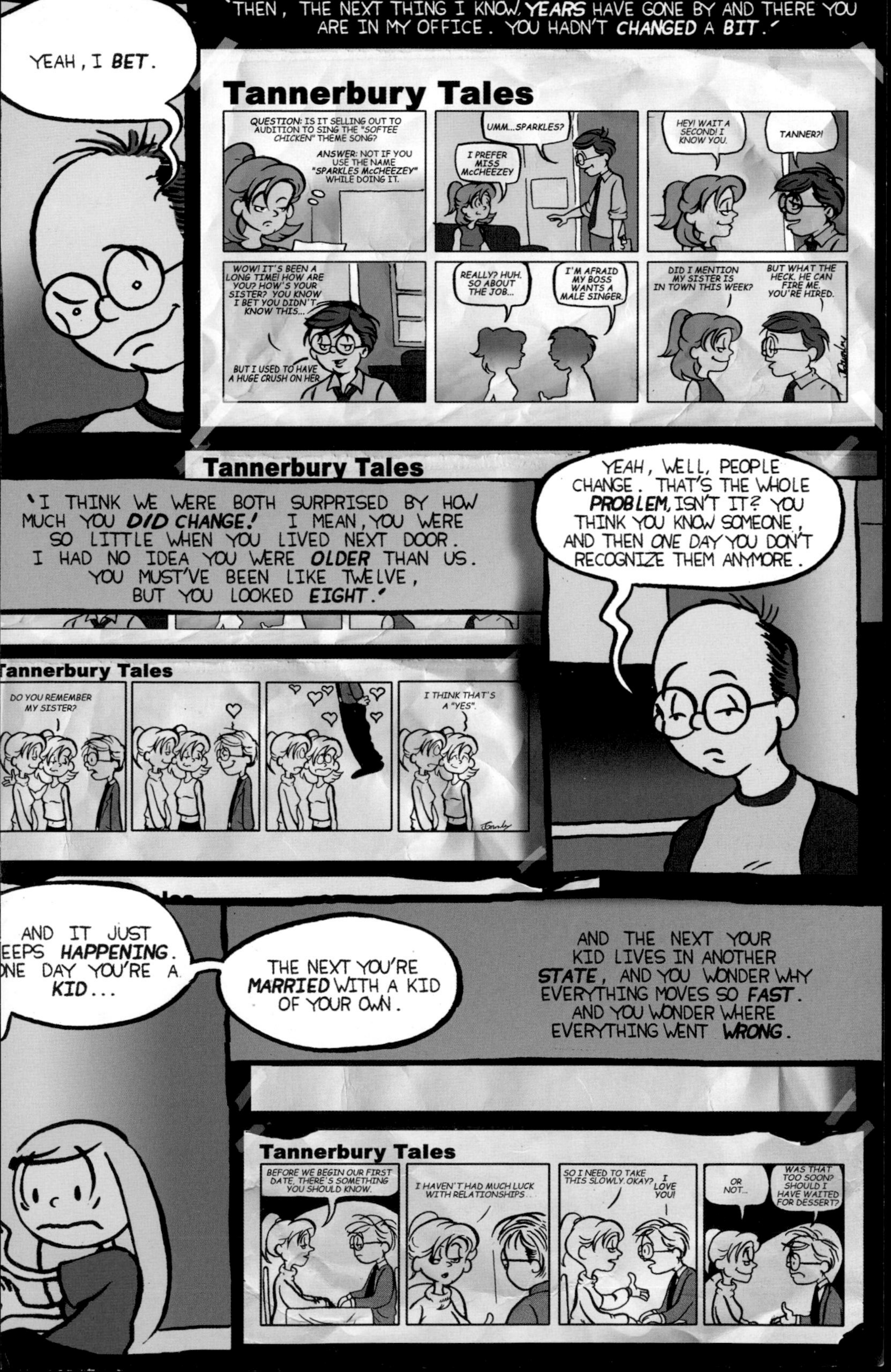
'THEN, THE NEXT THING I KNOW, YEARS HAVE GONE BY AND THERE YOU ARE IN MY OFFICE. YOU HADN'T CHANGED A BIT.'
YEAH, I BET.
Tannerbury Tales
QUESTION: IS IT SELLING OUT TO AUDITION TO SING THE "SOFTEE CHICKEN" THEME SONG?
ANSWER: NOT IF YOU USE THE NAME "SPARKLES McCHEEZEY" WHILE DOING IT.
UMM...SPARKLES?
I PREFER MISS McCHEEZEY
HEY! WAIT A SECOND! I KNOW YOU.
TANNER?!
WOW! IT'S BEEN A LONG TIME! HOW ARE YOU? HOW'S YOUR SISTER? YOU KNOW I BET YOU DIDN'T KNOW THIS...
BUT I USED TO HAVE A HUGE CRUSH ON HER.
REALLY? HUH. SO ABOUT THE JOB...
I'M AFRAID MY BOSS WANTS A MALE SINGER.
DID I MENTION MY SISTER IS IN TOWN THIS WEEK?
BUT WHAT THE HECK. HE CAN FIRE ME. YOU'RE HIRED.
Tannerbury Tales
'I THINK WE WERE BOTH SURPRISED BY HOW MUCH YOU DID CHANGE! I MEAN, YOU WERE SO LITTLE WHEN YOU LIVED NEXT DOOR. I HAD NO IDEA YOU WERE OLDER THAN US. YOU MUST'VE BEEN LIKE TWELVE, BUT YOU LOOKED EIGHT.'
YEAH, WELL, PEOPLE CHANGE. THAT'S THE WHOLE PROBLEM, ISN'T IT? YOU THINK YOU KNOW SOMEONE, AND THEN ONE DAY YOU DON'T RECOGNIZE THEM ANYMORE.
Tannerbury Tales
DO YOU REMEMBER MY SISTER?
I THINK THAT'S A "YES".
AND IT JUST KEEPS HAPPENING. ONE DAY YOU'RE A KID...
THE NEXT YOU'RE MARRIED WITH A KID OF YOUR OWN.
AND THE NEXT YOUR KID LIVES IN ANOTHER STATE, AND YOU WONDER WHY EVERYTHING MOVES SO FAST. AND YOU WONDER WHERE EVERYTHING WENT WRONG.
Tannerbury Tales
BEFORE WE BEGIN OUR FIRST DATE, THERE'S SOMETHING YOU SHOULD KNOW.
I HAVEN'T HAD MUCH LUCK WITH RELATIONSHIPS...
SO I NEED TO TAKE THIS SLOWLY. OKAY?
I LOVE YOU!
OR NOT...
WAS THAT TOO SOON? SHOULD I HAVE WAITED FOR DESSERT?

HEY, HOW'S THE *MOVIE*? DID I MISS MUCH?

OH... I SEE... OH, WELL.

I guess I should learn to... to stop... counting on... on...

SNIFF

PAT PAT PAT

THE NEXT DAY WAS **GREAT**. DAD TOOK US TO THE **PARK** AND THE **MUSEUM**.
AND WE RAN AROUND THE OLD NEIGHBORHOOD PLAYING. BUT OF COURSE...

LIONS AND TIGERS AND BEARS OH MY! LIONS AND TIGERS AND BEARS OH MY! LIONS AND TIGERS AND BEARS OH MY! LIONS AND TIGERS AND BEARS OH MY! LIONS AND TIGERS AND BEARS OH MY! LIONS AND TIGERS AND BEARS OH MY! LIONS AND TIGERS AND BEARS OH MY! LIONS AND TIGERS AND BEARS OH MY! LION

AMELIA...

?

I CALLED US A CAB AND BROUGHT OUT YOUR BAGS.

WE REALLY NEED TO BE GETTING BACK.

;OH!;

Oh...

TIME TO SAY GOODBYE. OKAY?

OKAY.

OKAY.

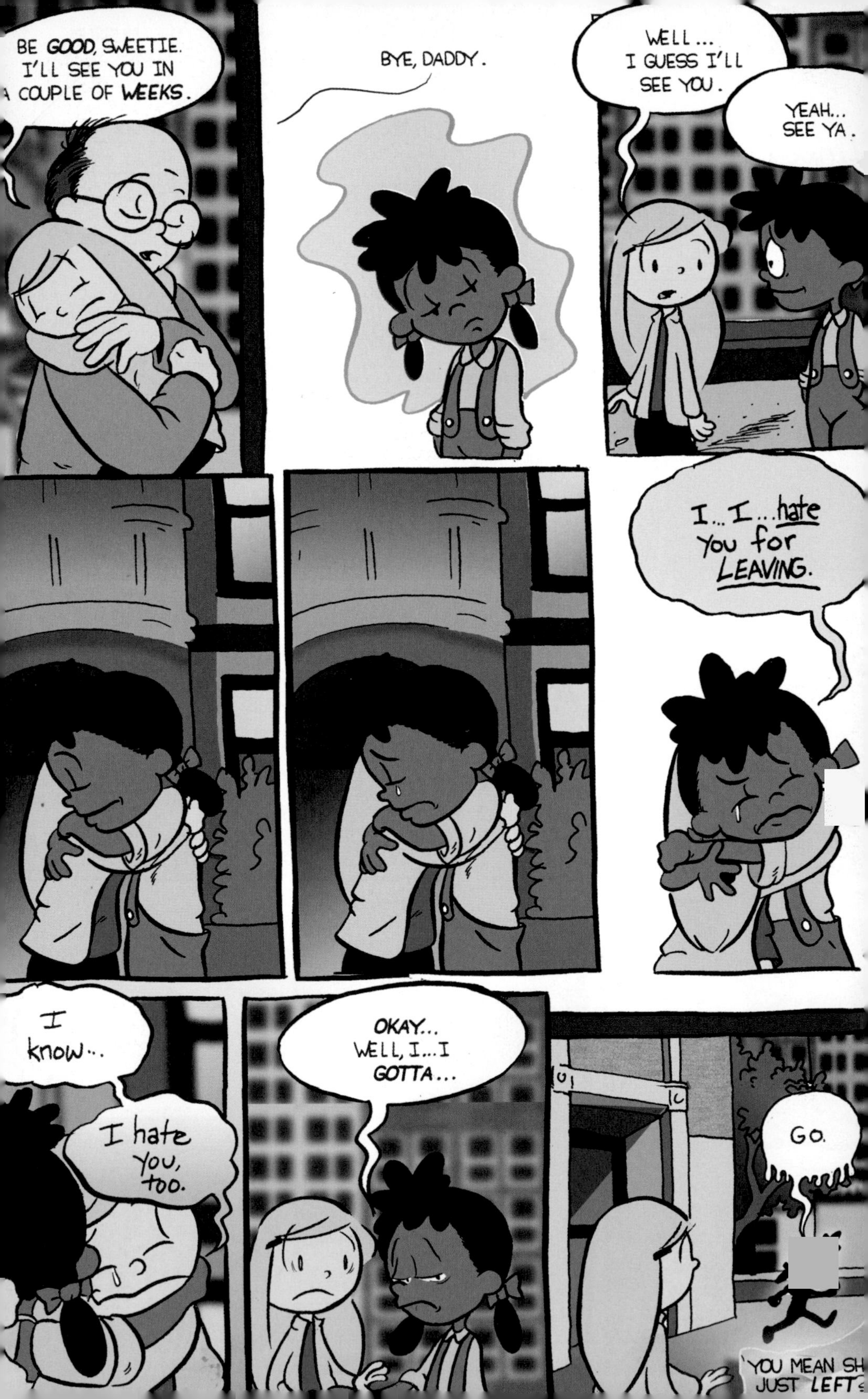

BE GOOD, SWEETIE. I'LL SEE YOU IN A COUPLE OF WEEKS.
BYE, DADDY.
WELL... I GUESS I'LL SEE YOU.
YEAH... SEE YA.
I... I... hate you for LEAVING.
I know...
I hate you, too.
OKAY... WELL, I...I GOTTA...
GO.
YOU MEAN SH JUST LEFT

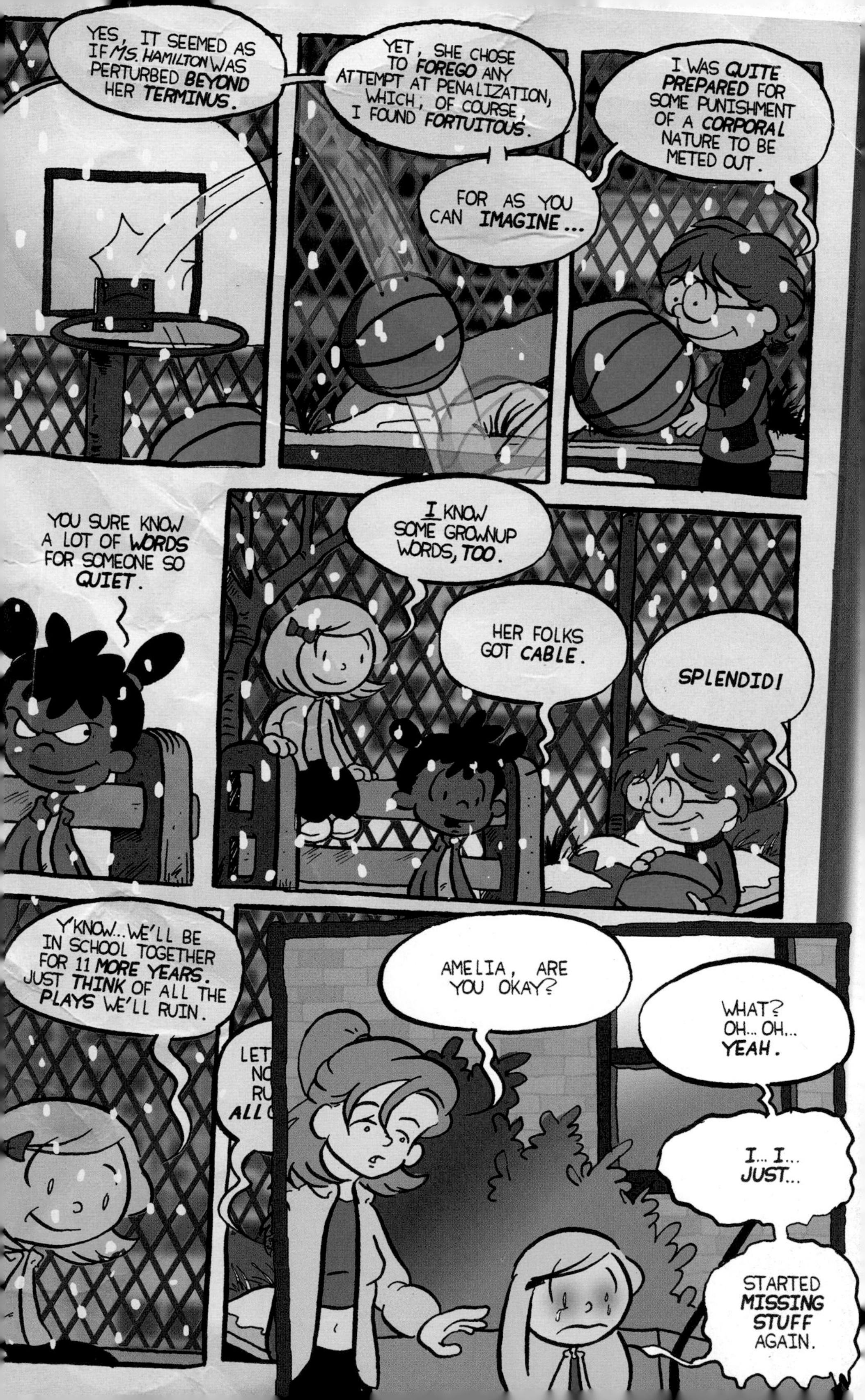
YES, IT SEEMED AS IF MS. HAMILTON WAS PERTURBED BEYOND HER TERMINUS.
YET, SHE CHOSE TO FOREGO ANY ATTEMPT AT PENALIZATION, WHICH, OF COURSE, I FOUND FORTUITOUS.
FOR AS YOU CAN IMAGINE...
I WAS QUITE PREPARED FOR SOME PUNISHMENT OF A CORPORAL NATURE TO BE METED OUT.
YOU SURE KNOW A LOT OF WORDS FOR SOMEONE SO QUIET.
I KNOW SOME GROWNUP WORDS, TOO.
HER FOLKS GOT CABLE.
SPLENDID!
Y'KNOW... WE'LL BE IN SCHOOL TOGETHER FOR 11 MORE YEARS. JUST THINK OF ALL THE PLAYS WE'LL RUIN.
AMELIA, ARE YOU OKAY?
WHAT? OH... OH... YEAH.
I... I... JUST...
STARTED MISSING STUFF AGAIN.

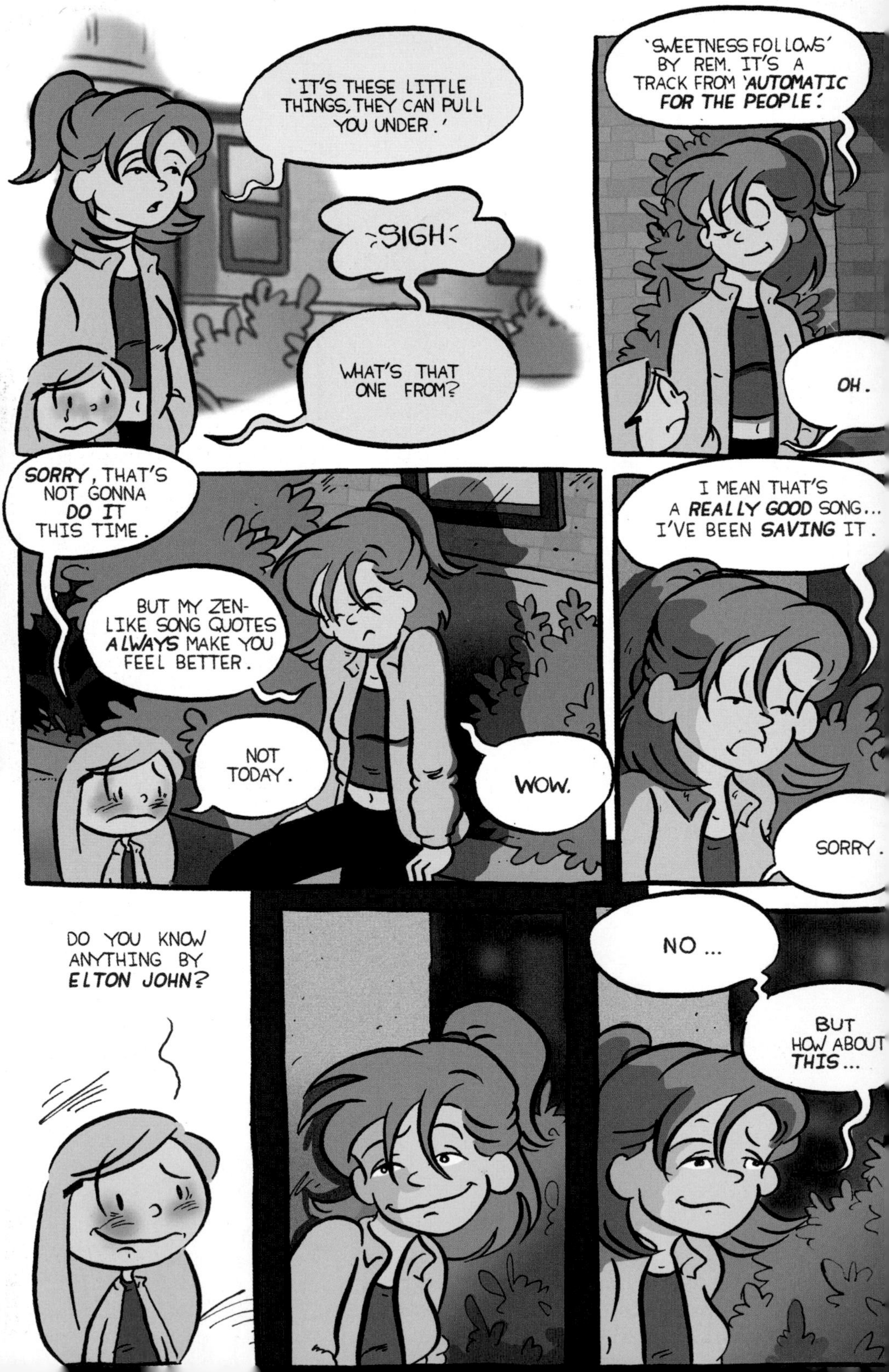
'IT'S THESE LITTLE THINGS, THEY CAN PULL YOU UNDER.'
SIGH
WHAT'S THAT ONE FROM?
'SWEETNESS FOLLOWS' BY REM. IT'S A TRACK FROM '**AUTOMATIC FOR THE PEOPLE**.'
OH.
SORRY, THAT'S NOT GONNA **DO IT** THIS TIME.
BUT MY ZEN-LIKE SONG QUOTES **ALWAYS** MAKE YOU FEEL BETTER.
NOT TODAY.
WOW.
I MEAN THAT'S A **REALLY GOOD** SONG... I'VE BEEN **SAVING** IT.
SORRY.
DO YOU KNOW ANYTHING BY **ELTON JOHN**?
NO...
BUT HOW ABOUT **THIS**...

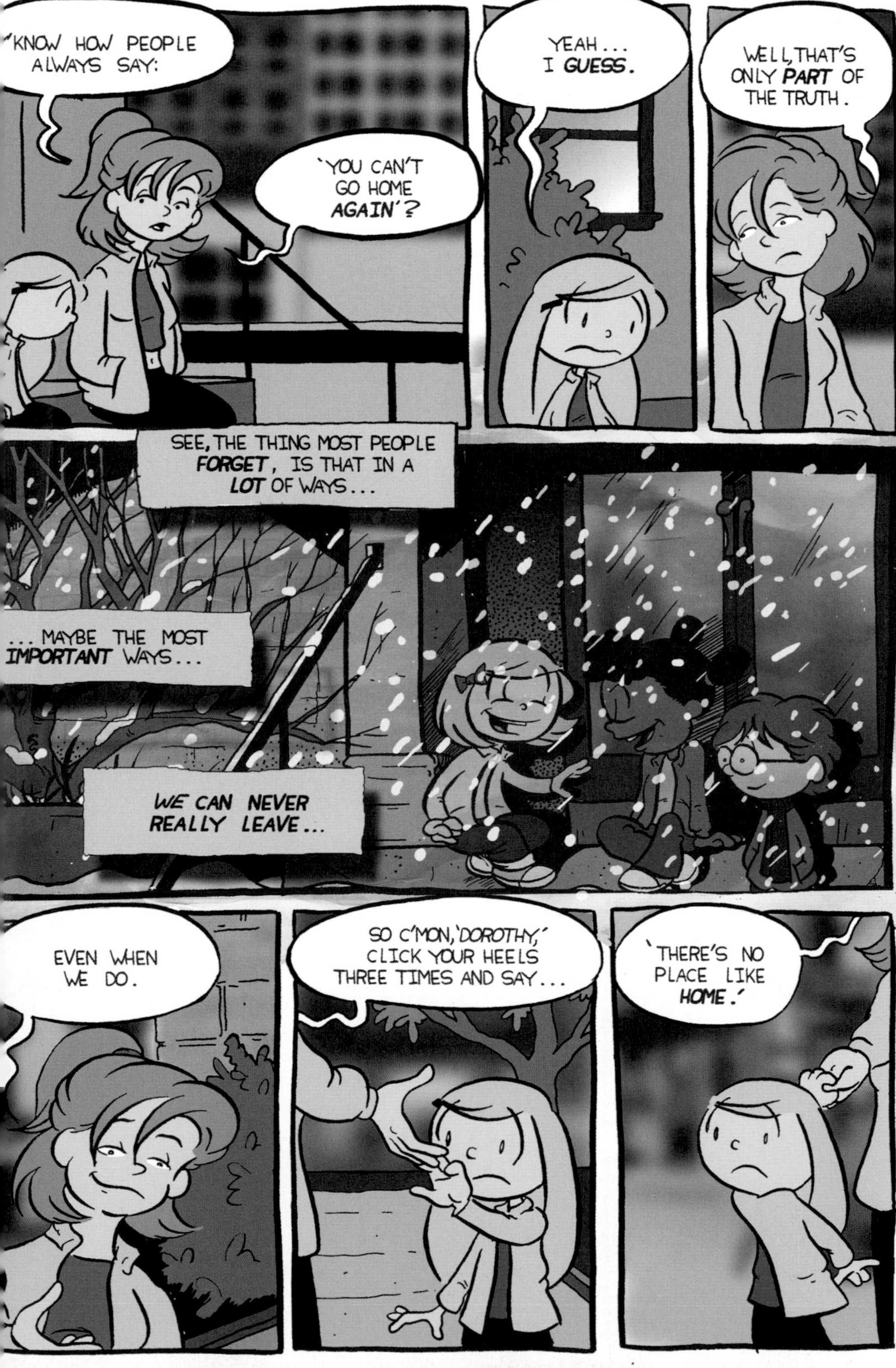
'KNOW HOW PEOPLE ALWAYS SAY:
'YOU CAN'T GO HOME AGAIN'?
YEAH... I GUESS.
WELL, THAT'S ONLY PART OF THE TRUTH.
SEE, THE THING MOST PEOPLE FORGET, IS THAT IN A LOT OF WAYS...
...MAYBE THE MOST IMPORTANT WAYS...
WE CAN NEVER REALLY LEAVE...
EVEN WHEN WE DO.
SO C'MON, 'DOROTHY,' CLICK YOUR HEELS THREE TIMES AND SAY...
'THERE'S NO PLACE LIKE HOME.'

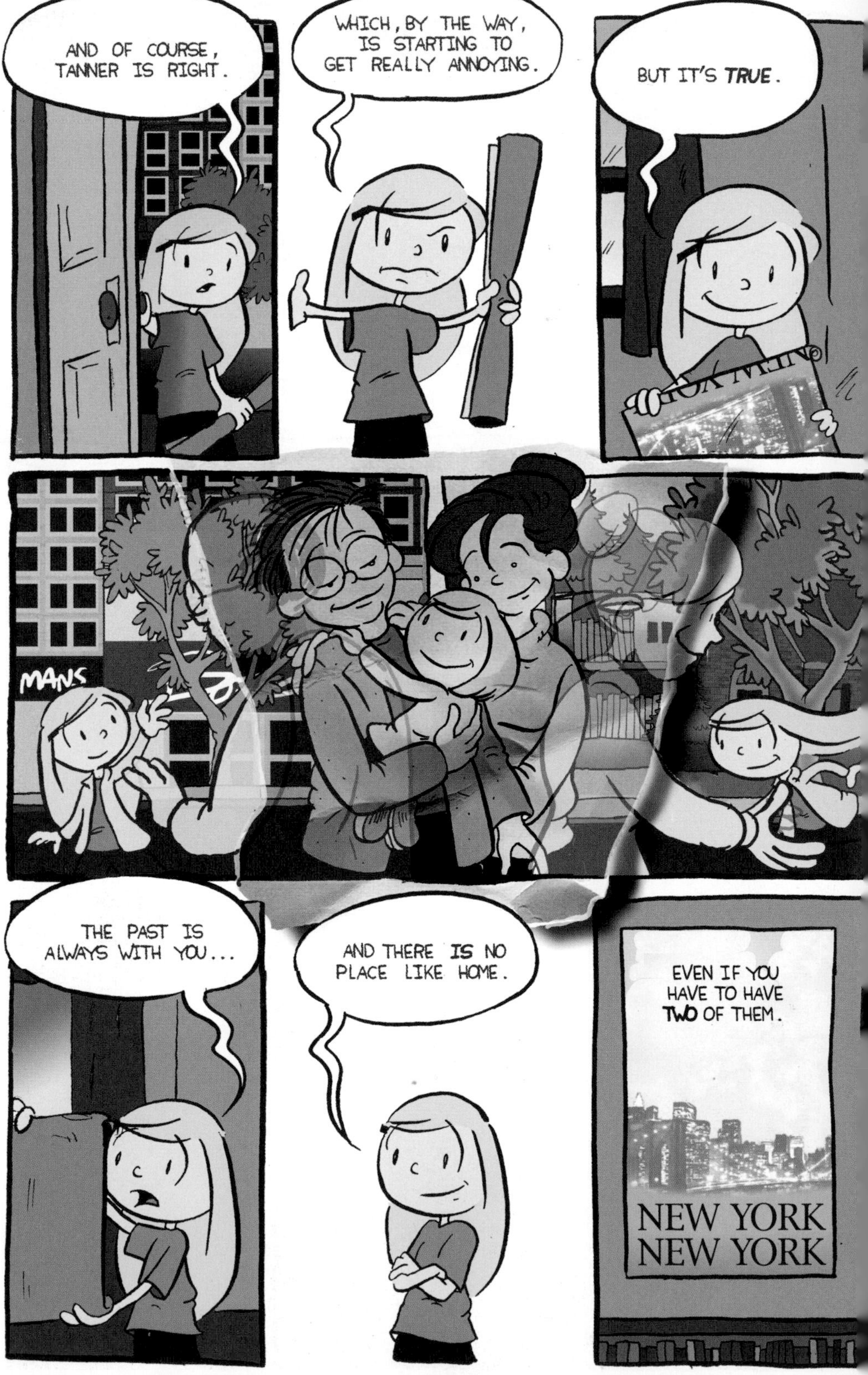
AND OF COURSE, TANNER IS RIGHT.
WHICH, BY THE WAY, IS STARTING TO GET REALLY ANNOYING.
BUT IT'S TRUE.
MANS
THE PAST IS ALWAYS WITH YOU...
AND THERE IS NO PLACE LIKE HOME.
EVEN IF YOU HAVE TO HAVE TWO OF THEM.
NEW YORK NEW YORK

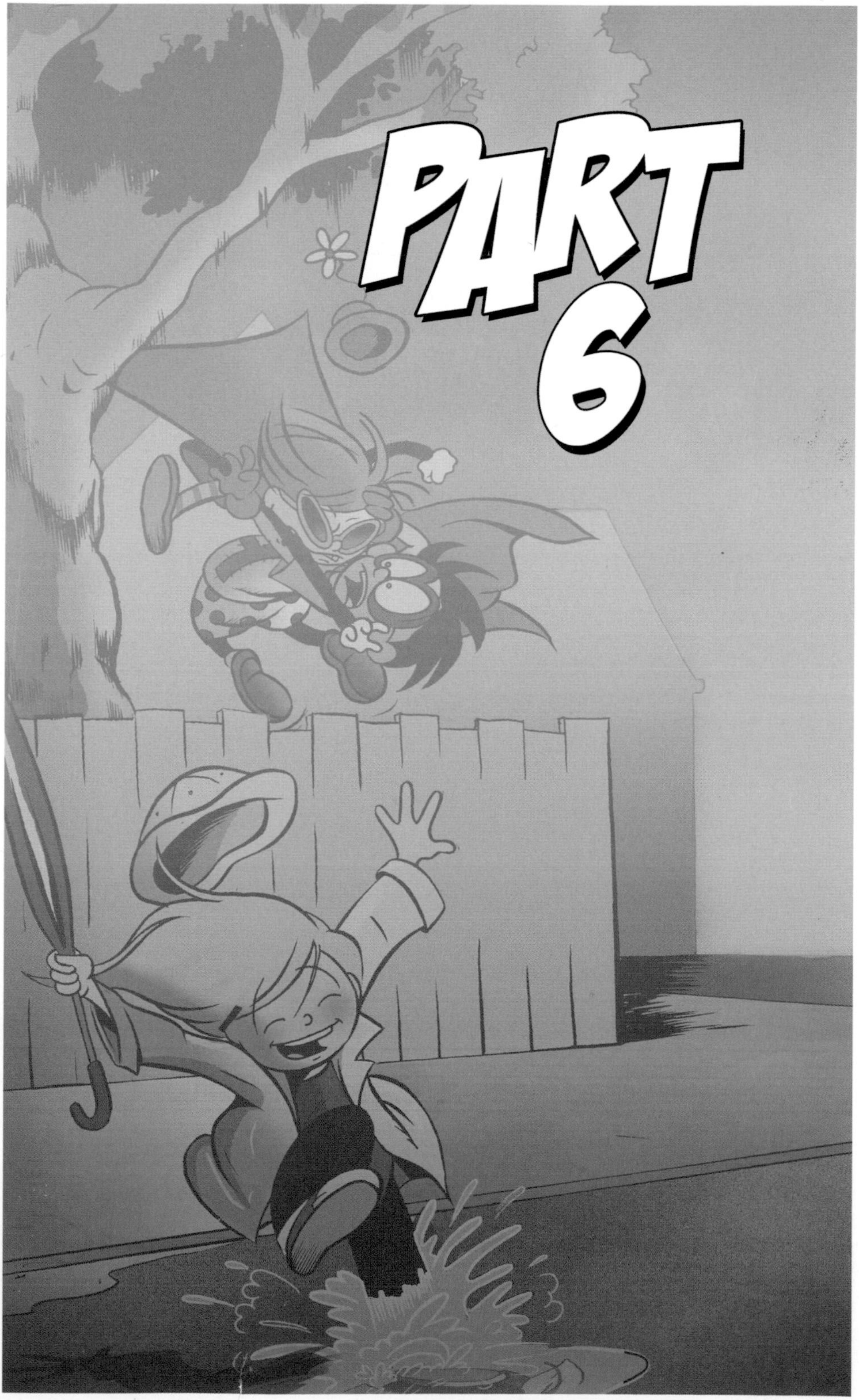
PART
6

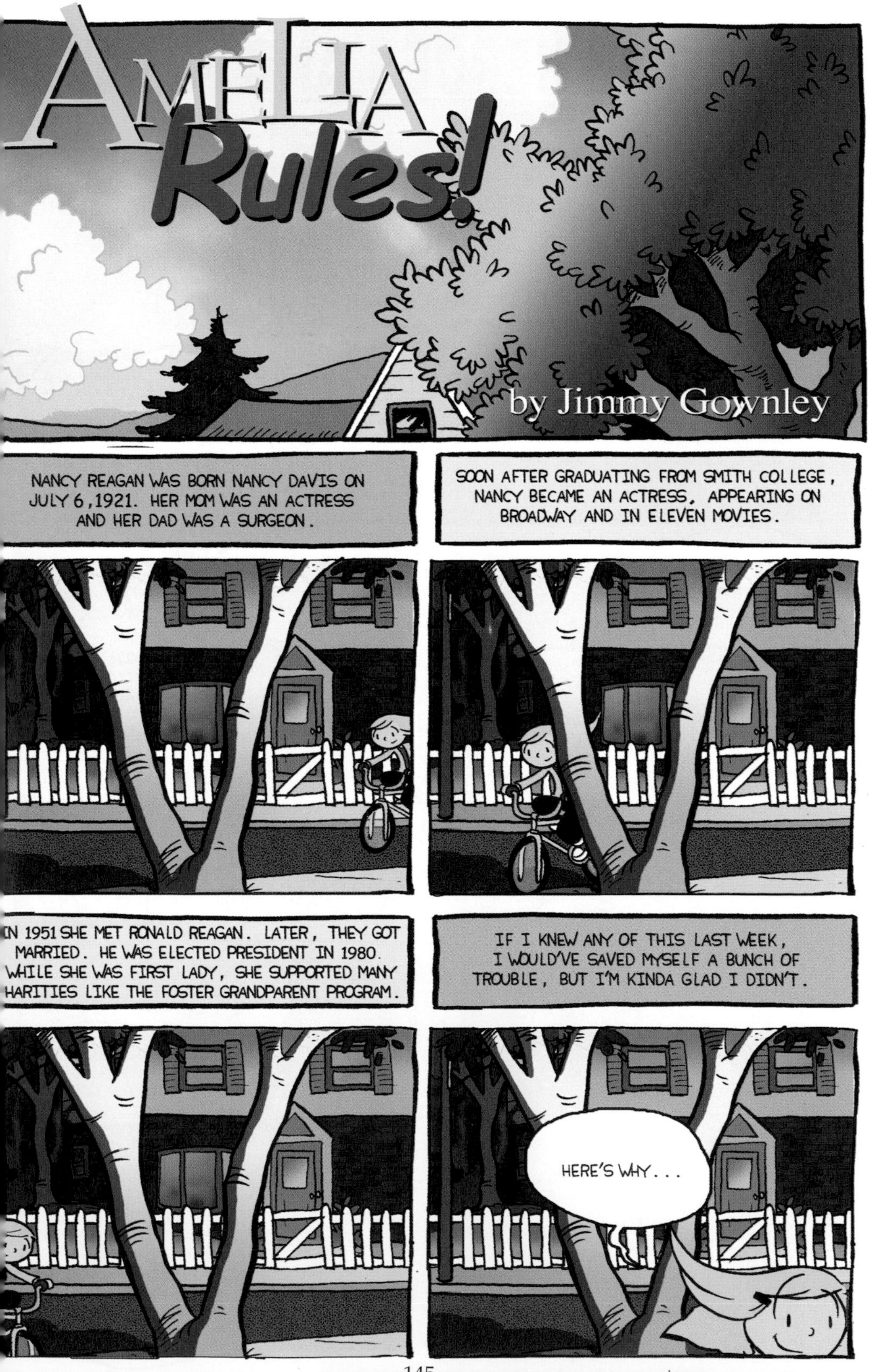
Amelia Rules!
by Jimmy Gownley
NANCY REAGAN WAS BORN NANCY DAVIS ON JULY 6, 1921. HER MOM WAS AN ACTRESS AND HER DAD WAS A SURGEON.
SOON AFTER GRADUATING FROM SMITH COLLEGE, NANCY BECAME AN ACTRESS, APPEARING ON BROADWAY AND IN ELEVEN MOVIES.
IN 1951 SHE MET RONALD REAGAN. LATER, THEY GOT MARRIED. HE WAS ELECTED PRESIDENT IN 1980. WHILE SHE WAS FIRST LADY, SHE SUPPORTED MANY CHARITIES LIKE THE FOSTER GRANDPARENT PROGRAM.
IF I KNEW ANY OF THIS LAST WEEK, I WOULD'VE SAVED MYSELF A BUNCH OF TROUBLE, BUT I'M KINDA GLAD I DIDN'T.
HERE'S WHY...

"FOR THE HEROES AND VILLAINS"

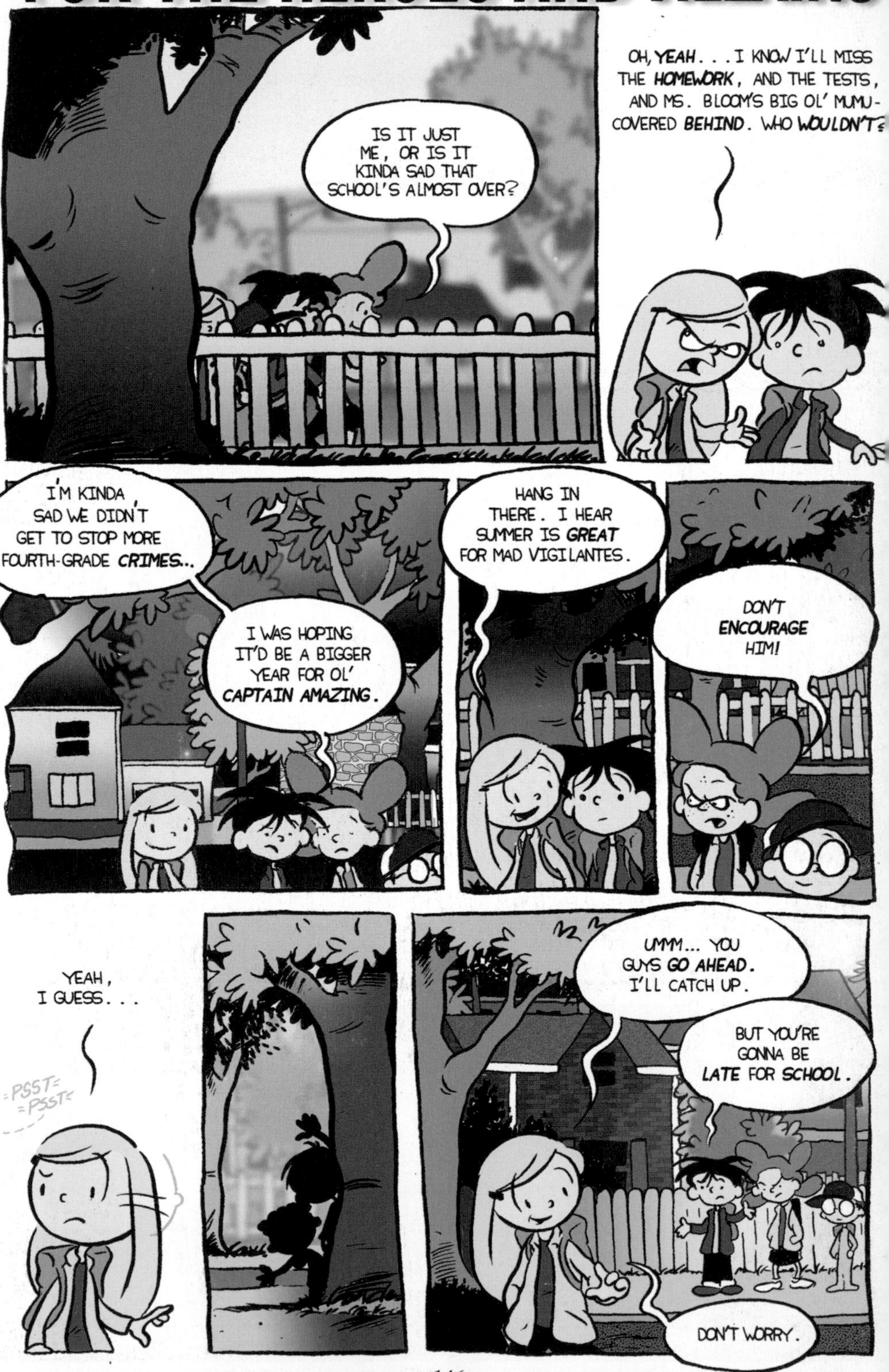
IS IT JUST ME, OR IS IT KINDA SAD THAT SCHOOL'S ALMOST OVER?
OH, YEAH. . . I KNOW I'LL MISS THE HOMEWORK, AND THE TESTS, AND MS. BLOOM'S BIG OL' MUMU-COVERED BEHIND. WHO WOULDN'T?
I'M KINDA SAD WE DIDN'T GET TO STOP MORE FOURTH-GRADE CRIMES...
I WAS HOPING IT'D BE A BIGGER YEAR FOR OL' CAPTAIN AMAZING.
HANG IN THERE. I HEAR SUMMER IS GREAT FOR MAD VIGILANTES.
DON'T ENCOURAGE HIM!
YEAH, I GUESS. . .
=PSST=
=PSST=
UMM... YOU GUYS GO AHEAD. I'LL CATCH UP.
BUT YOU'RE GONNA BE LATE FOR SCHOOL.
DON'T WORRY.

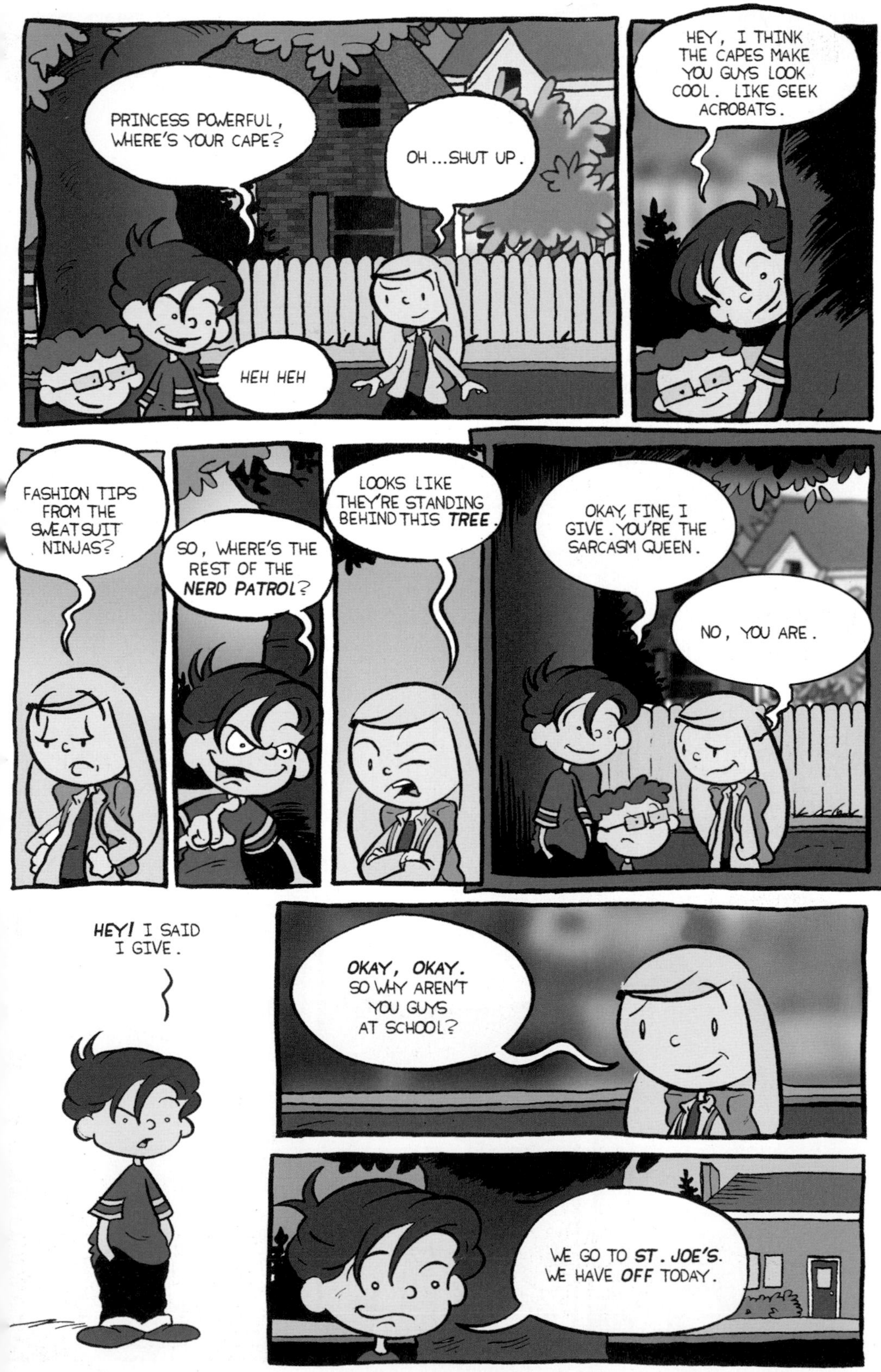
PRINCESS POWERFUL, WHERE'S YOUR CAPE?
HEH HEH
OH ... SHUT UP.
HEY, I THINK THE CAPES MAKE YOU GUYS LOOK COOL. LIKE GEEK ACROBATS.
FASHION TIPS FROM THE SWEATSUIT NINJAS?
SO, WHERE'S THE REST OF THE NERD PATROL?
LOOKS LIKE THEY'RE STANDING BEHIND THIS TREE.
OKAY, FINE, I GIVE. YOU'RE THE SARCASM QUEEN.
NO, YOU ARE.
HEY! I SAID I GIVE.
OKAY, OKAY. SO WHY AREN'T YOU GUYS AT SCHOOL?
WE GO TO ST. JOE'S. WE HAVE OFF TODAY.

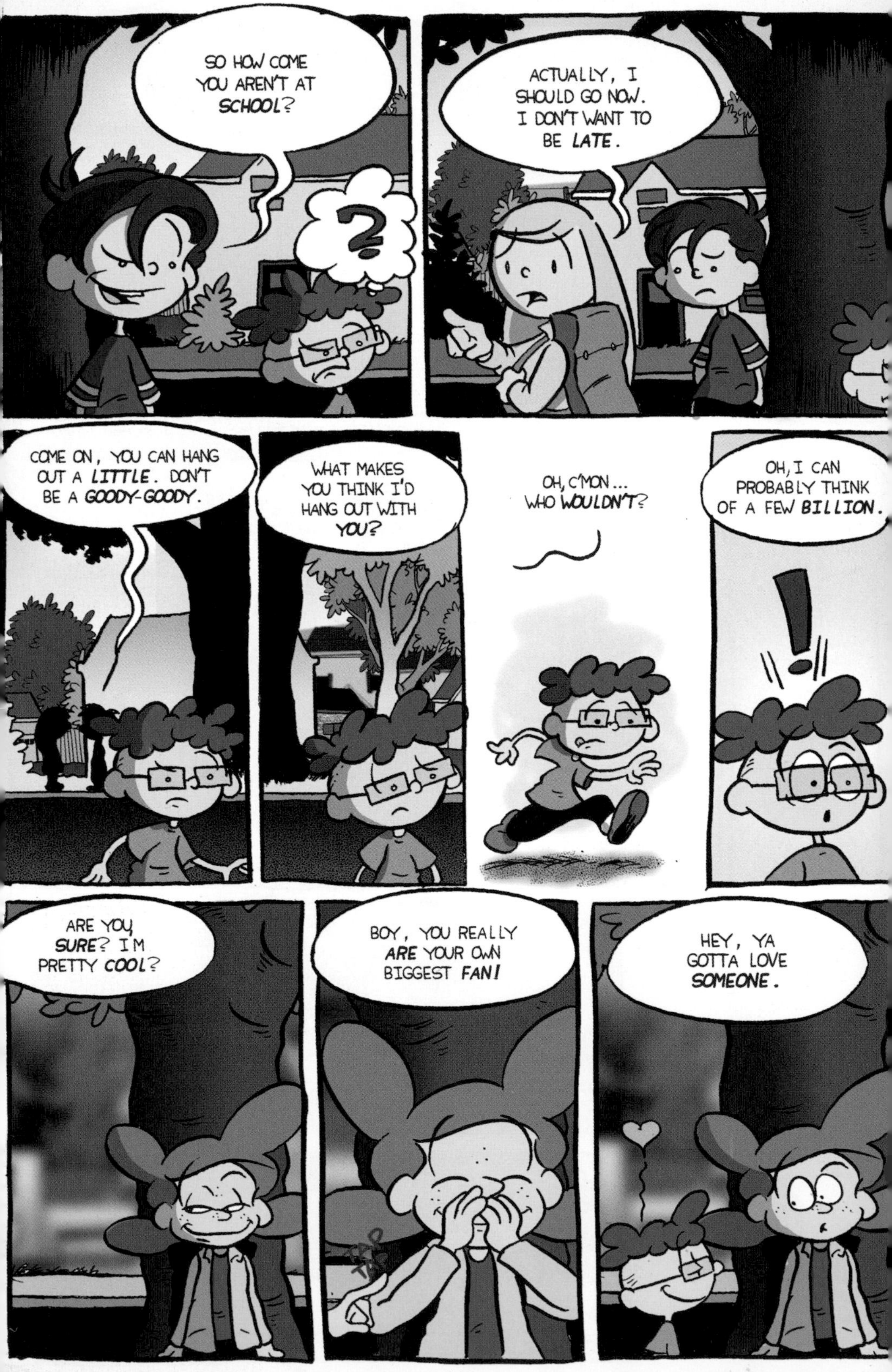
SO HOW COME YOU AREN'T AT SCHOOL?
?
ACTUALLY, I SHOULD GO NOW. I DON'T WANT TO BE LATE.
COME ON, YOU CAN HANG OUT A LITTLE. DON'T BE A GOODY-GOODY.
WHAT MAKES YOU THINK I'D HANG OUT WITH YOU?
OH, C'MON... WHO WOULDN'T?
OH, I CAN PROBABLY THINK OF A FEW BILLION.
!
ARE YOU SURE? I'M PRETTY COOL?
BOY, YOU REALLY ARE YOUR OWN BIGGEST FAN!
HEY, YA GOTTA LOVE SOMEONE.

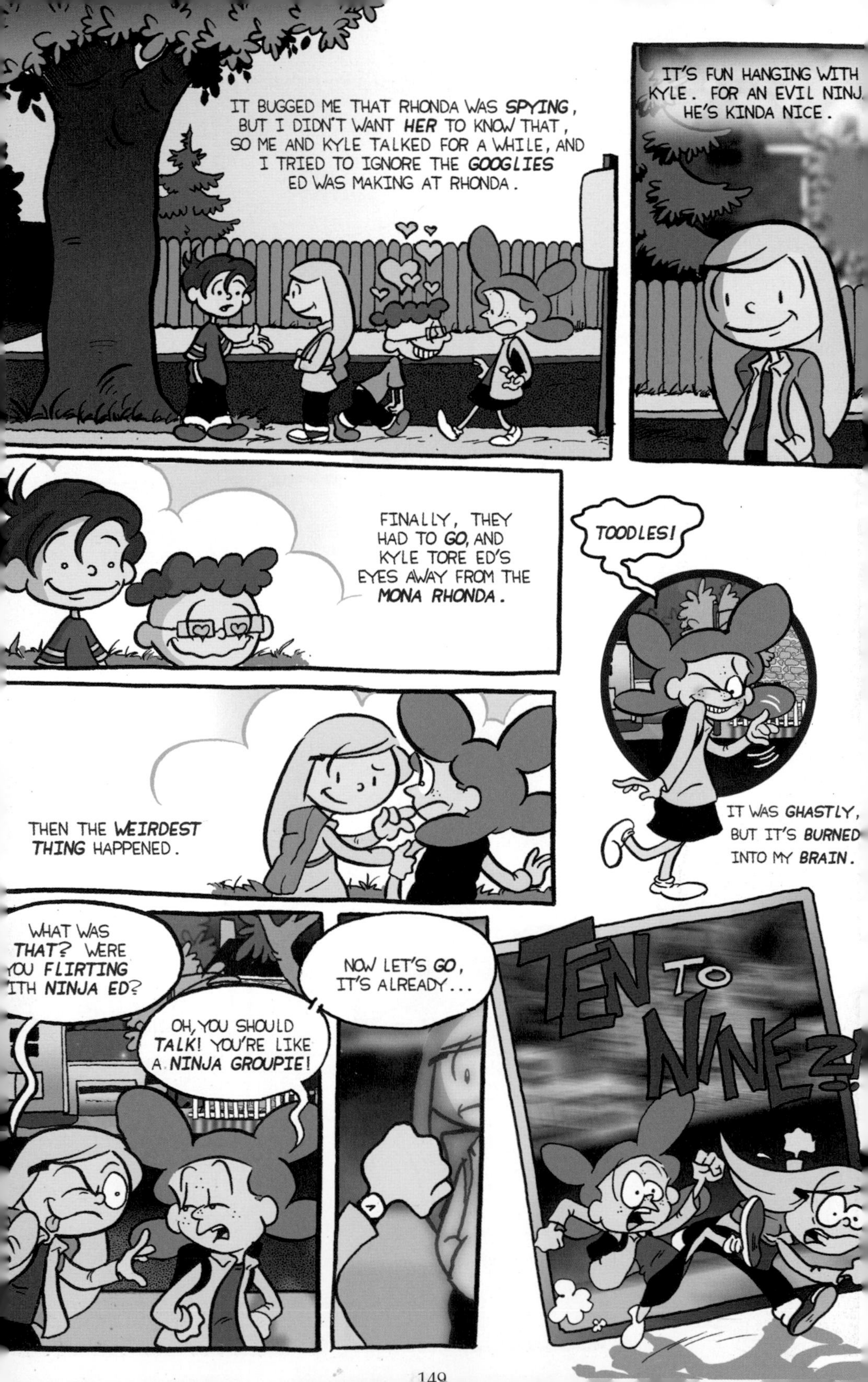
IT BUGGED ME THAT RHONDA WAS SPYING, BUT I DIDN'T WANT HER TO KNOW THAT, SO ME AND KYLE TALKED FOR A WHILE, AND I TRIED TO IGNORE THE GOOGLIES ED WAS MAKING AT RHONDA.
IT'S FUN HANGING WITH KYLE. FOR AN EVIL NINJ HE'S KINDA NICE.
FINALLY, THEY HAD TO GO, AND KYLE TORE ED'S EYES AWAY FROM THE MONA RHONDA.
TOODLES!
THEN THE WEIRDEST THING HAPPENED.
IT WAS GHASTLY, BUT IT'S BURNED INTO MY BRAIN.
WHAT WAS THAT? WERE YOU FLIRTING ITH NINJA ED?
OH, YOU SHOULD TALK! YOU'RE LIKE A NINJA GROUPIE!
NOW LET'S GO, IT'S ALREADY...
TEN TO NINE Z!

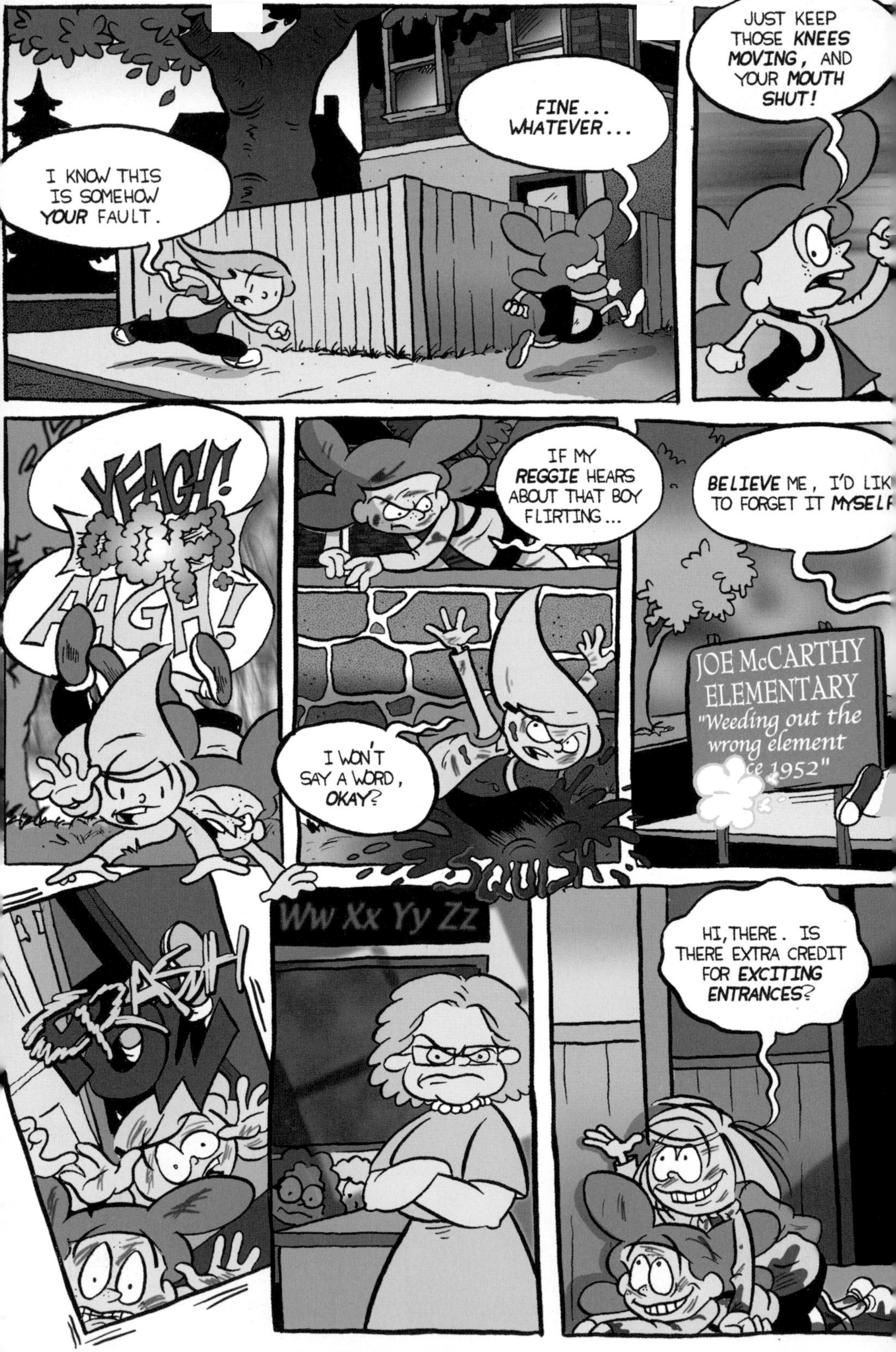
I KNOW THIS IS SOMEHOW YOUR FAULT.
FINE... WHATEVER...
JUST KEEP THOSE KNEES MOVING, AND YOUR MOUTH SHUT!
YEAGH!
OOF
AAGH!
IF MY REGGIE HEARS ABOUT THAT BOY FLIRTING...
I WON'T SAY A WORD, OKAY?
BELIEVE ME, I'D LIK TO FORGET IT MYSELF
JOE McCARTHY ELEMENTARY
"Weeding out the wrong element
ce 1952"
Ww Xx Yy Zz
HI, THERE. IS THERE EXTRA CREDIT FOR EXCITING ENTRANCES?

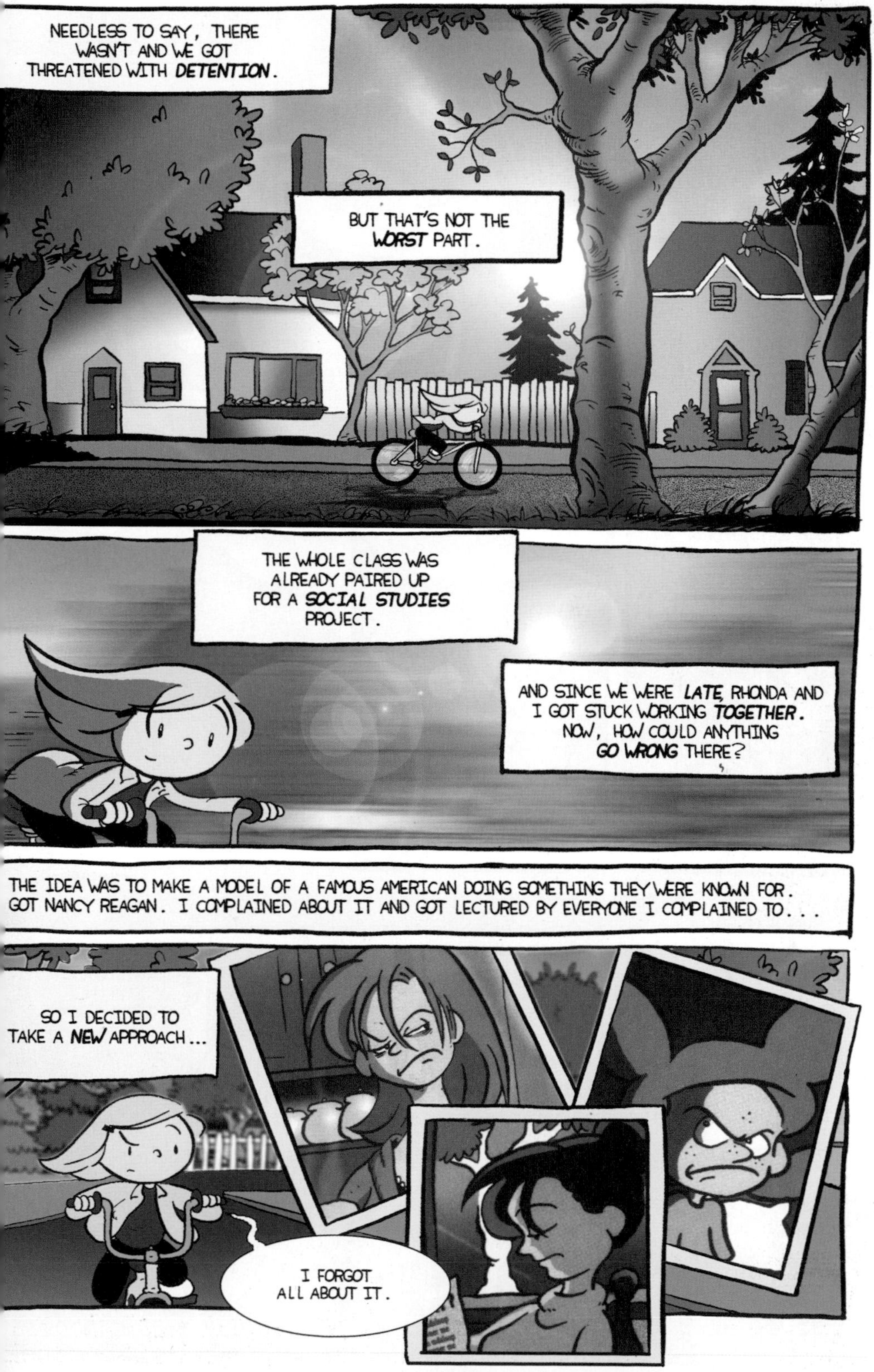
NEEDLESS TO SAY, THERE WASN'T AND WE GOT THREATENED WITH **DETENTION**.
BUT THAT'S NOT THE **WORST** PART.
THE WHOLE CLASS WAS ALREADY PAIRED UP FOR A **SOCIAL STUDIES** PROJECT.
AND SINCE WE WERE **LATE**, RHONDA AND I GOT STUCK WORKING **TOGETHER**. NOW, HOW COULD ANYTHING **GO WRONG** THERE?
THE IDEA WAS TO MAKE A MODEL OF A FAMOUS AMERICAN DOING SOMETHING THEY WERE KNOWN FOR. GOT NANCY REAGAN. I COMPLAINED ABOUT IT AND GOT LECTURED BY EVERYONE I COMPLAINED TO . . .
SO I DECIDED TO TAKE A **NEW** APPROACH ...
I FORGOT ALL ABOUT IT.

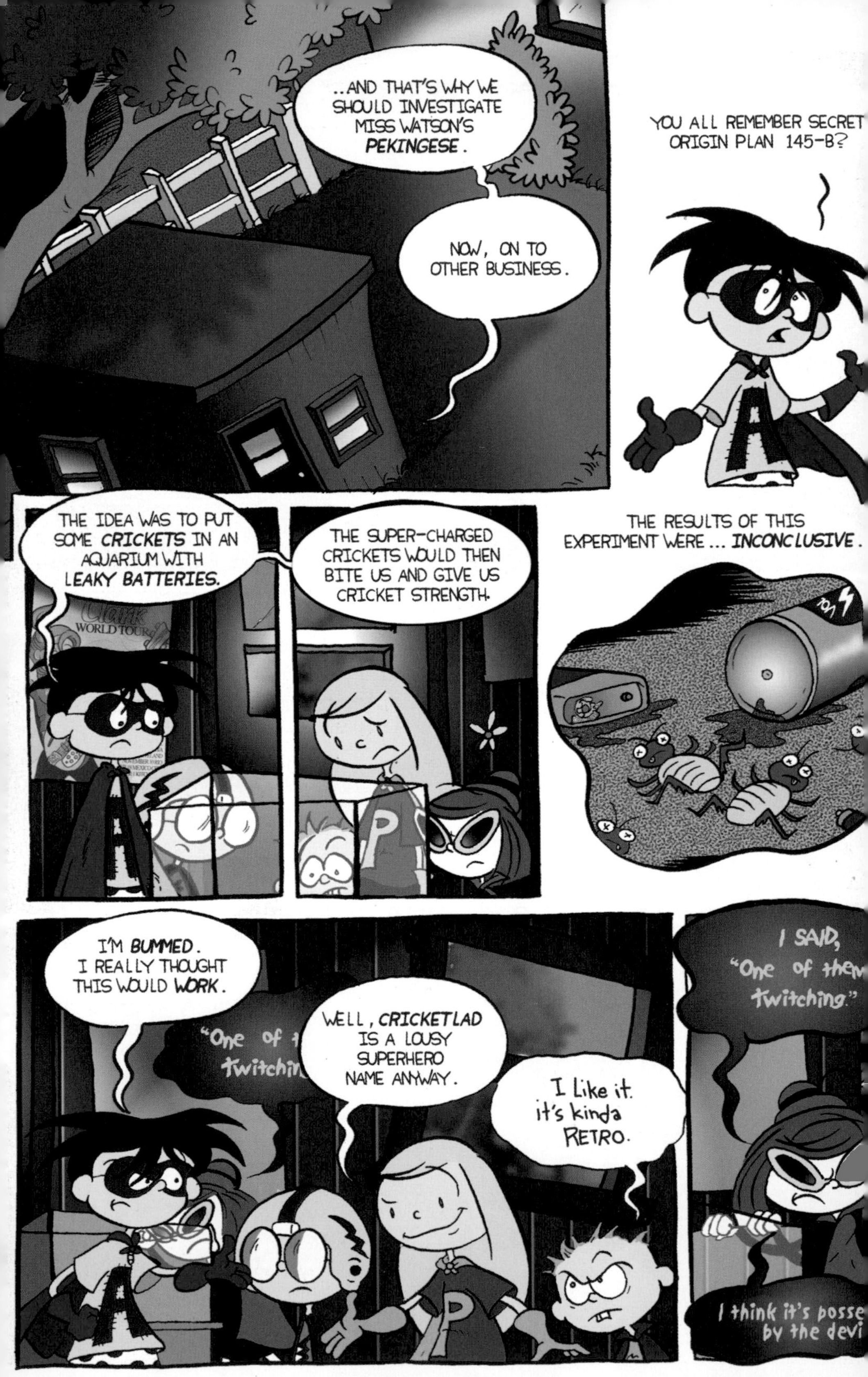

...AND THAT'S WHY WE SHOULD INVESTIGATE MISS WATSON'S PEKINGESE.
NOW, ON TO OTHER BUSINESS.
YOU ALL REMEMBER SECRET ORIGIN PLAN 145-B?
THE IDEA WAS TO PUT SOME CRICKETS IN AN AQUARIUM WITH LEAKY BATTERIES.
WORLD TOUR
THE SUPER-CHARGED CRICKETS WOULD THEN BITE US AND GIVE US CRICKET STRENGTH.
THE RESULTS OF THIS EXPERIMENT WERE... INCONCLUSIVE.
I'M BUMMED. I REALLY THOUGHT THIS WOULD WORK.
"One of t
twitchin
WELL, CRICKETLAD IS A LOUSY SUPERHERO NAME ANYWAY.
I Like it. it's kinda RETRO.
I SAID, "One of them twitching."
I think it's posse by the devi

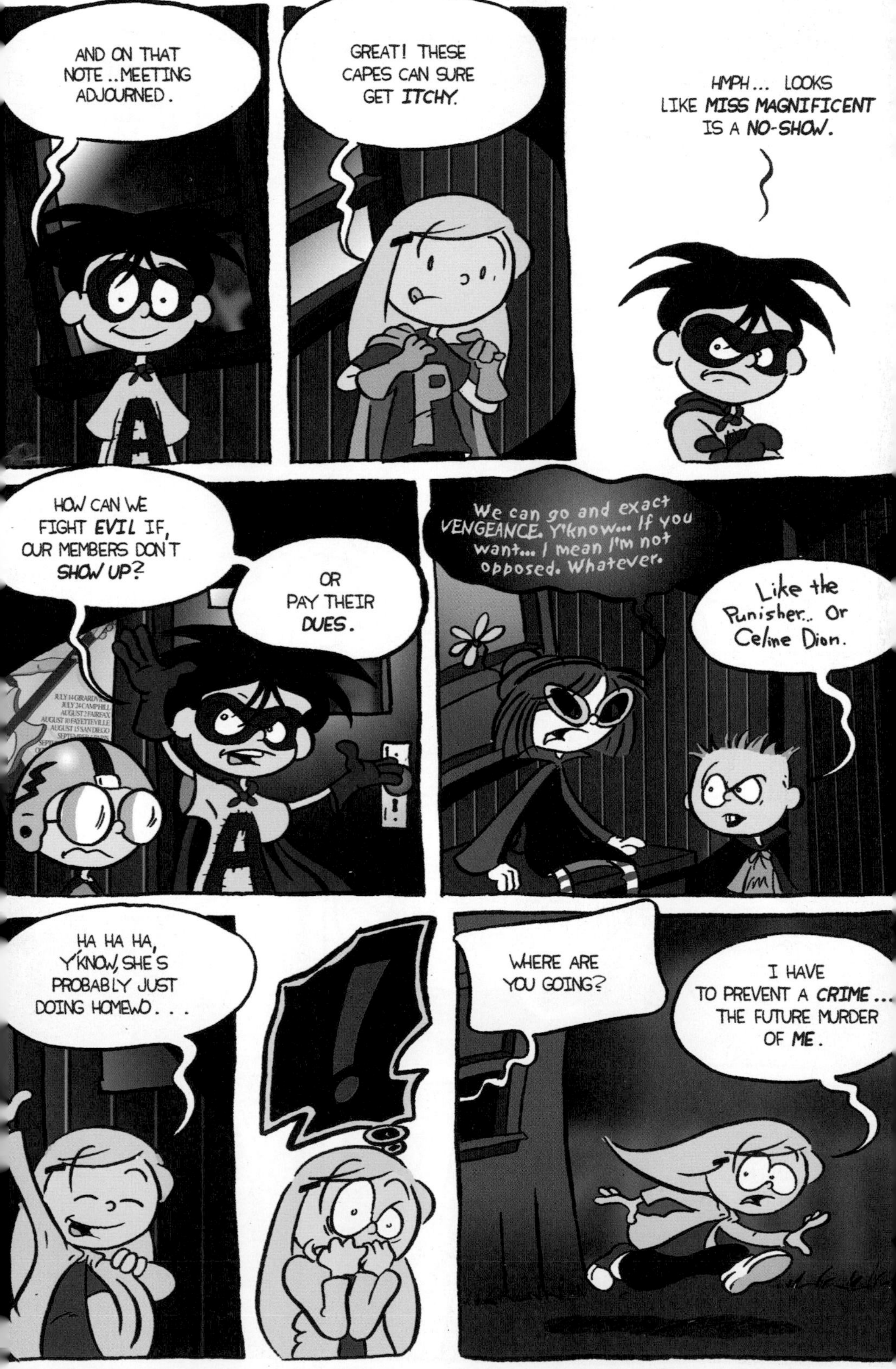
AND ON THAT NOTE ..MEETING ADJOURNED.
GREAT! THESE CAPES CAN SURE GET ITCHY.
HMPH... LOOKS LIKE MISS MAGNIFICENT IS A NO-SHOW.
HOW CAN WE FIGHT EVIL IF, OUR MEMBERS DON'T SHOW UP?
OR PAY THEIR DUES.
We can go and exact VENGEANCE. Y'know... If you want... I mean I'm not opposed. Whatever.
Like the Punisher... Or Celine Dion.
HA HA HA, Y'KNOW, SHE'S PROBABLY JUST DOING HOMEWO . . .
!
WHERE ARE YOU GOING?
I HAVE TO PREVENT A CRIME... THE FUTURE MURDER OF ME.

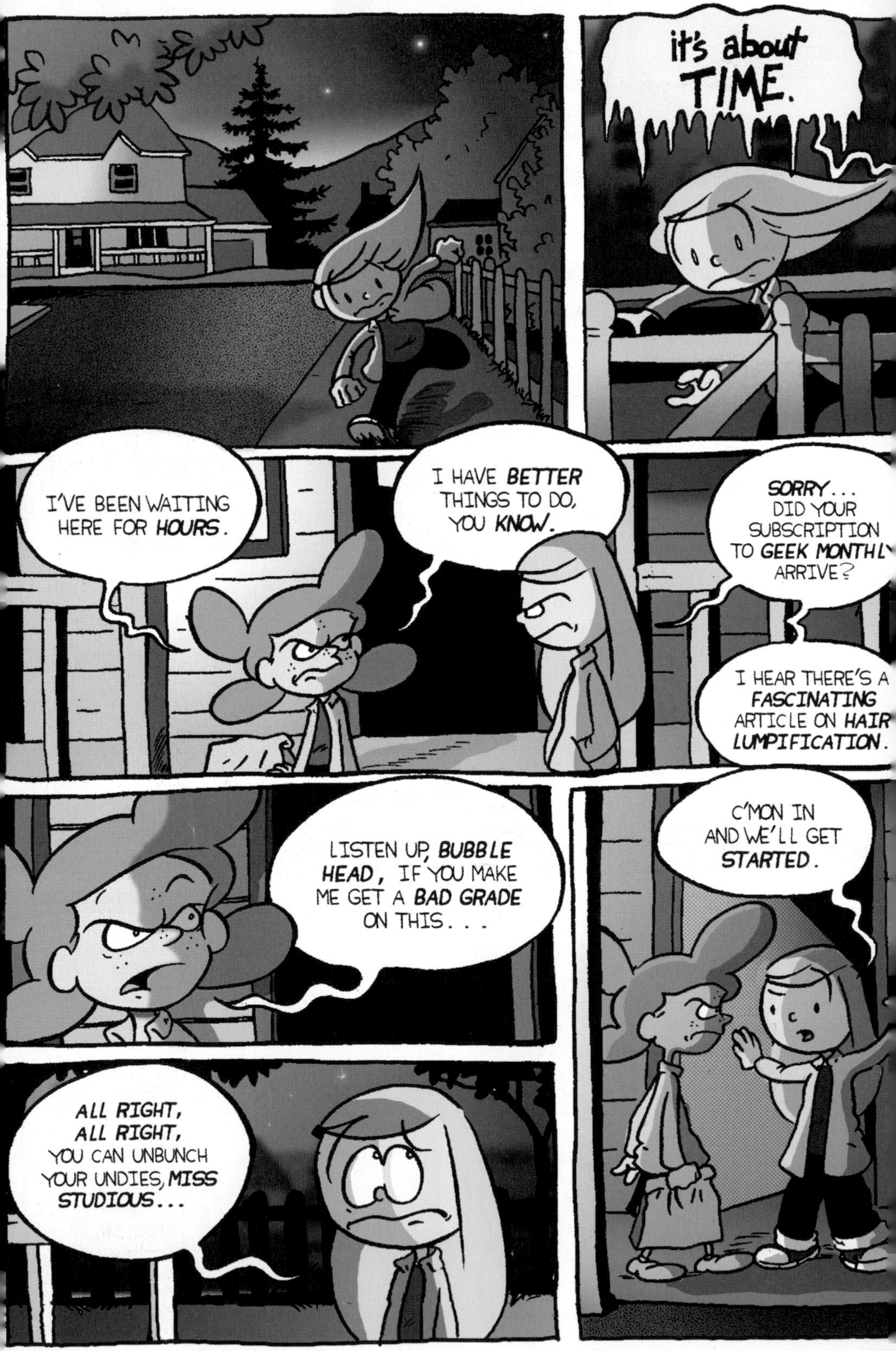
it's about TIME.
I'VE BEEN WAITING HERE FOR **HOURS**.
I HAVE **BETTER** THINGS TO DO, YOU **KNOW**.
SORRY... DID YOUR SUBSCRIPTION TO **GEEK MONTHLY** ARRIVE?
I HEAR THERE'S A **FASCINATING** ARTICLE ON **HAIR LUMPIFICATION**.
LISTEN UP, **BUBBLE HEAD**, IF YOU MAKE ME GET A **BAD GRADE** ON THIS...
C'MON IN AND WE'LL GET **STARTED**.
ALL RIGHT, ALL RIGHT, YOU CAN UNBUNCH YOUR UNDIES, **MISS STUDIOUS**...

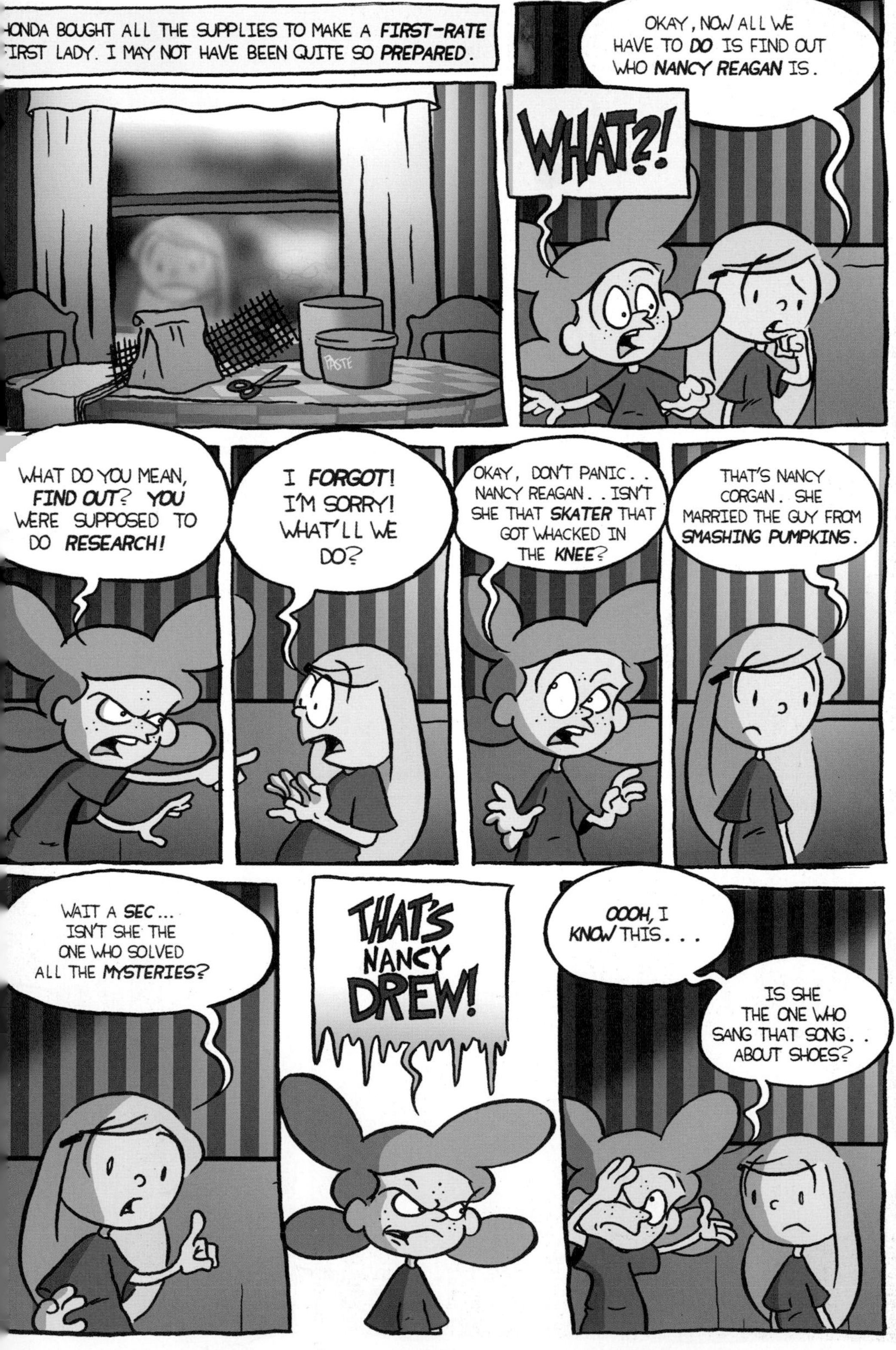

HONDA BOUGHT ALL THE SUPPLIES TO MAKE A FIRST-RATE FIRST LADY. I MAY NOT HAVE BEEN QUITE SO PREPARED.
PASTE
OKAY, NOW ALL WE HAVE TO DO IS FIND OUT WHO NANCY REAGAN IS.
WHAT?!
WHAT DO YOU MEAN, FIND OUT? YOU WERE SUPPOSED TO DO RESEARCH!
I FORGOT! I'M SORRY! WHAT'LL WE DO?
OKAY, DON'T PANIC.. NANCY REAGAN.. ISN'T SHE THAT SKATER THAT GOT WHACKED IN THE KNEE?
THAT'S NANCY CORGAN. SHE MARRIED THE GUY FROM SMASHING PUMPKINS.
WAIT A SEC... ISN'T SHE THE ONE WHO SOLVED ALL THE MYSTERIES?
THAT'S NANCY DREW!
OOOH, I KNOW THIS...
IS SHE THE ONE WHO SANG THAT SONG.. ABOUT SHOES?

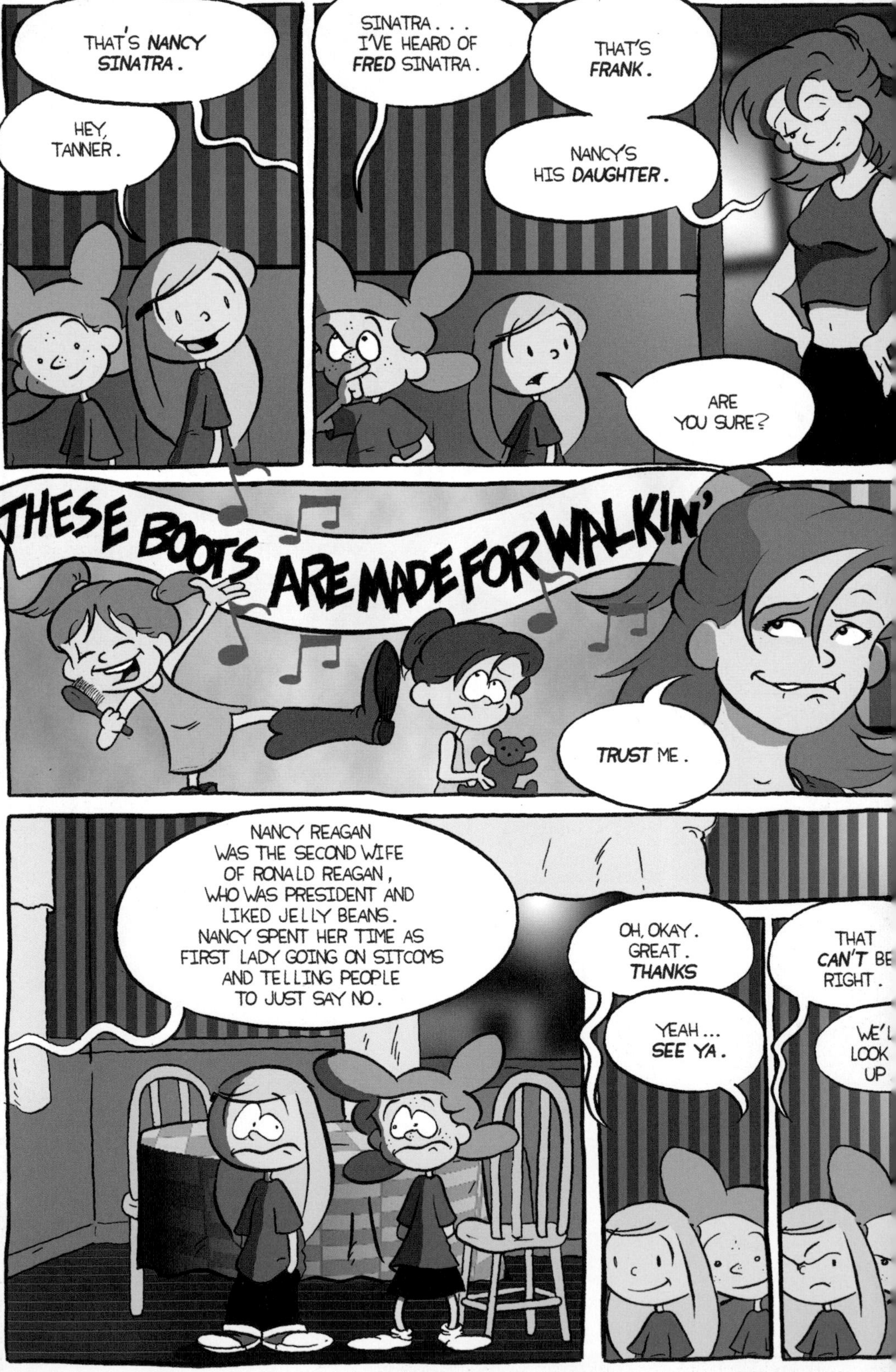
THAT'S NANCY SINATRA.
HEY, TANNER.
SINATRA... I'VE HEARD OF FRED SINATRA.
THAT'S FRANK.
NANCY'S HIS DAUGHTER.
ARE YOU SURE?
THESE BOOTS ARE MADE FOR WALKIN'
TRUST ME.
NANCY REAGAN WAS THE SECOND WIFE OF RONALD REAGAN, WHO WAS PRESIDENT AND LIKED JELLY BEANS. NANCY SPENT HER TIME AS FIRST LADY GOING ON SITCOMS AND TELLING PEOPLE TO JUST SAY NO.
OH, OKAY. GREAT. THANKS
YEAH... SEE YA.
THAT CAN'T BE RIGHT.
WE'L LOOK UP

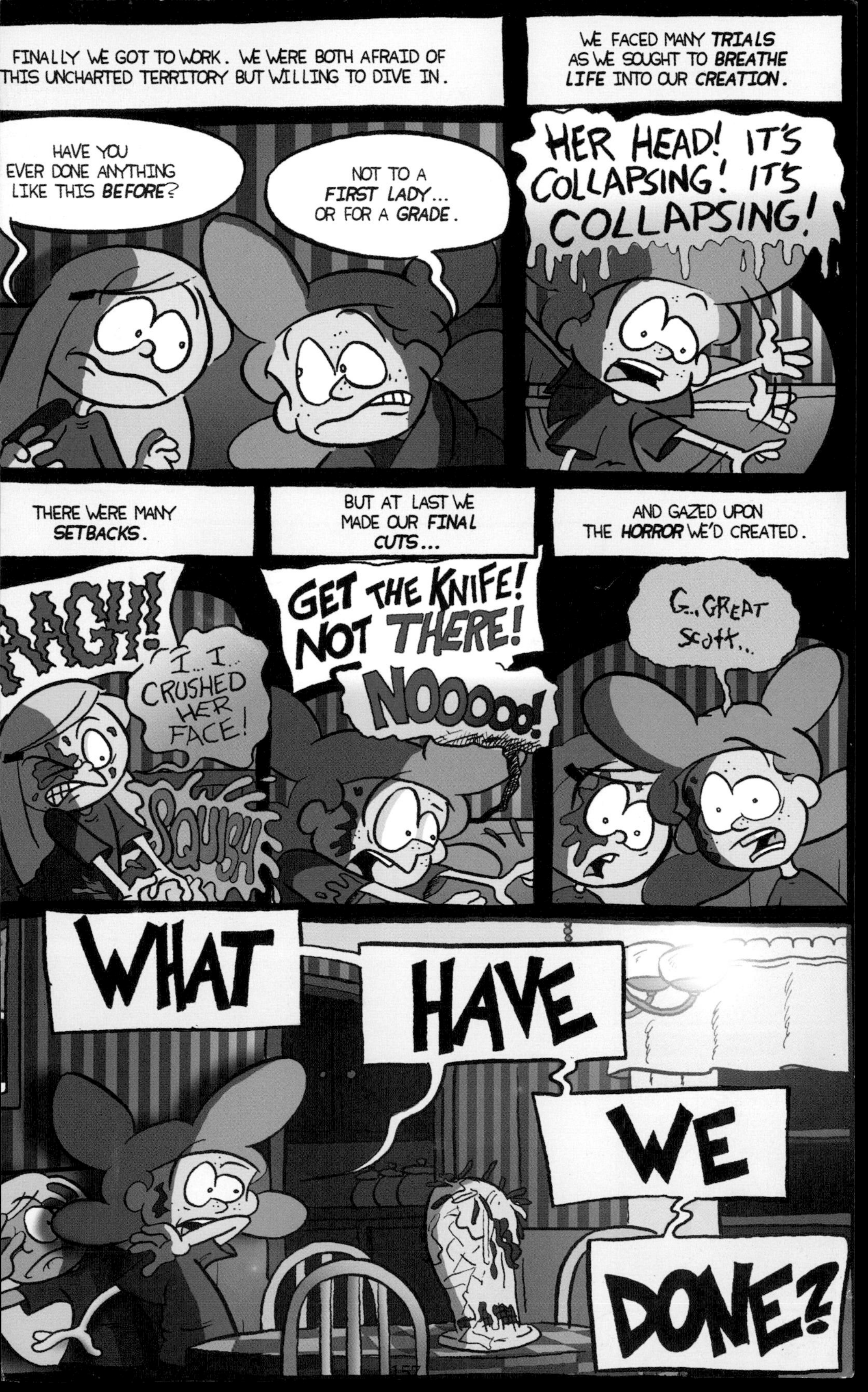
FINALLY WE GOT TO WORK. WE WERE BOTH AFRAID OF THIS UNCHARTED TERRITORY BUT WILLING TO DIVE IN.
HAVE YOU EVER DONE ANYTHING LIKE THIS BEFORE?
NOT TO A FIRST LADY... OR FOR A GRADE.
WE FACED MANY TRIALS AS WE SOUGHT TO BREATHE LIFE INTO OUR CREATION.
HER HEAD! IT'S COLLAPSING! IT'S COLLAPSING!
THERE WERE MANY SETBACKS.
RAGH!
I... I... CRUSHED HER FACE!
SQUISH
BUT AT LAST WE MADE OUR FINAL CUTS...
GET THE KNIFE! NOT THERE!
NOOOOOO!
AND GAZED UPON THE HORROR WE'D CREATED.
G... GREAT SCOTT...
WHAT HAVE WE DONE?

THE NEXT DAY AT SCHOOL, EVERYONE BROUGHT THEIR PROJECTS IN. THEY WERE ALL DISPLAYED IN THE FRONT OF THE CLASS.

THERE WAS AN *ABE LINC* WITH A *CD* THAT RECIT THE *GETTYSBURG ADDR*

4 SCORE AND 7 YEARS AGO

A+   Abe Lincoln

I SHOT THE MAKERS A *LOOK* THAT WAS HALF `I'M IMPRESSED' AND HALF `I'M PLOTTING YOUR DOOM.'

REGGIE AND *PAJAMAMAN* DID *WASHINGTON CROSSING THE DELAWARE* OUT OF ACTION FIGURES. *IT WAS COOL.*

BUT THEY GOT DOCKED *POINTS* FOR HISTORICAL INACCURACIES.

WHICH I'M PRETT SURE WERE *REGGIE'S* FAULT

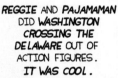

B-   G. Washington and Friends

MARY VIOLET AND EARTHDOG MADE *JACKIE KENNEDY* OUT OF A HONEYDEW.

THEY GOT BONUS POINTS 'CUZ THE HAT WAS A REAL *CHANEL*.

THEN, AT THE END OF THE LINE, SLIGHTLY *APART* FROM THE *OTHERS*...

WAS NANCY.

A   Jackie Kennedy

NO

F-   Nancy Reagan

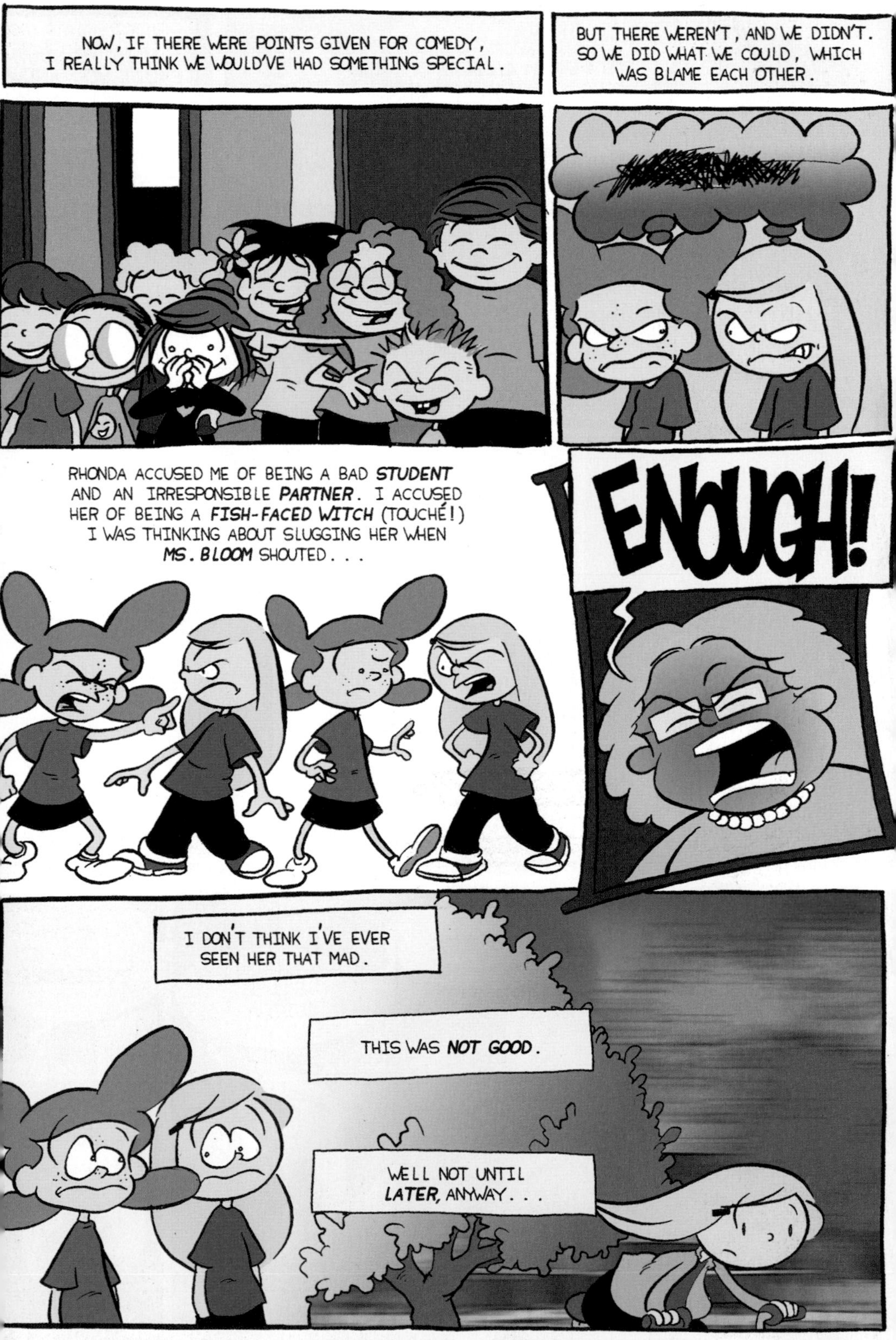
NOW, IF THERE WERE POINTS GIVEN FOR COMEDY, I REALLY THINK WE WOULD'VE HAD SOMETHING SPECIAL.
BUT THERE WEREN'T, AND WE DIDN'T. SO WE DID WHAT WE COULD, WHICH WAS BLAME EACH OTHER.
RHONDA ACCUSED ME OF BEING A BAD STUDENT AND AN IRRESPONSIBLE PARTNER. I ACCUSED HER OF BEING A FISH-FACED WITCH (TOUCHÉ!) I WAS THINKING ABOUT SLUGGING HER WHEN MS. BLOOM SHOUTED . . .
ENOUGH!
I DON'T THINK I'VE EVER SEEN HER THAT MAD.
THIS WAS NOT GOOD.
WELL NOT UNTIL LATER, ANYWAY . . .

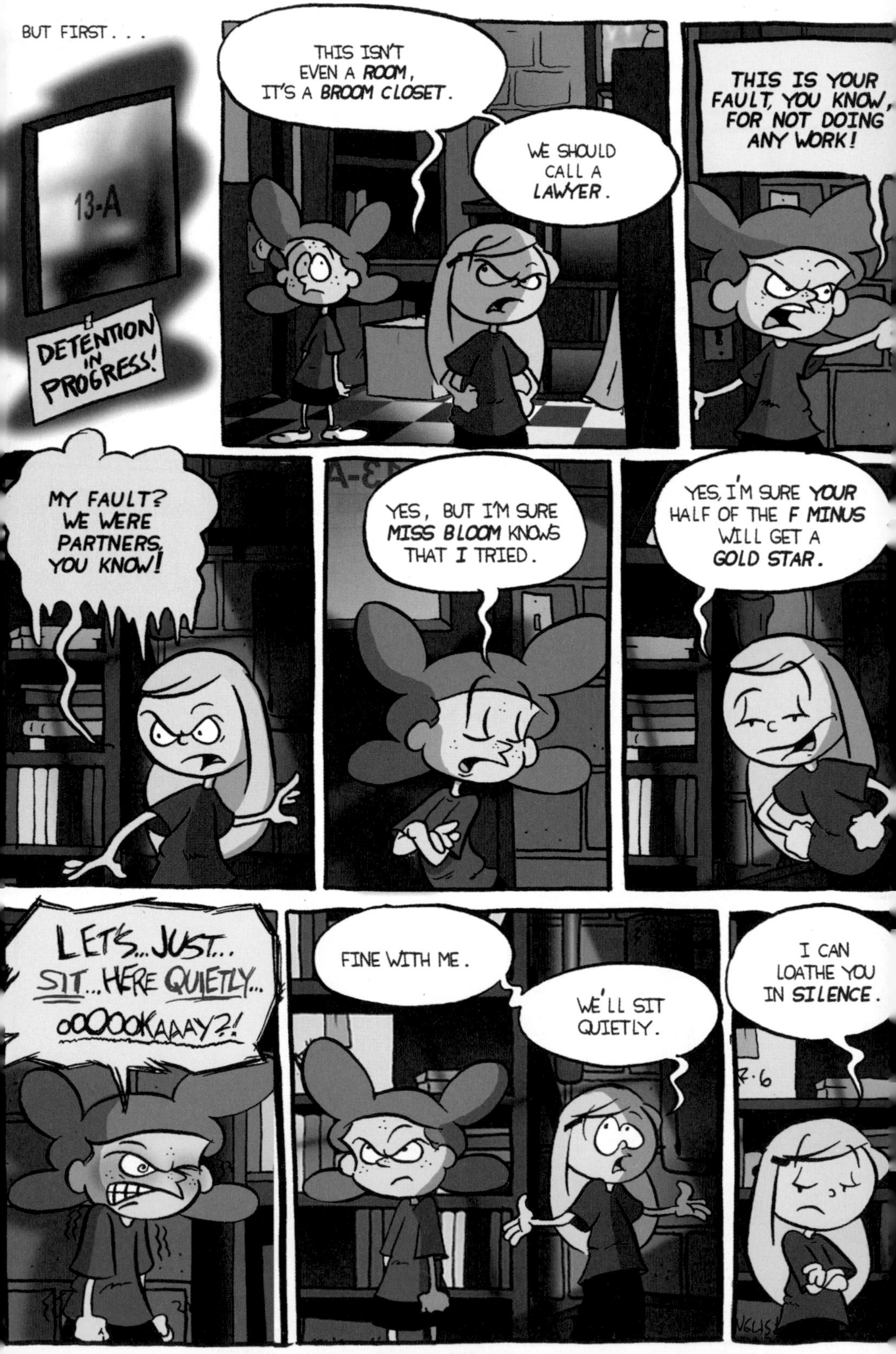
BUT FIRST . . .
13-A
DETENTION IN PROGRESS!
THIS ISN'T EVEN A ROOM, IT'S A BROOM CLOSET.
WE SHOULD CALL A LAWYER.
THIS IS YOUR FAULT, YOU KNOW, FOR NOT DOING ANY WORK!
MY FAULT? WE WERE PARTNERS, YOU KNOW!
YES, BUT I'M SURE MISS BLOOM KNOWS THAT I TRIED.
YES, I'M SURE YOUR HALF OF THE F MINUS WILL GET A GOLD STAR.
LET'S...JUST... SIT...HERE QUIETLY... OOOOOKAAAY?!
FINE WITH ME.
WE'LL SIT QUIETLY.
I CAN LOATHE YOU IN SILENCE.

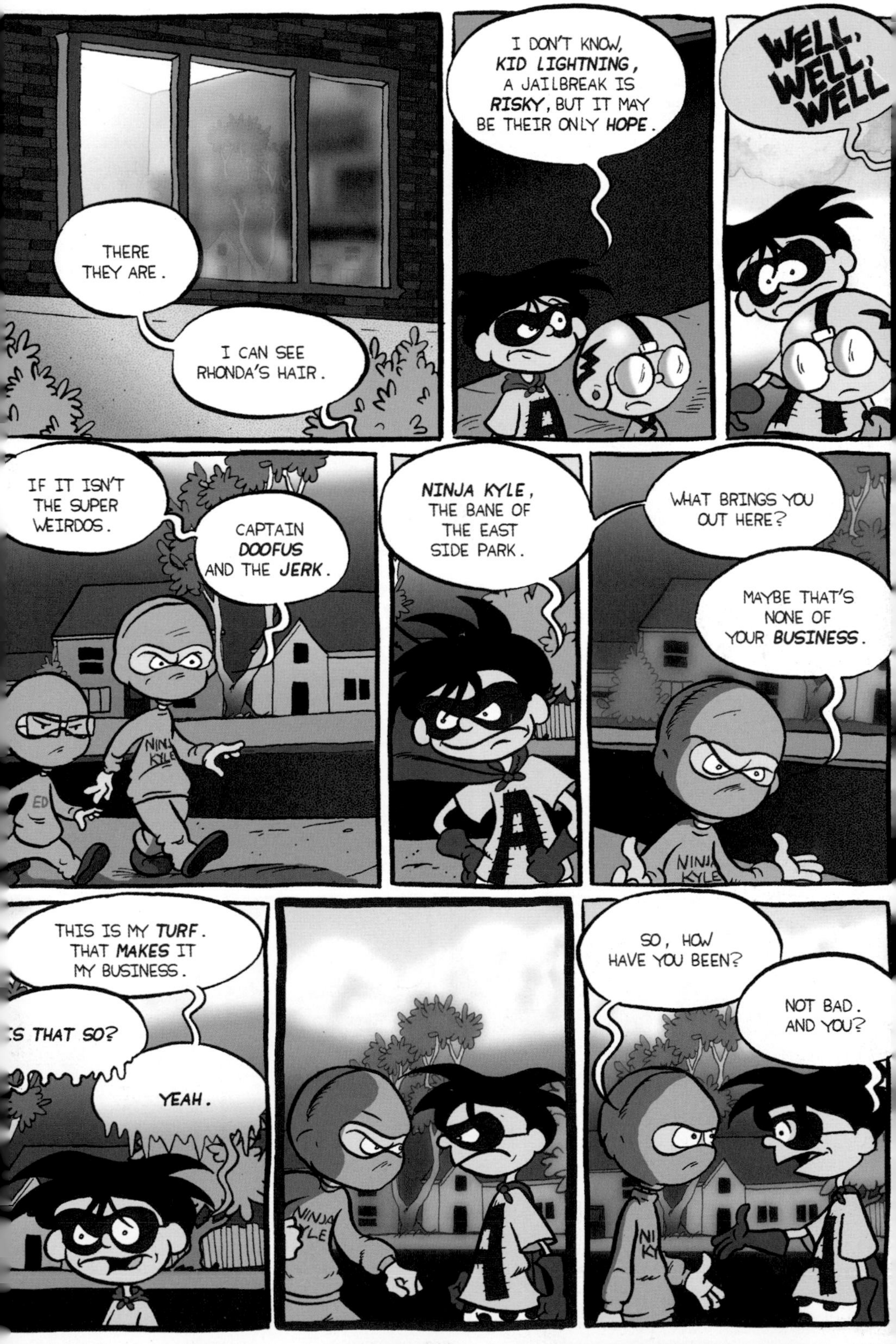

THERE THEY ARE.
I CAN SEE RHONDA'S HAIR.
I DON'T KNOW, **KID LIGHTNING**, A JAILBREAK IS **RISKY**, BUT IT MAY BE THEIR ONLY **HOPE**.
WELL, WELL, WELL
IF IT ISN'T THE SUPER WEIRDOS.
CAPTAIN **DOOFUS** AND THE **JERK**.
NINJA KYLE
ED
NINJA KYLE, THE BANE OF THE EAST SIDE PARK.
WHAT BRINGS YOU OUT HERE?
MAYBE THAT'S NONE OF YOUR **BUSINESS**.
NINJA KYLE
THIS IS MY **TURF**. THAT **MAKES** IT MY BUSINESS.
IS THAT SO?
YEAH.
NINJA KYLE
SO, HOW HAVE YOU BEEN?
NOT BAD. AND YOU?

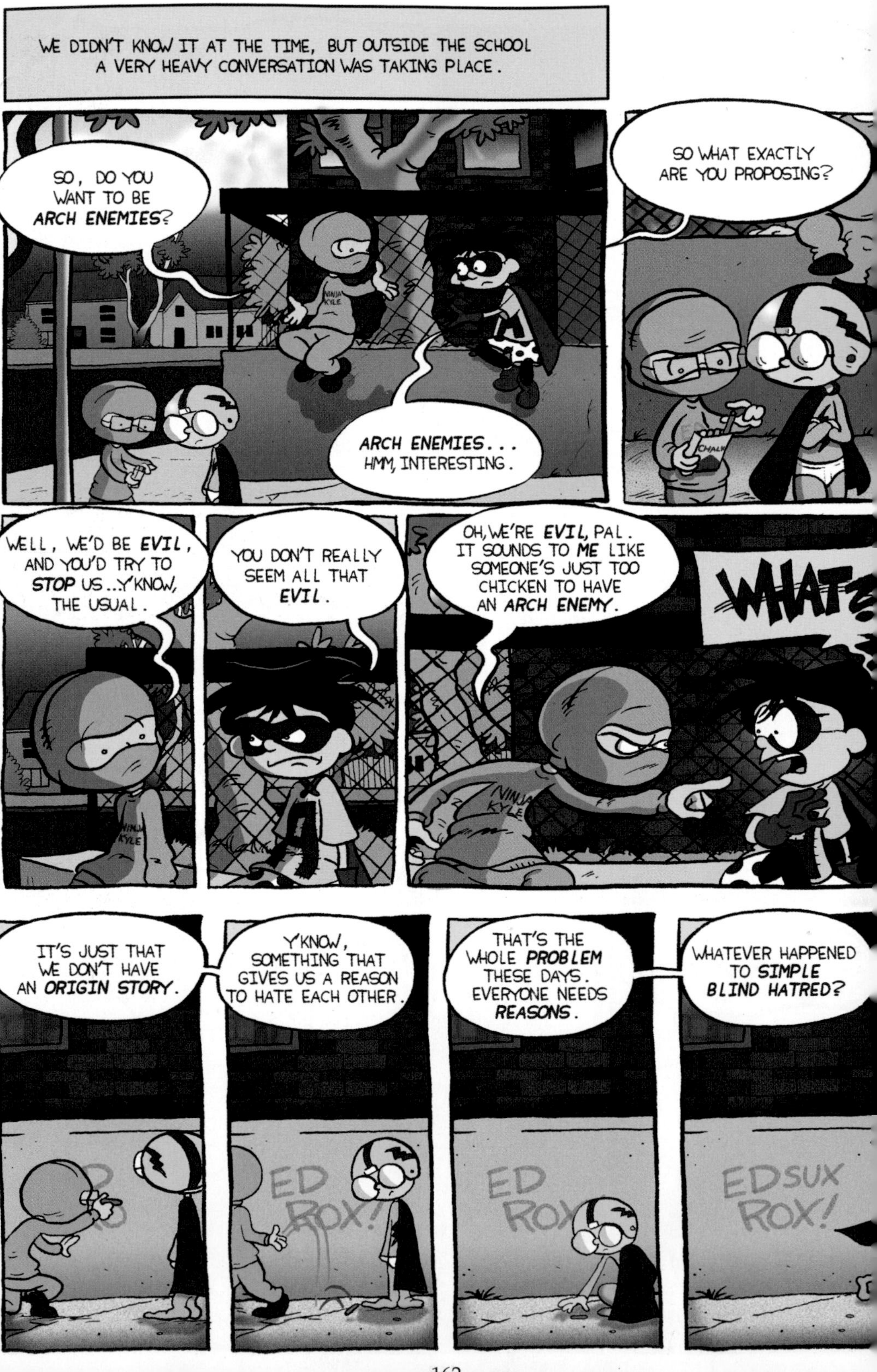
WE DIDN'T KNOW IT AT THE TIME, BUT OUTSIDE THE SCHOOL A VERY HEAVY CONVERSATION WAS TAKING PLACE.
SO, DO YOU WANT TO BE ARCH ENEMIES?
NINJA KYLE
ARCH ENEMIES... HMM, INTERESTING.
SO WHAT EXACTLY ARE YOU PROPOSING?
CHALK
WELL, WE'D BE EVIL, AND YOU'D TRY TO STOP US...Y'KNOW, THE USUAL.
NINJA KYLE
YOU DON'T REALLY SEEM ALL THAT EVIL.
OH, WE'RE EVIL, PAL. IT SOUNDS TO ME LIKE SOMEONE'S JUST TOO CHICKEN TO HAVE AN ARCH ENEMY.
NINJA KYLE
WHAT?
IT'S JUST THAT WE DON'T HAVE AN ORIGIN STORY.
Y'KNOW, SOMETHING THAT GIVES US A REASON TO HATE EACH OTHER.
ED ROX!
THAT'S THE WHOLE PROBLEM THESE DAYS. EVERYONE NEEDS REASONS.
ED ROX
WHATEVER HAPPENED TO SIMPLE BLIND HATRED?
EDSUX ROX!

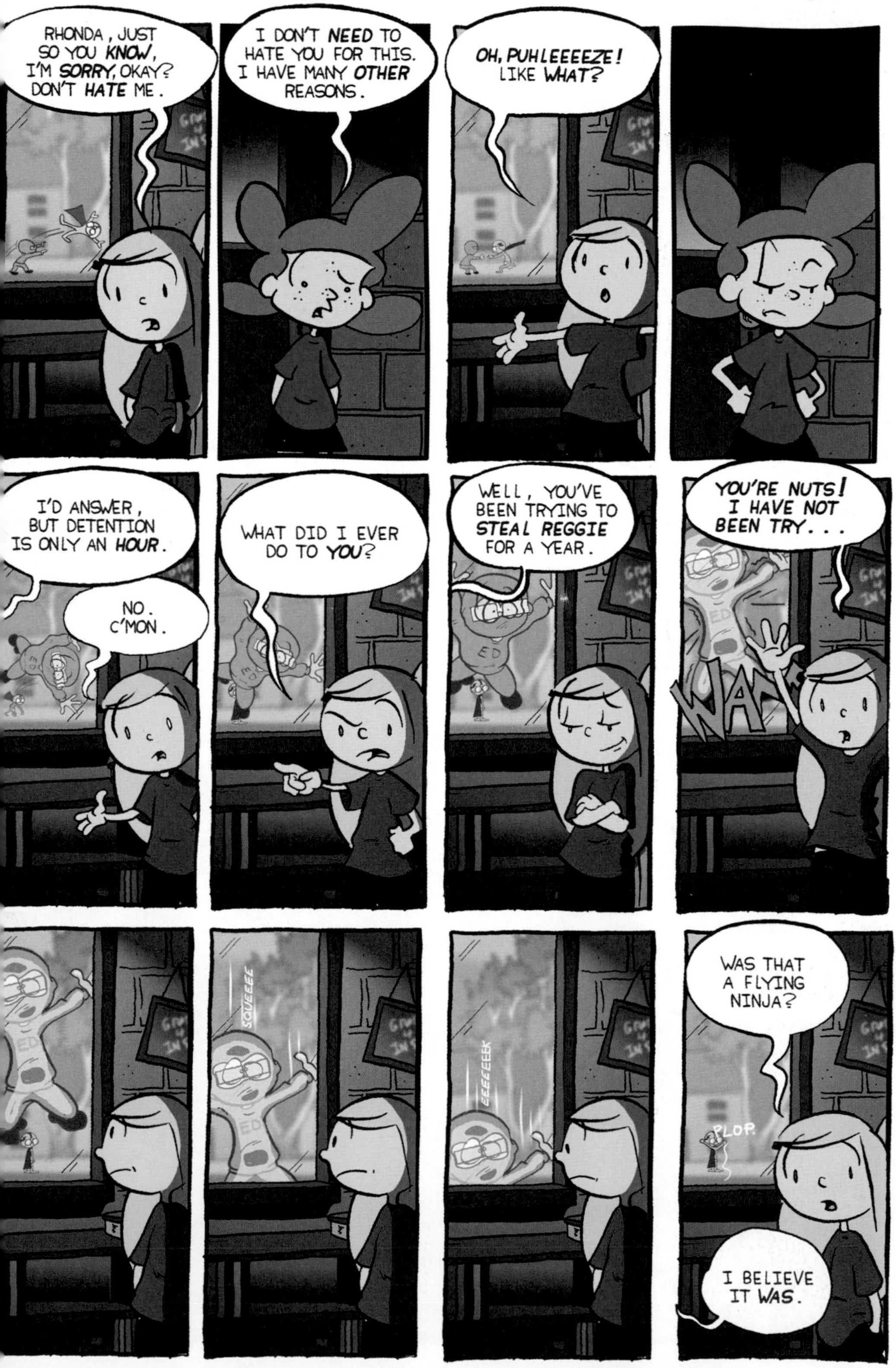
RHONDA, JUST SO YOU KNOW, I'M SORRY, OKAY? DON'T HATE ME.
I DON'T NEED TO HATE YOU FOR THIS. I HAVE MANY OTHER REASONS.
OH, PUHLEEEEZE! LIKE WHAT?
I'D ANSWER, BUT DETENTION IS ONLY AN HOUR.
NO. C'MON.
WHAT DID I EVER DO TO YOU?
WELL, YOU'VE BEEN TRYING TO STEAL REGGIE FOR A YEAR.
YOU'RE NUTS! I HAVE NOT BEEN TRY...
SQUEEEEE
EEEEEEEK
PLOP
WAS THAT A FLYING NINJA?
I BELIEVE IT WAS.

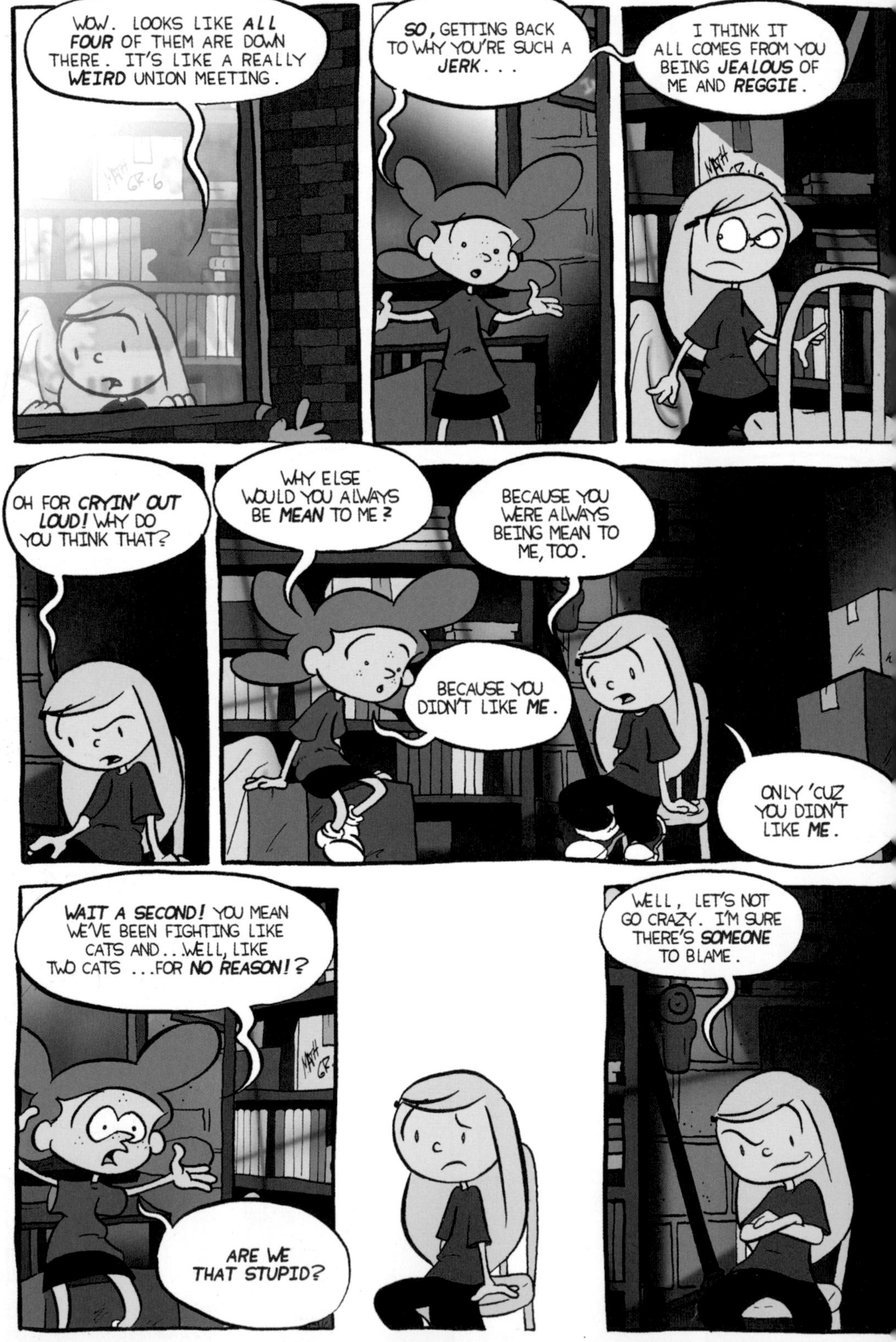
WOW. LOOKS LIKE **ALL FOUR** OF THEM ARE DOWN THERE. IT'S LIKE A REALLY **WEIRD** UNION MEETING.
MATH GR. 6
SO, GETTING BACK TO WHY YOU'RE SUCH A **JERK**...
I THINK IT ALL COMES FROM YOU BEING **JEALOUS** OF ME AND **REGGIE**.
OH FOR **CRYIN' OUT LOUD!** WHY DO YOU THINK THAT?
WHY ELSE WOULD YOU ALWAYS BE **MEAN** TO ME?
BECAUSE YOU WERE ALWAYS BEING MEAN TO ME, TOO.
BECAUSE YOU DIDN'T LIKE **ME**.
ONLY 'CUZ YOU DIDN'T LIKE **ME**.
WAIT A SECOND! YOU MEAN WE'VE BEEN FIGHTING LIKE CATS AND...WELL, LIKE TWO CATS ...FOR **NO REASON!?**
ARE WE THAT STUPID?
WELL, LET'S NOT GO CRAZY. I'M SURE THERE'S **SOMEONE** TO BLAME.

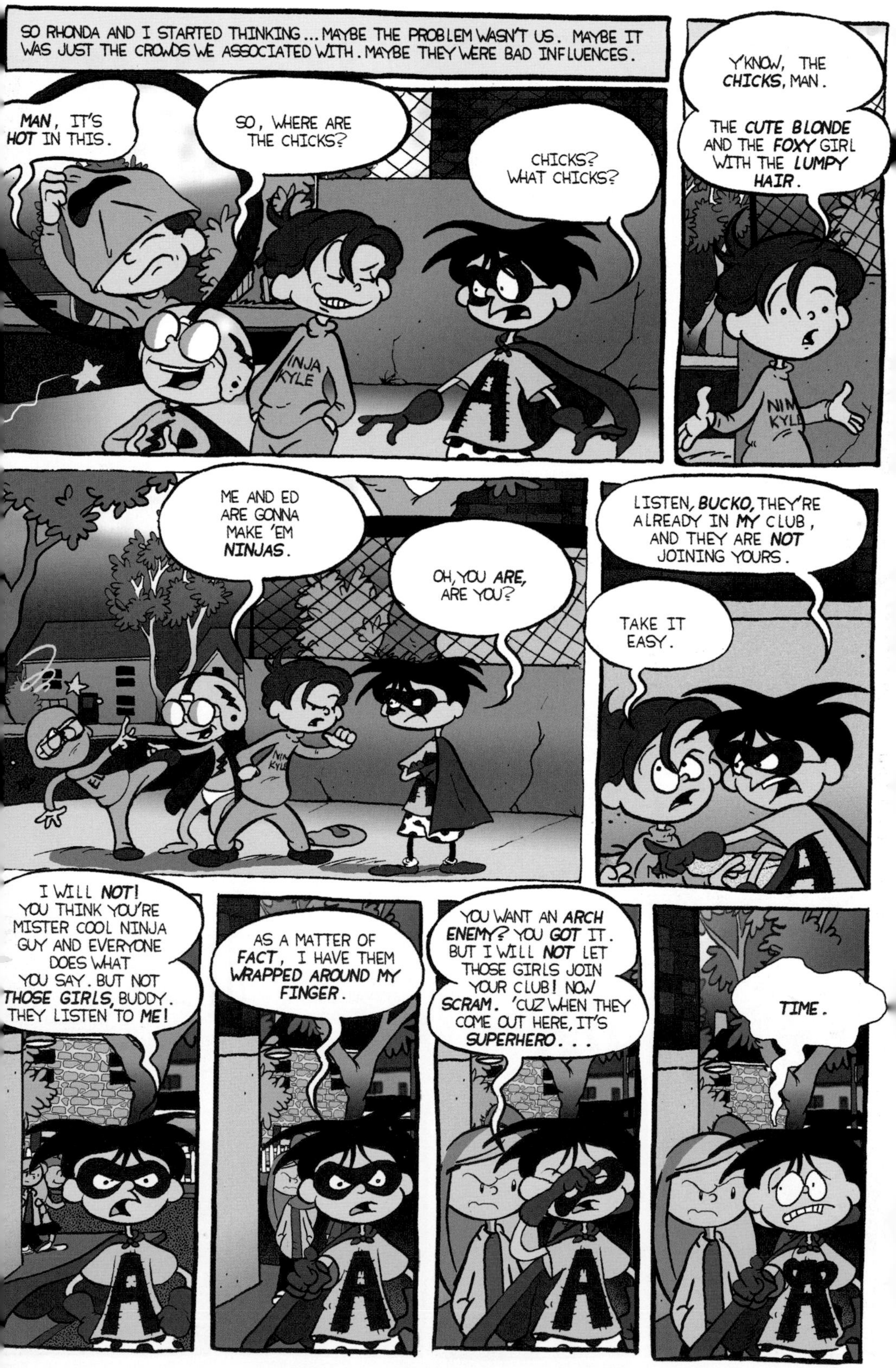
SO RHONDA AND I STARTED THINKING... MAYBE THE PROBLEM WASN'T US. MAYBE IT WAS JUST THE CROWDS WE ASSOCIATED WITH. MAYBE THEY WERE BAD INFLUENCES.
MAN, IT'S HOT IN THIS.
SO, WHERE ARE THE CHICKS?
CHICKS? WHAT CHICKS?
Y'KNOW, THE CHICKS, MAN.
THE CUTE BLONDE AND THE FOXY GIRL WITH THE LUMPY HAIR.
NINJA KYLE
ME AND ED ARE GONNA MAKE 'EM NINJAS.
OH, YOU ARE, ARE YOU?
LISTEN, BUCKO, THEY'RE ALREADY IN MY CLUB, AND THEY ARE NOT JOINING YOURS.
TAKE IT EASY.
I WILL NOT! YOU THINK YOU'RE MISTER COOL NINJA GUY AND EVERYONE DOES WHAT YOU SAY. BUT NOT THOSE GIRLS, BUDDY. THEY LISTEN TO ME!
AS A MATTER OF FACT, I HAVE THEM WRAPPED AROUND MY FINGER.
YOU WANT AN ARCH ENEMY? YOU GOT IT. BUT I WILL NOT LET THOSE GIRLS JOIN YOUR CLUB! NOW SCRAM. 'CUZ WHEN THEY COME OUT HERE, IT'S SUPERHERO...
TIME.

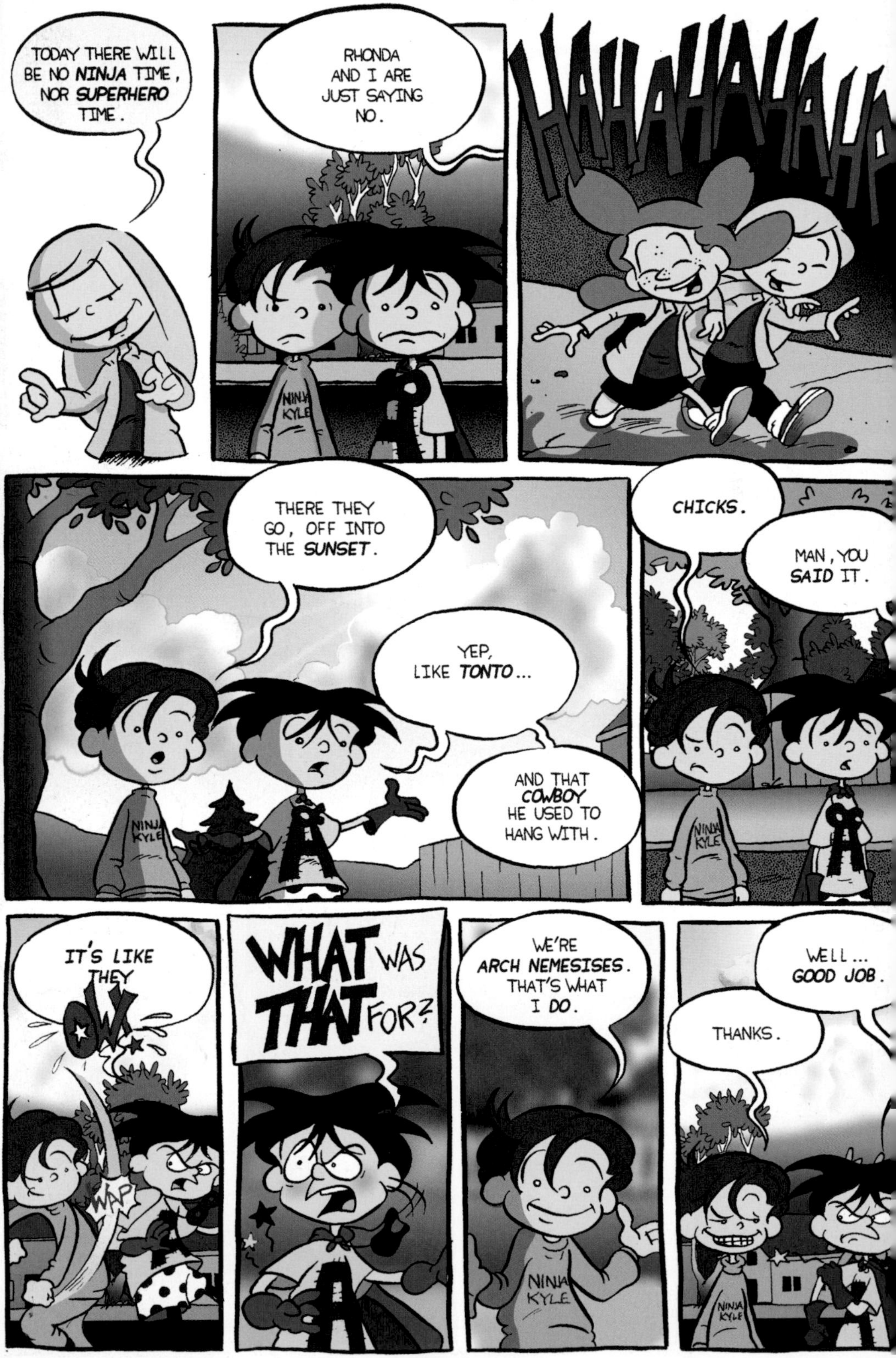
TODAY THERE WILL BE NO NINJA TIME, NOR SUPERHERO TIME.
RHONDA AND I ARE JUST SAYING NO.
HAHAHAHAHAHA
THERE THEY GO, OFF INTO THE SUNSET.
YEP, LIKE TONTO...
AND THAT COWBOY HE USED TO HANG WITH.
NINJA KYLE
CHICKS.
MAN, YOU SAID IT.
IT'S LIKE THEY
OW
WAP
WHAT WAS THAT FOR?
WE'RE ARCH NEMESISES. THAT'S WHAT I DO.
WELL... GOOD JOB.
THANKS.

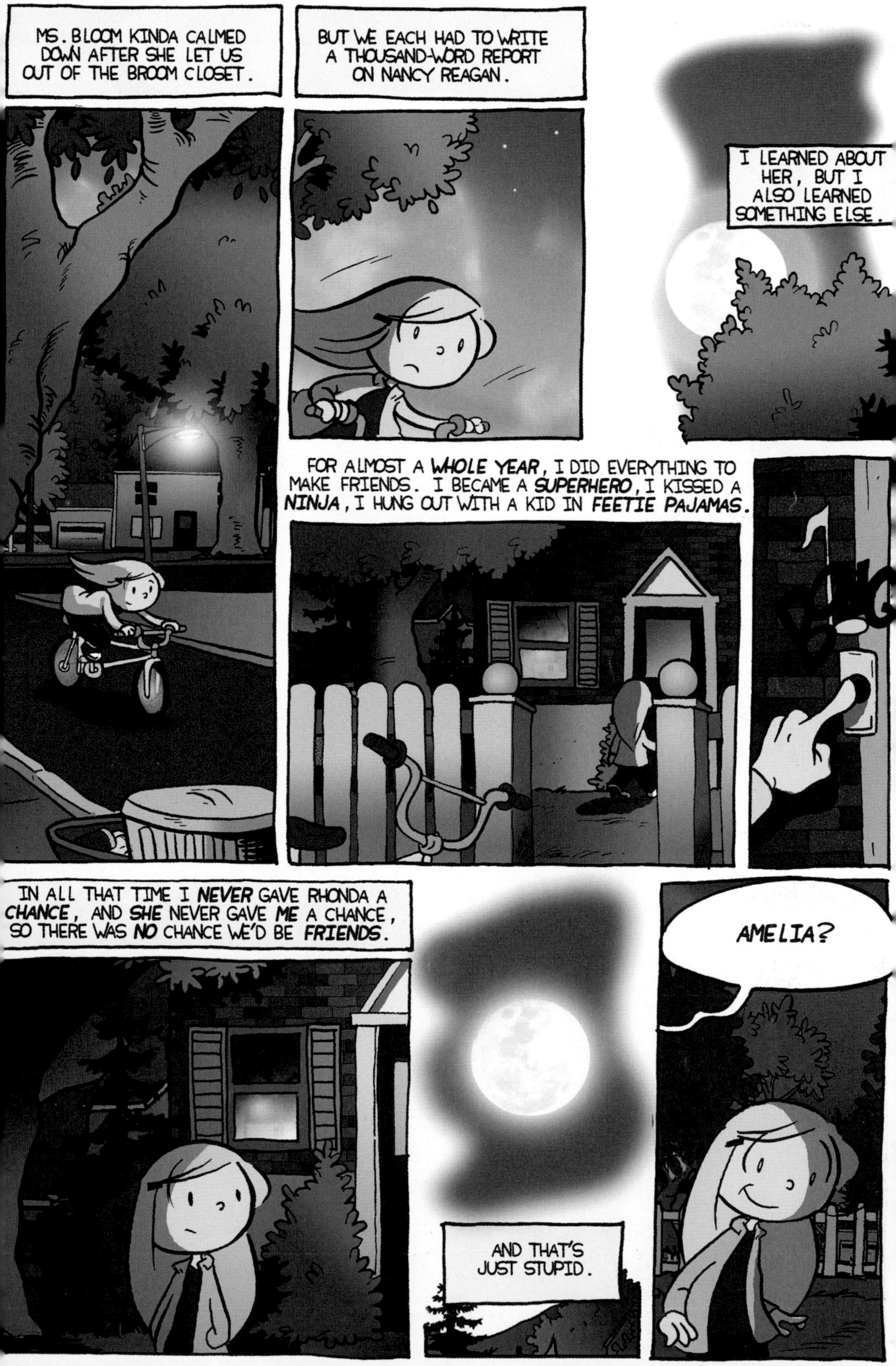
MS. BLOOM KINDA CALMED DOWN AFTER SHE LET US OUT OF THE BROOM CLOSET.
BUT WE EACH HAD TO WRITE A THOUSAND-WORD REPORT ON NANCY REAGAN.
I LEARNED ABOUT HER, BUT I ALSO LEARNED SOMETHING ELSE.
FOR ALMOST A **WHOLE YEAR**, I DID EVERYTHING TO MAKE FRIENDS. I BECAME A **SUPERHERO**, I KISSED A **NINJA**, I HUNG OUT WITH A KID IN **FEETIE PAJAMAS**.
IN ALL THAT TIME I **NEVER** GAVE RHONDA A **CHANCE**, AND **SHE** NEVER GAVE **ME** A CHANCE, SO THERE WAS **NO** CHANCE WE'D BE **FRIENDS**.
AND THAT'S JUST STUPID.
AMELIA?

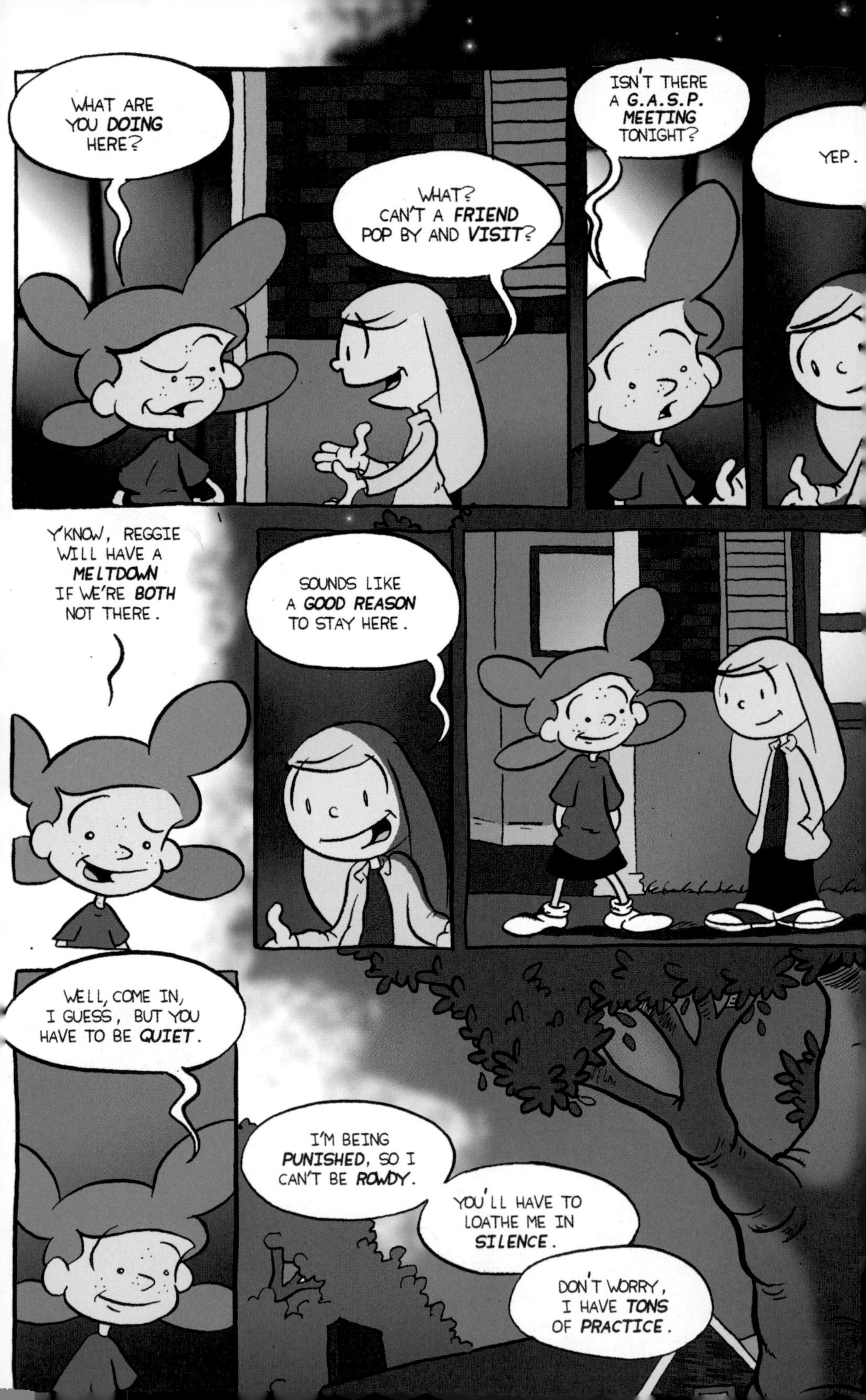

WHAT ARE YOU DOING HERE?
WHAT? CAN'T A FRIEND POP BY AND VISIT?
ISN'T THERE A G.A.S.P. MEETING TONIGHT?
YEP.
Y'KNOW, REGGIE WILL HAVE A MELTDOWN IF WE'RE BOTH NOT THERE.
SOUNDS LIKE A GOOD REASON TO STAY HERE.
WELL, COME IN, I GUESS, BUT YOU HAVE TO BE QUIET.
I'M BEING PUNISHED, SO I CAN'T BE ROWDY.
YOU'LL HAVE TO LOATHE ME IN SILENCE.
DON'T WORRY, I HAVE TONS OF PRACTICE.

Cartoonist Jimmy Gownley developed a love of comics at an early age when his mother read *Peanuts* collections to him. Not long after, he discovered comic books (via his dad) and developed a voracious appetite for reading any and all things comic-related.

By the age of 15, Gownley was self-publishing his first book, *Shades of Gray Comics and Stories*. The black & white slice-of-life series ran 16 issues and was recently collected by *Century Comics*.

The idea for *Amelia Rules!* came about several years ago while Gownley was still working on *Shades of Gray*. The goal was to create a comic book with comic strip sensibilities that both traditional and nontraditional comic book fans could enjoy. He also wanted to provide good, solid entertainment for kids that didn't talk down to them.

Since its debut in June 2001, *Amelia Rules!* has become a critical and fan favorite and has been nominated for several awards, including the *Howard Eugene Day Memorial Prize*, the *Harvey Award*, and the *Eisner Award*.

34-year-old Gownley lives in Harrisburg, Pennsylvania with his wife Karen and twin daughters Stella and Anna.

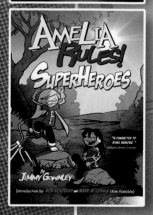